M000102401

TEXTUALITIES

TEXTUALITIES

BETWEEN HERMENEUTICS AND DECONSTRUCTION

Hugh J. Silverman

ROUTLEDGE: NEW YORK AND LONDON

Published in 1994 by

Routledge
29 West 35th Street
New York, NY 10001

Published in Great Britain in 1994 by

Routledge
11 New Fetter Lane
London EC4P 4EE

Copyright © 1994 by Routledge

Printed in the United States of America on acid-free paper.

All rights reserved. No part of this book may be reprinted or reproduced or utilized in any form or by any electronic, mechanical or other means, now known or hereafter invented, including photocopying and recording, or in any information storage or retrieval system, without permission in writing from the publisher.

Library of Congress Cataloging-in-Publication Data

Silverman, Hugh J.
    Textualities: between hermeneutics and deconstruction / Hugh J. Silverman.
        p. cm. — (Continental philosophy: 6)
    Includes bibliographical references and index.
    ISBN 0-415-90818-3—ISBN 0-415-90819-1 (pbk.)
    1. Philosophy, European—20th century. 2. Philosophy, Modern—20th century.
    3. Hermeneutics. 4. Deconstruction. 5. Literature—Philosophy. 6. Semiotics.
    I. Title. II. Series.
    B804.S566 1993
    190'.9'04—dc20   93-38481
                                                          CIP

British Library Cataloging-in-Publication Data also available.

For my mother

Eleanore R. Silverman

CONTENTS

ACKNOWLEDGMENTS

With the frame of the present book in view, a number of the chapters were delivered as invited lectures in Europe and North America. Many colleagues, students, and friends have commented upon preliminary versions of what now constitutes this volume. Initial forays were presented at the Merleau-Ponty Circle, the Heidegger Conference, the American Society for Aesthetics, the Semiotic Society of America, the Nietzsche Society, the Society for Phenomenology and Existential Philosophy, the Centre International d'Études Françaises (Nice, France), the Collegium Phaenomenologicum (Perugia, Italy), the Warwick Continental Philosophy Summer Workshops (Coventry, England), the Internationales Wissenschaftsforum (Heidelberg, Germany), the Österreichische Gesellschaft für Philosophie (Vienna, Austria), and the Wrocław Institute of Philosophy Faculty Seminar (Poland).

Grateful acknowledgment is made to the following for publishing portions of this book prior to their appearance here: *Journal of the British Society for Phenomenology* (Wolfe Mays, editor), *Research in Phenomenology* (John Sallis, editor), *Phänomenologische Forschung* (Ernst Wolfgang Orth, editor), *Phenomenology + Pedagogy* (Max van Manen, editor), *Semiotica* (Richard Lanigan, special guest editor), *Boundary 2* (William V. Spanos, editor), *Journal of Aesthetics and Art Criticism* (John Fisher, editor), *Time and Metaphysics*, ed. David Wood and Robert Bernasconi (Coventry: Parousia Press, 1982), *Deconstruction and Philosophy*, ed. John Sallis (Chicago: University of Chicago Press, 1987), *Horizons of Continental Philosophy*, gen. ed. Hugh J. Silverman (Dordrecht: Kluwer, 1988), *Continental Philosophy-II: Derrida and Deconstruction*, ed. Hugh J. Silverman (London and New York: Routledge, 1989), *Ontology and Alterity in Merleau-Ponty*, ed. Galen A. Johnson and Michael B. Smith (Evanston: Northwestern University Press, 1990), and *Merleau-Ponty Vivant*, ed. M. C. Dillon (Albany: SUNY Press, 1991).

William Melaney and Erik Vogt read the whole manuscript in an early draft. Gertrude Postl reviewed it carefully as it was nearing completion. The final product is surely much improved as a result of their many detailed comments. Although I am extremely grateful to each of them for their interest in this work, they are not however responsible for any infelicities in the text. At various stages, Patricia Athay, George Noble, Martin Dillon, David Holdcroft, Gianni Vattimo, Jean-François Lyotard, Graeme Nicholson, Wilhelm Wurzer, Dalia Judovitz, and Gary Aylesworth have discussed this work with me. I am deeply indebted to all of them for their friendship and good will.

Stratford Caldecott convinced me that a sequel to *Inscriptions* was not only a good idea but also worth undertaking. He even selected a magnificent medieval postcard that would have been an ideal cover for the book. Anita Roy encouraged the project while she was with Routledge in London and, as always, Maureen MacGrogan, my Routledge editor in New York, has been a source of encouragement and generous support.

My appreciation is also due to Evanthia Speliotis, who copyedited the manuscript for Routledge. Her careful reading of the linguistic *Spielräume* as well as whatever philosophical *profondeur* is achieved here has surely improved the ultimate effect of this work. Only in matters of hyphenation did we disagree. Hence, the presence of hyphens in many instances are at my own insistence.

A visiting professorship at the University of Leeds (England) in Spring 1988 and at the Università di Torino (Italy) in Fall 1990, and a sabbatical leave from SUNY at Stony Brook during part of the 1990–91 academic year permitted a modicum of time in which I was able to advance this project, but without the peace and distance of summers in Vienna, I would not have been able to finish it.

This book has been completed amidst extreme turmoil in the Stony Brook Philosophy Department. I am glad for my colleagues David B. Allison, David A. Dilworth, Patrick A. Heelan (now executive vice-president for the Main Campus at Georgetown University), Donald Kuspit, François Raffoul, and Victorino Tejera for making it all still seem worthwhile.

My children Claire and Christopher were in their own ways supportive of this project and will be glad to see *Textualities* in published form.

ABBREVIATIONS

Throughout the text, the following abbreviations have been used. Full bibliographical information is given for each item when first cited in the Endnotes. When two dates are listed for the same item, the first is the date of original publication, the second is that of the translation. Only items which are quoted more than once are included below.

AF	Derrida, *Archeology of the Frivolous* (1973/1980)
Carte postale	Derrida, *La Carte postale* (1980/1987)
Cézanne	*Conversations avec Cézanne* (1978), ed. P. M. Doran
DC	Bloom, *Deconstruction and Criticism* (1979)
Degree Zero	Barthes, *Writing Degree Zero* (1953/1967)
Différance	Derrida, "Différance" (1968), in *Speech and Phenomena and Other Essays* (1973)
Dissemination	Derrida, *Dissemination* (1972/1981)
DP	Blanchot, "Le 'Discours Philosophique,'" *L'Arc: Merleau-Ponty* (1971)
EGT	Heidegger, "Logos (Heraclitus, Fragment B 50)" (1944/1951), in *Early Greek Thinking* (1975)
EH-RHtr	Nietzsche, *Ecce Homo* (1888/1979), trans. R. J. Hollingdale
EH-WKtr	Nietzsche, *Ecce Homo* (1888/1967), trans. Walter Kaufmann
EM	Merleau-Ponty, "Eye and Mind" (1961), in *The Primacy of Perception* (1964)
Grammatology	Derrida, *Of Grammatology* (1967/1975)
HHS	Ricoeur, *Hermeneutics and the Human Sciences* (1981)
Holz	Heidegger, *Holzwege* (1950)
IMT-DA	Barthes, "The Death of the Author" (1968) in *Image/Music/Text* (1977)
IMT-FWT	Barthes, "From Work to Text" (1971), in *Image/Music/Text* (1977)
Inscriptions	Silverman, *Inscriptions: Between Phenomenology and Structuralism* (1987)
IOG	Derrida, *Introduction to the Origin of Geometry* (1962/1978)
LWA	Ingarden, *The Literary Work of Art* (1931/1973)

Margins	Derrida, *Margins of Philosophy* (1972/1982)
NGH	Foucault, "Nietzsche, Genealogy, History" (1971), in *Language, Counter-Memory, Practice* (1977)
OE; EM	Merleau-Ponty, "L'Oeil et l'esprit" (1961); and "Eye and Mind," in *The Primacy of Perception* (1964)
OWL	Heidegger, *On the Way to Language* (1959/1971)
Pheno&Lit	Magliola, *Phenomenology and Literature: An Introduction* (1977)
PLT-L	Heidegger, "Language" (1950), in *Poetry Language Thought* (1971)
PLT-OWA	Heidegger, "The Origin of the Work of Art" (1935–36/ 1950/1960), in *Poetry Language Thought* (1971)
Positions	Derrida, *Positions* (1972/1982)
PR	Derrida, "The Principle of Reason: The University in the Eyes of Its Pupils," *Diacritics* (Fall 1983)
Prose	Merleau-Ponty, *Prose of the World* (1969/1973)
PT	Said, "The Problem of Textuality: Two Exemplary Positions" (1980), in *Aesthetics Today* (1981)
QB	Heidegger, *The Question of Being* (1958)
RB	Barthes, *Roland Barthes* (1975/1981)
Retrait	Derrida, "The *Retrait* of Metaphor" (1978)
RPL	Kristeva, *Revolution in Poetic Language* (1974/1984)
Sartre: Images	Sendyk-Siegel, *Sartre: Images d'une vie* (1978)
S/Z	Barthes, *S/Z* (1971/1974)
SE; UB	Nietzsche, *Schopenhauer as Educator* (1874/1965) Nietzsche, *Unzeitgemässe Betrachtungen* (1873–76)
Signs	Merleau-Ponty, *Signs* (1960/1964)
SNS; SNS-tr.	Merleau-Ponty, "Le Doute de Cézanne," in *Sens et non-sens* (1947); and "Cézanne's Doubt," in *Sense and Non-Sense* (1964)
SP	Derrida, *Speech and Phenomena* (1973); *La voix et le phe-nomène* (1967)
Spurs	Derrida, *Spurs: Nietzsche's Styles* (1976/1979)
StrucPoetics	Cullers, *Structuralist Poetics* (1975)
TM	Gadamer, *Truth and Method* (1960)
TT	Lévi-Strauss, *Tristes Tropiques* (1955)
Validity	Hirsch, *Validity in Interpretation* (1967)
Verité; TP	Derrida, *La Verité en peinture* (1978); and *The Truth in Painting* (1987)
VI; VI-tr.	Merleau-Ponty, *Le Visible et l'invisible* (1964); and *The Visible and the Invisible* (1968)
VN	Dante Alighieri, *Vita Nuova* (1290)
Walden	Thoreau, *Walden: Or Life in the Woods* (1854)
Words	Sartre, *The Words* (1963/1964)

INTRODUCTORY REMARKS

"Thinking the between" was the prevalent concern of *Inscriptions: Between Phenomenology and Structuralism* (Routledge, 1987). *Textualities: Between Hermeneutics and Deconstruction* elaborates further on strategies and examples for "thinking the between" by developing "difference"—as a philosophical, theoretical, methodological, textual, and institutional enterprise. Like its predecessor, *Textualities* is located in a specific historical and philosophical context. And like *Inscriptions*, it is both an account of recent developments in continental philosophy and a demonstration of continental philosophy at work as a distinctive theoretical practice of its own.

In the first aspect of its double function, *Textualities* can be read as a presentation and evaluation of continental philosophy from Heidegger and Merleau-Ponty to Foucault and Derrida. On the periphery of this historical account, the reader will also find considerations of Nietzsche, Sartre, Barthes, Blanchot, and Kristeva. In this respect, *Textualities* can be read as a report on the principal concerns of continental philosophy from the mid-1930s—especially Heidegger's essay "The Origin of the Work of Art" (1935–36)—to Derrida's writings on truth in painting and on the university. *Textualities* is a kind of sequel to *Inscriptions*, which interprets continental philosophy from the later work of Edmund Husserl and the early Heidegger through the early Merleau-Ponty and Sartre. The subsequent treatment of Foucault and Derrida in *Inscriptions* addresses the problem of the displacement of the self and the human subject in contemporary thought. *Textualities* returns to the question of the self and the human subject as textualized—namely as inscribed in autobiography, in painting, in photography, in literature, and in the institutions of philosophy, such as the university.

In the second aspect of its double function, *Textualities* is itself a philosophical practice. It demonstrates how to "think the between" not only by juxtaposing alternative philosophical methods and indicating how to philosophize between hermeneutics and deconstruction but also by examining various philosophical texts—bringing out the signification of the "place between." In *Inscriptions*, this practice of "thinking the between" was announced as a "hermeneutic semiology."

1

At various points in the present study, this same practice is named and invoked as a link with the work of *Inscriptions*. A hermeneutic semiology can be formulated as the understanding of a set of signs ordered into a coherent textual complex. Such an understanding will disclose the aspects of a particular text or textualization but always in relation to (or in the context of) alternative texts and textualizations. *Inscriptions* is concerned with the link between existential phenomenology (Sartre and Merleau-Ponty) and structuralism (Lévi-Strauss, Lacan, Barthes, Piaget, et al.). The idea of a hermeneutic semiology is built upon Heidegger's ontological hermeneutics as an advance over Husserl's transcendental phenomenology, and upon Foucault's archaeologies of knowledge along with Derrida's textual deconstructions. Similarly, here, the notion of a hermeneutic semiology moves toward the "place between" hermeneutics and deconstruction. That it could also be called a kind of deconstruction itself would depend upon a clear understanding of how deconstruction works. It would have to be clear—as shown in chapter six—how the name of the alternative position is given to the "between practice" without adopting the identity of the alternative but rather by articulating the features of the difference(s) between the two. In this respect, a hermeneutic semiology can be read as a type of deconstruction. To be more precise, a hermeneutic semiology could also be characterized as a "juxtapositional deconstructive reading." The practice of a deconstructive juxtaposition elaborates a place of difference as a place of understanding and is crucial to the philosophical enterprise offered here in *Textualities: Between Hermeneutics and Deconstruction.*

While *Inscriptions* identifies the places of difference—the slashes, the borders, the belonging-together of alternatives—*Textualities* reiterates the "place between" as the locus of multiple textualities. In many of the chapters of the present study, there are attempts to articulate the nature and function of textualities. Examples of textualities are developed in determinate regions, such as in "autobiographical textuality," "photobiographical textuality," "visible textuality," "scriptive textuality," "philosophical textuality," and "institutional textuality." The question will recur: what is a textuality? In short, a textuality is one of various meaning-structures of a text. But such a translation is too simple, for a textuality is a differential notion and not a matter of identity. For instance (as developed in chapter ten), the autobiographical textuality of Nietzsche's *Ecce Homo* does not define the text as an autobiography. Indeed, the question as to whether *Ecce Homo* is in fact an "autobiography" is very much at issue. And yet its autobiographical textuality is hardly disputable. Its autobiographical textuality is distinctly different from the text itself. And yet autobiographical textuality operates throughout the text, along with many other textualities (such as philosophical textuality, religious textuality, literary textuality, etc.). What is meant here is that the question of an authorial self is written in the text as a possible reading of its textual interests.

A textuality is disclosed through a "juxtapositional deconstructive reading." This is accomplished in Part I by bringing alternative philosophical methods into relation with one another, in Part II by examining a number of oppositions in order to develop a theory of textuality, and in Parts III-V by exploring examples of autobiographical, visible/scriptive, and institutional textualities—all with respect to philosophical textuality.

In Part I, four current ways of practicing continental philosophy are considered: hermeneutics, semiotics, interrogation, and deconstruction. The first chapter provides a historical overview of the development of continental theory from transcendental phenomenology through hermeneutic phenomenology and semiology to deconstruction. Here the theory of difference is elaborated in terms of this historical development of continental philosophy. The subsequent three chapters are juxtapositional in strategy. Semiotics is juxtaposed with hermeneutics in order to indicate the place of a hermeneutic semiology. Heideggerian and Gadamerian hermeneutics are juxtaposed with Merleau-Ponty's later method of philosophical interrogation. And Merleau-Ponty's philosophical interrogation is juxtaposed with Derridean deconstruction—and specifically with respect to the question of painting. Like Heidegger's "Origin of the Work of Art," which interweaves work and thing, thing and art, art and truth, these three chapters bring out the interwovenness of the four dominant continental theories and how the texture of their differences constitutes a "hermeneutic semiology" or more precisely a "juxtapositional deconstruction."

Part II takes the question of a theory of textuality by the horns. In this section, building upon the issue of the work of art raised in the last chapter of Part I, the place of textuality in Heidegger's account is set forth. Heidegger does not have a theory of textuality. He doesn't even have a theory of the text. Yet the place of disclosure, the Open, the differential space elaborated in his aesthetic hermeneutic circle delineates the "transversal" place in which a topology of the text and the origination of textuality can be explored. Chapter six, the second chapter of the second part, takes the instance of metaphysics building again on the Heideggerian example and outlines in detail the strategies of deconstruction: how it functions, and the tools of its practice. The seventh chapter moves from metaphysics to literature. Here by raising the question of a human science of literature, the possibility of a hermeneutic semiology in literary study is explored and developed in terms of an example from Roland Barthes's reading of Balzac's "Sarrasine" in *S/Z*. And finally the last chapter of the second part is an attempt to elaborate the various frameworks in which textualities occur—as occasioned by a reading of a number of binary oppositions including: visible/invisible, inside/outside, presence/absence, text/context, and unity/multiplicity.

The largest portion of what follows is devoted to a detailed exploration of different textualities in order to display how a juxtapositional deconstructive reading works in the specific. These last three parts are what Deleuze would call a rhizomal study rather than an arborescent one. They do not begin from a stem and branch out from there. Rather they offer a number of grouped instances of textualities at work. Part III concerns "autobiographical textuality" and takes the modernist conception of the human subject into the frame of a textualizing of the self or subject in quasi-autobiographical texts. Each of the instances selected is of marginal relation to the official genre of "autobiography." The first chapter in this part places autobiography among other genres and focuses on Thoreau's *Walden* in detail. *Walden* is as much an American transcendentalist philosophical treatise as an account of Thoreau's two years in the Concord woods. Although written in the first person singular, *Walden* lacks many of the features of a standard autobiography—and yet it is rife with autobiographical textuality. Similarly Nietzsche's *Ecce Homo*, as already indicated, is only marginally autobiographical. Lévi-Strauss' *Tristes Tropiques* provides access to the question of time in autobiographical textuality. The juxtaposition of Sartre's *Words* and Barthes's *Roland Barthes* examines autobiographical inscription at a point of radical divergence: Sartre's narrative stops at the age of twelve with his "fundamental project" when he decides to become a writer and Barthes's text interrupts the chronological prejudice of an autobiography in favor of an alphabetical one. The final chapter on autobiographical textuality takes an instance which, on the surface, has little to do with self-inscription, namely, Heidegger's reading of Van Gogh's painting of "Old Shoes with Laces." However, with the help of Meyer Schapiro and Jacques Derrida, it becomes evident that Heidegger's interpretation of the painting is largely autobiographical in its textuality. The connections now with the first chapter of Part II and the last chapter of Part III on autobiographical textuality become clear.

The second set of textualities (Part IV) is developed in terms of photographs of philosophers' bodies (specifically those of Sartre and Heidegger), the status of self-portraiture in painting (as in Merleau-Ponty's reading of Cézanne), the question of the speaking subject (as textualized differently in Merleau-Ponty and Kristeva), and the instance of writing (as a distinctive style for Merleau-Ponty and as textual practice for Derrida). Each of these cases of visible or scriptive textuality could be regarded as a borderline case of the autobiographical—and yet the question of the autobiographical is not central to any of them.

The last set of textualities (Part V) returns in a certain sense to the issues of the first part but now no longer as philosophical methods per se but rather as the textualization of philosophy itself—textualization in terms of specific institutions, most notably, the university. The first and last chapters of this last section are concerned with philosophy inside and outside the university. The first is in terms of Nietzsche's confrontation with Schopenhauer, the last, in relation to Derrida's reading of the role of philosophy and research in the university. The first explores the role and status of judgment when conducted inside the university and when considered from the outside. The last considers the topology of various universities and its significance for the practice of philosophy in the contemporary university. In effect, the reasons (or grounds) for philosophy are re-examined no longer historically but specifically in terms of a juxtapositional deconstructive reading. Between these two framing chapters are considerations of philosophical discourse (as exemplified by Merleau-Ponty's writings and as understood by the writer Blanchot); the inscription of the line— the locus of "thinking the between" (as drawn out and marked by the place between Heideggerian thinking and Derridean strategies); and the question of origin(s) in history (as circumscribed in Foucault's archaeology of knowledge and Derrida's deconstructions). These three concerns: "philosophical discourse," "the line between," and "the origin(s) of history" mark off the edges of metaphysics. They show that philosophical textuality operates with marginalities—its capital interest lies around the frames of educational institutions, in the formulations of theoretical and scientific concerns, and in the elaboration of the very foundations of history. But this should not be an occasion for philosophical despair—indeed quite the contrary, for, at the borders of these dominant practices and concerns, philosophy can review their various commitments, understand their preoccupations, and reassess their limitations. In this respect, the interest in philosophical textuality is perhaps of even greater import than in philosophy itself.

I

Continental Philosophy and the Texture of Theory

1

FROM HERMENEUTICS TO DECONSTRUCTION

Two roads diverged in a wood, and I—
I took the one less traveled by,
And that has made all the difference.
        —Robert Frost, "The Road Not Taken" (1915)

The divergence between descriptive phenomenology and hermeneutic phenomenology is a difference which arises within the entire enterprise of phenomenology. Semiology is another route altogether. Deconstruction makes all the difference. My thesis is that only by looking outside phenomenology to a parallel, yet dissimilar, theoretical practice will it be possible to establish the place (or at least *a* place) in which deconstruction operates. This place is the place of difference where Heideggerian ontological difference and Gadamerian aesthetic non-differentiation confronts the Saussurian system of differences. I shall consider in turn: (1) the distinction between descriptive phenomenology and hermeneutic phenomenology; (2) the divergence between hermeneutics (as opposed to the descriptive approach) and semiology; and (3) the difference that deconstruction makes, namely, the strategic choice of operating in terms of the divergence.

DESCRIPTION/INTERPRETATION

From its original formulation in Husserlian phenomenology, the form of constitution involves an act of directedness toward particular things of the world, toward some object of consciousness. At best, this act of directedness is not simply oriented from an ego to some empirical thing but at the same time also includes features of the thing presented to the constituting self. Effected in the phenomenological attitude, the intentional act produces a content. This content is the objective meaning of the thing as given in an act of constitution. A proper

9

description of that objective meaning as performed by a knowing (or describing) self produces an account of the thing or object under consideration. Various procedures are employed by the describing self so as to ascertain and affirm that the description is properly carried out. The goal is to produce an accurate and incontrovertible narrative or verbal account of the thing or object. The account is a description of the meaning of the thing or object.

The character of description has undergone some modification in the existential phenomenologies of Sartre and the early Merleau-Ponty. For Sartre, what is described is the essence of an existing thing. The description is not performed by a transcendental ego but rather by an existing situated being. Such an existing situated being is both for-itself and yet also conscious of the existing thing in terms of its essence, its essence as an in-itself. Although description is description of an essence, Sartre offers an account of the paradoxical situation in which a description of the existence which underlies a particular essence is attempted. But how does one describe existence? Already Sartre's description of an essence is an account of what is out there, the object of a conscious act. In the novel *Nausea*, Sartre's character Roquentin describes existence as a certain unsettling feeling, the very absence of certainty and security. But is the description of existence like the description of an essence? It seems to be in a category all its own—unlike all other descriptions, which are descriptions of essences. The description of existence comes in the form of a feeling of nausea rather than in terms of specific objective characteristics. A road may be described as "grassy" and "wanting wear" or a wood may be characterized as "yellow," but existence, it seems, must be described by the horrifying sense of nausea which arises when confronting it. Phenomenological description is to be extolled for its accuracy, effectiveness, and aptness. The quality of its language may be scientific or literary, circumspect or figurative. Its goal is to represent the content of experience clearly and distinctly, and without error.

The value of Merleau-Ponty's contribution to the theory of phenomenological description (as developed prior to his formulation of "interrogation" and specifically in the 1945 *Phenomenology of Perception*) lies in his view that, since consciousness must be embodied, any full account must survey the phenomenal field in terms of motility, spatiality, gesture, and expression. When the speaking subject describes the field of an experienced object, it must account for the tendency toward expression in much the same way that Husserl would have one consider the horizons of internal time-consciousness. However, what Merleau-Ponty adds is the kinesthetic and synesthetic aspect of what is described. And in sympathy with Sartre (unlike Husserl), description cannot be carried out from a transcendental, bird's eye *(pensée de survol)* point of view. The describer is already embodied and involved—incorporated—in the perceptual or experiential field. The meaning or content of experience is already corporeal. Suppose, for instance, a forest road were to be described. Not only would its length, width, distance, texture, and undergrowth be offered in the narrative, but also one would provide an account of the leaves covering the terrain to be traversed, the untrodden quality of their distribution over the road, and the place of the traveler tentatively leaning in the direction of one of two alternate paths. For the early Merleau-Ponty, the vision, stance, movement, hesitation, crackling of twigs underfoot, the lightness of leaves spread over the wooded path, the yellowish tint of the autumn trees, the moisture in the air, and the sense of alternative are all features worthy of phenomenological description.

Whereas phenomenological description is concerned with the contents of experience (whether transcendental or existential), phenomenological interpretation (or hermeneutics) stresses the act of mediation between an interpreter and the interpreted. Interpretation is a placing-between: like the path delineated by Hermes the messenger who travels between Zeus and the other gods. Interpretation is an act that, if successful, produces understanding. The task of interpretation is to understand that which is to be interpreted. To produce an interpretation is to come up with an understanding of the interpreted. Interpretation cannot operate with the transcendental presuppositions that descriptive phenomenology would require if it were to remain in the Husserlian mode. Interpretation must be able to operate freely between the interpreter and the interpreted. The barrier established between the transcendental position and the empirical domain makes such commerce difficult, if not impossible. Furthermore, consistent with the Sartrian and Merleau-Pontean positions, interpretive phenomenology (or hermeneutics) denies a transcendental status to the interpreter. However, to employ Husserlian terms—without the transcendental prejudice, which, some may argue, is to be non-Husserlian—descriptive phenomenology is primarily concerned with the noematic component of experience, while interpretive phenomenology stresses the noetic dimension. The description of the noema is an account of the meaning content of experience, while the interpretation of something is the act of knowing it and the understanding that is provided by it. Hence, while phenomenological description is an account of the meaning of something, phenomenological interpretation is the act of producing or establishing a meaning.

Just as phenomenological description seeks to narrate the meaning of something—the leaf-covered northern New England road, for instance—hermeneutics is concerned with interpreting the road, the road as a work or text, or more commonly, a poem about (or a painting of) the road. Hermeneutics was initially developed to interpret the Bible. The Bible regarded as a work—a work of divine inspiration—presents not only things, places, and people, but also situations, choices, and actions. At the same time that the Bible is a work of divine inspiration, it is also a book, a book to be read and interpreted. The problem of what Gadamer calls romantic hermeneutics—referring to the writings of Schleiermacher—is the relation between the book of Scripture and the whole context of one's life. Does interpretation concern itself simply with an understanding of the work of divine inspiration? Is the interpretation to be an account of what is recounted in the Bible? Does the Bible represent events in the lives of the ancient Hebrews and the coming of Christ? In that case, an interpretation of the book of Scripture is an understanding of those events per se and of the historical passion of Christ. Or is an interpretation of the Bible to be an understanding about the whole context of the life of the interpreter's relation to the events of the Bible? Indeed, hermeneutics takes this latter alternative as the focus of its attention. Romantic hermeneutics *qua* biblical interpretation is engaged in understanding not simply the exegetical considerations of the Bible but also the relation between the interpreter and Scripture, namely the significance of the Bible in one's life in general. Interpreting the Bible is already an interpretation of the Bible. The act of interpreting Scripture is the production of its significance in the life of the interpreter and in the lives of those who engage in that interpretation. The stress is not upon the subjective interests of the interpreter nor upon the objective features of the work itself, but on the act of interpreting and the significance of the interpretation that is produced.

But what if the interpretation is not of the Bible, but of a northern New England leaf-covered road in the woods? Clearly a description of the meaning of the road would be helpful. For an account of things or even of existence itself, phenomenological description is valuable, since its meaning can be characterized in various ways. Interpreting a road or perhaps a fork in the road in the tradition of romantic hermeneutics involves understanding the significance of the diverging roads in the context of human life. Diverging roads might signify division, fission, alternative, choice, or the multiplicity of possibilities.

A third example, besides the scriptural work and the divided road in the wood, is a poem about two roads dividing in the forest. Consider now Robert Frost's poem, "The Road Not Taken" (first published in *The Atlantic Monthly* in 1915 and included a year later in the little volume entitled *Mountain Interval*). In the present context, an American poem is surely called for. So often we look at the Hölderlin, Rilke, Trakl, and George poems (which Heidegger admired) or the Rimbaud, Mallarmé, Baudelaire, and Valéry poems (which figure in Sartre's philosophy). Frost's "The Road Not Taken" begins with the following lines:

> Two roads diverged in a yellow wood,
> And sorry I could not travel both
> And be one traveler, long I stood
> And looked down one as far as I could
> To where it bent in the undergrowth;
>
> Then took the other, as just as fair,
> And having perhaps the better claim,
> Because it was grassy and wanted wear...

Hermeneutics is reputed to be most effective at literary or textual interpretation. With its formative stages addressed to biblical interpretation, and vying with phenomenological description as an approach to things in the world, hermeneutics is more at home in the interpretation of poems such as Robert Frost's "The Road Not Taken." If we remember that hermeneutic phenomenology is primarily concerned with the act of interpreting, rather than with a description of the meaning of the thing under scrutiny, it becomes evident that the interpretation of a text such as "The Road Not Taken" should produce an understanding of the poem.

In phenomenological description, the meaning precedes, and is a necessary condition for, the description that is offered. In hermeneutics (or phenomenological interpretation), the meaning results from an interpretive act. The meaning is integral to the understanding that follows from the interpretation. Two major attempts at applying phenomenological description to the study of literary works (one by E. D. Hirsch[1] and the other by Roman Ingarden[2]) indicate the general inappropriateness of the method with respect to texts and raise difficulties which also arise when interpreting things in the world. E. D. Hirsch, in his *Validity in Interpretation*, tries to show that the model of Husserlian phenomenological description can be used to deal with literary texts. Hirsch's difficulty arises when he claims that there is a single "objective meaning" for any particular poem. This meaning is the meaning of the author's intention. He is not suggesting that one need fall into the intentional fallacy, but that the intentionality of the author makes an objective meaning available for the interpreter's own intentional act. He cites the example of John Donne's "A Valediction Forbidding Mourning," which is often taken to be "spoken by a dying man and to concern spiritual communion in death and after death." He claims that the mistake or "misconstruction" arises because the lines suggest that particular misunderstanding:

> As virtuous men pass mildly away,
> And whisper to their souls to go,
> Whilst some of their sad friends do say,
> "Now his breath goes," and some say "No,"
>
> So let us meet and make no noise,
> No tear-floods nor sigh-tempests move.

Hirsch claims that, in fact, "the poem is almost certainly about a temporary absence, and the speaker is almost certainly not a dying man" (*Validity*, pp. 73–74). Taking something like a transcendental stance, he argues that meaning in a text is determinate and that one need only—although not without diligence—find out what it is. In this way, Hirsch assumes that interpretation is really phenomenological description—taking an attitude toward the poem such that the meaning can be examined and described. The view is that the meaning is fixedly there—it need only be grasped and validated. In phenomenological interpretation or hermeneutics, the interpretive act must take priority. It cannot concern itself with the author's intention, nor even with some essence produced in the author's creative act. Rather it must focus on the interpreter's relation to the poem, a relation in which a meaning is produced, produced through a new and different language. The possibility of multiple meanings and interpretations is surely available just as long as they can be shown to constitute an effective understanding of the poem or text.

Although Hirsch makes no such attribution, it could be argued that the kind of position he takes with respect to interpretation is really a description of a literary product in the tradition of Ingarden's *The Literary Work of Art* (1931). Certainly both positions take their inspiration from Husserlian phenomenology. Ingarden is concerned with the literary work as given in a transcendental complex of strata: (1) the stratum of word sounds and the phonetic formations; (2) the stratum of meaning units of various orders; (3) the stratum of manifold schematized aspects, aspect continua, and series; and (4) the stratum of represented objectivities with their vicissitudes (*LWA*, p. 30). Built upon these four levels is a fifth: the stratum of metaphysical qualities, which permeates the previous four. The point is that these various strata all occur on the transcendental plane, particularly the strata of meaning units, the manifold of schematized aspects, and the multiplicity of represented objectivities. They are all available for phenomenological description. Interpretation is not the principal concern in the Ingardian formulation.

By following phenomenological description into the domain of literary and textual study, Hirsch (and Ingarden before him) introduces a rigidity inherent in the priority of the meaning claim such that interpretation becomes difficult if not impossible. However, interpretation seems to have better access to literary objects than is available to description. The richness, multiplicity, and even ambiguity of the literary object, as well as the need to produce meaning rather than find it, is inherent in the interpreted. To claim that Robert Frost's intention was to offer a poem about choice and decision as the meaning of "The Road Not Taken" is both limiting and perhaps even inappropriate, given the full interpretive framework. At least Ingarden's phenomenological description allows for multiple meaning units and represented objectivities, but the primary function of hermeneutics is to stress the interpreter's relation to the interpreted and the understanding that arises out of that relation. Thus interpreting "The Road Not Taken" produces the sense of alternative, the necessity of choice, the possibility of selecting the uncommon path, and the likely irreversibility of decision. Furthermore, there are also those paths that meet somewhere in the woods, bringing the ongoing traveler to a halt. The sense of awe, hesitation, selection, determination, and resignation might well result from the confrontation with a fork in the road. The Frost poem might even lend itself to an interpretive act such as that proposed in the thirteenth century by Dante Alighieri in a letter to Can Grande della Scala in which he appeals to Hugh of St. Victor's fourfold method of interpretation. Dante remarks that, in addition to reading his own *Divine Comedy* literally, it can also be read as an allegory, a moral account, or an anagogical (that is, religious) version of the very same poem. Although Dante suggests four possible levels to interpretation (and "The Road Not Taken" could certainly also embody these four levels), he hints at the importance of interpretation and the significance of the interpretive act which had to be revived later in the hermeneutic tradition. Suppose Frost's poem is interpreted in the fourfold way: literally, it is the selection of one of two paths with the concomitant recognition that the other is irretrievable. Allegorically, it is an account of choice in the face of alternatives. Morally, it is the lesson that, when one chooses, one cannot turn back. Anagogically, it is the recognition that, when one opts for the life that Christ has shown, the way is not easy but surely worthy. Whether or not any of these interpretations were part of the author's original intention (as they presumably were in the writing of Dante's *Divine Comedy*), they could well be invoked in an interpretation of the poem.

In this dichotomy or divergence between description and interpretation, what, it may be asked, is the missing link between the Husserlian conception of phenomenological description and the Gadamerian version of hermeneutics? The answer is well-known. For Heidegger, hermeneutics is concerned with the business of interpreting. However, although the fundamental conditions of phenomenology are preserved, Heidegger puts the whole transcendental turn into question. In the eidetic reduction, the meaning or *eidos* is offered as an appearance, *phainomenon, Schein*. However, Heidegger elides the transcendental reduction, in which meaning is relegated to a special, purified realm where existence is placed in suspension. Interpretation is concerned with truth (and produces an *eidos*) in its project of uncovering the meaning of Being and the general structures of Dasein. To uncover the meaning of Being, the interpretive act must situate itself in the relation to Being, namely in the ontico-ontological difference (*Differenz*) between Being and beings. This space of difference is characterized by the genitive form in the Being of beings. By interpreting the Being of beings, phenomenology makes the general structures of Dasein appear. Interpretation is the act of bringing the meaning of the relation of beings to Being out of concealment. Yet the meaning of this relation does not antedate the act by which it is disclosed. The meaning arises in the interpretation of the Being of beings. Dasein is the Being-here (also Being-there) of a being in its relation to Being. Dasein exists in that it always has Being on the horizon. Interpretation is the act of bringing out the fact of Dasein's Being. Interpretation of this sort brings out the existentiality of existence. Unlike Sartre and Merleau-Ponty, Heidegger does not propose to describe the meaning of Dasein, but rather to interpret it. The meaning of Being-here is disclosed through the interpretive act; it is not simply already there.

Heidegger himself makes the move from the interpretation of the Being of beings as the meaning of Dasein to the interpretation of the artwork's relation to the artist as the disclosure of the meaning of Art. Just as the interpretation of the difference between Being and a particular being can be understood in terms of Dasein, so too the difference between the work of art and the artist can be understood in terms of Art. In each case, the hermeneutic circle discloses the truth *(aletheia)* of a being's relation to Being and the work's relation to the artist. Hence, in Heidegger, one finds the shift from interpretation as concerned with a being to interpretation as concerned with a work of art. Just as one is already here in the interpretive situation in which one's own being is related to Being, so too the work of art as an origin of the artist is interpreted in the artist's origination of the work. Just as Dasein's authentic mode of Being-in-the-world is disclosed in the interpretive situation, so too Art is disclosed in the interpretation of the relation between the artist and the artwork. Heidegger's way is the path of interpretive phenomenology. It was the road less traveled when he set it forth in the late 1920s. And, given the choice of description by phenomenologists such as Sartre and Merleau-Ponty, it retained a fairly isolated status until Gadamer offered his own version of hermeneutics in *Truth and Method* (1960),[3] and Ricoeur[4] (primarily in the 1970s) gave it generalized currency in his study of various kinds of texts. Description was the road not taken (by Gadamer and Ricoeur) and that has made a significant difference.

SEMIOLOGY/HERMENEUTICS

A proper assessment of the place of deconstruction in its relation to hermeneutics demands a consideration of the role of semiology or semiotics. Imagine another fork further along the road—yet without a corresponding temporal distance. Saussure (1859–1913) gave his famous lectures in general linguistics at the University of Geneva from 1906 to 1911, just when Husserl (1859–1938) was giving his lectures on the "idea" of phenomenology at the University of Göttingen. Saussure's lecture notes were published by his students in 1916.[5] However, Saussure's semiology was hardly noticed outside linguistics for almost three decades, while transcendental phenomenology grew and even spawned its existential versions, most notably in Sartre and Merleau-Ponty. Semiology was by far the road less traveled.

Semiology is "the general science of signs." A sign is a combination of a signifier and a signified, a word and a concept. The particular connection between a particular word (or sound-image) and a particular concept is arbitrary. A sign, however, has no signification in isolation from other signs in the same language system. A sign has signification because of its place in a system of differences. Such a system of differences is extended horizontally across a chain of signifiers constituting a signifying chain.

According to Saussure, linguistics is a part of semiology. Hence the study of language is part of the general study of signs (some of which are non-linguistic). When Roland Barthes takes up semiology anew in his *Elements of Semiology* (1964), he states that semiology is a part of linguistics,[6] that is, all sign systems are incorporated into a language of some sort. Semiology distinguishes *langue* (language) from *parole* (speaking or the act of speech). The enactment of a sign *(parole)* with its signification in a language *(langue)* involves the whole signifying chain in which the sign is located. Human speech, parlance, or discourse *(langage)* is the delimited field of a particular language in a specified domain. The language *(langage)* of roads, paths, ways, routes, and so forth are articulated in the *langue* English. The network of roads, paths, ways, routes, etc. with the concomitant highways, roadways, byways, freeways, airways, waterways, or the metaphorically associated ways of truth and appearance, mind's road to God, paths of least resistance, routes to freedom, trials of thought, and channels of communication are each encoded within a delimited discursive system of signs.

And (by the way) although signs may occur in the language of travel, the signposts, stoplights, road signs, direction indicators, billboards, and so on, are only specific cairns or markers within a coded system of signs. They have signification in the sentences and syntagms in which they occur, but also in the associative paradigms of which they partake.

These signs do not have signification because someone constitutes them, nor because they are experienced in an act of interpretation or an intentional act. They have signification because they participate in a signifying chain, not through the vertical constitution of an object by an act of consciousness. Semiotic significations are proliferated horizontally across a chain of signifiers or as part of an associative system. Phenomenological meaning is available either for description as given in an intentional act or as produced (disclosed) in an interpretive act. Although the semiological notion of the signified may correspond to the phenomenological notion of the noema, essence, idea, or meaning, the signified as a concept has no importance in an experiential act (except to the extent that Saussure is interested in *parole* or the spoken enactment of a particular sign). And indeed the signified is only a concept combined with a specific word in a particular language. It has no signification apart from the whole signifying chain. Although phenomenological constitution and hermeneutic interpretation appeal to the horizons of meaning, the difference that is relevant is the differentiation between subject and object, interpreter and interpreted, the difference in which meaning is found or produced, and not the system of differences that gives signification to any particular sign.

Nevertheless, a concept of difference is operative in both the hermeneutic formulation and the semiological understanding. In semiology, difference is deferral, a sliding off or passing on to a contiguous, subsequent, or prior sign. Difference is what gives any particular sign's signification its identity. Difference is not restricted to any particular temporal sequence. Difference links the various elements (both syntagmatic and paradigmatic) in the whole sign system. Difference is also that which distinguishes and identifies any particular element in the system. Difference is not simply the intervals between each unit (signifier plus signified) as if each sign were an atomic unit. In those traditional linguistic accounts in which the sign is identical with the word, the absolute character of difference as the interval between words could be invoked. However, in the semiological view, the relation between the signifier and the signified is often imbalanced. Metaphor produces a situation in which there is an overdetermination of signification, namely a multiplicity of signifieds for a given signifier. Metonymy leads to an underdetermination of signification. Synecdoche involves only a portion of the full signified even though the signification could be complete. These are just some examples in which rhetorical tropes produce an imbalanced and off-center signifier-signified relation. The fluidity and flexibility occur in the place of difference.

In hermeneutics, difference is theoretically spatial and vertical—located in the in-between where interpretation occurs. The understanding offered by Heidegger establishes the place of difference where Being stands at the horizon of each particular being. The difference between the ontic and the ontological is the difference that Dasein makes. Dasein interprets—stands between—and renders a meaning in its response to the call of Being. In responding to the call of Being, Dasein establishes itself as authentic, as proper to itself, as its own. To be here is to belong in the belonging together of Being and beings. Dasein is here, fallen, thrown, and in-the-world, yet with others and endowed with the possibility of care. Although Dasein is one type of being, it is distinct from other types. As in semiological sign systems, this distinction *(Unterschied)* of one being from another is horizontal in that one being is marked off from others. However, this notion of distinction does not involve the difference of meaning that Saussure attributes to the system of differences. In Heidegger, the difference that makes meaning possible is more specifically the vertical ontico-ontological difference which hermeneutics identifies and enacts.

The ontico-ontological difference is the place in which truth occurs. Truth, for Heidegger, is an event, a disclosure, a bringing out of concealedness. Truth is what can occur in the understanding that interpretation provides. Truth as *aletheia* is an emergence from forgetfulness and a creation of new meaning (a meaning which is imbedded in the very Western tradition that has covered it over). In that truth is a disclosing of what is in its relation to Being, truth is the proper response to the call of Being, the full hearing of Being, and therefore the accomplishment of the belonging together of Being and beings.

In *Being and Time*, Heidegger understood language as an ontic feature—idle chatter, banter, just talking.[7] Discourse could be authentic but only when it hears the call of Being. In his essays of the post-war period, Heidegger understood language *qua logos* to be situated in the ontico-ontological difference, in the Open where the event, appropriation, and the ownness of Being and beings occur. "Language," "speech," and "the word" are already authentic, already the fullest articulation of the meaning of a being's relation to Being.[8] Language is located in the ontological difference just as Art is characterized as the origin of both the work of art and the artist. The work, Heidegger claims in "The Origin of the Work of Art,"[9] is the origin of the artist, the artist is the origin of the work, and Art is the origin of both the artist and the work. This circle, referred to as the hermeneutic circle, delineates the place of Art in the place of difference, just as truth and language are articulated in the ontico-ontological difference. This vertical interpretive difference constitutes the place of Dasein, the place of Art, and the place of language as *logos*.

In Gadamer's *Truth and Method*, this notion of ontological difference is examined in terms of the recent history of aesthetic experience. Aesthetic differentiation *(aesthetische Unterscheidung)* in the Kantian tradition sets up the dichotomy between the subjective and the objective, between a transcendental and an empirical realm. The subjectivization of aesthetics occurs because the conception of the work is abstracted from the form. Genius and taste become the conditions for the possibility of artistic creation and critical judgment, for the subject is given the full power of discrimination. This notion of aesthetic differentiation is carried over into twentieth-century aesthetics in that the interpreter must offer an interpretation of the work. However, aesthetic differentiation in Gadamer's view is the establishment of a difference in which interpretation situates itself and in which an aesthetic non-differentiation occurs, namely, the identity of difference. Aesthetic differentiation sets up the space in which interpretation, and then understanding, can arise. Thus, aesthetic experience is not located in the subject, nor is it located in the object. Aesthetic experience is not in the place of the interpreter nor in that of the interpreted. Aesthetic experience occurs in the place of interpretation, the place between, the place where difference becomes identity. This place of difference, which becomes aesthetic non-differentiation, is the space in which "play" occurs. The playing of play is the interpreting of interpretation. The playing of play is what Gadamer calls the "transformation of structure." In this activity of play, aesthetic meaning and ultimately understanding arise. Play is the movement of interpretation. And in the final part of Gadamer's *magnum opus*, he indicates that this place of play, this place of interpretation, is also the place of language. Language is the horizon of a hermeneutic ontology. Language is the locus for the play and transformation of structure which occurs in interpretation. As Gadamer says, "everything that is language has a speculative unity: it contains a distinction (*Unterscheidung*), that between its being and the way in which it presents itself, but this is a distinction that is really not a distinction at all" (*TM*, p. 432). The distinction (*Unterscheidung*) is not really a distinction since it does not occupy an actual space. It is only marked out by the relation between the interpreter and the interpreted. It is only the playing of the play, the interpreting of the interpretation; it is pure act with meaning as its non-differentiation and understanding as what it produces. Language constitutes the horizon for the being of interpretation. Language establishes the domain of interpretation. Its ontological limits are set by what Heidegger calls the ontico-ontological difference.

If this place of language in the ontico-ontological difference, at the horizon of a hermeneutic ontology, is juxtaposed with the semiological conception of language (particularly *langage*) as the "discourse," "human speech," or "parlance" in which signification is derived from a system of differences, a curious dichotomy occurs. On the one hand, language sets the limits of aesthetic experience by placing itself in the space of interpretive difference (which is no distinction at all). On the other hand, language is situated at the conjuncture of a language and the speaking of that language. In the first instance, language is the opening up of the historical presentation (*Darstellung*) of works in the interpretive space. In the second case, language (*langage*) is constituted in the time-slice (synchrony) which cuts across its historical (diachronic) development. For the later Heidegger language speaks while for Gadamer language distinguishes itself from itself. By contrast, for Saussure language is a convention and a social product, while for Barthes language is both materiality and articulated usage. Jacques Lacan, who draws upon structural linguistics for his psychoanalysis, says that the unconscious is structured like a language, ex-centric and dispersed. The language of the self is the language of the speaking subject as other or, as Lacan writes: *ça parle* (it speaks; the id speaks).[10]

Confronted with the divergence between the hermeneutic view that language speaks—speaks in the ontico-ontological difference, in the place of presentation, play, and the non-differentiation of aesthetic differentiation—and the semiological view that I am spoken—spoken in the fabric and texture of language, the system of differences comprising the signifying chain—there is a sense of regret that both paths cannot be chosen at once. One is even led to wonder whether some third position which is not an alternative—a hermeneutic semiology,[11] for instance—might be possible.

HERMENEUTIC SEMIOLOGY AND DECONSTRUCTION

A hermeneutic semiology would operate at the intersection of the vertical interpretive, constitutive, meaning-forming experience and the horizontal dispersive, differential system-articulating signifying chain. At the zero degree of phenomenological meaning and semiological signification, the respective differing functions overlap and cooperate. At the zero degree of interpretive differentiation and significatory differentials, language in each view acquires its identity. However, the very prospect of hermeneutic semiology suggests a positive science for which there are only further theoretical practices and juxtapositional strategies. Deconstruction, however, offers a way of reading texts such that the zero degree and point of departure for a hermeneutic semiology can itself be decentered and disseminated in a field of writing, differance, and indecidables.

The task of deconstruction is to offer a theoretical practice of reading texts. Its fundamental activity is that of reading, and not interpretation as in hermeneutics, nor analysis as in semiology. Deconstruction is a reading of texts which leaves aside the interpretation of artworks. As Barthes has shown, the move from work to text is the shift not only from hermeneutics to semiology, but also the transfer from a fragment of substance to a methodological field.[12] The work is an object of interpretation, that which is produced by an artist, and that which finds itself on shelves alongside other works by the same artist or other artists. The text is not that which is interpreted but rather the domain in which the interpretation occurs. It is the space of both writing and reading: the network of sign systems, codes, and systems of knowledge production, but also of frames, margins, edges, limits, and borders. The text is self-circumscribing, its outside (pre-texts, con-texts, inter-texts) implies its inside. At the hinge or borderline between the two, at the meeting place of the oppositional relation, the reading of writing and the writing of a reading take place.

The text is writing. The writing calls for a reading. The reading requires a writing in order for it to have a status of its own. Writing is the textuality of the text. Writing is the text taken to its limits. Writing is neither the act of producing a text nor that which is produced but rather that which happens at the hinge between the two. Writing is not that which is opposed to speech. Writing is that originary space in which a text is communicated, disseminated, displayed, incorporated, limited, contexted, and so forth. As Derrida has demonstrated in

"Plato's Pharmacy,"[13] writing is neither a remedy nor a poison, yet as *pharmakon* it has features of both. It supplements in that it adds on to what has been written elsewhere, yet it also supplements in that it repeats and takes the place of what it recounts. Writing is an indecidable.

Writing is a play of differences. Whereas play in Gadamer is serious—the activity of interpreting—and whereas difference in Saussure is a linking function, Derrida, by contrast, puts the play of differences into the very strategies of deconstruction. In his essay *"Différance,"*[14] Derrida notes that *différer* means both to differ, to separate, to make different, and to defer, to put off, to postpone. *Différance* is neither separation nor postponement. *Différance* is the temporal movement of a spatial separation. Yet we will remember that this is also the difference that hermeneutics and semiology make. *Différance* is the indecidable which does not choose one road or the other. *Différance* is, in effect, the difference that the divergence makes.

Différance is neither the inside nor the outside, neither the intelligible nor the sensible, neither the metaphorical nor the literal, neither the true nor the false, neither the text nor the outside-text, neither good luck nor bad fortune, and more. Yet *différance* is, in a certain sense, the conjuncture of these oppositional terms as they are located in the history of metaphysics. *Différance* requires the divergence, the opposition, the meeting of two distinct ways. Yet it is not the ways that matter. The path one takes, either this or that, is not what counts, for to take one route is not to take the other, to imply one is to imply the other, to incorporate one is to incorporate the other, to limit in terms of one is to limit in terms of the other, to make one present is to make the other absent, and so on. What counts is the difference that is made between them. Robert Frost writes this difference (his *Differenzschrift*) at the end of "The Road Not Taken." He writes the difference by marking out the traces of the path not followed as well as those of the one selected. Yet the poem itself inscribes not one choice or the other, not one path or the other, but the hinge, the intersection, the meeting place, the copula, the veil, the seam, the fork, the difference between the two. He concludes—as I do here—with a sigh, not a sign; with a future, not a past; with a trace, not an experience; with a tale, not a fiction; with an I, not a footprint:

> I shall be telling this with a sigh
> Somewhere ages and ages hence:
>
> Two roads diverged in a wood, and I—
> I took the one less traveled by,
> And that has made all the difference.

2

SEMIOTICS AND HERMENEUTICS

The conjunction of semiotics and hermeneutics is a difficult space to occupy. A hermeneutic semiology, as I have called it,[1] is open to criticism from both sides. Advocates of hermeneutics require that one situate oneself in the hermeneutic circle, that one enter into the interpretive activity of meaning production and meaning disclosure. Advocates of semiotics—or semiology as Saussure and Barthes have called it—insist that "unended semiosis" (following Peirce) or "unlimited semiosis" (according to Eco) is the endless chain of sign relations and sign production. The semiotician wants to argue that the proliferation of signs and sign systems goes on irrespective of any interpretive activity. An interpretive semiology, which some—such as the Italian philosopher Carlo Sini[2]—offer as a complementarity of hermeneutics and semiotics, will have to be practiced in relation to the well-known opposition between hermeneutics and semiotics.

The commitment to hermeneutics as the art of interpretation is directed toward the production of understanding (*Verstehen*). Semiotics as the general science of signs offers a method for acquiring knowledge about the underlying structures of language and languages. Hermeneutics is criticized for its subjective orientation whereas semiotics is criticized for its excessive objectivity. At the intersection of the two, however, the dynamic processes of signification and signifiability open up the space in which a hermeneutic semiology might operate. While Heidegger and subsequently Gadamer offer formulations for the nature and character of hermeneutics, Paul Ricoeur stretches the hermeneutic enterprise to its limits. Sini appeals to the American semiotician Charles Sanders Peirce as his model for semiotics, but might equally well cite Saussure and Barthes on the one hand or Hjelmslev and Eco on the other. In order to develop the possibility of a hermeneutic semiology, I propose to examine: (1) the features and function of the hermeneutic circle—especially in the interpretation of *works* (Heidegger), the play of aesthetic non-differentiation (Gadamer), and discourse as the mediation of self-understanding (Ricoeur); (2) the status of texts—especially the sign systems which constitute them (Barthes), the theory of codes which identifies them (Hjelmslev and Eco), and the pleasure or enchantment (Sini) which happens in them. This inquiry will lead to the question of a theory of textuality whose domain of operation is located in the meaning structurations of texts and the topological frameworks of interpretive knowledge production.

THE HERMENEUTIC CIRCLE

There is no reason to suppose that the hermeneutic circle is vicious. To enter the hermeneutic circle is to hope for the disclosure of truth in the space of difference produced by an interpretive activity. In the early Heidegger (most notably in *Being and Time*), this space of difference is delineated by the ontological difference which arises in the relation of beings to Being. To recognize that every being *(ein Seiendes)* is something which is and that beings must also manifest what is common to all of them, namely Being *(das Sein)*, is to mark out the space of difference described by the Being of beings (or the ontological genitive). The ontico-ontological difference, established by the Being of beings *(das Sein des Seienden)*, the particular being which is here *(Da)* gives identity to this difference. *Da-sein* is the name given to the being which is *here* in the ontological difference. *Dasein* is the existing self—which both interprets itself and gives sense to the understanding it has of itself. *Dasein* is a kind of third term in the relation of beings to Being. *Dasein* both fills the space of difference and gives meaning to itself in the interpretive activity in which it engages. *Dasein* constitutes itself as Being-in-the-world and at the same time discloses its thrownness in the world. The triadic relationality can be outlined as follows: beings are the source of Being, for without that which is, Being would not make sense. But Being is also the source of beings since beings obtain their being-like character from the general condition known as Being. Furthermore, both beings and Being obtain their identity from the being which is here and which constitutes them or understands them in an act of self-interpretation. The being which is *here* is *Dasein,* human existence itself. However, *Dasein* achieves its status as a being which is here by its situatedness in the relation of beings to Being in the ontico-ontological difference. This circular triadic relation is the hermeneutic circle in which the meaning of Being is disclosed. The disclosure occurs in terms of the language of the relation to Being—what Heidegger later calls *logos*[3]—the speaking, calling, naming of Being, as well as the hearing *(hören)* and belonging-together *(Zusammengehörigkeit)* of Being and beings. Thus, in the essay "Language" (1950–51), we learn that not only does "man speak," for "language belongs to the closest neighborhood of man's being," but also "language speaks."[4] Language speaks in this place of difference delineated by the hermeneutic circle.

In the "Origin of the Work of Art" (1935–36),[5] the triad of Being, beings, and *Dasein* (in which language speaks) is repeated in the structures of artist, artwork, and Art. The hermeneutic circle is repeated in this other triad (or threeness). The artist is offered as the origin of the artwork and the artwork is announced as the origin of the artist (since there would be no artist without the production of particular works). To the question: what is the origin of the artist and the artwork, the answer given is "Art." But then Art is what makes both the artist and the work possible. Here again, the hermeneutic circle—into which one must enter if meaning is to be disclosed—provides a context for situating oneself and one's thinking in the interpretive activity.

Moving around the circle, across the spaces of difference, origination, and relationality, the interpreter lets the being or the work (depending on which is in question) speak for itself. But if the being or the work truly speak for themselves, then the interpreter is also spoken by them. The disclosure is at the same time self-disclosure. The understanding of the meaning of Being or the meaning of the artwork is also self-understanding. Hence, something happens in the hermeneutic circle. One cannot suppose that the hermeneutic circle is vicious. Rather, the hermeneutic circle discloses the truth of being or the truth of the artwork. But what is the meaning of this disclosed truth? If we wish to appropriate that meaning, we must consult semiotics.

Before asking about the role of semiotics in this connection, however, consider the function of language and play in what Gadamer calls "aesthetic non-differentiation." Dante's *La Vita Nuova* shall serve as the guide and the occasion. As an artwork (in Heidegger's sense), the *Vita Nuova* is the result of the activity of Dante the artist or poet. The poet Dante is an artist-writer-author by virtue of having produced not only the *Vita Nuova* but also the *Convivio*, the *De Monarchia*, the *Divina Commedia*, and so on. But what of his Art? His Art is the disclosure of what Heidegger calls "poetry," the presentation of life, a life—that of Dante himself—but also life itself, illuminated through the beatific vision of God's grace. The disclosure, the truth laid bare, brought out of concealment, is not simply the personal itinerary of a young man in the late thirteenth and early fourteenth centuries. A meaning is disclosed: the meaning of poetry, the meaning of love (and not just infatuation)—love for Beatrice—love of God, and personal transfiguration through the experience of the two loves. This multifaceted meaning discloses a world—a late medieval world—based in Florence, developed out of elaborate classical learning and theological conviction, but also out of political involvement in the conflicts that necessitate leaving a city, journeying away, veiling one's true convictions, and so on. Heidegger's Fourfold—*das Geviert* (earth, sky, mortals, and divinities)—is the context of this disclosure: the Florentine soil against the trinitarian illuminated sky, the all-too-evident finitude of human life—the death of Beatrice, the importance of her mortality, and the *visio Dei* that her death occasioned for the young poet.

Just as Heidegger in *Unterwegs zur Sprache*[6] recognizes the importance of language in the speaking of poetry, so Gadamer announces language as the horizon of a hermeneutic ontology. Language is not the ontic, idle, everyday chatter as the early Heidegger first proposed. Rather it is the very call of Being—the *logos*—through which one can pass from the abyss *(Ab-grund)* to the ground *(Grund)*. Although Heidegger delineates the shift from the abyss *(Ab-grund)*, which Hölderlin announces as a "destitute time" and out of which Rilke indicates a way (to Nature as *Ur-grund)*, it could be said that Dante's poetry also points the way out of an abyss. His ground is other: it has all the trappings of medieval religiosity, but it also opens up a space for poetry. In this sense, language can be regarded as the horizon of a hermeneutic ontology. In language, the interpretive experience is the specification of the substitution of interpreter for artist, author, or poet. In the Heideggerian hermeneutic circle, the position of the interpreter must necessarily occupy that of the artist-author-poet and thereby enter into the hermeneutic circle as interpreter of the artwork and as involved in the disclosure of Art, Literature, Poetry. When language (*logos*)—as "Word" or *Verbum*—is invoked by Heidegger in the *Logos* essay and again in the *Language* essay, he identifies that which speaks: "language speaks." The language of the *Vita Nuova* speaks:

> In the book of my memory, after the first pages, which are almost blank, there is a section headed *Incipit vita nova*. Beneath this heading I find the words which it is my intention to copy into this smaller book, or if not all, at least their meaning. (*In quella parte del libro de la mia memoria dinanzi a la quale dice: Incipit vita nova. Sotto la quale rubrica io trovo scritte le parole le quali e mio intendimento d'assemblare in questo libello, e se non tutte, almeno la loro sentenzia.*)[7]

The opening words speak from the work as the interpreter interprets them by placing them between the work and his own interpretive position. The interpretation stresses the vernacular prose language which is set off against the poetic sonnets which are to come. The interpretation notes the language of memory as a book—a large book—which is to be copied into a smaller one. A correspondence or *resemblance* between the book of memory and the written book bespeaks the common activity of copying from one book into another. Accordingly, the second book is illuminated with vivid and colorful images. What is copied is not so much words as their meaning *(sentenzia)*. Thus, in the newly written work, when language speaks, the meaning is what is spoken. The interpretative, mediating activity in its relation to the written work brings out this articulated meaning in the work. What Gadamer adds is that this language is the medium of the hermeneutical experience.

For Gadamer, the interpretive consciousness seeks to distinguish itself from the work. In the nineteenth century, this position went under the name of "aesthetic consciousness." Gadamer seeks to demonstrate that the theory of aesthetic consciousness presupposes a function of "aesthetic differentiation" through which "the work loses its place as well as the world to which it belongs insofar as it belongs to aesthetic consciousness" (*TM*, p. 79). And Gadamer goes on to say, "this is paralleled by the artist also losing his place in the world" (*TM*, p. 79). Aesthetic consciousness distinguishes the position of the interpreter from that of the work. The work is abstracted from its world and taken as the object of a consciousness in which an "aesthetic differentiation" *(Unterscheidung* not *Differenz)* takes place between the interpreter and the work. Gadamer opposes this sort of "aesthetic differentiation" in favor of aesthetic non-differentiation—namely, the non-distinction between the representation or presentation and that which is represented or presented. However, the non-differentiation occurs in the place delineated by the conception of aesthetic differentiation. Or, to put it another way, the differentiation is imposed upon a space of non-differentiation. This is the space of play—Merleau-Ponty referred to it as a *Spielraum*—the domain in which the interpretive activity occurs as it situates itself in the place of language. There, the distinctions between speaking and the spoken, representing and the represented, voice and content do not assume an oppositional form. The play of language involves a "transformation of structure" and a "total mediation" such that the work and its meaning are not distinct. Hence one finds the following lines opening the first sonnet of the *Vita Nuova*:

> To every captive soul and gentle lover
> Into whose sight this present rhyme may chance,
> That, writing back, each may expound its sense,
> Greetings in Love, who is their Lord, I offer.
> (*A chiacun'alma presa e gentil core*
> *nel cui cospetto ven lo dir presente,*
> *in chiò che mi rescrivan suo parvente,*
> *salute in lor segnor, choè Amore.*) (*VN*, p. 32).

Here it becomes evident that both the presentation of Love and its inscription are not different. The sense of meaning may be multiple in that it is often repeated in many contexts—there are, one hopes, many who love. In Gadamer's view, however, the sense of Love and the writing of it in the interpretation of Dante's poem are not distinct. The distinction between the being of language and the way in which it presents itself is really not a distinction at all (*TM*, p. 432). The language of the sonnet is conjoined with a prose section in which Dante announces: "As I had already tried my hand at the art of composing rhyme, I decided to write a sonnet in which I would greet all Love's faithful servants; and so, requesting them to interpret my dread, I described what I had seen in my sleep. This was the sonnet beginning: To every captive soul..."(*VN*, p. 32). Here the language of narrative, recitative, and explication leads into the language of poetry. The meaning of the language (namely, the greeting of those servants of Love) is not distinct from the prose description on the one hand or the poetic version on the other. In both cases, the language constitutes a horizon of meaning in which the being of language speaks and renders the sense that is presented. The interpretation of language and horizon in each case, and in conjunction with its horizon produces understanding. Or, as Ricoeur further elaborates, interpretation develops the intentional orientation toward a world and the reflexive orientation toward a self (*HHS*, p. 171).

Curiously, near the end of *Truth and Method*, Gadamer substitutes the term "text" for "work." The substitution seems to be entirely arbitrary. Furthermore, it does not seem to imply a full recognition of its rationale. However, the very function of the "work" results from the activity of the artist (or by a different substitution) that of the interpreter. The "work" the *Vita Nuova* is the work of Dante the poet and writer. The shift to understanding the *Vita Nuova* as a "text" is an important move—indeed one that opens up the space in which the conjuncture of hermeneutics and semiotics is made possible. The place in which the *Vita Nuova* can be understood as a text in Gadamer's formulation is the place where he locates language. The text is not the work. The text is at best in the place of language as the horizon of a hermeneutic ontology. The text is, in this respect, the limit of the being of the interpretive activity. The text is not the product of the artist's creative skills. The text is also not identical with Gadamer's notion of language. The text does not incorporate its textuality in the same way that Gadamer's notion of language incorporates its meaning. But Gadamer says nothing of textuality, a fundamental feature of any hermeneutic semiology.

In Ricoeur's hermeneutics, the text acquires a more definite specification. However, by considering works as texts Ricoeur seems to maintain a nostalgia for the artist-author-poet. Indeed, he claims that "a text is any discourse fixed by writing" (*HHS*, p. 145). Discourse, whose basic unit is the sentence, is realized as an event and understood as meaning. The event in which discourse is realized could be either speaking or writing. However, when discourse is text, it is preserved in an impoverished form—namely, the fixing of an anterior speech. Text is writing and thereby impoverished speech. The *Vita Nuova* is the fixing of Dante's voice by writing. But Ricoeur does not want to take the simple view that writing was initially speaking. Rather, he wants to suggest that the text is written precisely because it is not said. There is no dialogue between writer and reader (as Jean-Paul Sartre calls for in *Qu'est-ce que la littérature?*). This emancipation of the text from the oral situation interrupts the relations between language and the world (*HHS*, p. 148). Language cannot simply refer to the world in the name of the text. For Gadamer, language and its meaning-horizon might be a more plausible way to understand the text than to equate it with, or substitute it for, the work. However, Gadamer does not make the move which Ricoeur proposes. For Ricoeur, the text is an autonomous space of meaning which is no longer animated by the intention of its author. The author has been cut off from the text: this is why it seems odd to say that works (which are not cut off from their author) might be considered as texts. But again, this view implies a nostalgia for the author as origin and source of meaning in the text. The *Vita Nuova* is autonomous; it "speaks" in its own name, develops its own structures of meaning, and even inscribes its own interlocutors (as in the first sonnet, where other lovers are invited to reply or write back to the poet). The positions of the author Dante and the narrative voice—the "I" who writes, who remembers, who loves, etc.—are not the same.

For Ricoeur, however, discourse is produced in an event—either spoken or written. The meaning of the text (written discourse) is supported by the structure of the *proposition* (that is, singular identification and general predication). The event of the text is not the authorial event, nor is the meaning the author's meaning. Both the event and meaning are available for interpretation or explanation. Explanation concerns the "sense" or immanent pattern of discourse. Interpretation develops reference (that about which something is said) in that the text applies itself to an extralinguistic reality about which it says what it says. Interpretive activity involves a dialectic of distanciation and appropriation. Distanciation concerns the way in which a text is addressed to someone (for instance, the *Vita Nuova* sonnet, as addressed to lovers). Appropriation involves a playful transposition of the text, in which the reader—who unlike the author is not cut off from the text—enters into the text and makes it his or her own. This does not entail the traditional psychological identification of reader with characters or features described, but rather an adoption of the postures of the text. Appropriation involves a gathering together of meaning features that are proper to the text. The fact that Ricoeur allows for the cooperation of interpretation and explanation of texts indicates the proximity of his position to that of a hermeneutic semiology.

TOWARD A HERMENEUTIC SEMIOLOGY OF THE TEXT

The text is located and operates at the intersection of semiotics and hermeneutics. The text is neither strictly nuclear nor explicitly marginal. It is neither pure differential event nor pure sign function. The text is active at the place of conjuncture between semiotics and hermeneutics, the place in which it elaborates its meaning structures, its textuality, whose features are the province of a hermeneutic semiology.

The semiotic concern with texts—at least in the version offered by Roland Barthes—arises out of his earlier theory of writing *(écriture)*. In the *Degré zero de l'écriture* (1953),[8] Barthes explores the intersection of the writer's individual idiosyncratic style and the language of the epoch in terms of which that writer writes. This meeting-point of a horizontal (Cartesian coordinates x-axis) language and a vertical (y-axis) style designates the neutral, zero degree place of *writing*. In this way, Barthes's theory of writing invokes neither the subjective intentional concerns of the writer nor the objective causal conditioning introduced by the language which the writer employs. Each *écriture* is repeatable not only in the same period but in others as well. The exploration of writing at zero degree ([0,0] in Cartesian coordinates—the place of intersection) opens up the space of the text, which Barthes subsequently replaces with writing, but it says nothing about *how* writing is to be read or interpreted or understood. Only when Barthes develops his notion of *text* (in contrast to that of *work* such as in Heidegger) does he begin to develop his view of the death of the author. In the essay entitled "The Death of the Author," Barthes claims that "writing is the destruction of every voice, of every point of origin." "Writing," he continues, "is that neutral, composite, oblique space where our subject slips away, the negative where all identity is lost, starting with the very identity of the body writing."[9] The death of the author brings with it the birth of the reader. The author is rigidly excluded from consideration. And in Barthes, there is no apparent nostalgia for the author-artist-poet as in Ricoeur. "Linguistically," Barthes writes, "the author is never more than the instance writing, just as *I* is nothing other than the instance saying *I*" (*IMT-DA*, p. 145). The "I" of the *Vita Nuova* is the instance of a youthful poet seeking to verbalize his experience of love and to perfect the act of doing so through writing. The *énoncé* (statement or enunciation) of the text does not depend upon the temporal and spatial conditions of the author: "There is no other time than that of the enunciation and every text is eternally written *here* and *now*" (*IMT-DA*, p. 145).

But what happens where the text is located? In *S/Z* (1971),[10] Barthes claims that there are fundamentally two types of text: those which are *lisible* and those which are *scriptible*. The readerly *(lisible)* text, however, is the text rewritten in terms of its codes, sign systems, and structures. Here the enunciations are entered into a categorial, coded, scheme. In his reading of Balzac's *Sarrasine*, Barthes offers five such codes: the semic, the referential, the hermeneutic, the action, and the symbolic. Each lexia of the narrative is read in terms of some scheme of encoding. The codes are not those of Hjelmslev or Eco (as in his theory of code production), but they motivate the reading of this particular text. That they could be employed in the reading of most texts is worthy of mention.

The text—as is evident from recent developments in hermeneutics—is not the work. The work, Barthes points out, "is a fragment of substance, occupying a part of the space of books (in a library for example). The text is a methodological field" (*IMT-DA*, p. 157). The text practices the infinite deferment of the signified—its field is that of the signifier—the signifying chain" (*IMT-DA*, p. 158). It has none of the processes of filiation that prevail in the work (with the author in a paternal position) and determined by world, race, History, etc. When the author returns to the text, it is as a guest. The text is plural; its multiple meanings are neither centered nor closed off.

The text, then, is an open field participating in the proliferation of sign production. In Peircean terms,[11] the text would be a complex of signs with their tripartite interpretant, object, and ground. However, despite his highly elaborate theory of signs, Peirce does not propose an explicit theory of the text. Yet, were one to read the sign in its triadic set of relations (icon, index, and symbol), its relation to the object might denote the fundamental features of the text. According to Peirce, the *icon* denotes merely by virtue of characters of its own; the *index* is really affected by the object; and the *symbol* is the performance of a law. In this case, the text would correspond to that which lies outside its domain—namely, the domain of the object and the ground that accompanies it. The sign, in its proliferative function, would be what Peirce calls the interpretant. The interpretant incorporates a reading of the relation to the object and its ground in terms of icon, index, or symbol. In proposing the conjunction of hermeneutics and semiology, Carlo Sini cites the Peircean interpretant as the basis for such a connection. Although not identical with the Saussurean *signifier*, the *interpretant* (like the *signifier*) establishes the conditions for a description of the text. Both signifier and interpretant raise the problem of denotation, or the question of the relation to the object. In the Saussurian tradition, the signified (whether concept or object) remains ambiguous whereas in Peirce it becomes unequivocal. Peirce's sign involves a clear relation to the object. If the text is, for example, the *Vita Nuova*, the clear relation to the object poses problems for the purely semiotic theory of the text as a complex of signs. However by allowing for various ways in which the sign as interpretant can refer to the object, Peirce makes it evident that signs cannot be read simply in terms of their signifiers. Here then we find the basis for Sini's view that Peircean semiotics can be combined with hermeneutics in that the theory of signs can operate in relation to the world with its objects and grounding by situating itself within the hermeneutic circle.

If, by contrast, one were to focus on the theory of the text rather than on the theory of signs, the place of intersection between hermeneutics and semiotics assumes a different shape. Text, in the hermeneutic understanding of Gadamer and Ricoeur, is located where language (in Gadamer) opens up a horizon of interpretive meaning. In Ricoeur, language is given further specificity as discourse. For Ricoeur, writing is autonomous in terms of its meaning. However, it is also available for the appropriative and distancial activities of an interpretation.

On the side of semiology, the text is an open system of signs with plural meanings. The plurality of meaning arises because the semiological notion of signification (based on the act or process of a signifier combined with a signified) has been broken open by the stress on the chain of signifiers. The signifying chain produces multiple significations which even Dante (building upon Hugh of St. Victor's fourfold method of interpretation) proposes for the reading of his own texts. The text, in hermeneutics, is that which offers its meaning through the *event* of the text as it is interpreted in relation to the world and as a reflection back upon the interpreting self. The text, in Peircean semiotics, would refer to the world iconically, indexically, and symbolically, but the reflection upon the self would be left in suspension. In semiology, the text would offer its own multiple readings in its *atopic plurisignificational* dimensions. A hermeneutic semiology would seek to offer a reading of the text in terms of its meaning structures as they relate to elements in the world and as they refer back not to a centered self but to the interpretive activity itself. Such a reading of meaning structures in their plurisignificational character occurs in a cultural/natural, social/individual, etc. *milieu* as a *reading* of the textuality (or textualities) of the text.

3

HERMENEUTICS AND INTERROGATION

Ask me no questions, I'll tell you no lies.
—Goldsmith, *She Stoops to Conquer*

Interpretation develops the aspect of meaning which we have called "reference," that is, the intentional orientation towards a world and the reflexive orientation towards a self.
—Ricoeur, "Metaphor and the Problem of Hermeneutics"

In sum, philosophy interrogates the perceptual faith—but neither expects nor receives an answer in the ordinary sense, because it is not the disclosing of a variable or of an unknown invariant that will satisfy this question, and because the existing world exists in the interrogative mode. Philosophy is the perceptual faith questioning itself about itself.
—Merleau-Ponty, *The Visible and the Invisible*

Interpretation and interrogation are not the same. Yet they occupy the same space. The hermeneutics of Heidegger, Gadamer, and Ricoeur offer an account of interpretation that moves away from the egocentric, subject-based, self-directed conception that is most commonly associated with Husserlian phenomenology. There is no authority here, only authenticity and authorization. Similarly Merleau-Pontean interrogation opens up a field in which questioning takes priority, where the answers are located neither in the questioner, nor in that which is questioned. In both cases, interpretation and interrogation happen in the space of difference where the production of discursive meaning is decentered and "praxical." Their task is to raise questions rather than answer them, to ask about rather than conclude for, to make a place where positions *can occur* rather than speak *from* positions.

The task here is to understand: (1) this displacement of positionality; (2) the opening up of a space of difference; and (3) the reading of the truths and lies that constitute the textualities of experience. This threefold understanding will demonstrate both the commonality and the differential marks of the hermeneutic enterprise and the interrogative practice. Although the epistemological features of the two continental philosophies (namely, hermeneutics and interrogation) are similar in many ways, the implications of their respective enactments are distinct albeit complementary.

ABDICATING THE THRONE

The subject has been sitting on the throne. Husserl called it the "transcendental ego," William James called it the "pure ego," and Freud simply invoked the ego as the centerpiece of the psychical realm. In each case, this modernist conception takes the subject as the center, foundation, source, point of departure, last court of appeal, and determinate authority for all conscious life. The subject reigns supreme and, although sometimes limited by material conditions, social restraints, and unconscious desires, its rational demands cannot be questioned. In this modernist outlook, to question the subject is to compromise its groundedness, to uproot its right to assert formal conditions for the expression of any content, to undermine its absolute authority over what it knows, understands, and performs. However along with this supremacy and dominance comes the possibility of its failure and displacement. In the literature of modernism, the authority of the ego is placed in question. Dostoyevsky's underground man, Joyce's Ulyssean wanderer, Kafka's castle seeker, Woolf's ego-splitting Clarissa Dalloway, and Eliot's wasteland inhabitants are the constructions of an ego in crisis. The subject that is given the philosophical throne is placed in doubt across a field of literary formulations. The ego's "divine right of kings" is almost at once matched up with a revolutionary spirit in which the subject's position calls for a reassessment and restructuring of its self-assertions. Encased within the force of the subject is the self-recognition and self-understanding in which the self does not have the power that it might have wished to claim for itself. Its position on the throne is no longer certain, no longer determinate, no longer beyond question, no longer apodictic and complete unto itself. The self shows itself to be incomplete, uncertain, and explicitly dubitable.

The subject is forced to abdicate the throne. The self cannot simply prevail. The center cannot hold. The ego cannot speak for all its acts. The cogito can no longer proclaim itself supreme. Like semiology (or semiotics), both hermeneutics and interrogation have been engaged in an enterprise in which the ego must surrender its authority. The position of understanding can no longer stand at the subjective pole, in the place which opposes itself to the objective pole. Knowledge can no longer be produced as if it were a ball shot from a cannon. Rather, as hermeneutics comes to show, knowledge is more like placing the activity of the knowing self in the track of the trajectory. In hermeneutics, the self abdicates when it says that it is not the source of authority. Rather the interpreter operates in the "between," in the space of difference which is neither that of the subject nor that of the object. In hermeneutics, the "in-between" is the place where the subject says that it is not supreme. Its knowing is neither what it knows nor what does the knowing. Knowledge and understanding (which is derived from knowledge) are not the province of the knowing subject. Rather they belong to the place in which the knowing occurs, namely where the self stands up against *(Gegen-stand)* the thing (constituted as an object). Knowing and understanding occur (if they are to occur) in the relation of the self to its objects. And that place of relation has no content. Unlike the position propounded by transcendental phenomenology (and its relatives), hermeneutics tries to apprehend its activity as located in the place *between,* in the space of difference. Interpretation is indeed the very activity of placing between: the messenger who travels back and forth between Zeus and the other gods, or between Zeus and human beings. This Hermes is a go-between. Hermeneutics is a philosophy of go-betweenness. Hermeneutics does not speak from a throne. Its job is to carry the message, to bring out the Word, to disclose what is unspoken, to uncover the sub-floor. Hermeneutics cannot speak from a ground. It must place itself where the ground sets itself off against the absence of ground (or abyss). The task of hermeneutics is to operate in the space of difference between subject and object, ground and non-ground, thinker and thought, speaker and spoken about, knower and that which is to be known.

Just as hermeneutics cannot operate from the position of the subject, it also cannot situate itself in the place of the thing itself. The thing wants to present itself as nature. The thing seeks to function as if it were the source of knowledge, as if it were the source of authority for all science. It is not that the thing provides no data, but it is also not that the thing is what knowing is all about. The thing can be an object, but it cannot be the inter-pretation. Inter-pretation—not the thing and not the subject—renders knowledge and understanding.

Similarly in interrogation. The asking is not an activity of the subject, self, or ego, nor is it initiated by the visible thing. The subject has no authority here. The thing cannot constitute or direct or determine what the interrogative activity will be. Philosophy interrogates. Philosophy places itself in the between. It does not offer itself as a transcendental subject nor even as the condition for transcendental subjectivity. Philosophy as interrogation surrenders any right to speak with absolute authority, to present itself as the condition for all knowledge, to look down from above. With Merleau-Pontean interrogation, there is no longer any need to abdicate the throne—it has already displaced its authority. Questioning simply happens in the place between—if it is to happen at all.

OPENING A SPACE

The space of difference opened up by the practice of hermeneutic interpretation is established by the act of *placing between.* Inter-pretation takes authority away from the subject and at the same time away from the thing. Just as the self places itself between, so the thing operates in that context of betweenness. As Ricoeur puts it, "interpretation develops the aspect of meaning which we have called 'reference,' that is, the intentional orientation towards a world and the reflexive orientation towards a self" (*HHS*, p. 171). The "meaning" or "reference" is neither that toward which the interpretive act is directed nor that from which it is directed. Interpretation, then, is the activity of understanding that provides meaning. But meaning itself is not a focus, an identity, a single unity. Meaning here is a practice, an activity, an elaboration of a field.

This field is opened up as "difference" in the Heideggerian formulation. This difference is the difference between the ontic and the ontological, between that which is present *(Anwesend)* and the presence *(Anwesen)* of that which is present, between the abyss or non-ground *(Ab-Grund)* and ground *(Grund)*, between the inauthentic *(Uneigentlich)* and the authentic *(Eigentlich)*. This ontico-ontological difference has no content, yet it is precisely where interpretation must take place. But what happens in this space of difference?

Heidegger says that the being which is here *(Da-sein)* calls out the relation to Being, names the ontico-ontological difference as a difference—but it does not "call" or "name" from the outside. Rather it occurs by situating itself there *(Da)* in the difference itself. But this difference is not an inside any more than it is an outside. To name this difference is to name what the later Heidegger simply calls "the Open." By naming the difference, *Da-sein* places itself in this Open. There it is able to engage in the very act of interpretation. Interpretation happens in this clearing *(Lichtung)*. Yet it has no authority there. Interpretation occupies the space of difference by spreading into all the cracks and corners of what is to be interpreted. However, it is not the interpreted that occupies the space of difference. Nor is it the interpreter who occupies this space. To the extent that the interpreter and the interpreted are dis-placed into the Open, they lose their independent identities. Interpretation takes the position of the non-position. In this way, the multiple meanings and dimensions of what is interpreted can disclose themselves, make themselves evident, and bring out their features—without being derived from either the interpreter or the interpreted. The interpretation is the belonging *(Zu-gehörigkeit)* which is heard *(gehört)* when the calling, naming, speaking of the interpretation takes place. The interpretation speaks for itself. It is its own meaning, its own referentiality, its own text. The task of hermeneutics is to make the interpretation speak, to elaborate the framework, encirclements, and delimitations that mark out the space of difference in which the interpretation is located. If an event, or an idea, or an experience, or a poem is interpreted, the interpretation will bring out the respects in which the event, idea, experience, or poem means, speaks, and discloses its limits. The achievement of the interpretation is the appropriation of a space which is neither that of the interpreter nor that of the interpreted, but one which uncovers what most needs to be said with respect to that which is interpreted.

Heidegger writes: "The intimacy of world and thing is present in the separation of the between; it is present in the dif-ference" (*PLT-L*, p. 202). The thing—as that which is to be interpreted—discloses a world. This world, which separates itself from the thing and grants the thing its independence, opens up the very space of difference in which the interpretation as appropriation can occur. The world is, of course, also not the subject. The world differs from the thing, but does not constitute it:

> World and thing do not subsist alongside one another. They penetrate each other. Thus the two traverse a middle. In it, they are at one. Thus as one they are intimate. The middle of the two is intimacy—in Latin, *inter*. The corresponding German word is *unter*, the English *inter-*. The intimacy of world and thing is not a fusion. Intimacy obtains only where the intimate—world and thing—divides itself cleanly and remains separated. In the midst of the two, in the between of world and thing, in their *inter*, division prevails: a *dif-ference* (*PLT-L*, p. 202).

Heidegger calls a "worlding" what goes on in this dif-ference. "Worlding" is an activity of providing meaning without offering an identity of content and concept. "Worlding" is an interpretive disclosure in which the interpreted (the thing) opens up an understanding that does not belong to the thing. In the dif-ference of world and thing, the thing is appropriated by disclosing its meaning, by rendering it no longer complete and identical unto itself. Indeed, the thing is ex-propriated in order for the worlding, interpreting, disclosing to take place.

Merleau-Pontean interrogation takes the next step. It not only places meaning in the space of difference, it animates a questioning that places what is to be interpreted (or interrogated) in the interrogative mode. Merleau-Ponty writes:

> Philosophy does not raise questions and does not provide answers that would little by little fill in the blanks. The questions are within our life, within our history: they are born there, they die there, if they have found a response, more often than not they are transformed there; in any case, it is a past of experience and of knowledge that one day ends up at this open wondering. Philosophy does not take the context as given; it turns back upon it in order to seek the origin and meaning of the questions and of the responses and the identity of him who questions, and it thereby gains access to the interrogation that animates all the questions of cognition, but is of another sort than they.[1]

"Interrogation animates all the questions of cognition, but is of another sort than they." This means that by seeking the meaning and origin of questions, interrogation distinguishes itself from the visible world. Interrogation operates in what Heidegger calls the Open. An intertwining of the visible and invisible, of what sees, touches, hears, says, understands and the seen, touched, heard, said, understood sets up the chiasmatic space in which interrogation occurs. Here, then, interrogation provides the life of cognition. It is not itself cognition. Interrogation is also not interpretation cum cognition; rather it is the questioning that makes interpretation possible. Philosophy interrogates so that something can be seen, something can be said, something can be known, something can be understood, something can be interrogated. As a fundamental ontology, interrogation operates in the open space of difference so that meaning, reference, and cognition can happen. But interrogation is not itself another ground, a foundation that replaces the transcendental subject. Interrogation is the questioning that makes the position of the subject as well as the isolated position of the objective visible world untenable. When philosophy interrogates it operates in the interwoven, intertwined—textual—space in which visible things and invisible subjects, objects known and the knowing of them are differentiated and yet looked into, asked about, placed—not in doubt but—in question.

READING TRUTHS AND LIES

In Oliver Goldsmith's eighteenth-century play *She Stoops to Conquer*, one finds the now well-known line: "Ask me no questions, I'll tell you no lies."[2] If no questions are asked, no lies will be produced. If no questioning takes place, no lies can be provided. Of course, it is also the case that if no questions are asked, no questioning takes place, and no truths will be brought forth either. Without questions, without questioning, there will be neither truths nor lies. As we have come to think since Heidegger, truth is disclosure. *Aletheia* is a bringing out of concealment, uncovering that which is hidden, covered up, unavailable to activities of understanding. *Aletheia* is the move away from oblivion, forgetfulness, ignoring that which is most important. Truth is this abandonment of the oblivious, forgotten, ignored features of our daily lives, encounters with things, relations with other people, historical conditions, examination of the natural world, construction of ideas. Truth in the hermeneutic account is a "revealing-concealing-gathering which lights everything present in its presencing."[3] By revealing-concealing-gathering, interpretation makes truth happen. But is this also how lies happen?

Interpretation seeks to disclose that which is hidden, to make a place for truth—in the clearing, the lighting, the Open. Interpretation happens in the space of difference. But it happens there in the space of difference—not by asking *me* questions. To ask *someone* questions is to establish a place of authority, a transcendental signified, a place of final resort. But as we have seen, the subject is not up to such confidence. It would be a mistake to invest it with such confidence. The task is not to ask *someone* questions. To do so could produce either truths or lies. Yet it is also the case that if the someone—transcendental subject, source of knowledge, position of sovereignty—were even a conditional point of reference, that self could not itself know whether it was producing truths or lies. Not to ask at all would be one way to solve the problem. If there are no questions, then there is nothing to worry about: neither lies nor truths will be offered. Yet this can hardly be the most appropriate solution.

The production of truths and lies is the production of discourse. As Heidegger puts it, "Language speaks. Its speaking bids the dif-ference to come which expropriates world and things into the simple onefold of their intimacy"

(*PLT-L*, p. 210). When language speaks in the place of difference, it produces a discourse in which truths and lies are possible, for discourse is the speaking of truths and lies, scientific, nonfictional, reliable writing and literary, fictional, creative writing. The speaking of language is the speaking of truths and lies. Indeed, "man speaks," writes Heidegger, "only as he responds to language. Language speaks. Its speaking speaks for us in what has been spoken" (*PLT-L*, p. 210). The production of discourse, the dissemination of knowledge, occurs in the speaking of language, in the appropriated space of difference. It is not possible not to speak. Language cannot not speak. Discourse cannot not produce truths and lies.

Insofar as discourse cannot not produce truths and lies, there must also be questions. Questions, as the Goldsmith character makes perfectly clear, render it possible for there to be lies as well as truths. By questioning, language opens up a space for both scientific language and poetic language, nonfiction and fiction to happen. Questions happen in the Open, in the clearing, in the lighting, in the place of the appropriation itself. They happen where interpretation interposes itself. Interpretation, hermeneutics, thinking the relation to Being, listening to the poetry that speaks in the place of difference—these are the activities that are the context delineated by interrogation. Interrogation is asking in the between, in the chiasmatic intertwining of visible and invisible, in the place where visibility makes interpretation possible.[4] Visibility arises in the space of difference, in the place between. It also occurs where language speaks, where discourse is produced, where language in its most indirect character can announce itself as the place for questioning, as the place for disclosure, as the place for the production of nonfiction and fiction, in short, as the place of textuality.

4

INTERROGATION AND DECONSTRUCTION

In 1945, Maurice Merleau-Ponty published an article entitled "Le Doute de Cézanne."[1] Cézanne's experience of his world, his reservations about his work, and his views concerning the epistemology of painting are explored in detail. The sources for this information include documented conversations with and letters to Émile Bernard during the last years of Cézanne's life (1904–1906). Merleau-Ponty returns again to the postimpressionist painter's projects and perspectives in *Eye and Mind* (1961).[2] There, as in the posthumous *The Visible and the Invisible*, he develops the philosophical practice which he calls "interrogation."

Seventeen years later, Jacques Derrida publishes a piece in the art journal *Macula*, nos. 3/4, entitled "Restitutions de la verité en peinture."[3] The essay is then expanded and collected as the fourth of four forays "*around* painting" and published under the title *La Verité en peinture* (1978).[4] Although the essay is concerned with Martin Heidegger and Van Gogh's shoes as developed in the 1965 correspondence between Heidegger and the art critic Meyer Schapiro,[5] Derrida quotes (in epi-gramme) Cézanne's eighth of nine letters addressed to the painter Émile Bernard: "*Je vous dois la verité en peinture et je vous la dirai.*"[6] From this statement, cited by the philosopher and art critic Hubert Damisch, Derrida derives his title *La Verité en peinture*. In that text, as in previous writings, Derrida puts into practice the critical strategies of "deconstruction."

THINKING (TRUTH) IN PAINTING

For the statement, "*Je vous dois la verité en peinture, et je vous la dirai,*" Derrida cites Damisch (*Verité*, p. 6). Damisch was a student of Merleau-Ponty in the late 1940's. When the *Bulletin de Psychologie* collection of Merleau-Ponty's 1949–52 Sorbonne Lectures was published in 1964, Damisch was selected to produce the "Foreword."[7] Furthermore, while the statement (which Derrida cites) occurs at the end of the eighth letter (*Cézanne*, p. 46), in "Le Doute de Cézanne" Merleau-Ponty quotes the initial lines of the ninth letter (*SNS tr.*, p. 9).[8] There,

Cézanne describes a state of mental disorder, accompanied by a period of intense Provençal heat, after which more clement weather ensued and with it the sense that he could see better and think more clearly.

Merleau-Ponty repeats this association of seeing with thinking in *L'Oeil et l'esprit*, claiming that Cézanne "*pense en peinture*" (*OE*, p. 60; *EM*, p. 178).⁹ Merleau-Ponty interrogates Cézanne's world by noting that he "thinks in painting." Thinking, if we can invoke Heidegger, is necessary for the disclosure which is the very essence of truth. Thinking is a precondition for the production of truth. "Truth in painting," it could be claimed, is brought about by "thinking in painting." In any case, Cézanne asserts that he has a commitment to render the former ("truth") and that he engages in the latter ("thinking"). Derrida cites the former in order to develop his deconstructive strategies; Merleau-Ponty cites the latter in order to demonstrate the virtues of interrogation.

It is no accident that Merleau-Ponty's account of Cézanne focuses on his "thinking in painting" and that Derrida appeals to Cézanne's statement that he "owes truth in painting." For Merleau-Ponty, the task of philosophy is to interrogate the visible world of things. Philosophy is thinking. In that thinking is an interrogation of the visible world of things, it is not done as if by a third person witness of one's own vision nor like a geometrician who reconstitutes and surveys the visible world (*OE*, pp. 58–59; *EM*, p. 178). The visible world, when thought, is not interrogated from the outside. Interrogation operates at the "zero degree of spatiality." Interrogation situates itself in the place where the spatial and visible world of things is located. Thinking this spatial and visible world is not "speaking about space and light but rather making the space and light which are there speak" (*OE*, p. 59; *EM*, p. 178). For the painter to think in painting is for him to put what he sees into action, gesture, painting. The philosophy of thinking which animates the painter is not the sort in which opinions about the world are expressed, rather it is of the variety in which the painter transforms what he sees into a painting. The task of philosophy is thinking. Thinking is interrogating. The painter philosophizes in that he interrogates the visible world. He interrogates the visible world by painting what he sees, by transforming his vision into painting.¹⁰ According to Merleau-Ponty, Cézanne is thinking in painting.

Merleau-Ponty could well have taken up Cézanne's claim (issued to Émile Bernard) that he owes "truth in painting" and that "he will say it." Indeed, he does indicate that the painter makes space and light, which are already there, speak. In making space and light speak, Cézanne interrogates the visible world; he *says* the visible world in painting. But is he thereby saying "truth in painting"? Derrida suggests in the introductory essay to *La Verité en peinture*, entitled "Passe-partout," that perhaps Cézanne's speech act (in which he writes that he owes truth in painting) is the promise of a "painting act" in which he indicates that he will "say" truth in painting.

According to Derrida, the painting act would be the saying of the truth in painting, the performance of the truth in the act of painting. Truth occurs in the production of the painting. But this version is different from the account

Merleau-Ponty offers in which the painter makes space and light speak. For Derrida, Cézanne is promising to produce a discourse of truth in painting. For Merleau-Ponty, Cézanne is in fact making it possible for the visible world itself to speak. For Derrida, Cézanne writes a promise to render truth in what he does, namely painting, in such a way that visible things themselves speak. In Derrida's view, Cézanne proposes to say the truth in painting. According to Merleau-Ponty, Cézanne seeks to make visible things say what and how they are. Is the truth what and how things are? If so, then in Merleau-Ponty's version, visible things say the truth in painting; in Derrida's version, Cézanne writes his debt or self-imposed obligation to say the truth that already exists (or that he will render) in painting. Following Derrida, Cézanne writes what he will say; following Merleau-Ponty, Cézanne paints what things say. With Derrida, Cézanne writes a promise to say the truth (what and how things are); with Merleau-Ponty, Cézanne paints things and thereby says the truth (what and how things are). Merleau-Ponty interrogates the painting of visible things so that they might speak the truth; Derrida deconstructs the writing of the act of promising to say in painting what and how visible things are. In one case, the philosopher interrogates the painter interrogating the truth of visible things; in the other case, the philosopher deconstructs the painter's written commitment to paint the truth (of visible things).

How does the interrogation of an interrogation of the truth of things differ from the deconstruction of a writing of the painting of the truth (of things)? Interrogation is the asking about what is. Interrogation places itself between the asking and what is asked about. Interrogation makes it possible for what is asked about to speak. Interrogation places in question what is asked about so that it can speak for itself, so that it can announce itself, so that it can make itself known. When Merleau-Ponty asks about Cézanne painting visible things, he is offering an interrogation of an interrogation. The end, however, is for visible things to speak, for visible things to make their truth known. Interrogation brings out "the origin of truth," which after all was one of the preliminary titles for *The Visible and the Invisible*.

A deconstruction of a writing of the painting of the truth (of things) is a writing of a writing. Deconstruction is a writing performative. Writing about writing is putting writing into play, exploring its margins, limits, frontiers, and borderlines. Deconstructing Cézanne's "*je vous dois la verité en peinture et je vous la dirai,*" or, in short, "truth in painting," involves an examination of the limits and supplements to the written statement. For instance, in the fourth essay of *La Verité en peinture*, Derrida appeals to what he calls "*la verité en pointure*" (*Verité*, pp. 291–436). "Pointure" has to do with shoe size. So when looking at the correspondence between Meyer Schapiro and Martin Heidegger concerning Van Gogh's painting entitled "A Pair of Shoes," Derrida concerns himself with truth in shoe size. A supplement to the matter of "truth in painting" is the matter of "truth in shoe size." Along with the statement from Cézanne, Derrida cites a similar passage from Van Gogh. It reads: "*Mais elle m'est si chère, la verité, le chercher à faire vrai aussi, enfin je crois, je crois que je préfère encore être cordon-*

nier à être musicien avec les couleurs" (*Verité*, p. 291). ["But truth is so dear to me that to seek to make it true as well, in the end, I believe, I believe I still prefer to be a shoemaker (or shoemender) than to be a musician with colors."] Like Cézanne, Van Gogh wants to produce truth in painting; but truth cannot be a construct. If it were necessary to make the truth true, he would rather be a mender of shoes than a musician with colors. The connection between truth in painting and truth in shoes is already established in Van Gogh's statement. Thus Heidegger's account of truth as disclosure through the painting of "peasant shoes" is already available in Van Gogh's own writings. A deconstruction of "truth in painting" readily incorporates, along with Cézanne's promise, Van Gogh's abhorrence of verisimilitude in favor of shoemending as a vocation, Heidegger's claim about the disclosure of a being *(ein Seiende)* in its relation to Being *(Sein)* in Van Gogh's painting of "a pair of peasant shoes," Meyer Schapiro's dispute with Heidegger over the identity of the painted shoes (claiming simply that the shoes are those of the painter and not of a peasant), and the dictionary definition of "*pointure*" (shoe points or shoe sizes) which Derrida offers in epigrammatic form.[11]

The deconstruction of truth in painting introduces a whole chain of supplementarity with respect to the "initial" statement by Cézanne. The deconstruction of the writing of the painting of the truth (of things) is then an examination of the dissemination (spreading out, sending forth, publication) of Cézanne's writing into that of Van Gogh, Heidegger, Schapiro, and so forth. The interrogation of the interrogation of the truth of things (it will be remembered) asks about the visible things themselves.

VISIBILITY AND SUPPLEMENTARITY

What, it may be asked, is at issue in the opposition between interrogation and deconstruction? The question is different from the one which asks what is at issue in each practice respectively. The former presupposes the latter. At issue in interrogation is the logic of visibility; at issue in deconstruction is the logic of supplementarity. In juxtaposing the two, one finds that visibility is a sort of phenomenological supplementarity and supplementarity is a sort of textual visibility. Such a claim is tenuous and requires elaboration. Nevertheless, in order to make sense of the claim, each logic must be considered in its own right.

In the later writings, Merleau-Ponty's project is to bring out the logic of visibility. Visibility arises out of the conjuncture of the visible and the invisible. Visibility is situated at the horizon of the visible. Visibility is both that which arises out of seeing visible things in the world and the condition of the possibility of such seeing. Visibility both identifies visible things as seen, as visible, and distributes them throughout the field of vision. Accompanying visible things is the invisible vision which sees. For Merleau-Ponty, this visibility is located in and passes through the locus of the body. Visible objects surround us, and even enter into us as embodied seers in the world. One's fleshly situatedness in the world makes one particularly susceptible to the sensuous qualities of the texture of things. We see things, we touch things, we feel things—we thereby incorporate them into our daily existence. Visibility is our incorporation of things and that which renders it possible for us to, in fact, incorporate things.

Visibility occurs where there is vision. We encounter things through vision in general. However, we also form a "constant style of visibility" (*VI*, p. 192; *VI tr.*, p. 146) according to which we operate in the world. Visibility establishes the intertwining or chiasm in which this style is given expression, in which the visible is brought into relation with the invisible, with seeing itself, with vision and touch. This style is allusive, elliptical, as is any style, but also inimitable and inalienable like any style (*VI*, pp. 199–200; *VI tr.*, p. 152). In seeking to reproduce the visibility of a vision in its relation to visible things, the painter transforms the visibility of the painting. But what is at issue is not simple reproduction. From the crossing over which occurs between the seeing and the seen, the touching and the touched, the eye and the other, one hand and the other, the painter transforms this curious system of exchanges into paint.

The manifest visibility of our experience of the visible world of things is doubled in a secret visibility (*OE*, p. 22; *EM*, p. 164) in which the painter brings forth a new visibility. In this sense, painting "gives visible existence to that which profane vision believed to be invisible" (*OE*, p. 27; *EM*, p. 166). Painting renders visible what many who might have seen did not really see. When Cézanne paints the Mont Saint-Victoire, many who have traveled through Aix-en-Provence, and even those who have lived there all their lives, will not have seen the mountain as Cézanne sees it. The mountain is visible to them. They see it; but they do not have access to the visibility that the painter sees and produces until it has unfolded through the painting. The visibility of the actual mountain is doubled in the visibility of the painting and a new visibility arises.

Painting has this effect of a new visibility whether it is figurative or not. In a certain sense, with the appearance of the painting, a new visibility occurs because there is a new visible thing. But this would be too simple. Merleau-Ponty makes the point in a radical way: "painting never celebrated any other enigma than that of visibility" (*OE*, p. 26; *EM*, p. 166). His claim is that painting is the celebration of visibility in that it calls attention to the visibility of things, makes the thematization of vision possible, and opens up hidden features of the already visible world of things.

Interrogation operates according to a logic of visibility. Visibility is what interrogation ultimately seeks to identify and characterize. To interrogate visible things is to examine their visibility. To interrogate vision is to explore its visibility. To interrogate painting is to reveal its visibility. The interrogation of visible things is the asking after their truth. The interrogation of vision is an inquiry concerning its truth. The interrogation of painting places its truth in question. To interrogate the visibility of painting is to interrogate truth in painting.

It is curious that Merleau-Ponty does not cite Cézanne's statement: "*Je vous dois la verité en peinture et je vous la dirai.*" Merleau-Ponty could well have written, because Cézanne interrogates the visibility of the visible world through his painterly vision, that he thereby owes (has a commitment to render) truth in painting (i.e., the visibility of painting). For Cézanne to produce *truth* in painting would be for him to produce the visibility of visible things in the visibility of painting. However, Merleau-Ponty notes, in "Cézanne's Doubt," that Cézanne "writes as painter what has not yet been painted and he renders it absolutely (as) painting" (*SNS*, p. 30; *SNS-tr.*, p. 17). The painter writes the visibility of things and transforms it into the visibility of the painting. That is, the painter sees the truth of visible things and produces truth in painting. Truth in painting, as we gather from Derrida's deconstructive reading of Cézanne's dictum, is what the painter has an obligation to produce. The interrogation of the visibility of painting, in Merleau-Ponty's account, becomes the deconstruction of "truth in painting" in the Derridean reading.

Merleau-Ponty, in *Eye and Mind*, remarks that the painter experiences an "urgency" which surpasses all other urgencies. Later he asks, "What is this dimension according to which Van Gogh wants to go 'further'?" (*OE*, p. 15; *EM*, p. 161). Derrida demonstrates that he (Derrida), Heidegger, Meyer Schapiro, and we might as well add Merleau-Ponty, have an interest in Van Gogh. The logic of supplementarity suggests that there is always the "further" that one can go but at the same time that there are limits to where one has gone. Derrida does not incorporate—at least not explicitly—Merleau-Ponty's notion that Van Gogh wants to go further. To incorporate Merleau-Ponty here, in fact, is to go further than where Derrida operates. Yet Derrida accounts for this "going further" in his logic of supplementarity. In that Merleau-Ponty is also concerned with the "origin of truth" and at the same time with "the painter's inscriptions," it is not unreasonable that he too should be incorporated here.

Merleau-Ponty's remark about Van Gogh is itself a supplement to what Derrida, Heidegger, and Schapiro have to say about Van Gogh. As we already know, they are not concerned with Van Gogh per se. Rather their interest lies in Van Gogh's shoes. For Heidegger, Van Gogh's shoes are the shoes of a peasant who lives close to the earth and who makes use of their equipmentality as a being-in-the-world. For Schapiro, they are Van Gogh's own shoes. For Derrida, they are the subject of a correspondence between Schapiro and Heidegger. They are also, for Derrida, what stands outside any particular determinate being. They are, if you will, the shoe size that never quite fits. Just as truth in shoe size *(la vérité en pointure)* is what never quite fits, so too truth in painting is never quite all there; for in coming out of concealment, the disclosure inherent in *aletheia* carries what is not disclosed along with what is disclosed. Along with every being, there is also Being. Truth as disclosure makes this ontico-ontological difference evident.

According to Heidegger, the work of art or painting uncovers what the pair of shoes is, but there is always something more. For Derrida, this logic of supplementarity operates at the textual and intertextual plane. The something more lies at the edge of the text, at the borders of the painting, in the framing *[Gestell]* of the work of art. At the edge of *la vérité en peinture* stands *la verité en pointure*. At the margin of *la vérité en pointure*, one finds Van Gogh stating that if he is obliged to make the truth true, he prefers the role of the cobbler to that of the musician. At the frontier of Van Gogh's statement about truth lies his own paintings of shoes. At the limit of Van Gogh's paintings of shoes are those of René Magritte and Richard Lindner as well as Van Gogh's own alternative versions of shoes. Each version involves a limit and an excess. The logic of supplementarity takes the fact just one step further.

The logic of supplementarity is like a master key *(un passe-partout)* that opens many different doors. It not only surrounds and delimits but also opens the possibility of entering a new room. The supplement is both an addition to and a replacement for something. In *Dissemination* (1972), Derrida characterizes both writing and the *pharmakon* as a supplement (*Dissemination*, p. 126; tr., p. 110). Just as writing and the *pharmakon* are indecidables (either speech or writing, remedy or poison) so too "truth in painting" is an indecidable (either truth in the act of painting or painting what is true). To deconstruct "truth in painting" is to bring out not only its indecidability but also its supplementarity. That the supplement itself is also an indecidable (either addition or replacement) is only an additional feature of the deconstructive strategy. To deconstruct "truth in painting" is to look for its limits and its excesses, to look for what is not fully disclosed in the disclosure, to look for the invisible among the visible. The invisible is a phenomenological supplement to the visible rendered evident through interrogation. The supplement is a textual invisible that hovers at the limits of any particular text and that is brought into play through deconstructive practice.

INTERROGATIVE AND DECONSTRUCTIVE PRACTICES

Interrogation invokes a philosophical practice whether it occurs in philosophy, in one's gaze over things, or in painting. Deconstruction involves a critical practice whether it be that of the philosopher, the literary theorist, the historian, or the critic. The task of interrogation is to become the experience of the things which it interrogates. The task of deconstruction is to become writing, namely another text, a critical text which supplements and incorporates the one or ones in question. Interrogation is concerned with visible things and their significations. Deconstruction is concerned with texts and their inscribed interrelations. Interrogation requires that what is interrogated be placed in question. Deconstruction requires that the text be examined for its differences (from other texts) and its deferrals (into other texts). Interrogation explores the visible as intertwined with the invisible. Deconstruction examines textual traces, marks, traits, signatures, and differences as they occur in writing. For Merleau-Ponty, what is not there is the seeing itself. For Derrida, what is not there is either at the borderlines of a particular text (at the hinge of this text and another text) or within the frame of (an)other text(s).

When philosophy interrogates, it interrogates what Merleau-Ponty calls "perceptual faith" (*VI*, p. 139; *VI-tr.*, p. 103). When philosophy interrogates, it neither expects nor receives an answer in the ordinary sense. This is because there is no variable or unknown invariant whose disclosure would satisfy the question. It is also because the existing world already exists in an interrogative mode. Philosophy *is* perceptual faith interrogating itself. It is faith because there is the possibility of doubt (as Merleau-Ponty stresses in his account of Cézanne). Philosophy is an indefatigable ranging over things—a continuous interrogation—which operates in global rather than piecemeal fashion. As perceptual faith, philosophy engages in a fundamental interrogation which informs the others. Philosophical interrogation probes for and awaits a signification which will achieve its ultimate conclusion: the answer to questions such as "what is the world?" or "what is Being?" Philosophical interrogation appeals to the elucidation of what we know—without asking about the idea of knowledge (*VI*, p. 171; *VI-tr.*, p. 129). Philosophical interrogation is the faith that things are in accordance with the significations they render.

When our gaze interrogates, it interrogates the things themselves. We are a continuous question. We ourselves are in question in the unfolding of our lives. The one who questions is a being who questions. In both "*Le Doute de Cézanne*" and in *L'Oeil et l'esprit*, Merleau-Ponty cites Cézanne's frequent remark "*c'est effrayant la vie.*" We look out over the world of visible things and we ourselves are placed in question—not reflexively, not as a turning back on ourselves, but as a looking over, around, and through things as they surround and envelop us.

When the painter interrogates, "the mountain itself, from over there, makes itself seen by the painter; and the painter interrogates it with his gaze" (*OE*, p. 28; *EM*, p. 166). Here the painter is not simply interrogating his own life, but rather the world of the mountain. Merleau-Ponty writes, the painter "discloses the means, which are nothing other than visible things, by which the mountain makes itself a mountain beneath our very eyes" (*OE*, pp. 28–29; *EM*, p. 166). The painter's interrogation aims at "the secret and feverish genesis of things in our body" (*OE*, p. 30; *EM*, p. 167). This condition holds whether what the painter is looking at is a mountain off in the distance or the mirror image of himself in the act of self-portraiture. The painter's interrogation, like that of the philosopher and the everyday perceiver, aims at bringing out the visibility of visible things in terms of their significations.

When deconstruction is practiced, it establishes the place(s) of difference already inscribed in the text. It seeks to restore (make restitution for) what is left out of the text. But what is left out of the text is already a feature of the text. What is left out of the text is found in another text or produced in another writing. To restore, to provide restitution for what is not in the text is to juxtapose one text alongside another and to identify the chiasm between them. The place of chiasm is the hinge, border, frontier, margin, limit of the text. Just as Van Gogh, Heidegger, Schapiro, Cézanne, and Merleau-Ponty want to restore truth in painting, so too Derrida wants to restore truth in texts by exploring (deconstructing) their laws and practices of supplementarity. In *Glas,* he juxtaposes a text on Hegel and a text on Genet; in "The Double Session," a text on Mallarmé matches up with one on Plato; in "Living On: Border-Lines," the text in the footnotes accompanies the main text, just as Shelley's "Triumph of Life" is juxtaposed with Blanchot's *L'Arrêt de mort.* Derrida's textual juxtapositions proliferate. Each one indicates the constellation and dissemination of texts in general as well as the limits and frames of particular texts.

Deconstruction does not operate only at the multitextual level. The logic of supplementarity is not just a logic of restoration and incorporation of texts and signature. *Différance* is not just deferral. *Différance* is also distinction, opposition, pairing. Just as Derrida deconstructs Heidegger's account of Van Gogh's "Pair of Shoes," he also deconstructs a whole history and gallery of binary pairs, including intelligible/sensible, inside/outside, metaphorical/literal, signifier/signified, speaking/writing, transcendental/empirical, Being/beings—and (one might venture) invisible/visible.... The deconstruction of the text of metaphysics renders the place of difference *qua* distinction rather than difference *qua* deferral or displacement. The place of difference in traditional metaphysical binary oppositions signals the end of metaphysics, the closure of the book of metaphysics and the beginning (origin) of writing. But writing is at most a system of traces, textual limits, and intertextual interweavings. Writing does not fall on the side of speaking nor on the side of writing (as opposed to speaking). Deconstruction neither constructs writing nor destroys it. Deconstruction examines traditional binary oppositions just as it explores textual differentiations.

Deconstruction goes to the place of indecidables such as communication (oral presentation/transmission of messages), *écriture* (speaking/writing), difference (distinction/deferral), *pharmakon* (poison/remedy), trace (footprint/imprint), correspondence (exchange of letters/matching of similarities), supplement (addition/replacement), and so forth. In addition to the horizontal proliferation and displacement of one text into another, and in addition to the vertical reexamination of traditional binary oppositions, the deconstruction of texts requires the elucidation and elaboration of indecidables and their indecidability. The indecidability of texts is a feature of their textuality.

Supplementarity involves the incorporation and displacement of texts, the inversion of traditional binary oppositions, and the unfolding of indecidables. Visibility involves the elaboration of the texture of visible things, the intertwining of the visible and the invisible, and the opening up of the significations of vision. The logic of supplementarity is a logic of textuality. The logic of visibility is a logic of perception and the disclosure of brute Being. Just as Cézanne claims that he owes truth in painting and paints it, Merleau-Ponty "owes" visibility in philosophy as it becomes experience, and he "says" it. Derrida owes supplementarity in the inscription and dissemination of texts and "writes" it.

II

Toward a
Theory of Textuality

5

ENFRAMING THE WORK OF ART

Why did Heidegger seek after the origin of the work of art in the first place? What is there to be gained by knowing the *origin* of the work of art? What kind of access would one have if one could find out where the work of art *(das Kunstwerk)* springs from *(der Ur-sprung)*? Such access would not give its essence, nor its objectives, nor its destination, nor its fate. The preoccupation with the origin of the work of art could be characterized as an academic concern. Only academics are interested in where things "come from," where they arise, where they take their initial shape. Surely only academics want to know the lineage, the genealogy, the history of things. A geometrician is not likely to care about the origin of geometry; but a philosopher (such as Husserl) might. You do not need to know where geometry comes from in order to do geometry. You do not need to know where an artwork comes from in order to create paintings, poems, or sacred temples. Historians of art sometimes ask about the sources of a particular work. And philosophers ask about the nature of such appeals to source and origin, but in this regard, the philosopher is retracing the steps of the historian of art. When Heidegger, however, asks about the origin of the work of art, he is not retracing the steps marked off by the historian of art. Heidegger is asking about "that from and by which the work of art is what it is and as it is" *(PLT-OWA*, p. 17). Heidegger does not want to find out the influences on, or the ancestors to, any particular work of art. Indeed his concern is not one of historical filiation in any of the historiographical senses of the term. In asking about the origin of the work of art, Heidegger is asking about the structural interconnections among the artwork, the artist, and Art. This form of origination is considered apart from history itself. As Heidegger poses it, the question of origin is a question of relation.

In Heidegger's formulation—as already introduced in chapter two—the origin of the artwork is the artist. The artist creates the artwork and the artwork is the product of that creative activity. In this sense, the artist is the origin of the work of art. This sort of origination is of the seminal sort that paternity inaugurates. On this basis, one might assume that Heidegger is appealing to a process of filiation. However, when he then asks about the origin of the artist, and when he claims that the artwork is the origin of the artist, the direct filial chain is broken. The mutual origination of artist and artwork is structural-synchronic and no longer historical-diachronic. But this becomes even clearer when Heidegger announces that there is also an origin to the artist and the artwork, namely Art. Art makes it possible to speak of artist and artwork. Since Art is the origin of the artist and the artwork, the triangular relationality of multiple origination sets up a framework in which, in fact, there is no point of origin.

Without a point of origin, without a place which can be designated as the single source, the artwork becomes part of a complex structure or set of interactions. Although origination often has a dynamic aspect—specifically, the act of originating, coming forth from somewhere—there cannot be a single somewhere in this instance. However, in the triadic interconnections among artwork-artist-Art, there is a dynamic. The path of origination moves from artist to artwork, from artwork to artist, from artwork and artist to Art, from Art to artwork. This path of origination is not linear (though it could be said that lines connect the three points in various ways). Since at least three points are required to draw a circle, the path of origination could perhaps best be characterized as a circle. But it is only a circle in that the three points make the construction of a circle imaginatively possible. The movement of up-down, down-up, across from both, and back to down again is not *as such* a circular movement. It is circular only in the sense that it may be repeated. But this is not a circle; it is a repetition and an iteration.

Why then does Heidegger say: "Anyone can easily see that we are moving in a circle" (*PLT-OWA*, p.18)? It seems clear that this is not a circle at all. If one were to proceed from artwork to artist to Art, then it might be construed as a circle. But in the first account Heidegger does not do this. Perhaps this is because he is committed to the hermeneutic circle which he outlined in *Sein und Zeit*. As already developed, the ontological hermeneutic circle goes as follows: things have their being, their is-ness. But what is the nature of their is-ness, their being? It must be Being itself *(Sein)*. Thus beings *(Seiendes)* get their being from Being *(Sein)*—the essence of the being of things. At the same time (or at some related time), Being gets its being—its fundamental condition—from beings. But both Being and beings get their nature from the difference between them—the in-between which Heidegger calls the ontico-ontological difference. This is not the difference between two different beings, but the basic difference between beings and Being (in general). This ontico-ontological difference gives rise to the relation to Being and the Being of beings. Heidegger calls this triadic relationality: the hermeneutic circle. Is it a circle because there are three points which make it hypothetically possible to draw a circle? In a certain sense, one might claim that this is all there is to any circle. But then by comparing the artwork-artist-Art relational structure to the beings-Being-ontico-ontological difference relational structure, an apparent distinction can be identified. The former third term—Art—seems to be a positive term, while the latter third term—the ontico-ontological difference—seems to be negative (in that "difference" is sometimes understood as "negative.") However, the ontico-ontological difference is not really negative. Rather it establishes the very identity of both beings and Being, for without that difference, they would not have independent status in relation to each other. Thus the ontico-ontological difference (although differential in character) does provide the meaning of Being in its relation to beings. Furthermore, the structural comparison suggests something very interesting about Art. Since the artwork and the artist are, like beings and Being, positive terms, it would be odd (while structurally plausible) if the ontico-ontological difference were to be negative and Art were to be positive. Consider, then, the possible differential character of Art.

When the ancient conception of Art was distinguished from beauty and the sublime, Art was relegated quite precisely to the domain of *technē*, craft, skill, artfulness. Art had to do with making *(poetikē)*. In his *Inferno* (canto xi), Dante, the late medieval, remarks:

> Philosophy…
>
> springs from the Ultimate Intellect and Its Art:
> and if you read your *Physics* with due care,
> you will note, not many pages from the start,
>
> that Art strives after her by imitation,
> as the disciple imitates the master;
> Art, as it were, is the Grandchild of Creation.[1]

Dante demonstrates that Art involves creation. Art imitates Nature, but Nature imitates the creativity of God. Like Plato, Dante thinks of Art as copying (imitating), as doubly removed from the forms, from perfection. Like Aristotle, Dante presents Art as making. But for Dante, Art is creative and aspires to repeat perfection. When the Renaissance artist takes Art as a means of approximating, approaching, moving closer to the Ideal, Art has reversed its direction: it no longer turns away from perfection but rather orients itself toward ideality. Alberti, Michelangelo, and Leonardo all want to approach God through Art. And their Art is not just craft. Kant's account of Art in relation to the beautiful and the sublime is the last phase of an epoch in which Art is still conceived as craft-like, yet it is also the beginning of the identification of Art with the beautiful and the sublime. In the nineteenth-century, Théophile Gauthier's "Art for Art's sake" achieves the full conflation and suppression of the difference between craft and beauty (or the sublime). The suppression of the difference in what Gadamer calls "romantic aesthetics" is nevertheless the incorporation of the difference into the identity of Art.

A nostalgia for the divergence between the artist's craft and the artistic product remains in the modern conception of Art. Abstract expressionism, twelve-tone music, stream of consciousness novels extol the artist's skills in producing the purely sublime, spiritual, expressive content of the work. For the modernist artist and theorist, Art internalizes the differential structure of the relation between craft and product, between artist and artwork. Gadamer's "aesthetic non-differentiation" demonstrates that, in the early twentieth century version of Art, a tension, a disjunction, a sense of difference still haunts the concept of Art. In this respect, it is not in any way implausible that Heidegger should implicitly suggest an association between Art (in the aesthetic circle) and the ontico-ontological difference (in the ontological circle). Art embodies an ancient difference. Just as Art is the origin of the artist and the artwork, the difference that they make (namely the difference between craft and beauty or the sublime) serves as the origin, of Art.

THE CIRCLE/THE TRANSVERSAL

The question of the circle has not yet been resolved. We have noted the repetition of circles (aesthetic and ontological). The differential feature of Art—in its non-differentiation—has been identified. But what of these circles which do not seem to be circles?

"We are compelled to follow the circle," Heidegger writes (*PLT-OWA*, p. 18). Why "compelled"—especially when it is not clear that there is a circle, especially when it is more like a zigzag? Yet Heidegger goes on to state: "Not only is the main step from work to Art a circle like the step from Art to work, but every separate step that we attempt circles in this circle" (*PLT-OWA*, p. 18). It is as if Heidegger were trying to smooth out the zigzag by making it into a circle, tracing the path from work to artist to Art and then reversing it: traveling from Art to artist to work. But this circling and reverse circling is at best a reconstruction. It cuts out the intricacy of the movement.

Why should Heidegger feel obliged to turn the detailed zigzag character of his account into a circular movement? There is the matter of repeating the ontological circle by means of an aesthetic one. But there is another reason to turn the zigzag into a circle. Circles can be traveled smoothly. The movement of filiation and paternity requires smoothing over the rough edges. With three points, a circle can be drawn. But above all, the circle opens up a space, a clearing, a domain in which the artist is not identical with the artwork and in which Art can be named.

But what is the nature of this space within the circle? Certainly, it is enclosed by the artwork-artist-Art interconnection. Yet the space within is not any one of these points. The space within the circle is also not without meaning. Consider, for instance, a transversal, cutting across the circle on a horizontal, diametrical plane. At this juncture, suffice it to call this transversal *the text*. Although Heidegger does not offer a theory of the text, his account does leave room for such a reading.

Most of "The Origin of the Work of Art" is not concerned with this question of circles. Rather it weaves a fabric: (1) thing and work; (2) work and truth; and (3) truth and Art. The texture of the essay is carefully interwoven as it fills out the circle. Heidegger begins with the thingly character of the work. The work is identified in its thingliness, its groundedness in the ground. The work is at the bottom of the circle for a reason. It touches base with the earth, with the world of things, with other natural objects. In this respect, the questions to be asked are: how useful is it? how reliable is it? what kind of material is it? what is its form? and how is it different from other things which have these features as their defining characteristics? The point is, of course, that although some works are on occasion useful (De Stijl furniture, Le Corbusier architecture, even certain high moral tone novels, and some therapeutic music), it is not their usefulness or reliability that matters. What matters is not even simply their form or their material. Certainly they must have a form and they must have a particular material aspect. And the form they have, the matter they require are essential to any work's being what it is. However, what really matters—for Heidegger—is what the work discloses, namely, its truth.

Heidegger elaborates: "The art work opens up in its own way the Being of beings. This opening up, this de-concealing, i.e. the truth of beings, happens in the work. In the artwork, the truth of what is has set itself to work" (*PLT-OWA*, p. 39). What really matters about the artwork is its de-concealing, its bringing out of concealedness, its disclosure, its making truth happen in the place that it (the work) occupies. From its place at the bottom of the circle, the rest of the circle is set into motion. From its place at the bottom of the circle, the zigzag movement which Heidegger turns into a circle is set into motion. From its place at the bottom of the circle, the open space circumscribed by the circle is opened up. Truth happens. This place of disclosure, this place of openness, this clearing, this *Lichtung*, is the space of the circle, the space of truth as disclosed in and by the work. With the artwork, something very important happens, something other than usefulness and reliability. What happens is what also happens in the ontico-ontological difference, in the Being of beings, in the other circle.... What happens is truth. Just as the Being of beings discloses what is, renders the truth of what is, so too the artwork discloses what is. But the artwork discloses in its own particular way. Being *as such* does not disclose. The artwork, however, opens up onto the whole circle. The truth disclosed by the artwork is the Open itself of the aesthetic circle. The Greek temple in Paestum, Van Gogh's peasant shoes, Henry Moore's sculptures—all open up a world: the world of the aesthetic circle, the world of the truth that the artwork discloses. But, one might ask: "what truth?" Answer: "whatever truth the particular work discloses." Each one starts from a different place, hence the particular disclosure is different, but each one starts from the bottom of the circle. Only the content, the meaning of the disclosed itself, is different.

What of the relation to Art? The artwork discloses, the artwork makes truth happen, the artwork opens up the space of the circle. But the circle would not be a circle if Art were not a place on its circumference. For the hermeneutic traveler, Art is the next-to-last stop on the circle prior to a return to the beginning, namely the artwork. From the standpoint of the journey, Art is the next-to-last point in the zigzag before the last line is drawn back to the artwork. The next-to-lastness of Art is due to what Heidegger calls the "createdness" and "preserving" features of Art. The artist creates; the artwork preserves; and Art is "the creative preserving of truth in the work" (*PLT-OWA*, p. 71). Passing through the preserving of the work and the creating of the artist, the circle comes to Art itself. Art is located 270° around the circle. Yet it is also located 90° around the circle as well, for Art is in the place of difference between work and artist. Thus Art appears at the next-to-last point whichever way the circle is drawn. Art is affirmed in the place of the creative preserving of truth in the work. This place is repeated on both sides of the circle. Thus it is not that there are three points, forming a circle, but in fact there are four. Only, the third is repeated on the other side as the fourth. The fourth is a repetition of the third. Wherever one begins—whether with the preserving feature of the work or with its createdness—a different path along the circle is drawn. In either case, one comes to Art last. The determination of Art as Art is the establishment of a disclosure, that is, the establishment of the openness formed by the circle.

WORK / TEXT

The delineation of the transversal from the place of Art at 90° to that at 270° identifies the place of the text. The text is the transversal. It cuts across the circle from the place marked by Art on both sides. It is a line, a diameter of the circle. The text is not in the place of the artist nor in that of the artwork. The text is not produced—as such—by the artist, nor is it the product—as such—of an artistic production. The text is not unrelated to the productive activity of the artist nor to the createdness of the work. Yet it is also not identical with either.

Heidegger makes no appeal to the text. The text does not figure in the Heideggerian vocabulary. When Heidegger speaks of artworks such as the Greek temple, the Van Gogh painting, or the Hölderlin poem, he is not referring to texts. The closest he comes to designating the place which belongs to the text is when he announces the primacy of poetry: "*All art*," he writes, "as the letting happen of the advent of the truth of what is, is, as such, *essentially* poetry *(Dichtung)*" (*PLT-OWA*, p. 72). In effect, Heidegger locates poetry *(Dichtung)* in the place where truth happens, namely in the space of the circle. Poetry is not the transversal which cuts across the circle and joins the points marked out by Art. Rather it fills the complete Open—with meaning and sense. Poetry is the saying, calling, naming, speaking of truth—the language of the work. For Heidegger, poetry incorporates the other arts. It makes sense of them. The text however has no such powers. The text cannot incorporate the various arts. It cannot even fill the whole space delineated by the aesthetic hermeneutic circle that Heidegger describes as an abbreviation for the zigzag structure of the art-work-artist-Art relation. The text is in the in-between of the artwork and the artist. The text is a differential structure comparable to Heidegger's Art in its nostalgia for difference. Yet the text only traverses the space opened up by the truth of the work. The text cuts across that truth, that disclosure, that bringing out of concealedness. The text embodies the disclosure, but it does not fulfill it.

The text is, in a sense, a fragment of that disclosure. The text is a statement of the work of art: it is the self-presentation of the work, but without the direct, almost causal connection with the artist.

The text does not replace the work, it reinterprets it. The work remains where it is. The text traverses Heidegger's notion of Art. It makes a story out of the work. The text is the *mythos* or narrative, the fabric or web according to which the work is enunciated. The story need not be coherent, need not be a reconstruction of reality, need not be a tale that is told. Rather it is the coded, structured, enunciated version of the work.

Heidegger initially presented "The Origin of the Work of Art" in 1935–36. This was too early for a proper theory of the text. Roland Barthes, in his 1971 essay, elaborates the shift from work to text. Barthes points out that the work is a "fragment of substance, occupying a part of the space of books (in a library for instance)" (*IMT-FWT*, pp. 156–57). Although Barthes focuses on written works, the point would hold for other artworks as well—in that they are part of a world of things, a world of substances, and a world of entities. Thus the work, in its thingly character, is very much of the order which Heidegger recounts. This becomes especially evident when Barthes remarks that "the work is caught up in a process of filiation...the author is reputed to be the father and the owner of his work" (*IMT-FWT*, p. 160). This coincides with the account Heidegger offers when he says that the artwork is the origin of the artist and the artist is the origin of the artwork. The former is a case of filiation. The latter is one of paternity (—or is it maternity?). The work then cannot be understood apart from the artist or author.

The text, however, is "a methodological field" (*IMT-FWT*, p. 157). It exists "only in the movement of a discourse" (*IMT-FWT*, p. 157). It is "experienced only in an activity of production" (*IMT-FWT*, p. 157). It is not understood in any direct causal or originative relation with the author or artist. The text is a *network* of plural interconnections which cut across the space delineated by the work's relation to the artist. While the work "closes in on a signified" (*IMT-FWT*, p. 158), opening up the space of truth with its disclosures, the text "practices the infinite deferment of the signified" (*IMT-FWT*, p. 158). The text evades any univocal meaning, any singular sense of what it signifies. The text's plurality produces a metonymical dispersal of meaning across its field or network. The text is the production of a signifying chain, a chain that even extends beyond the confines of the aesthetic hermeneutic circle. The text insinuates itself in a context with other texts, other networks, other frameworks, which are not confined by the circumference of the circle.

FOCUS/FRAME

For Heidegger, Art—as the origin of the artist and the artwork, as the midway point along the circumference of the circle (whichever way it is traversed)—is not limited to the particular artwork in question. Thus Art is not just the art exemplified by Van Gogh's postimpressionism, or the Paestum Greek temple's classical style, or Henry Moore's contemporary primitivism. The Art that originates the artist and the artwork is much more general than that. It extends beyond the instance of artist and artwork which—together—announce its truth. The text, for Barthes, is hardly identical with Art in Heidegger's sense. Yet its indication and incorporation of what lies outside the frame of the circle is repeated in both cases. Where Art locates itself along the circumference of Heidegger's circle, the text cuts across it and extends out beyond it, bringing together a whole network of intertextuality which has nothing to do with the worlding of worlds.

So the question remains—a question which has not yet been posed—what sort of textuality is it that the text offers? What is the nature of a textuality of the text that takes it beyond its own frame? And furthermore, is there an identifiable place for the very notion of textuality in the framework that Heidegger offers?

In the 1960 "Addendum" *(Zusatz)* to "The Origin of the Work of Art," Heidegger attends to two notions: the "*thesis*" and the "*Ge-stell.*" For short, these two notions might be called the "focus" and the "frame." The thesis is what Heidegger calls "the existing human being's entrance into and compliance with the unconcealedness of Being" (*PLT-OWA*, p. 84). This "compliance" is the "letting happen of truth"—this letting happen occurs in *both* the clearing and the concealing, the opening up and the keeping from view. In that the thesis or focus is the setting forth, the fixing of what has been hidden from view, it is the specification of what is central to the space opened up by the aesthetic hermeneutic circle. One might say that the thesis is what gives focus to the truth which arises in the work's disclosure, or one might even say that the thesis cuts across the circle of disclosure. This would suggest that the text might be a kind of thesis—a thesis that has come into its own, a thesis whose time has come. In this sense, then, the text is something posited.

However, as Roland Barthes demonstrates in *The Pleasure of the Text* (1973),[2] the text is not so much a setting forth as it is a site—a locus for the pleasure that is derived from a reading of it, or, even more *a propos*, it is the place where *jouissance* happens, where, as Heidegger puts it, "the existing human being enters into and complies with" "the letting happen of truth." In other words, Heidegger's account incorporates both the pleasure of the text (Barthes's *lisible*) and the *jouissance*, the ecstasy or bliss, that happens in the site or locus of the text.

But if the text is a kind of thesis, a place where truth (or a fragment of it) happens as discourse, as narrative, as story, it must also set its own limits. This is Heidegger's second item for his "Addendum": the *Ge-stell.* The putting forth of the text is also the limiting of its frame. The thesis is also its margins, its bordering, its framing, its framework. The framework is not an "outwork," a supplement or remainder to the work. The text itself is already an "outwork," a supplement, a what-is-not-part-of-the-work, and a yet-not-unrelated-to-it. The framework is what enframes the text. It is the *encadrement*, the circumscription of the text at its borders. Thus the framework, the *Ge-stell*—is what gives form to the focus, what identifies the text as different from other texts. The framework is a kind of supplement, a leftover which doesn't quite belong to the text which it enframes, which is not identical with the text, and which is itself an addition to the work in its relation to the artist and their mutual relation to Art. The framework, then, is what marks the textuality of the text. The framework is what serves as the border to the text and hence makes possible the intertextuality and contextuality of the text. The framework is what identifies the text as the text that it is—with its limits, borders, beginnings, endings, middles, and edges.

6

WRITING AT THE EDGE OF METAPHYSICS

The debate about deconstruction in philosophical circles has come to take on significant proportions. Literary scholars have confronted the question because a dominant feature of the deconstructive enterprise involves the reading of texts. Literary theorists in particular have come to recognize deconstruction because, as a theory of reading, it challenges conventional and established modes of approaching literary writing.

Among phenomenologically-oriented philosophers both on the European continent and in the English-speaking world, deconstruction is regarded as a critique and threat to the philosophy of presence and experience. Semiologists and structuralists who have drawn their resources from linguistics in the tradition of Saussure, formalists who rely heavily upon the work of Jakobson and the Russian formalist school, and semioticians who appeal to Peirce and the corresponding classical American philosophical context find that deconstruction not only incorporates their predominant concerns and principal modes of operation but also undermines their project as a science. Furthermore, psychoanalytically-inclined philosophers, psychologists, and social theorists find that the deconstructive enterprise inspects and undoes the Freudian or post-Freudian (especially Lacanian) corpus. Even philosophers sometimes described as "post-analytic" have come not only to take deconstruction seriously but also to incorporate certain strategies and concerns into their modes of argumentation.

Is deconstruction identical with the "work" of Jacques Derrida? Certainly Derrida has produced a body of writing which offers deconstruction as a description of what he does and as a characterization of his enterprise. Certainly deconstruction has come to be considered a "method of approach" or a style of philosophizing since the 1967 publication of Derrida's first three "books" (*Speech and Phenomena*, *Writing and Difference*, and *Of Grammatology*).[1] [The only other publication of magnitude published prior to 1967 was the long introduction to his French translation of Husserl's *Origin of Geometry* (1962).[2]] Although Derrida cites deconstruction in the 1967 writings—for instance in an interview with Henri Ronse he talks about "deconstructing philosophy"—only in 1972 does he embrace deconstruction as a critical enterprise. A number of years later deconstruction has come to be cited alongside phenomenology, semiology, hermeneutics, pragmatism, ordinary language philosophy, linguistic analysis, and so forth as a contending philosophical approach. Indeed before the 1971 publication of the *Promesse* interview with Jean-Louis Houdebine and Guy Scarpetta (which appeals to the "general strategy of deconstruction"), Derrida more commonly offered the name "grammatology" as the calling card for his enterprise. In *Of Grammatology*, grammatology is cited as the positive science of writing. In a 1968 response to Julia Kristeva, grammatology is set off against semiology (for which Kristeva was a particularly strong advocate at the time).[3]

Derrida offered grammatology as "the science of textuality," claiming that it "must simultaneously go beyond metaphysical positivism and scientism, and accentuate whatever in the effective work of science contributes to freeing it of the metaphysical bonds that have borne on its definition and its movement since its beginnings" (*Positions*, p. 35). Furthermore, he proposed that grammatology "must pursue and consolidate that which, in scientific practice, has always already begun to exceed the logocentric closure" (*Positions*, p. 36). By this he means that scientific practices which take *logos* as central, which assert the prevalence of the spoken word, the voice of calling, the speech act, the ontico-ontological interpretation of language, etc. need to be examined and explored at their limits. Grammatology takes up science as *logos* and considers the extent to which it can still take itself to be science, the extent to which it can affirm itself as self-circumscribing. Hence, grammatology "*inscribes* and *delimits* science" (*Positions*, p. 36). Grammatology writes or rewrites the features and conditions of a particular science and at the same time demonstrates the limits, edges, places of closure which a particular science sets for itself by its very practice. Its "fundamental condition is the undoing of logocentrism" (*Grammatology*, p. 74), namely, the stretching of a particular science or even science-in-general to its extreme conditions, establishing the status of those limits and the character of its closure. Closure here is the correlate of origin. Closure is not, as such, the same as end. Closure means closing off—perhaps arbitrarily, but certainly as delimitation. Closure does not necessarily imply termination. It may signal achievement or fulfillment. It is more likely to be the self-circumscription which the science in question performs upon itself in order to give itself identity, boundaries, and a determinate form. Grammatology explores the historical and conceptual limits established in the various forms of closure.

In the interview with Kristeva, Derrida responds: "Grammatology must deconstruct everything that ties the concept and norms of scientificity to ontotheology, logocentrism, phonologism" (*Positions*, p. 35). Hence in 1968, Derrida asserts that "deconstruction" is what "grammatology" does. By 1972 when he published not only *Positions* (comprising the three interviews) but also *Dissemination* and *Margins of Philosophy*,[4] it was clear that deconstruction was the more appropriate way for Derrida to place his signature on his writings. The three essays in *Dissemination* date from the late 1960s: "Plato's Pharmacy" (1968); "The Double Session" (1970); and "Dissemination" (1969). The "preface," which prefaces by placing "prefacing" in question and which goes under the name of "Hors-livre" (translated as "Outwork" but, more literally, "outside the book"), dates from 1971 and announces that "deconstruction involves an indispensable phase of *reversal*" (*Dissemination*, p. 6). The pro-gramme is one of deconstruction, its operation involves reversal. (More will be said about this notion of reversal later.) As Derrida writes: "to put old names to work, or even just to leave them in circulation, will always, of course, involve some risk: the risk of settling down or of regressing into the system that has been, or is in the process of being, deconstructed" (*Dissemination*, p. 5). Here again, deconstruction is cited as that operation or set of operations undertaken with respect to a specific system or science. In the 1974 essay-fragment entitled "The Parergon" (subsequently incorporated into *Truth in Painting* in 1978), Derrida continues (now in connection with Kant's third *Critique*): "Philosophy wants to examine this 'truth,' but never succeeds. That which produces and manipulates the frame sets everything in motion to efface its effect, most often by naturalizing it to infinity, in God's keeping (to be confirmed in Kant). Deconstruction must neither reframe nor fantasize the pure and simple absence of the frame. These two apparently contradictory actions are precisely the systematically indissociable ones of that which is presently deconstructed."[5] As a pro-gramme deconstruction places interdictions upon itself. Deconstruction negatively operates in relation to frames and actual production. It must not itself re-frame what is already framed, nor must it fantasize what is already actually produced. The systematic association of framing and fantasizing constitutes the work which is to be deconstructed.

The deconstructive enterprise—in name and practice—has held on. In another interview, included in *La Carte postale* (1980), entitled "Du Tout" (1978), when asked about the confrontational aspect of his writing, Derrida replies that the "confrontational 'effect' [of his writing] keeps to the deconstruction of the so-called psychoanalytic institution."[6] Deconstruction operates within institutional frameworks. Although Derrida would not have put it quite that way six or seven years earlier, his claim is that institutions are systems: self-delimiting, self-circumscribing, and self-affirming. Hence, he argues, "deconstruction is not a discursive or theoretical matter, but rather a practico-political one; and it is always produced in structures which are called (perhaps a bit summarily and rapidly) institutional" (*Carte postale*, p. 536). Similarly when writing in 1981 about the apocalyptic tradition, Derrida notes that if one were to assess "the limit of demystification, a limit which is perhaps more essential and which would *perhaps distinguish* a deconstruction of a simple progressive demystification in the Enlightenment style, then [he] would be tempted by another procedure."[7] The demystification itself is a systematic, institutional, scientific self-circumscription. Such written self-delimitations are necessarily available for deconstruction.

But the question remains: who does the deconstruction? Is deconstruction identical with Jacques Derrida's work? In "The *Retrait* of Metaphor,"[8] he responds to (or even confronts) Paul Ricoeur on his critique of Derrida's notion of metaphor in "White Mythology." In support of his response to Ricoeur, Derrida affirms what he is doing in the "deconstruction of metaphysical rhetoric" and the treatment of what Ricoeur calls "the deep-seated unity of metaphoric and analogical transfer of visible being to intelligible being in, let's say for the sake of speed, a deconstructive mode" (*Retrait*, p. 13). Or again, with respect to the chapter entitled "Exergue," Derrida points out that he was not proposing a schema, but "deconstructing a philosophical concept, a philosophical construction erected on [a] schema of worn out metaphor or privileging, for significant reasons, the trope named metaphor" (*Retrait*, p. 14). Here Derrida adds that what he does is carried out in what can be called "for the sake of speed" deconstruction or a deconstructive mode. Or elsewhere, he says it is done as a deconstructing of "what is already dogmatized or accredited in problematic regions (let's say, for the sake of speed: psychoanalytic, economico-political, genealogical in the Nietzschean sense)" (*Retrait*, p. 13).

Deconstruction then is the general name—one that constitutes a short-cut, a matter of brevity, a provisional inscription—for the practice in which Derrida engages. In practicing deconstruction, however, Derrida does not make it his own property. It is his own when he practices it, but it is an activity of appropriation when he does so. Indeed, the particular form of appropriation is one in which he inscribes the deconstructive practice in a text which is itself the writing of a reading of another text. Perhaps its danger in the literary domain is more paramount and immediate due to the possibilities entailed by: (1) the appropriation of that which can be appropriated by others in the writing of a reading of a text, and (2) the institution of a practice which is repeatable. In the first case, the possibility of appropriation becomes especially evident where Derrida offers a deconstruction of Lacan's "Seminar on Poe's Purloined Letter,"[9] which is subsequently read deconstructively again by Barbara Johnson in an essay on "The Frames of Reference."[10] The second case follows from the first in that if deconstruction can be appropriated as a writing of a reading, then the repeatability of the practice is evident. It is not unreasonable therefore that a volume of essays entitled *Deconstruction and Criticism* (1979)[11] was published as a kind of *théorie d'ensemble* including contributions from Derrida and other members of what was then the Yale group. All the essays treat (in some fashion or another) Shelley's "The Triumph of Life." Paul de Man's contribution was closest to that of Derrida in the character of its practice. (The memory of that closeness has been subsequently and posthumously reassessed in considerable detail.) Harold Bloom admits that he is not practicing deconstruction per se. Together the four, who also include Geoffrey Hartman (who has himself written a book on Derrida) and J. Hillis Miller (who indicates explicit sympathies with the deconstructive enterprise), are in a position to be incorporated into the practice which is most commonly associated with Derrida. Indeed, it goes without saying that many books and articles written by literary scholars in America (not to mention Philippe Lacoue-Labarthe, Jean-Luc Nancy, Sarah Kofman, and others in France) take up Derrida's style or his deconstructive practice.

To a certain extent, deconstruction is a banner, a flag, an aegis under which a whole series of practices are conducted—by Derrida, but also by others. To imitate Derrida's style—employing the linguistic play, *double entendre*, etc.—does not as such make for a deconstructive practice. One may even wonder whether Derrida is always operating in a deconstructive mode. It may be suggested that in many of his interviews—where he explains his practice—their published version does not necessarily demonstrate what could be called deconstruction. Hence one can—albeit with difficulty—dissociate deconstruction from Derrida. In order to offer an account of the features of deconstruction per se, a full consideration would have to assess: (1) the problematics which are in question; (2) the strategies employed; and (3) the particular deconstructive indicators which identify the practice and its elements.

PROBLEMATICS

With respect to philosophy, the problematics of deconstruction are basically threefold. Deconstruction concerns itself with: (a) the limits of the history of metaphysics; (b) the consequences and effects of metaphysical thinking; and (c) the necessity and limits of the science of writing (namely grammatology).

(a) In order to assess the limits of the history of metaphysics, it is necessary to understand the character of the history in question. A history opens up the possibility of a beginning and an end. Western metaphysics is often cited as having a beginning with the writings of the pre-Socratics. In his *Introduction to Husserl's Origin of Geometry* (1962), Derrida takes up the question of historicity and origin. Beginning is not the same as origin—just as end is not the same as closure. The origin which concerns Derrida is the origin of geometry: the respect in which geometry can be said to have a point of origin—particularly if its contents are said to be eternal. Can it be that geometry came into being at a particular moment in time? If so, it must have a beginning whose origin can be established. Beginning then is the moment when geometry as a science comes into being. Its origin is the condition of its genesis: where it comes from, how it got from there to here, and what makes it possible for it to come into being. Geometry both comes-into-being and does not come-into-being, in that it is already there—eternal and accessible to trained mathematical thinking. Its origin is situated at the place where its temporality meets its atemporality. The history of metaphysics follows a similar pattern. Its origin is located where the writing of metaphysics meets the being that is inscribed in it. Being, substance, matter, form, essence, and so forth are inscribed in the writing of metaphysics— that begins with the pre-Socratics. The horizon of metaphysics is also its origin—the place where its non-being comes into being. Its origin, then, is one of the limits of the history of metaphysics—a feature of its historicity.

Unlike geometry, whose ideality meets its history at the place of origin, metaphysics is already first philosophy and hence its more significant concerns are with its ends. In *The Archaeology of the Frivolous* (1973),[12] Derrida confronts the respects in which a first philosophy can be second (i.e., following, or subsequent to, Condillac's 1746 *Essay on the Origin of Human Knowledge*). One of the fundamental features of a first philosophy is that it be first and that any other philosophy come after. Metaphysics, as Aristotle writes it, is indeed "first" philosophy. But if Condillac is to write *first philosophy,* he is confronted with the dilemma of writing first philosophy *after* Aristotle. Even Aristotle considered metaphysics *after* physics. And if Condillac can write first philosophy second or third or at some other place after Aristotle, what of the "ends" of metaphysics? Or will the writing and rewriting of metaphysics go on endlessly? Or alternatively, after Hegel (who claims to have given a complete account of metaphysics, to have fulfilled its promise, to have written it to its completion) is there any place for the writing of metaphysics? In asking about the overcoming of metaphysics, Heidegger raises just such a concern. At the same time that he announces what has been forgotten in Western thought and what merits being thought *(Denkwürdige),* he tries to assess the end as the accomplishment, achievement, fulfillment, and success of metaphysics. For Heidegger, the overcoming of metaphysics is the incorporation of metaphysics into a new beginning. The ending of metaphysics is not its termination and extinction, but rather its opening onto the re-establishment of the truth of the Being of beings. The recovery of truth in the ontological difference and in the thinking of that difference involves a calling, hearing, belonging—all of which Derrida sees as identified with *logos* and logocentrism. It will be remembered that Derrida states, "grammatology must deconstruct everything that ties the concept and norms of scientificity to ontotheology, logocentrism, phonologism" (*Positions,* p. 35). In announcing the ontological difference as the place where truth can be unveiled, Heidegger offers a logocentrism imbued with ontotheology, in that the ontico-ontological difference is the difference that arises in the Being of beings. Heidegger (in *The Question of Being*)[13] writes this ontological genitive as a crossing out of Being (namely B̶e̶i̶n̶g̶). The effacing of Being is the writing of the trace of Being. As such it takes the very history of Being to its limits by setting the frame outside of which metaphysics cannot wander.[14] Furthermore, in the tradition of Rousseau, who places speech over writing, and Saussure, who gives prominence to *parole* over *langue,* Heidegger understands *logos,* truth, ontological difference as that which is called, heard, listened to—in short, another case of the prevalence of *phonē* and hence phonologism. In offering both an *Introduction to Metaphysics* and a statement of the "Overcoming of Metaphysics,"[15] Heidegger circumscribes the whole history of metaphysics in such a way that he takes it to its limits. Deconstruction construes as one of its primary concerns that very history and its limits.

(b) The consequences and effects of metaphysical thinking are manifold. How does metaphysics inscribe itself into Western thinking and what are the after-effects of such thinking? Derrida seems almost obsessed with that very concern. Metaphysical thinking takes itself to be at the very limits of scientific thought. The Kantian program was to show the conditions of the possibility of metaphysical thinking as it sets itself off from scientific knowledge. But this is to suggest that metaphysical thinking stands outside scientificity. In order for metaphysics to stand outside science, dogma, system, it must affirm and mark out just such domains. In other words, in order for metaphysics to accomplish anything, it must go beyond the limits of science. But in going beyond the limits of science, metaphysics only reinserts itself back into the very spaces in which science prevails. The outside presumes the inside, the consequence and effect of metaphysical thinking is to give a space for scientific thinking to operate. Deconstruction goes to the hinge between the two, at the place of interface between that which writes itself as outside and that which it delineates as inside.

(c) It is sometimes claimed that deconstruction is a type of negative theology. It is argued that deconstruction makes no positive assertions, that it only marks out the limits of metaphysical thinking, the limits of the history of metaphysics, and so forth. Yet in *Of Grammatology*, Derrida does offer grammatology as a positive science of writing; and elsewhere, as the science of textuality. The point is that deconstruction situates itself at the places where writing—the particular archē-writing which is not reducible to the opposition between speech and writing—is located. Grammatology is a positive science only in the sense that it delimits itself. It can only operate in the field in which traditional binary oppositions proclaim themselves to delineate the spaces of metaphysical thinking. Yet these oppositions are inscribed everywhere in the history of Western philosophy and literature. Hence deconstruction takes as its domain the whole history, corpus, and multiplicity of texts. Deconstruction operates on these texts as writing and assesses the marks, traces, and boundaries of metaphysical thinking as they appear, as they occupy a determinate place.

Metaphysics necessarily textualizes itself. It is written. The whole history of metaphysics is in fact the history of the writing of metaphysics. Hence if metaphysics is to be studied, it must be examined in terms of what and how metaphysics is written. Deconstruction concerns itself with texts as the writing of metaphysics. Since metaphysics could not be otherwise—Plato makes Socrates write, as Derrida demonstrates in *La Carte postale*—deconstruction affirms its own field of operation in its very practice.

STRATEGIES

The question of strategy is the question of how one goes about doing deconstruction, or rather how deconstruction operates. I have already indicated elsewhere that deconstruction is neither destruction nor construction.[16] It is neither an attack upon established, written, advocated systems nor a building of such systems. It takes neither a position like that of Hegel where systems are constructed nor like that of Kierkegaard where systems are placed under attack. In this respect, deconstruction is more like analytical philosophy in that it explores the *limits* of scientific knowledge without itself proposing to offer a replacement metaphysical scheme. However, deconstruction provides no examination of the validity of propositional content. Rather deconstruction situates itself at the juncture of attack and system building, at the place where a scientific scheme is offered and where it circumscribes itself in writing, in a philosophical text, in the production of textuality. Heidegger characterizes his own work as involving an *Abbauen*—an "unbuilding" which means going back to the origins of Western thinking, recovering what has been forgotten, and retrieving the very foundations of metaphysics. Although Heidegger's own writing takes metaphysics to its limits, brings its history to the very frontier of its trajectory, nevertheless Heidegger's unbuilding is not yet the deconstruction which operates where Heidegger leaves off, where Being *sous rature* (under erasure) inscribes itself in the history of metaphysics. Hence when Derrida states that "Grammatology *inscribes* and *delimits* science" (*Positions*, p. 36), this holds for metaphysical science or knowledge as well.

The deconstructive strategy is essentially threefold: (a) to identify the conceptual oppositions that operate within metaphysical discourse and overturn the implicit hierarchy established by the opposition; (b) to inscribe one's own writing at the place of indecidables by demonstrating their differential function; and (c) to account for the deferral and effects of the deconstructive enterprise. To know the strategy is not necessarily to be able to practice it. Although features of the moves, outlines of the positions, and markings of the practice can be recounted, a deconstructive competence is also required. It has been argued that this competence is not the sole property of Derrida, for that would make deconstruction at most a highly original philosophy in its own right—but this is not easily practiced. Skill, care, and expertise are necessary. Perhaps it can be learned by reading—watching Derrida work (write)—but then again what is compelling about deconstruction is not that it offers a substitute for thinking and philosophizing on one's own, a method which can be followed as a technology of thought, or a strategy which can be employed in tight situations. What is compelling about deconstruction is that it opens up a way of reading texts—philosophical, literary, etc.—so as to identify the framework of their scope and ultimately the extent of their theoretical domain. As a poststructuralism, postphenomenology, postpsychoanalysis, postmodernism, etc., deconstruction offers a reading of the frames, boundaries, and limits of writing whether they be contemporary or imbedded in the history of writing.

(a) As to the strategy itself, the first item is to identify the conceptual oppositions that operate within metaphysical discourse and overturn the implicit hierarchy established by the opposition. The binary oppositions—noticed particularly by Saussure and subsequent semiological writers such as Roland Barthes—are manifold within the history of Western metaphysics. They include such oppositions as sensible/intelligible, speech/writing, passivity/activity, signifier/signified, inside/outside, literal/metaphorical, presence/absence, form/substance, and so on. In "Plato's Pharmacy," Derrida assesses the status of writing as recounted by Plato in the *Phaedrus*. He shows that Plato gives primacy to speech by reading the tale of King Thamus who—as king, father of speech—asserts his authority over Theuth, father of writing. Derrida claims that Plato operates an ambiguity, which through the mouth of King Thamus proclaims dominance and mastery "by asserting its definition into simple, clear-cut oppositions: good and evil, inside and outside, true and false, essence and appearance" (*Dissemination*, p. 103). Derrida goes on to indicate that "it is

not enough to say that writing is conceived out of this or that series of oppositions. Plato thinks of writing, and tries to comprehend it, to dominate it, on
the basis of *opposition* as such. In order for these contrary values (good/evil,
true/false, essence/appearance, inside/outside, etc.) to be in opposition, each of
the terms must be simply *external* to the other, which means that one of these
oppositions (the opposition between inside and outside) must already be
accredited as the matrix of all possible opposition" (*Dissemination*, p. 103).
That Plato writes the predominance of the inside/outside opposition over the
others is to say that he sets one term of the opposition outside the others, but
in so doing he incorporates it within the whole system of metaphysical oppositions which are introduced in order to provide a place for writing itself. Hence
Derrida shows that the outside of the inside/outside opposition is already an
inside and that the king's speech about writing is inscribed in Plato's text. And
furthermore a deconstruction of the whole system of oppositions allows
Derrida to situate his own enterprise—his own placing between—at the site
where the elements of each of these oppositions confront each other and where
the interfaces are proliferated, dis-seminated, spread out, dispersed, throughout
the whole text of metaphysics. The A/not-A opposition is in fact an (A/not-
B)/(B/not-A) oppositional structure which is repeated in the case of each
opposition and linked by the inscription of the bar, slash, interface between
each particular pair.

(b) The second aspect of the deconstructive strategy is the inscription of
one's own writing at the place of "indecidables" by demonstrating their differential function. In *Positions*, Derrida offers something like a definition of
indecidables. He describes them as "unities of simulacrum, 'false' verbal proper-
ties (nominal or semantic) that can no longer be included within philosophical
(binary) opposition, but which, however, inhabit philosophical opposition,
resisting and disorganizing it, *without ever* constituting a third term, without
leaving room for a solution in the form of speculative dialectics" (*Positions*, p.
43). Indecidables operate where philosophical oppositions arise. They are not
elements of the oppositions, yet they mark the oppositions and relate different
oppositions to one another. Indecidables have a double character. They seem to
raise the possibility of turning in either direction within a whole variety of
philosophical oppositions, yet they do not assume the position of either side of
such oppositions. Their double character does not necessarily draw upon the
elements of the binary pair in the metaphysical opposition which they inhabit.
They avoid becoming a third term: an *Aufhebung*, a synthesis of two dialectically
related terms. They do not carry the possibility of resolve that a Hegelian third
term permits. The indecidable is precisely "the limit, interruption, destruction
of Hegelian *Aufhebung*" (*Positions*, p. 40).

Examples of indecidables include: sign, structure, writing, communication,
genre, difference, and so on. And Derrida characterizes some others as follows:

"the *pharmakon* is neither remedy nor poison, neither good nor evil, neither the inside nor the outside, neither speech nor writing: the supplement

is neither a plus nor a minus, neither an outside nor the complement of an inside, neither accident nor essence, etc.; the *hymen* is neither confusion nor distinction, neither identity nor difference, neither consummation nor virginity, neither the veil nor unveiling, neither the insider nor the outsider, etc.; the *gram* is neither a signifier nor a signified, neither a sign nor a thing, neither a presence nor an absence, neither a position nor a negation, etc.; *spacing* is neither space nor time; the *incision* is neither the incised integrity of a beginning, or of a simple cutting into, nor simple secondarity. Neither/nor, that is, *simultaneously* either/or; their mark is also the *marginal* limit, the *march*, etc." (*Positions*, p. 43).

Each of these indecidables is highlighted in at least one of Derrida's many essays (texts). The neither-nor/either-or placement situates the indecidables at the horizontally proliferated dissemination of the sign structure throughout Western metaphysics. The sign itself carries the signifier/signified pair and is therefore also inscribed within the text of metaphysics, the text of philosophy. The indecidable itself is not undecidable—not passively incapable of resolution nor fully active in not working out resolution.

(c) The third task of the deconstructive strategy is to account for the deferral and effects of the enterprise itself. Since indecidables can arise without end—as long as there is writing, they trace the very limits and boundaries of metaphysical discourse itself. They postpone and put off any determination, any circumscription, any completion of the system of scientificity itself. One of the key indecidables is "*différance.*" *Différance* is neither (both) separating nor (and) deferring, neither (both) distinguishing nor (and) postponing. *Différance* both makes itself other than either of two elements of a binary pair and brings itself to generate the move to another place, another opposition, another time.... For instance, Derrida claims that "subjectivity—like objectivity—is an effect of *différance* an effect inscribed in a system of differences" (*Positions*, p. 28). The determination of the place of subjectivity is the marking out of its pair: objectivity. In *différance*, subjectivity is put off until a later objective determination, which itself calls into question the subjectivity from which it distinguishes itself. The effects of *différance* therefore are the production of metaphysical oppositions as they repeat themselves and as they determine themselves in relation to other such oppositions.

DECONSTRUCTIVE INDICATORS

Deconstructive indicators are not entities. Rather they are the earmarks of a deconstructive practice. They can be noticed, introduced, put into operation, and themselves deconstructed. Unlike indecidables, they do not as such bear the character of the neither-nor/either-or. They are the very line or border between the inscriptions of writing and other indecidables as they move about the text. Although deconstructive indicators may themselves have indecidable character, they are not as such indecidables. Some examples include: trace, mark, margin, referral, blank, edge, etc. Each of these indicators is the marking out or writing in the place where a limit occurs. In each case, a filled space occupies both sides. Remarking what is outside the limit is at the same time a marking and an incorporation of the inside. What is on one side—this side, for instance—of the history of metaphysics indicates the possibility of *the other* side. The limit, mark, border, margin, etc. is the writing of that difference. Deconstructive indicators link one side to the other; they serve as the hinge between—bringing together and at the same time separating off the two.

Deconstructive indicators break the ground, come to the surface, and cut through the ice in readings of philosophical, literary, and critical texts. They are sometimes the devices for indicating the places where a deconstructive strategy must operate and sometimes they signal sites where a deconstructive practice has already been. Traces and margins are trademarks of the very type of reading which deconstruction offers. Traces are like footprints which indicate that someone was once there and which are themselves a being-there. But traces are also like lines drawn on see-through (often known as "tracing") paper—they both replicate what they reiterate and they produce a new outline, a new form. They are both re-presentation and presentation at once, both repetition and replacement. Traces are also inscriptions of the place between binary oppositions—they are neither the one nor the other and yet they note the co-givenness, co-operation, and co-incidence of the two. As tools of the trade, traces, marks, notes, inscriptions, etc. indicate the places where deconstruction is both engaged in the preservation of the history of metaphysics and committed to the reservations which metaphysics makes for itself.

Reading the history of metaphysics is a re-writing of its epoch of prevalence. Deconstructive indicators are not only disseminated throughout the text of metaphysics but they also indicate and perform at its edges, frontiers, borders, margins, and limits. While metaphysics cites its own limits and frontiers, deconstruction re-marks these end-points, self-circumscriptions, and auto-delimitations. As a practice, deconstruction cites these places where metaphysics writes them off. But it is metaphysics itself which writes itself in and writes itself off. Deconstruction offers a reading of the loci of this dual practice. Deconstructive indicators note these loci in the note-books of deconstruction, which themselves take the form of essays, texts, and critical writings.

Does deconstruction itself "sign" (or "re-sign," itself to) the possibility of a post-deconstruction? In a certain sense, a post-deconstruction is not only feasible but already written into the contract. If, however, deconstruction has no space of its own, no place to call its own, no limit to its activity, then there cannot be any post-deconstruction. However, if deconstruction is a determining of limits, spaces, effects, then it must *itself* be limited, spaced, and effect-bearing.... By coming into its own, deconstruction could also come to an end. By coming into its own, deconstruction can circumscribe itself. As long as it remains disseminated—sending out, publishing elsewhere, reproducing itself—it can go on, it can continue to produce deferrals and effects. Its post-ponement is simultaneously one step ahead of its own inscription into the history of philosophy. As a reading of the history of philosophy—namely, the text of philosophy—deconstruction provides a pro-gramme, but the gramme is writing itself, the text itself deconstructed as textuality. The pro-gramme, by keeping itself at the limit of writing, keeps itself from becoming a post-gramme.

7

TEXTUALITY AND LITERARY THEORY

To what extent is a philosophical theory of textuality also a literary theory? A philosophy of the text would necessarily also cross into the domain of the literary. A literary theory of the text would also be a matter of concern for philosophy. A theory of textuality would require both the methodological interests of philosophy and the theoretical practice of literary concerns. A deconstructive hermeneutic semiology would raise the question of textuality without offering a general account of the text. The theoretical practice of reading textualities would provide an account of the limits of literature, the logics of literary study, the status of the text along with the role of meaning, and an account of the relationship between interpretation and reading.

LIMITS OF LITERATURE

For an understanding of textuality in a literary context, the question of the scope, status, and limits of literature must be raised. In short, what is the space of literature? If literature is equivalent to the literary object, how is the literary object different from other "objects" such as symphonies, paintings, human beings, and canyons? If literature is a form of expression, how is it different from other types of expression, such as ideas, images, pictures, and gestures? If literature is a language, how is it different from other "languages," such as corporeality, sight, fashion, and the self? In each case, the concern is to establish the space which is particular to literature. In each case, the effort to place literature in the scheme of things is to mark out a space which is all its own, to identify it according to its difference from other domains.

Efforts at identifying literature according to "what it is" often produce an inappropriate space. In *What is Literature?* (1947), Sartre sets limits by distinguishing prose from poetry.[1] For Sartre, only prose-writing seriously counts as literature or writing. Poetry is self-reflection, verbal absolutizing, and its own end. Prose introduces the collaboration of writer and reader, it motivates communication and achieves the bridge between two or more freedoms. Thus Sartre establishes the literary space by division: literature is on the side of prose, its mode of existence is non-poetic. Since poetry is not engaged, it is an "inferior" (and non-literary) verbal type. By contrast, in responding implicitly to Sartre, Roland Barthes in *Writing Degree Zero* (1953) identifies literature as writing and establishes that it holds a position between language and style.[2] Writing is at the zero degree—the intersection of the x and y axes of Cartesian coordinates, where language (the x-axis) is a horizontal display and style (the y-axis) is a vertical pronouncement. Form and value also occur at this point of intersection. Here writing is silent, neutral, and indicative. The spoken level of language in writing—written speech—anticipates a homogeneous social state,—one in which literature is continually placed on trial. At this level, literature seeks to establish its significative function as a complex of signs, codes, and paradigms. Here literature sets its own space and limits.

Between these two extremes of delimitation: one in which literature is distinctly and narrowly defined according to its communicative function and the other in which literature is identified with the open field of zero degree writing, the literary space sets its own boundaries. Border disputes hinge on whether this space includes folktales and slogans as well as poems, epics, plays, and novels and whether what is known has the status of writing, text, intentional object, significant form, grammatical structure, etc. Hence definitions of literature range from fiction, myth, complex, system, rhetorical device, and vision to lie, illusion, tale, frivolity, and diversion. Criteria such as consistency, intricacy, complexity, universality, depth of meaning, endurance, and the like have been invoked. But such criteria are not likely to resolve whether to exclude Lévi-Strauss's account of the Pueblo Zuni myth[3] as nonliterary and to include Homer's *Iliad* and Sophocles's *Oedipus Rex* as literary. They would not permit the claim that Kafka's short stories are literature while Kierkegaard's *Either/Or* is not, that La Fontaine's fables are literature while the Grimms' fairy tales and Mother Goose rhymes are not. Hence literary space is determined according to the manners in which it is known, read, and studied.

LOGICS OF LITERATURE

A literary logic establishes the underlying conditions for knowledge of a text. Such conditions operate within a particular literary space and they presuppose an understanding of how the text is to be interpreted. Therefore a logic of literature operates at the juncture of the literary space and the various approaches to literature. It articulates the limits of the literature which it elucidates and it forbids itself from becoming one among the many independent ways of interpreting the text. The function of a literary logic is to indicate how a text is constructed and how it is unraveled for the reader. Its achievement prescribes the type of knowledge appropriate to a particular text. Logic here is conceived as the systematic account of what is appropriate to a literary text. To know Dante's *Divine Comedy* is to presume that it can be known in a particular way and that a particular way of knowing the poem will enhance the understanding of it. The logic in question is not entirely there in the text, nor does it simply pertain to the inquiry itself. It interweaves the crucial aspects of each in order to affirm and inform a particular reading and interpretation.

A wide variety of approaches accompany literary logics. The most common are of the historical variety. Historical studies tend to define periods, styles, and movements. They are sometimes supplemented by critical approaches where questions of influence, authorship and allusion are embellished with axiological judgments concerning style, meter, genre, theme, plot, and importance of the work in question. Linguistic studies determine "optional slots in grammar,"[4] as well as syntactic structures, [5] intertexts,[6] and tropes.[7] On occasion they stress the speech act function of a literary statement.[8] In other instances linguistic studies spill over into computerized assessments of literary language.[9] Hermeneutical studies[10] tend to (but do not always) build upon historical, critical, and linguistic accounts in that they offer an interpretation of the meaning of the text. Psychological and sociological accounts may also take precedence. In each case, however, the approach itself has an identity of its own just as the literary text has its own space and limits.

A logic of literature depends upon particular texts, but it also announces a particular type of reading. In order for literature to be a human science, the logic in question must condition an approach to the text. Thus although Sophocles's *Oedipus Rex* and Shakespeare's *Hamlet* have a space independent of Freudian psychoanalysis, and psychoanalysis has an identity of its own without ever making reference to Sophocles or Shakespeare, nevertheless the conjunction of the two opens up a specific literary logic.[11] Similarly, although Baudelaire, Mallarmé, and Genet do not depend upon Sartre's account of them to establish their own space, their juxtaposition with existential psychoanalysis does provide a rather unique logic of literature.[12] The sociological studies of Lukács on Goethe, Horkheimer and Adorno on Homer, Goldmann on Pascal and Racine, and Kott on Shakespeare [13] determine a unique literary logic which is distinct from the particular texts and from the philosophical approach which animates the studies. One could also appeal to Northrop Frye's myth studies,[14] René Girard's quasi-anthropological accounts,[15] Geoffrey Hartman's early Heideggerian interpretations of Wordsworth and other poems,[16] and so on. In each of the above cases, the literary logic pertains to the conjuncture of a text or texts with an approach. Each time, the logic is a logic of a reading, or of an interpretation. It establishes its own coherence, consistency, and methodological rigor. Such a logic only allows for particular readings or interpretations to be followed, understood, appreciated, and proliferated. Even if each study is entirely unique, the logic of such a study will be the establishment of its own identity. It is much more customary for such logics to overlap and even reproduce themselves in new readings and interpretations—sometimes forming whole schools of approach. If the psychoanalytical, existential, mythological, sociological, phenomenological, structuralist, poststructuralist, feminist, and deconstructionist orientations are the more common, it is only because they have similar logics, with similar modes of reading and interpreting.

Many current logics are singular in character. Indeed, for a logic to be consistent it must be singular. Typically logics achieve their singularity from the uniqueness of the approaches that condition them. Although critics are wont to draw upon a wide range of approaches and styles of literary understanding, the result is often eclectic or confused. A multiple logic however is different from the employment of a multiplicity of approaches. A multiple logic bears its own singularity due to its special concatenation of features, aspects, and functions. In offering a deconstructive hermeneutic semiology of literature as a multiple logic, I now propose to indicate its place at the juncture of literary spaces and literary approaches.

A hermeneutic semiology of literature is based on a bicontextual multiple logic of literary study, namely, a theoretical practice for reading textualities. Although purity of method and unidimensionality of approach are possible in the human sciences as in the natural sciences, the specifically polyvalent features of literature tend to demand a theory and logic which accounts for the expected ambiguities, complexities and multidimensional orientations present within the literary work of art. Such a theory announces and even performs the type of practical criticism necessary for reading the textuality of literary works. A hermeneutic semiology is itself *a* theory—even though it incorporates (but is not reducible to) aspects arising out of semiological-structuralist and hermeneutic-phenomenological approaches as well as deconstructionist strategies along with their concomitant logics. However, a hermeneutic semiology is already, at the very least, poststructuralist and postphenomenological. The task of a hermeneutic semiology is to offer concepts and strategies of reading and interpreting which account for signifying textualities (that are not otherwise accessible).

A textuality is the condition according to which a text is a text. A text is a complex fabric of signs. Signification depends upon codes and structures arising from relations between signs as they occur within the development of the text. A reading of the codes and structures with their significations provides a context for interpretational modes and models. Such modes and models include the psychological, sociological, historical, political, and other logics or types of expression. These types are cognitively understood in terms of rhetorical tropes, epistemic systems, and symbolic formations. As the reading identifies the textuality of the literary work, the reading deconstructs the text such that, on the one hand, the signs actualize the signification, and, on the other hand, the signification actualizes a meaning through interpretation. Together these features constitute the architectonic for a hermeneutic semiology.

TEXT AND MEANING

The juncture between the ontological spaces and the epistemological concerns of literary study serves as the locus for a hermeneutic semiology of literature.[17] To the question "what is literature?" the answer now includes an appeal to a series, a grouping, or a culture of texts. Such texts might include the traditional canon of genres (plays, novels, poems, short stories, etc.), but they would also federate myths, autobiographies, science fiction, philosophical treatises, historical chronicles, and other forms of writing. Boundaries need not be set as to what may or must count as a literary text. Unlike the neoclassical era, varieties of textuality are now unlimited. Some texts offer themselves for the purposes of literary study because of their specifically fictional qualities, some for their stylistic features, some for their relationship to other texts, and some for their cultural contextuality. The epistemological function intersects with these texts at the point where they are read, interpreted, and understood.

Although the phenomenological notion of intentionality provides descriptions for the manner in which the text is known, this notion is severely limited. In the Husserlian version, intentionality is unidirectional (from a subject to the object under scrutiny). Hence the object under study is understood phenomenologically in terms of a mediating meaning. Ingarden extends this view by considering the various strata of the literary work of art at the noematic (mediating, meaning-laden) level. This level stresses the stratum of represented objectivities, though it also allows for the superimposition of content-oriented units and other intentional features.[18] When placed in the context of Dufrenne's phenomenology of aesthetic experience with his distinction between a literary work of art and the literary aesthetic object, the intentional relation is where the text (as mediating object) achieves meaning in the aesthetic experience—an experience which is filled with sensuousness and expressivity.[19] With Dufrenne, the notion of intentionality incarnates and gives meaning to the work of art. However, even though both Merleau-Ponty and Dufrenne allow for a bidirectional meaning-laden intentionality (from subject to object and from object to subject) and though they take experience as in-the-world along with the work or text, they nevertheless treat the meaning or sense as present to (but separate from) an interpretation of the text. In a phenomenological reading of the literary work, the reader constitutes the meaning of the work. Such an act of constitution is the manner according to which the text is known. In Ingarden's case, the text is different from both the literary work of art and the meaning. In Dufrenne, the text and the literary work of art are equivalent, but the meaning *qua* aesthetic object is distinct. In both cases the meaning is different from the text, for the meaning is constituted in the reading of the text.

Semiologically speaking, the text is a system of signs forming a set of structures and a variety of significations established by the conventionalization of nature. The text, in this case, is a complex of relations, both within a limited domain such as a novel or a poem and with respect to limited domains outside any particular set of relations (its "intertextuality"). By virtue of intertextuality, the semiological-structuralist's text is not simply "intrinsic" (to use Wellek and Warren's term).[20] The structuralist's text involves the possibility of other versions with similar structures (established by transformation), intertextual elements from other texts which are co-present with the text, and a *language* in which the text participates. Granted these "extrinsic" elements are not biographical, psychoanalytical, historical, or philosophical; nevertheless they do cut across the boundaries of the intrinsic/extrinsic distinction. According to the semiological account, signification arises out of the act or process of relating the signifier to the signified. However, signification can only occur within a context of signs where one is given in relation to another (textually or intertextually). A text is a set of signifying sign systems arising from the interrelationships between signs. Hence the signification is inseparable from the text. An act of reading would bring out the signification and consequently the text.

For semiology, the text is interwoven with signification. As Jonathan Culler puts it, "the poem cannot be *created* except in relation to other poems and conventions of reading. It is what it is by virtue of those relations, and its status does not change with publication. If its meaning changes later on, that is because it enters new relations with later texts: new works which modify the literary system itself."[21] The "meaning" which Culler describes is generally referred to as "signification." For hermeneutics, the text is interpreted at the level of meaning, which is distinct from the text and which is given in the intentional act.

What then is the relationship between semiological signification and hermeneutic meaning? E. D. Hirsch, for example, discriminates between "meaning" and "significance."[22] Meaning is the "verbal meaning" which is present in both the author's intentional act and that of the reader. Significance is drawn from the particular value which a reader gives to the text but which is unique to that reader. The meaning which is present in both the author's and the reader's intentional act must remain different from the referent (or *Bedeutung*) to which the meaning (for example: "unicorn in the garden," Dante's "Inferno," or Thoreau's "Walden Pond") refers. Nevertheless, the validity of any particular reading of the text with its referents *(Bedeutungen)* depends upon the invariability of the verbal meaning *(Sinn)*. If we associate Hirsch's "verbal meaning" *(Sinn)*, Ingarden's "stratum of meaning units," and Dufrenne's "aesthetic object" with the semiological account of "signification," we find a parallelism or even intersection of terms. Although we may locate the phenomenologist's meaning *(Sinn)* and the structuralist's signification *(signification)* in the same place epistemologically, their difference at the ontological level must be identified. Epistemologically, *hermeneutic-phenomenological meaning* and *semiological-structuralist signification* are equivalent because when the text is read, "meaning" or "signification" is what is known (i.e., interpreted).[23] Ontologically, however, meaning for the hermeneutic phenomenologist cannot occupy the same place with respect to the text as signification does for the semiological-structuralist. Meaning is the textuality of the text while signification is the performance or activity of the text in its textuality.

READING AND INTERPRETATION

A hermeneutic semiology of literature can resolve the difference in the ontological status of meaning or signification as developed by hermeneutic phenomenology on the one hand and by semiological-structuralism on the other. However, it does not suffice to claim simply that in a hermeneutic semiology the notions of "meaning" and "signification" are ontologically equivalent. We must turn to the epistemological, or interpretational, mode in order to demonstrate how the *meaning of the text* is read as *signification*. In this way, it can be shown that the cognition of the text need not pass through a concept, intentional object, or textual meaning by a subject who is other than either the meaning or the text. Rather the text is read in terms of its signification, and its signification is the interpreted meaning.

The hermeneutic phenomenological reading affirms that a text or literary work of art is placed there by the author and is to be interpreted by a reader. Thus Magliola, who associates the Geneva School of criticism with the phenomenological approach, claims that the subjective life-world of the author is that aspect of the author which passes into the text (*Pheno&Lit*, p. 9). In this respect, the meaning or "subjective life-world" is read by the interpreter as the meaning *(Sinn)* of the text. This meaning (or sense) of the text is nevertheless distinct from the text, for it is that which is ascribed to the author and his "experiential patterns" (*Pheno&Lit*, p. 30). The meaning of the text, for the phenomenologist, is the content of the text as it is revealed in a variety of different—psychological, sociological, political, and historical—modes. A hermeneutic of the literary text is an interpretation of the meaning which the reader reads there.

The semiological-structuralist reading of the text is a reading of its signification. The signification of the text is identical with the totality of its codes, connotations, and metalanguages. In *S/Z*, Barthes postulates five different codes which constitute the readability of the text. They include: (1) the *proairetic code*, which governs the reader's construction of plot; (2) the *hermeneutic* (not to be confused with the general sense of "hermeneutic" discussed in this chapter) *code* which deals with the formulation of an enigma and its resolution; (3) the *semic code*, which identifies the semantic features of the text; (4) the *symbolic code*, which follows the symbolic or thematic elements; and (5) the *referential code*, which accounts for the cultural background to which the text refers.[24] An elaboration of the way in which these five codes operate within a particular work constitutes Barthes's "writerly" text: the text as rewritten in a semiological reading of it. The "readerly" text accounts for the work as it is read in an everyday, conventional, sequential, and essentially syntagmatic fashion (*S/Z*, pp. 3–4). Culler characterizes a structuralist reading of the text (i.e., elaborating the "writerly") as "naturalization." He claims that "if one has made one-self aware of the various naturalizing operations that reading and criticism involve, one will become newly attentive to the ways in which the text resists the operations which one seeks to perform on it and exceeds the meaning which one can discover at any given level of *vraisemblance*. Consequently, the most interesting features of a text—the features on which a semiological-structuralist criticism may choose to dwell—become those by which it asserts its otherness, its difference from what is already dealt with by the cultural models of "literature as an institution" (*StructPoetics*, p. 160). Thus, what Culler develops as a notion of "literary competence" involves basically a reading of the text—a reading whose goal is to bring out "the underlying system which makes literary effects possible."[25] Literary competence permits the reader to "read the work *as literature*," to "convert linguistic sequences into literary structures and meanings" (*StructPoetics*, p. 114). Literary competence, then, is the means by which the text becomes the meaning (signification) which it already is. In this respect, rather than taking the phenomenological orientation in which the reader speaks by means of his interpretation, the structuralist alternative is to consider that the reader *is spoken* in the reading of the text.

The semiological-structuralist model of reading is an elaboration of a critical discourse. Citing Barthes, Culler states that structuralist poetics is not "a 'science of contents' which, in hermeneutic fashion, proposed interpretations for works, 'but a science of the conditions of content,' that is to say of forms. What interests it will be the variations of meaning generated and, as it were, capable of being generated by works; it will not interpret symbols but describe their polyvalency. In short, its object will not be the full meanings of the work but on the contrary the empty meaning which supports them all.'"[26] For the semiological-structuralist, meanings (significations) are generated by the literary works or texts themselves, while in the hermeneutic approach, the author or reader generates the meanings of the text in relation to a world. In the words of Magliola, "whereas the Geneva School sees language as the expression of self and world, structuralism recognizes and examines the converse of this: that self and world are shaped by the structure of language." "It seems to me," he goes on to say, "that these two intuitions, radically inadequate when treated disjunctively, best operate in conjunction with each other" (*Pheno&Lit*, p. 92). A hermeneutic semiology of literature will not provide that conjunction as such, since it must establish its own ground apart from either semiological-structuralism or hermeneutic-phenomenology. However, by moving to the question of meaning, it becomes evident that a new theoretical practice of reading and interpretation must account for the divergence.

In a hermeneutic semiology of literature, the language of the text must neither come from the self to the world nor from the codes, connotations, and metalanguages of the text back to the self or world. A hermeneutic semiology requires that there be both signifying structures and sign systems and the interpretative experience by which they are given expression. No priority can be claimed by the self-world axis as entering the text nor by the text as it fulfills the self-world axis. A bidirectionality, which both passes through the text as meaning-signification and by which the text textualizes, contextualizes, and intertextualizes, will constitute the interpretation of literary works. One must therefore look for the codes, messages, and expressions in the text—for that is the meaning of the work—but one must expect that the text itself is engaged in a textualizing process according to which a *reading competence* (to reformulate Culler's idea of "competent reader") is in effect. Only in this respect do the semiological-structuralist notion of signification and the hermeneutic-phenomenological notion of meaning intersect, for, in a hermeneutic semiology of literature, the literary text speaks us as we read it. Thus we, as readers or interpreters, and the text, as a reading or an interpretation, are meaningful activities within the general study of literature.

SIGNIFYING TEXTUALITY: THE VOICE OF THE READER

Roland Barthes's *S/Z* offers a semiological reading of Balzac's short story *Sarrasine*. In one section, which he entitles "The Voice of the Reader," Barthes examines the following passage:

> A girl was listening to a declaration of love unaware that she was spilling sherry on the tablecloth. In the midst of this disorder, La Zambinella remained thoughtful, *as though terror-struck*. She refused to drink, perhaps she ate a bit too much; however, it is said that greediness in a woman is a charming quality. Admiring his mistress's modesty, Sarrasine thought seriously about the future.[27]

Sarrasine, a sculptor, has fallen madly in love with La Zambinella and attends her performances regularly at the theatre. At last, in the passage cited above, he is invited to a party at which he meets his beloved in person. Sarrasine does not yet know that La Zambinella is a male eunuch.

The words "as though terror-struck," which I have emphasized, are the focus of Barthes's attention. He asks: "Who is speaking here?" and then explains: "It cannot be Sarrasine, even indirectly, since he interprets La Zambinella's fear as timidity. Above all, it cannot be the narrator because he knows that La Zambinella really is terrified. The modalization *(as though)* expresses the interests of only one character, who is neither Sarrasine nor the narrator, but the reader: it is the reader who is concerned that the truth be simultaneously named and evaded, an ambiguity which the discourse nicely creates by *as though*, which indicates the truth and yet reduces it declaratively to a mere appearance" (*S/Z*, p. 151). The code in which "as though terror-struck" participates is designed as the proairetic or action code, for "terror-struck" is associated with danger and fear on the part of La Zambinella. The message is that something is awry, for why should a woman be terrified by loving glances? What is expressed is a sense of horror: its content may take the form of rapid eating. When one is afraid or uncertain, there is often a tendency to eat more quickly than usual—though, in this case, it is somewhat unbecoming of a woman (and Sarrasine would surely interpret it as such).

In the passage under consideration, the language of the text is one of multiple significations. La Zambinella is thoroughly feminine in her dress, posture, and gestures. Amid this femininity is a masculine appetite and a terror which is not particularly sex-typed. Furthermore, significations of amorous affection, an overlooking of non-feminine qualities, and an ignorance of mockery among those at the party are manifestly present in the language of the passage. What do all these significations mean? They mean that something is wrong in the situation, but it is not clear what. Who interprets this meaning? It cannot be Sarrasine, for he does not notice any discrepancy between his expectations and what occurs. It cannot be La Zambinella, for she actively produces many of the significations. It cannot be any of those attending, for they are too thoroughly immersed in mirth and carousing. None of these people are in a position to specify a condition of enigmatic concern. In each case, the situation is clear-cut: for Sarrasine, it is love; for La Zambinella, it is fear of consequences resulting from the deception; for those attending, it is amusement. The text reads: "as though terror-struck." Therefore, it must be *the text* which "interprets" and *the interpretation* which textualizes. The reader places the text in the world through a textuality which can be called its meaning. But the text announces the multiplicity of signification *as* meaning through an interpretation—that which is "in-between" and that which incorporates subject and object, self and world, interpreter and interpreted—establishing the text itself, for the text provides both the significations and the meaning of the situation. The text as *textuality* is both interpreter and interpreted. Thus it is neither the author, as Hirsch proposes, nor the reader, as Barthes suggests, but the text which says, "as though terror-struck."

What is the role of the reader in such a deconstructive hermeneutic semiology? The reader is the one who signifies. The reader gives expression to the text, which itself asserts the interpretation. In what Barthes calls the middle voice,[28] the reader announces the various significations of affection, fear, and amusement. The text interprets these significations as a textuality of "as though terror-struck"-ness. The context of the statement is meaningful. The significations all crystallize here in this one statement. The reader "speaks" them by directing them to the interpretation which the text offers. There is a sense of terror pervading the situation: La Zambinella, Sarrasine, and those at the party are all in collusion. La Zambinella remains thoughtful—as though terror-struck—because the text interprets it as such. There is no reader outside the text by which the meaning can be said to enter the text. The meaning—the "verbal meaning" to stress Hirsch's expression—achieves its significance alongside other meanings in the world with its texture of languages. This particular textuality provides for a reader who signifies a meaning which the text enacts and interprets just as the text of this chapter enacts and interprets a deconstructive hermeneutic semiology to which the reader provides a multiplicity of meaningful significations that are already there and spoken for in what is written here.[29]

8

THE LANGUAGE OF TEXTUALITY

The text is an indecidable. The text's indecidability is elaborated in terms of and as an operative feature of its textuality. Indeed, the text's textuality is its indecidability. It is not that the text is one thing and that there is a problem of determining what that thing is—although an articulation of the status of the text is no easy matter and elucidating its textuality is not a simple procedure. The indecision is not a psychological state of the reader, although interpretation is usually necessary in order to make sense of the text's textuality. The reader often requires an interpretation in order to dispel any confusion that might arise in a reading, or *the* reading, of a text. However, the text's indecidability does not lie in the reader's confusion. Furthermore, the text's indecidability does not result from an indeterminacy of reference or a simple multiplicity of references. Many texts exhibit a world in which it is often unclear what (if any) reality, what (if any) experience, what (if any) event is cited or invoked. And many texts offer various possible worlds which do or could suit the narrative offered. But, neither of these features characterize the text's indecidability. The text's indecidability lies in its textuality or textualities through which the text (or a text) establishes its identity as a text.

A textuality constitutes a text as a text in a particular way. Textualities constitute the text as an indecidable. The textuality of a text produces knowledge about the text. The knowledge that it produces is of a particular sort; its particular decidability does not lie in the knowledge that is produced but rather in the status of the text in which the production occurs. Textuality (in general) is produced in the textualization of the text. In rendering itself text, the text offers up a textuality which is indecidability itself. The text is an indecidable because its textuality is indecidable. Its textuality is indecidable because textuality occurs at the place where the text escapes definition, particular determination, specification—where the text effaces itself in favor of what Paul de Man has called a "disfiguration."[1] Textuality occurs where the text off-centers itself. The text is off-center (ex-centric); its textuality is its decentering in specific ways.

A reading of the text occurs *through* its textuality or textualities. The text is *what* is read, but its textuality or textualities is *how* it is read. An interpretation of the text arises in that the textualities are understood as the meaning-structure(s) of the text. The interpretation of the text brings the textuality or textualities *in* so as to take them outside the text, so as to specify and determine the text in a particular fashion. The text is apart from its readings and interpretations. Its textuality or textualities are constituted in a reading of the text and identified through an interpretation of it. But, if the text is an indecidable and its textuality is its indecidability, then what can it mean to speak of a reading or an interpretation of a text? If indecidable, what sort of readings and interpretations are possible? If indecidable, why read or interpret?

In order to provide anything like an answer to these questions, both the nature of the indecidability and the place of the text will have to be assessed. By establishing the place of the text, the respect in which it is an indecidable will become evident. An assessment and elaboration of its indecidability will also be an assessment and elaboration of its textuality. As Edward Said has pointed out, textuality is a *practice*.[2] Through its textuality, the text makes itself mean, makes itself be, makes itself come about in a particular way. At the same time, through its textuality, the text makes itself other than what it is in a particular way or ways. Through its textuality and textualities, the text relinquishes its status as identity and affirms its condition as pure difference. Because of its textuality, the text elides itself, defines itself, or determines itself in particular ways. But, in that its textuality is other, the text "dedefines" itself (*PT*, p. 89), inscribes itself in a texture or network of meaning which is not limited to the text itself. By dedefining itself, the text offers the possibility of a definitive reading and a decisive interpretation. By the very nature of its textuality, neither the definitive reading nor the decisive interpretation succeeds. Although the reading may define and the interpretation may decide, the text neither defines nor decides. The text remains operationally and fundamentally indecidable. Its textuality as a practice is the text dedefining itself and rendering itself operationally and fundamentally indecidable. The text is difference itself; its textuality is its differing from itself, making itself different. Each text is different. In differing, it defers; it produces a textuality that is consistent with and even identical to the textuality of other texts. Hence through its textuality, the text brings in, incorporates, and invokes other texts. But because the text is indecidable, its textuality does not determine once and for all which meaning or meanings, which interpretation or interpretations, which reading or readings prevail and which do not.

The indecidability of the textuality of the text is different from the text as indecidable. The text as an indecidable is conditioned by the nature and function of indecidables. According to Derrida, indecidables are theoretical configurations which are marked and located in writing as highlighted "words" or "concepts." As already indicated, Derrida operates and employs a general strategy of deconstruction which avoids simply *neutralizing* the binary oppositions of metaphysics. It also "does not simply *reside* within the closed field of binary oppositions, for that would only confirm the binary field itself" (*Positions*, p. 41). Thus, indecidables perform a dual function. They keep notions from turning into a third term, which synthesizes and thereby neutralizes oppositional pairs, *and* they prohibit notions from occupying either one side or the other. In short, indecidables are not Hegelian *Aufhebungen* yet they also do not simply constitute antithetical (or oppositional) structural dyads. Indecidables situate themselves at the interface or slash between such oppositional pairs. They lean in each direction at once without affirming, with exclusivity, either one side or the other. Indecidables occur in the context of traditional metaphysical, philosophical, or literary terms and therefore within the general field of writing. Indecidables have no independent status apart from the general field of writing and the oppositional structures in which they take place. Furthermore, they are spread out—disseminated—throughout the general field of writing. They demonstrate the limitations of traditional notions and yet are inscribed within the very discourses in which such traditional notions are situated.

Derrida's deconstructive strategy practices a "double writing." This double writing, which he elaborates in the essay on the "Double Session," indicates the respect in which writing operates in two places at once (see *Dissemination*, pp. 173–286). The double writing is also a double science, a double seance, a double scene, and so forth. The double writing is the inscription of a binary oppositional structure within the general field of writing. Within that general field, with its traditional metaphysical concepts, hierarchies assert themselves. The deconstructive strategy produces and provokes an overturning or reversal of the hierarchy as affirmed within the tradition. In order to accomplish such an overturning, it is necessary to locate the relevant oppositional terms within the general field and thereby to locate the indecidables as well.

Derrida identifies a wide variety of indecidables.[3] The strategy is to operate at the indecidable interface between the "neither" and the "nor." The indecidable is not a third term, nor is it resolvable into either of the two sides. If now the text is an indecidable, it should be more readily apparent in what sense it is so.

The text is "exorbitant" (*PT*, pp. 93–4). The text goes out beyond itself. The text demonstrates its supplementarity by being something more than what is there. What is there sets limits to itself, establishes its own boundaries, margins, borderlines, frontiers, circumscriptions. Yet at the same time the text spills over those boundaries, frontiers, and circumscriptions. The text spills over into one or another definition of itself. It cannot and does not remain pure difference. There is always a remainder according to which the text affirms an identity for itself. The text tends to fall on one side or the other of a whole complex of binary oppositions. In this sense, the text is: (1) neither visible nor invisible, (2) neither inside nor outside, (3) neither present nor absent, (4) neither text nor context, (5) neither one nor many. By considering the respects in which the text is located at the interface of these oppositions, it shall become evident where the text's textuality occurs and how, specifically, it tends to spill over onto one side or the other as a resolution of one sort or another of its indecidability.

VISIBLE/INVISIBLE

The text is always hiding something: something of itself, something which it is not. As Said points out, unlike Foucault's view in which the text is invisible, there is something to be revealed, stated, brought to a certain visibility. For Derrida, however, the more that is grasped about the text, the more detail there is of what is not there (*PT*, p. 89). The view proposed here is that what is invisible or hidden in the text comes into view in terms of its textuality, but *qua* text the more that is affirmed about the text in terms of its textuality, the more the text effaces itself, evades definition, escapes visible determination. The text is visible in that it offers a narrative, discloses a world, opens up a clearing in which sounds, ideas, rhythms, and stories are made evident. But the text also tends to hide its very textuality or textualities. It tends to cover up its meanings and meaning structures. Readings only disclose the surfaces; interpretations are required to reveal its meaning, rendering its enigmatic and indecidable character more evident. It cannot be decided whether the text is visible or not. To opt for one or the other is to render its textuality determinate—though its textuality remains fundamentally indecidable. A text might be an epic novel or it might be a fragment; it might be a long poem or it might be a screenplay. The limits of Dante's *Divine Comedy* are clearly outlined in repeated triadic form: from the canzone to the canto and the canto to *terza rima* verse, from Hell to Heaven through Purgatory, from Virgil to Beatrice through Statius, and so on; yet many autobiographical textualities, historical textualities, and poetic textualities are hidden from view. The poem's triadics make certain theological textualities visible and open for inspection. Although at the fringes, the trinity turns into a unity, ninety-nine cantos engender a hundredth, along with a Hell, Purgatory, and Paradise. There is also a Rose or Empyrean, which englobes them all. What could be said about the trinity, about controversies among realists and nominalists, about the function of religious allegory in secular medieval romances, about Dante's inventions of a cosmological *Weltanschauung*, is not visible in the text. To take them as hidden and to claim that they constitute the text in some fundamental way is to decide on its theological textuality at a level where it is not decidable, where it operates at the border between what is visible and what is not visible in the text.

INSIDE/OUTSIDE

If it could be determined what is inside the text and what is outside, then the textuality or textualities of the text would also be decidable. Are the varoria to Shakespeare's plays inside the text or outside? Is the concluding portion of the *Roman de la rose* written by Jean de Meun and added onto Guillaume de Lorris's poem inside or outside the text? Is *Stephen Hero* part of Joyce's *A Portrait of the Artist as a Young Man* in the ways in which Kant's A and B versions are part of (inside) the *Critique of Pure Reason*? Are the spaces between the aphorisms in Nietzsche's *Gay Science* inside or outside the text? What is indecidable about each of these texts is also indecidable about the text. The text is neither a work nor a series of words, neither a book nor the content of its pages. The text is off-center, located were the intratextual meets the extratextual and dedefines its borders. Its textuality is precisely the condition of not setting clear lines of demarcation between the intratextual and the extratextual, between what counts as part of the text and what does not. Its textuality is also the practice of upsetting specifications as to where the borderlines occur. As Said puts it, the text "bursts through semantic horizons" (*PT*, p. 108). The practice of textuality is to traverse those limits of meaning and particularly those which arbitrarily set boundaries to the text.

PRESENCE/ABSENCE

The text is neither present nor absent, neither scription nor diction, neither writing nor speech. The text *is* neither the graphic writing nor the spoken sounds. The text *is* neither a substitute for something absent nor the immediate form of something present. What Derrida calls writing *(écriture) is* the indecidable between the present and the absent, between writing as graphic sign and speech as verbal sounds. Like *écriture*, the text operates at the interface between the oppositional polarities. Although there are specific texts, Derrida also says that there is a "general text" which "practically inscribes and overflows the limits of a discourse" entirely regulated by essence, meaning, truth, consciousness, ideality, etc." Derrida goes on to write:

> *there is* such a general text everywhere that this discourse and its order (essence, sense, truth, meaning, consciousness, ideality, etc.) are over-flowed, that is, everywhere that their authority is put back into the position of a *mark* in a chain that this authority intrinsically and illusorily believes it wishes to, and does in fact, govern. This general text is not lim-ited to writings on the page (*Positions*, p. 60).

The general text is not fully present in any particular text. Indeed, just as there is no way of deciding what *is in* a text, there is no way of deciding what is present in the text. What is present in the specific text is also present in the general text but what is absent in the specific text may not be absent in the general text. Features of the general text permeate the specific text, render themselves clear and present in the specific text; but in that they are also directly and explicitly absent from the text, they cannot be said to be present.

The text is a performance, a speech act in a sense. As a performance, the text renders itself present, but what is rendered present is strictly absent. Lodged per-haps in the general text, what is absent is spoken and even written, rendering what is absent present. Cartesian notions of clarity and distinctness are per-formed in Madame de Lafayette's novel *La Princesse de Clèves*; theories and conditions of alienation are spoken in Brecht's *Mutter Courage*; Kafka's *The Castle* exhibits a search for an ego ideal, which Freudian psychoanalysis had identified in the culture. The textuality of texts incorporates as present what is also absent; it incorporates these elements so that there is no way to decide whether they are present or absent—only that they are in play, in the play of differences which constitute the text.

TEXT / CONTEXT

The text sets its own limits. In setting its own limits, it also establishes what goes with it and what does not. But is a text distinct from its context? The context is what accompanies the text. It is also what is outside and therefore other than the text. In its otherness, it is context only in that it is signaled in the text as that which goes with it. As Derrida (1977) points out in "Limited Inc. a b c...,"[4] "context" in French can be heard as "*qu'on texte*"—that which one texts. In other words, the context is that which is rendered text. It includes the neologistic verb "to text." Context, then, is the making part of the text that which is not part of the text and that which remains other than the text. Context may be political, historical, literary, cultural, social, and so forth. Although many of these features are typically regarded as extrinsic to the text, outside the text, other than the text, nevertheless they accompany the text and are "texted," in that they are the context for the text in question. In that they are "texted," or with respect to their textuality, "textualized," they are also intrinsic to the text. The Second World War is textualized in Sartre's *Chemins de la liberté (Roads to Freedom)* novels; the American Civil War is given shape in Stephen Crane's *The Red Badge of Courage*. The condition of Blacks in America is textualized in Ralph Ellison's *Invisible Man;* apartheid is rendered text in Alan Paton's *Cry the Beloved Country*. Early twentieth-century social structure among the upper bourgeoisie is textualized in Virginia Woolf's *Mrs. Dalloway* with respect to England, and in Marcel Proust's *À la Recherche du temps perdu* with respect to France. In these cases, what is offered is not the representation of the outside world in the text, though the textuality of the text can be interpreted as such. Rather, although separate and other, the generalized context or milieu is incorporated into the framework of the text without thematization and specific identification.

Along with contexts, texts have intertexts. Although intertexts are texts which go along with texts, they are also identified and specified in texts. Intertexts are included within texts in that they become part of a complex of texts which constitutes the text in question. Because intertexts span the boundaries between text and intertext, there is no way to decide whether they are inside or outside, part of or separate from the text in question.

TEXTUALITY: UNITY OR MULTIPLICITY?

Textuality is the indecidability of the text. The text is situated at the interface between visible/invisible, inside/outside, presence/absence, text/context. The text is an indecidable. The text falls on neither side. It cannot be decided on which side it falls. Its indecidability is its textuality. Its character as difference is its indecidability. The textuality of the text is both a condition of the text and the practice of the text. Textuality, however, is not single. For each text, there are many textualities. These different textualities are read and interpreted. Textualities are not tied to particular texts. They are part of the general text. Yet particular texts exhibit, manifest, and operate particular textualities. Autobiographical textuality occurs in a marginal way in texts such as Thoreau's *Walden*, Nietzsche's *Ecce Homo*, and Lévi-Strauss's *Tristes Tropiques*,[5] but also in a more restricted domain in many biology textbooks or in psychological research papers. Historical textuality appears in texts as diverse as Tolstoy's *War and Peace*, Stendhal's *The Red and the Black*, and Dickens's *Tale of Two Cities*, but it also enters into Hegel's *Phenomenology of Mind* and Darwin's *Origin of Species*. Scientific textuality, psychological textuality, gastronomic textuality, and so forth, operate so as to produce the indecidability of texts. Certainly not all texts exhibit and practice all types of textuality. Some achieve dominance where others hold a minor status in specific texts. Particular textualities can be characterized and qualified apart from texts, but they achieve their practice and function in terms of particular texts. From their multiplicity they contribute to the indecidability of the text and acquire their own status in the place and places of difference.

III

Autobiographical
Textualities

9

AUTOBIOGRAPHICAL
TEXTUALITY AND
THOREAU'S *WALDEN*

Autobiographical textuality elaborates the autobiographical features (or meanings) of a text. It characterizes the respects in which a particular text develops autobiographical concerns. These concerns remain inherent in the text although they are not necessarily its central themes, issues, or foci of discussion. The elucidation of its autobiographical aspects informs about the function and features of the autobiographical in general. Thus an understanding of the autobiographical textuality of a text contributes to knowledge about the particular text and what constitutes the autobiographical per se.

An autobiographical textuality is an epistemological formation. It provides knowledge about how a text operates, what meanings the text incorporates, and the respects in which the text determines itself as enacting autobiographical considerations. As an epistemological formation, this particular type of textuality specifies dimensions, conditions, parameters, and determinations of the life narrated. The autobiographical text provides the narrative of a life. Its textuality establishes what is to be known about that particular life and the way it is to be known. An autobiographical textuality establishes a place in which essential knowledge about the autobiographical text can be made evident in terms of the relational elements, features, and signs of the narrated life. The textuality also calls into question what constitutes the life as this particular life. It circumscribes the limits of the life as narrated and sets itself off from the various forms and types of non-autobiographical textuality. The task of a deconstructive hermeneutic semiology is to explore textualities. In exploring them, it offers an understanding of the meaning of the sign systems operative in the text. The study of an autobiographical textuality is one such enterprise. Since autobiographical textualities are examined in relation to particular texts, the present consideration will take up Henry David Thoreau's *Walden: or, Life in the Woods* (1960 edition) in order to give a clearer account of autobiographical textuality in general.[1]

AUTOBIOGRAPHY AS PURE LIMIT

In autobiography, the self or subject is written as text. Auto-bio-graphizing is the writing of the self as text. In other words, the dialectic of selfhood is inscribed as textuality. Writing the self or subject is an activity in which the self or subject attempts to account for itself. The accounting is its textuality. Such an accounting approximates a *recounting*—though it will become evident that the self neither fully accounts for itself nor fully recounts itself. Yet the activity, the inscribing, the writing, the interface between accounting and recounting is autobiographical textuality. Autobiographizing is textualizing, its textuality is autobiographical signification—the act or process of textualizing the textualized self.

Although it may be possible to articulate the textuality of an autobiographical text, the placement of the textualized self is more problematical. Indeed, to indicate a distinctive space in which the textualized self is at home and in a place of its own is to provide a false sense of security, for the autobiographical is without space. What sort of space is in question here? It is most appropriately called topological space. Autobiographical textuality is a *topos:* neither a place nor a topic and yet situated at the intersection of the two. A *topos* is a discursive space. It has features derived from geography and features derived from rhetoric. Yet it occupies a domain all its own, for discursive spaces are at the same time delimited by texts and opened up by texts. A topology—the interpretation of *topoi*—maps out discursive spaces as they constitute texts and as they distinguish themselves from one another.

Autobiographical textuality is a *topos* in that it describes a unique topic and a place in the scheme of things. More specifically, autobiography involves a *topos* because it forms a type of discourse with an apparent space all its own. Writing the self as text has its own features just like other *topoi*, such as architecture, metaphysics, the body, political economy, etc. Yet under closer scrutiny, it becomes evident that autobiography as a genre is situated at the limits of discursive spaces and that it does not have a distinctive space of its own. This should not imply that autobiography is a counter-*topos*, an anti-discursive space, for a counter-*topos* or an anti-discursive space would already be a sort of *topos*. If the textuality of romanticism is a countertopos with respect to classicism, then romantic textuality is already a *topos*. If Rousseau's social contract theory is an anti-discursive space with respect to absolute monarchy, then social contract theory is already a discursive space. Rousseau's *Confessions*, however, is not an anti-discursive space with respect to any other—unless one were to distinguish it from all other autobiographies as a class. More specifically, Rousseau's *Confessions* is located at the limit of his particular enterprises. Considering all of Rousseau's adventures, theories, and personal contacts, none of these as such constitutes the autobiographical space, for they are each *topoi* in themselves.

The autobiographical in the case of Rousseau's *Confessions* is precisely at the limit of each of these *topoi*. The textuality of Rousseau's *Confessions* as autobiography is situated at the limits of the discourses of the text. However, the place of the autobiographical textuality is not located in any of the discourses of the text per se. And yet at the edge of all of these discourses is the achievement of autobiographical practice. The topology of the autobiographical occurs at the intersection of the autobiographical text and any other authorially linked texts, or at the limits of the author's theoretical, political, fictional, aesthetic, or other writings—as in the case of Rousseau's *Confessions* in relation to the *Discourse on the Origin of Inequality among Mankind, Émile, The Social Contract, La Nouvelle Heloïse,* etc. Although the autobiographical text may be juxtaposed with authorially linked non-autobiographical texts, the autobiographical space is located at the interface between autobiographical and non-autobiographical texts. To be located at an interface, in the intersection, is not to be located in any space at all. Autobiographical textuality is without space and therefore pure limit.

Consider now Thoreau's *Walden.* Here is a text written in large part between 1845 and 1847, while Thoreau lived in a wooden hut that he built himself near Walden Pond in Concord, Massachusetts. Published in 1854 with very little success, it represents one of two books that appeared during Thoreau's lifetime. Walden is a report of a two-year-and-two month experience. But the status of the text is in question. It is surely an account by an individual concerning his own life and thought. Writing his own life, Thoreau's text announces itself as autobiographical. The self is textualized in a pensive style and thereby presents itself as autobiography. The discursive space opened up by *Walden* is inscribed alongside *A Week on the Concord and Merrimack Rivers* (1849). Its textuality is autobiographical in that it is given in the first person singular as an "I" describing the "me." Its space is a non-space not only because Thoreau was hardly read during his lifetime, but also because in privileging the autobiographical, Thoreau prioritizes his experience and places himself outside the frame of the standard writer. Even his apparently non-autobiographical texts, such as the famous essay *On Civil Disobedience,* are nevertheless imbued with a first-person singular point of view. Hence autobiographical textuality takes a central place in the self-determination of his writing across a variety of texts.

If *Walden* is an autobiography, it is not the autobiography per se that is of interest. *Walden* carries the form of autobiography—a written report of one's own life. Yet it is rarely read as such. Unlike Rousseau's *Confessions,* Goethe's *Dichtung und Wahrheit,* and Sartre's *Les Mots*—to name just a few canonical autobiographies—Thoreau's *Walden* is more often read as a naturalistic treatise, as an essay characteristic of nineteenth-century American thought, as an enacted utopia, and as a segment of journals. Indeed, if one looks at Georges May's study of autobiography[2] in which he lists some seventy autobiographies, *Walden* is not among them. Nor have I found it included in the discussion of many general studies of autobiography.[3] In some cases, Thoreau is cited only in passing.[4] Thus the work is denied its important place among autobiographies—just as it was ignored when Thoreau first published it. Yet its reception and recognition is not what concerns us here, for autobiographical textuality does not rely upon statistics and classification for the establishment of its identity. The introductory paragraph of the text announces the autobiographical:

> When I wrote the following pages, or rather the bulk of them, I lived alone, in the woods, a mile from any neighbor, in a house which I had built myself, on the shore of Walden Pond, in Concord, Massachusetts, and earned my living by the labor of my hands only. I lived there only two years and two months. At present I am a sojourner in civilized life again (*Walden*, p. 7).

The textualized self is put into operation. Prior experience is reported and, according to the account, portions that were written while in the woods are incorporated into the autobiographical narrative. The self is dispersed into a textuality—the writing of Thoreau's own life. This autobiographical textuality is, however, at most a limit of the textualized self.

AUTOBIOGRAPHY AS GENRE

If autobiographical textuality is pure limit, what are its implications for autobiography as a type of writing? Poetry, fiction, drama, etc. are well known as literary genres. But what of autobiography? It is certainly the case that one can cite many examples of writers who have produced autobiographical texts along with their general literary writings. One need only mention Goethe, Stendhal, Tolstoy, Yeats, Ionesco, and so on. Then again some autobiographical texts occupy a dominant place in certain authorial productions. Marcus Aurelius's *Meditations*, Henry Adams's *Education of Henry Adams*, and Simone de Beauvoir's *Memoirs of a Dutiful Daughter, Prime of Life, Force of Circumstance,* and *All Said and Done* constitute an autobiographical textuality that preoccupies the authorial literary space. Furthermore, certain autobiographical texts have a home in non-literary places. One would not cite Freud, Stravinsky, and Lévi-Strauss as the literary figures of our age, and yet their autobiographical texts do participate in a topological domain that constitutes the autobiographical. They do not write epics, lyrics, tragedies, comedies, historical novels, etc.—all of which have entered the canon of literary genres. Just as the historical novel makes claims to the literary and the historical, autobiography is situated at the interface between literature and a whole range of writing, psychoanalysis, music, anthropology, politics, philosophy, history, and so on.

What is curious about autobiographical texts is that they occur in strange places—places distinctively outside the literary domain—in psychology (B. F. Skinner's *Particulars of My Life*), in philosophy (Bertrand Russell's *Autobiography* and A. J. Ayer's *Part of My Life*), in theology (Loyola's *Autobiography*), and in politics (De Gaulle and Eisenhower are as likely as Caesar). Yet, autobiography is writing and specifically writing one's own life. Autobiographizing, then, occurs at the limits of literature and at the limits of psychology, philosophy, theology, politics, music, anthropology, etc. The coincidence of these limits is the space characterized by the autobiographical. Yet, can the autobiographical determine a genre? If texts could be gathered together and grouped under one head, then surely the answer would be affirmative. Yet what are the rules of this category—other than the writing of one's own life? Clearly it must be peculiar to the authorial field, but when what could count as an acceptable field is open, autobiographical texts begin to appear everywhere. The concern for establishing autobiography as a genre, however, indicates a specifically literary concern. Thus if autobiography is a literary genre, it falls on the side of literature. Since, by contrast, so much autobiography is not produced by members of the literary establishment but by authors outside, autobiography is generally a non-literary type of textuality. The generic space of autobiography is located precisely at the interface between the literary and the nonliterary. But there is no such space; it is pure difference—a difference that can be approximated only at the limits of the literary and the nonliterary. Hence autobiography is a genre activity whose only proper place is that appropriated by its author—whose authority is achieved in the writing.

Walden is a text that enters the autobiographical field, not in relation to other important works by the same author, but rather as an elaboration of an identity that is pure difference. In a certain respect, *Walden* approximates a literary text. Its descriptions of sounds, the pond, solitude, the coming of spring, all approach the sort of romantic adulation of nature that one finds in Wordsworth, Lamartine, and Goethe's *Werther*. But Thoreau's corpus does not define itself as poetry, novel, drama, romance, or the like. If anything, it approximates first person singular fictional journals in the tradition characterized by Dostoevsky's *Notes from Underground* and Sartre's *La Nausée*. First person singular journalistic novels, however, where the "I" predominates, are written explicitly with devices to separate the "I" of the text from the authorial "I." For instance, editors are introduced as mediators. But in Thoreau's *Walden*, whatever editors there are have a real (rather than imaginary) status and they vary from edition to edition. The text itself is neither a novel nor a fictional journal. No distance stands between the author and the "I" in the text. Like John Dean at the Watergate trials, an eyewitness to an automobile accident, or a scientific researcher reporting his or her findings, the "I" in the narrative gives all appearance of veracity and identity with its author. Indeed, the project of *Walden* is one of non-deception and nonfictionalization. As to its genre, *Walden* is situated at the intersection of the first person novel or fictional journal and the various types of non-literary writing. The text appeals to navigation as Thoreau sounds the depths of the pond, to economics as he determines his expenses, to agriculture as he attends to his bean field, etc. *Walden*, however, is clearly not a scientific text—it hardly fulfills the genre of a treatise in navigation, economics, or agriculture. The place of *Walden* remains as a "limit genre" that has a marginal status in relation to the dominant literary types; on occasion it even risks falling into a scientific work. However, because it avoids both, in the end its status as genre is one of difference from each.

TEMPORALITY/SPATIALITY

The concern here has been oriented toward spatiality: the autobiographical domain whose limits constitute the place of autobiographical textuality, the place of autobiography as a genre neither within nor without literature but at the interface between the two. By contrast, autobiography is typically construed as a temporal activity whose textuality might appropriately be characterized as a stream, flow, career, or curriculum of life. Autobiography recounts that which occurs over time. Autobiography is marked by the diachronic—events followed by events, thoughts followed by thoughts, acquaintances and friendships followed by acquaintances and friendships. Not all autobiographies are specifically segmented according to definite year spans as in Loyola's *Autobiography* and Rousseau's *Confessions*, but most follow a chronological pattern.

By sharp contrast with many fictional narratives, which rely on a "flash-back" technique, a special feature of autobiographical temporality[5] is that it permits a "flash-forward" device. The Homeric epic, for example—particularly *The Odyssey*—makes ample use of the "flash-back" technique. Book after book of *The Odyssey* is devoted to Odysseus's narration of events that occurred previously—until the temporal place of the reader and that of Odysseus coincide. Autobiography allows for not only the "flash-back," but also the "flash-forward" technique. Consider the following passage from Freud's *An Autobiographical Study*:

> While I was writing my "History of the Psycho-Analytic Movement" in 1914, there recurred to my mind some remarks that had been made to me by Breuer, Charcot, and Chrobak, which might have led me to this discovery earlier. But at the time I heard them I did not understand what these authorities meant; indeed they had told me more than they knew themselves or were prepared to defend. What I heard from them lay dormant and passive within me, until the chance of my cathartic experiments brought it out as an apparently original discovery. Nor was I then aware that in deriving hysteria from sexuality I was going back to the very beginnings of medicine and following up a thought of Plato's. It was not until later that I learnt this from an essay by Havelock Ellis.[6]

Throughout this passage, Freud makes reference to perspectives that he holds at the time of the writing of the autobiography but that were unavailable to him at the time of the events in question. In other words, in the narrative itself, Freud refers forward to a future perspective that enhances the interpretation of the event at the time of its reportage. In the flash-back that is employed in epics, novels, and various other literary types, reference is made to events occurring prior to that which is under account. To flash forward, however, would alter the progressive feature of the specifically literary narrative. The autobiographical modality is one in which the autobiographer reports, in the narrative, that if something else had been done, or if some other knowledge had been available, then such and such an event would—or would not—have taken place. Or if the autobiographical narrator knew what he/she now knows, then the event or situation could have been interpreted differently. Hence the narrator can fill out an event with subsequent information that contributes to the full and polyvalent interpretation of the autobiographical textuality. No suspense is lost, no secrets are given away, no hidden motives await to be uncovered. In the tradition of Montaigne and Rousseau, the autobiographer wants to "tell all" and needs to do so by weaving the present with the past and, if desirable, with the future. This does not imply that a novelist cannot imitate the autobiographical narrative mode, but it does mean that the autobiographical is peculiarly temporal.

Yet, temporality is not the whole story. Autobiography institutes a distinctive spatiality as well. As already noted, autobiography does not have a generic spatiality of its own. And its textuality operates at the intersection of pure temporality and pure spatiality at the place of difference where they meet. The pure temporality of the autobiography is the autobiographer's own life. Autobiographical temporality is a structuring of time in the text in terms of its textuality. The pure spatiality of the autobiography is a work *(une oeuvre)* as it sits on the shelf or in one's hands and, hence, is distinguishable from others. Autobiographical spatiality is the account of the spaces in which the life takes shape. What is distinctive about autobiography is that it incorporates both time and space, while its textuality both occurs and is located at the interface of temporality and spatiality, at the limits of temporality and the limits of spatiality.

Walden reports Thoreau's life and thoughts over the period of a couple of years. At the end of the penultimate chapter, he writes: "Thus was my first year's life in the woods completed; and the second year was similar to it. I finally left Walden September 6th, 1847" (*Walden*, p. 212). In offering a report of his stay at the pond, Thoreau circumscribes a full year—a full cycle. Once the pattern was set, the rest would follow, and once he had confirmed the pattern with a second year, the cyclical repetition of the seasons would operate accordingly. In other words, the temporality of Thoreau's life in the woods was established according to the movements of nature. As for Thoreau himself, he notes in his conclusion: "I left the woods for as good a reason as I went there. Perhaps it seemed to me that I had several more lives to live, and could not spare any more time for that one" (*Walden*, p. 214). This setting in motion of a temporal pattern and the opening of the possibility of new ones in other contexts indicates the diachronic modality based upon an annual synchronic slice. Thoreau's consecration of one year to know his place and a second to verify its inductive validity indicates a temporality that Thoreau need not even recount for the second year. This sort of flash forward is similar to the one Freud reports—except that for Thoreau, it covers a whole year rather than a single event. Albeit curious, Thoreau need not even live the other years, for (in his view) he already knows their pattern and is able to predict their content.

The work itself is the spatiality of Thoreau's text. *Walden* establishes the space in which the repetition of the seasons is announced, interrogated, and even developed at length. This textual space opens the possibility of an autobiographical textuality in which the author's experiences are given a locus of expression.

The places frequented near the pond, away from the town, in the context of brute neighbors, establish the narrated autobiographical spatiality. The autobiographical textuality of Thoreau's *Walden* is neither seasonal temporality nor narrated spatiality, but rather the co-giveness and interleaving of the two.

FICTION/NONFICTION

Is autobiography fiction or nonfiction? When it is posed in this way, our task is to determine the character of the activities in question. Non-fictionalization presumes that the descriptions offered participate in a discourse of truth. These descriptions are engaged in knowledge production—informing rather than performing, pronouncing rather than announcing, analyzing rather than picturing. Non-fictionalization wants to be a science. It seeks confirmation by respectability—acquiring its place in the domain of discovery, news, and reportage. By contrast, fictionalization presents itself as a discourse of lies. Its activity entails the production of specious knowledge—knowledge that follows its own rules, that sets its own boundary conditions, that speaks its own language. Autobiographizing takes both fictionalization and non-fictionalization to their extreme boundaries.

Autobiographizing has elements of non-fictionalization: it proposes to tell the truth about a life. Montaigne's note to the Reader is paradigmatic. "If I had written to seek the world's favor, I should have bedecked myself better, and should present myself in a studied posture. I want to be seen here in my simple, natural, ordinary fashion, without straining or artifice; for it is myself that I portray."[7] Similarly, Rousseau remarks: "I have resolved on an enterprise which has no precedent, and which, once complete, will have no imitator. My purpose is to display to my kind a portrait in every way true to nature, and the man I shall portray will be myself."[8] In both cases the claim to veracity is explicit and unmitigated. The proposed autobiographizing presents a self that is true to nature. Without a doubt, what is offered is a discourse of truth, hence a variety of non-fictionalization.

One need not consider only texts that announce their claim to veracity and their fidelity to nature. Other accounts—such as a book of statistics or a textbook in history—stress the factual. Take the example of Vico's *Autobiography*. "Giambattista Vico was born in Naples in the year 1670 of upright parents who left a good name after them. His father was of a cheerful disposition, his mother of a quite melancholy temper; both contributed to the character of their child."[9] Or that of Goethe: "On the 28th of August, 1749, at midday, as the clock struck twelve, I came into the world, at Frankfort-on-the-Main. My horoscope was propitious: the sun stood in the sign of the Virgin, and had culminated for the day ...."[10] Or even *The Education of Henry Adams*:

Under the shadow of Boston State House, turning its back on the house of John Hancock, the little passage called Hancock Avenue runs, or ran, from Beacon Street, skirting the State House grounds; to Mount Vernon Street, on the summit of Beacon Hill; and there, in the third house below Mount Vernon Place, February 16, 1838, a child was born, and christened later by his uncle, the minister of the First Church after the tenets of Boston Unitarianism, as Henry Brooks Adams.[11]

In each case, the factual nature of the account prevails. These are autobiographies taking the role of nonfiction. Indeed, there is a sort of will to nonfiction at work in each case.

And yet in each case there is also an effort to portray, to offer a picture, to envision the self in a particular circumstance and to recount it in a unique way—or, in the case of Rousseau, to imitate Montaigne so explicitly that he can say that he has no imitator. Montaigne's function as an intertext undermines Rousseau's veracity and shows him to be engaged in a lie: he cannot be without an imitator since he is imitating Montaigne, and others could do the same with his claims. Hence, the irony in Rousseau's assertion of originality demonstrates his entry into a lie. Even Vico's report of the character of his parents (which he presents with conviction and assurance), Goethe's account of the auspiciousness of his birth, and Adams's geographical placement of his appearance into the world all have a claim to truth and the quality of a novel—one that is about to be unraveled and that the reader would do well to follow. Hence at the limit of non-fictionalization, autobiography spills over into fictionalization and at the limit of fictionalization, autobiographical textuality announces a non-fictionalization that can help the reader understand the other features of the autobiographer's experience, knowledge, and conviction.

Like Montaigne and Rousseau, Thoreau engages in autobiographizing that produces both a fictional lie and a nonfictional truth. *Walden* orients itself toward a direct full account of an individual's experiences:

> Some have asked what I got to eat; if I did not feel lonesome; if I was not afraid; and the like. Others have been curious to learn what portion of my income I devoted to charitable purposes; and some who have large families, how many poor children I maintained. I will therefore ask those of my readers who feel no particular interest in me to pardon me if I undertake to answer some of these questions in this book. In most books, the I, or first person is omitted; in this it will be retained; that, in respect to egotism, is the main difference. We commonly do not remember that it is, after all, always the first person that is speaking (*Walden*, p. 7).

Thoreau reassures the reader that his book is in response to some specific questions that have been posed concerning his stay near the pond. He is therefore providing a report as faithful as a grant application and as nonfictional as a response to a series of questionnaires. His use of the "I" is at most a concession to truth, since in the end every treatise is written from the first person singular—whether explicit or not. Admitting the first person as present even in scientific treatises, Thoreau indicates the respects in which his own discourse is non-fictional and even philosophical. Indeed, the philosophical pose tends to predominate. Thoreau philosophizes about how one should live one's life, about food, clothing, and shelter, about the seasons, the birds, the animals, and the bean fields, about the body, visitors, and neighbors. Thoreau's observations are as elaborate as those of Francis Bacon, as profound as those of Fichte, and as penetrating as those of Bergson.

But one should not be deceived—the employment of the "I" also opens the possibility of a fictional account. *Walden* is indeed a series of personal literary reflections with a style comparable to that of Epictetus, Montaigne, and Coleridge. *Walden* is a work of letters—it is replete with musings, descriptions of natural phenomena, and quasi-poetic formulas. Above all, it is read, studied, and treated as literature. Its delicate sensibility, its careful attention to detail, and its expressive flourish all indicate its orientation toward the fictional, toward literature. The work cannot be true: Thoreau's remarks are not available for scientific verification, his comments about nature do not serve as a model for research in agriculture, geography, or astronomy. *Walden* is a lie. Surely Thoreau's reflections were not repeated in precisely the same way the second year of his stay at Walden Pond: they are not the recounting of events that happened as such. Yet the lie is not with an intent to deceive. On the contrary, it is to offer perceptions that inform, delight, and provoke.

However when one attempts to situate *Walden* in relation to fiction and to nonfiction, it becomes quite evident that the text is not really either—even though it has features of each. Its autobiographical textuality situates *Walden* between fiction and nonfiction, between literature and philosophy. It is in fact precisely in the autobiographical tradition that the text articulates itself. Consider, for example, the passage at the beginning of the text where Thoreau writes:

> I should not talk about myself if there were anybody else whom I knew as well. Unfortunately, I am confined to this theme by the narrowness of my experience. Moreover, I, on my side, require of every writer, first or last, a simple and sincere account of his own life, and not merely what he has heard of other men's lives; some such account as he would send to his kindred far away on a distant land; for if he has lived sincerely it must have been in a distant land to me (*Walden*, p. 7).

The similarities between this statement and Montaigne's note to his reader, where he admits that he would have shown himself quite naked had he been able to do so, are remarkable. Thoreau's appeal to sincerity repeats Montaigne's assertion that his portrait is as natural as possible and not necessarily of interest to others. This appeal to sincerity also matches Montaigne's directness and Rousseau's version of his own enterprise in the *Confessions*. To be sincere about one's own life is to offer one's own identity in writing it as text. Such texts announce the autobiographical at the interface between fiction and nonfiction.

METAPHORICITY/LITERALITY

In the Aristotelian tradition of discussions about metaphor, a metaphor is the substitute for a literal situation. In this sense, an autobiography is metaphoricity itself—the substitution of a writing of one's life for the life itself. In the tradition of metaphor as transference, the autobiography can be conceived of as a transference of a lifetime from experience to writing, from experiencing to autobiographizing. Or, in the I. A. Richards tenor-vehicle and the Max Black focus-frame models, the life is the vehicle or frame, while the narrative of it as a discursive space is the tenor or focus—in other words, the metaphor. As Paul de Man would put it, autobiography is a translation, an *Übersetzung,* a passage, a transposition from the domain of individual experience to that of writing.[12] Autobiography is not just the substitution, transfer, tenor, focus, or translation of some lexeme, word, or element in a sentence. Rather autobiography is metaphoricity itself—the whole text is metaphorical. This does not mean that autobiography is an allegory for a life. On the contrary, when autobiography is allegory, as in Dante's *Vita Nuova,* then it is both a metaphor for Dante's own life and an allegory of salvation, the blissful vision and love of the divine. Writing one's own life is appropriating that life and at the same time forming it, giving it style and character. Henry Adams's report of his date of birth is only one aspect of a larger picture—yet the account provides a view of where he was born in the proximity of the State House on Beacon Hill. And above all the report is not given in a matter-of-fact way, but with a flourish almost comparable to a Balzac description of a house façade in *Père Goriot.*

An autobiography is neither an allegory nor a novel. And although an autobiography is imbued with metaphoricity, it is also necessarily literal. Autobiography that is devoid of literality is no longer autobiography. Autobiography must characterize the events of the individual's life more or less as they occurred. Without the letter of the life and the experience of the individual in question, the text would be a novel and no longer autobiography. The literality of autobiography is in its fidelity to what is, what has been, and what is reported to be. Autobiographies not only describe a past and present, but also a future on the way. Indeed, they occur at the limits of human temporality. Autobiographizing is literally the direct, unmediated report of one's life. It lacks both the mediation required in biography and the hypothetical features pertinent to a novel.

How, we might ask, can an autobiographical text incorporate both metaphoricity and literality? It might be said that the autobiographical text must be either one or the other—not both. And in a certain respect, it cannot be both metaphoricity and literality. It cannot be both the substitution, transfer, tenor, focus, and translation of the life and the life itself. In other words, an autobiography must situate itself at the place where metaphoricity meets literality, where the substitution of life is life itself, where the writing of a life is the life, where the activity of translating is living. In this respect, autobiographizing is textualizing, but textualizing is both activity and text, practice and account of practice.

Autobiographizing is writing, naming, signing, inscribing, and ultimately incorporating itself into the singularity of an individual's living itinerary—with all the vital signs marked along the way.

A reading of *Walden*, particularly in the contemporary situation, makes it evident that Thoreau is as much the figure in the text as the man who lived in the mid-nineteenth century. *Walden* is in some respects the substitute for the man—Thoreau lives in the Concord woods through his text. A biography of Thoreau would report his two years and two months, but it would also indicate his studies at Harvard, his days as a school teacher, his arrest for willfully not paying his taxes, and so forth. This would be the literal Thoreau that is matched inadequately by the autobiographical Thoreau of *Walden*. But the task of a metaphor is not to provide an exact match. Rather, it is a substitute for the life and hence another version. In this respect, *Walden* is literally a metaphor written as life in the woods, in the *Wald*. Its textuality, however, never quite fulfills either the literal life or the complete substitution for that life.

IMAGINATION/MEMORY

Perception is often cited as the locus of the intersection between imagination and memory.[13] When the writer entertains the possibility of remembering all that there is to remember, and when he/she considers the potential of envisioning how it all fits together—looking forward to the place of that ensemble of remembering—then the place of autobiography is invoked. Autobiographizing is not perceiving. It is perception textualized. To say that a novel such as *A La Recherche du temps perdu* is autobiographical is not to claim that Marcel Proust is reporting his perceptions as if he were giving a phenomenological description of his neighbors on either side. Rather it is to say that features of Marcel's experience resemble Proust's own, that Proust is imaginatively remembering and transforming his own experiences into the writing of a novel.

More explicitly, in the cases of specifically autobiographical texts, remembering the past and imagining the future are incorporated into an autobiographical textuality that is neither present, nor perceptual. Autobiographical textuality brings together the remembered and the imagined into a written personal account. Ionesco, for example, opens his *Présent passé/Passé présent* with the following passage:

> I search in my memory for the first images of my father. I see dark hallways. I was two years old, I think. In a train. My mother is next to me; her hair is done up in a big bun. My father is across from me, next to the window. I don't see his face; I see shoulders and a suitcoat.
>
> Suddenly there's a tunnel.
>
> I cry out.[14]

Ionesco is remembering. Ionesco is imagining. At the limit of his remembering is the autobiographizing that textualizes the memories. At the limit of his imagining is the autobiographizing that textualizes his projections of himself. The textualized self is a present, but not *this* one, only *that* one—the autobiographical present of Ionesco as autobiographizing text. The memoir is personal because it cannot belong to anyone else. It can be appropriated in a reading, but such a reading is obliged to follow, or at most rewrite (reinterpret), the textualized self. Hence once again, the autobiographical textuality has its place at the intersection, at the interface between remembering and imagining. Although Proust's *Recherche* or James Joyce's *Portrait of the Artist as a Young Man* could also reiterate this interface, when placed in the context of all the other interfaces that have been announced here (temporality/spatiality, fiction/nonfiction, and metaphoricity/literality), the delimitation of the nexus of these interfaces indicates a rather unique locale.

Like Montaigne's *Essays*, *Walden* is a patchwork of passages written at different times in Thoreau's life. Each one offers a perception of a specific event, thought, place, animal, or person. In all, it serves as a memoir of Thoreau's experience. The *Gestalt* constitutes the memory and the imaginative report of his days there. The memories derive from his recall of that period in his life; his imagination gives the multiplicity a unity. The autobiographical textuality of the text is a nonspatial perception of what is neither memory nor imagination, but the interface of the two.

AUTOBIOGRAPHER/AUTOBIOGRAPHED

One final opposition needs to be articulated. The inclusion of the opposition autobiographer/autobiographed finalizes and determines the place of autobiographical textuality at the slash between each of the aforementioned oppositions. The superimposition of the slash in each case is the repetition of the autobiographical *topos* as a unique topic and place, as what Sartre calls: "the singular universal."[15]

Autobiographizing is situated at the limits of the autobiographer and at the limits of the autobiographed. Thoreau *recounting* his stay at Walden Pond during the years between 1845 and 1847 is not there in the text—nor is Thoreau himself *recounted* there in the text. The text is the place where the autobiographizing takes place, where subject and object lose their independent status. The text is where autobiographical textuality affirms the place of the autobiographical self. The autobiographizing links the autobiographer and the autobiographed at the place where their limits intersect and coincide.

The autobiographer is not an author, nor is the autobiographed a character. The autobiographer is the one who writes his/her own life. The autobiographed is the one whose own life is written. The "I" in the text is the trace of the autobiographer; the "me" is the index of the autobiographed. In the chapter on "The bean-field," Thoreau writes:

> This further experience I also gained: I said to myself, I will not plant beans and corn with so much industry another summer, but such seeds, if seed is not lost, as sincerity, truth, simplicity, faith, innocence, and the like, and see if they will not grow in this soil, even with less toil and manurance, and sustain me, for surely it has not been exhausting for these crops. Alas! I said this to myself; but now another summer is gone, and another, and another, and I am obliged to say to you, Reader, that the seeds which I planted, if indeed they were the seeds of those virtues, were worm-eaten or had lost their vitality, and so did not come up. (*Walden*, p. 13).

The "I" who speaks to "himself" is not the autobiographer per se but only the trace of that position. The "I" is the author announcing himself as narrator and calling for the identity of the two. The "I" speaks in the name of the autobiographer and employs his signature. The "myself" and the "me" are not the autobiographed per se since, in a certain sense, the autobiographed permeates the whole autobiographical text. Yet the "myself" or the "me" does serve as an adequate index of the autobiographed, indicating that a self is portrayed and rendered up—in this case explicitly to a "Reader." The autobiographizing is the production of an autobiographical text as it matches the autobiographer against the autobiographed. In the place of the matching, at the hinge between the two, where the autobiographical text asserts itself, the autobiographical textuality of Thoreau's *Walden* is constituted. The autobiographical textuality establishes the discursive space that denotes the point of intersection between temporality and spatiality, fiction and nonfiction, metaphoricity and literality, imagination and memory, autobiographer and autobiographed. This unique point of intersection is not a point, but a slash. The slash is the decentering of the autobiographical self from its established place. The decentering of the autobiographical self is the incorporation of other autobiographical selves who might have approximated the same locale had their autobiographizing been the same. But the difference in the autobiographizing is what writes the difference that distinguishes the selves. Each autobiographical self delineates its own outlines, its own limitations, and its own modalities. Hence Thoreau's autobiographical textuality depends upon an autobiographizing in which specific limits are set by the activity itself. These limits that occur at the slash identify this particular autobiographical self as that of Henry David Thoreau. His particular autobiographical self, however, cannot be located anywhere except in the autobiographical textuality that is its signification and that decenters itself through *Walden* as an autobiographical text.

10

TRACES OF AUTOBIOGRAPHICAL TEXTUALITY IN NIETZSCHE'S *ECCE HOMO*

An autobiography is one's own life as written. Autobiographizing is writing one's own life. An autobiographical text is a particular written version, fragment, or account of one's own life. Autobiographical textuality is the feature of a text (autobiographical or otherwise) which characterizes the writing of a version, fragment, or account of one's own life. Since it has been argued that *Ecce Homo*[1] is unsuccessful as autobiography and since the concern here is more with the autobiographical textuality of Nietzsche's *Ecce Homo*, I defer at the outset the determination as to whether the text is, in fact, an autobiography.

This latter exclusion is occasioned by the introductory remarks of R. J. Hollingdale, the English translator for the Penguin edition: "It matters how you approach this book. If, under the guidance of the literature on the subject, you approach it as 'Nietzsche's autobiography' you will get very little out of it and probably won't even finish it, short though it is. As autobiography it is a plain failure. You cannot reconstruct Nietzsche's life even in its broad outlines from his 'autobiography'; it is in no way a narrative; it is not in the least 'objective.' "[2] Hollingdale is perhaps right: *Ecce Homo* is hardly Nietzsche's own life as written in any comprehensive sense. Of course, an autobiography need not provide a full account of one's own life. Sartre's *Words* recounts only the first twelve or so years of his life; Dante's *Vita Nuova* is limited only to the early years during which he admired Beatrice; and Descartes's *Discourse on Method* is a severely restricted inquiry into the course and development of his own mind. On the other hand, if autobiographies are reserved for the large-scale enterprises which are announced by Benvenuto Cellini's *La Vita*, Rousseau's *Confessions*, Simone de Beauvoir's multiple volumes, and Russell's *Autobiography*, then perhaps Hollingdale has a point. But if *Ecce Homo* does not match up to these epic autobiographies, is it necessarily a "failure"? If we assume that one must be able to reconstruct the broad outlines of the autobiographer's life, then Hollingdale is probably correct. In subsection 3 of "Why I Am So Wise," Nietzsche offers a brief sketch of his Polish ancestry, his mother's and his paternal grandmother's

Germanness, his father's date of birth and death when Nietzsche was only five years old, and the date of his own birth along with the reason why he was named after King Friedrich Wilhelm the Fourth of Prussia. Yet all this is no more than a scant report—hardly sufficient material to qualify it as an autobiography in which his own life is written. With the exception of the dates and names Nietzsche offers, it has been argued that his other facts might even be spurious. For example, he may not be at all of Polish descent. For this reason, Hollingdale denies the "objective" character of the work.

By contrast, however, *Ecce Homo* is very much a narrative. It is not a narrative in the sense of a nineteenth-century novel, but neither is Thoreau's *Walden* or Roland Barthes's *Roland Barthes*—and they both would qualify as autobiographical narration. What Nietzsche narrates is why he is so wise, why he is so clever, and why he writes such excellent books. This is not chronological narration but it does recount Nietzsche's views about himself and his work. This specifically non-chronological yet thematic narration is one feature of the autobiographical textuality of the text.

Since some question has been raised as to whether *Ecce Homo* can be classified as autobiography, one might wonder whether the same holds for its status as an autobiographical text. Composed in the first person singular, it concerns the author—at least in name—and not some fictitious character. *Ecce Homo* is fragmentary, but at the same time it is a written version of Nietzsche's own life. He does offer an account of "who he is." In these respects *Ecce Homo* is an autobiographical text even though it may not qualify specifically as autobiography. Since, furthermore, the text need not be autobiographical in order for it to demonstrate autobiographical textuality—Joyce's *Portrait of the Artist as a Young Man* is a case in point—I shall now restrict my examination to its autobiographical textuality, that is, the writing of features which characterize it as a version, fragment, or account of Nietzsche's own life. The text *Ecce Homo* introduces the problematic of writing one's own life as a persistent self-examination.

SELF/TEXT

The autobiographical textuality of Nietzsche's *Ecce Homo* arises and operates at the intersection of self and text. A pure textless account of Nietzsche's life is no longer available. Nietzsche, the man, died in 1900. The text in which a first person singular appears is surely quite distant from the self who lived from 1844 to 1900. Hollingdale's report that the text (albeit largely autobiographical) makes poor autobiography indicates the inadequacy of *Ecce Homo* as an elaboration of the self. Yet this is not to say that there is not some relation between the self and the text. In fact, the relation as written is the place of the autobiographical textuality.

Ecce Homo is filled with remarks such as the one which opens the text: "Seeing that before long I must confront humanity with the most difficult demand ever made on it, it seems indispensable to me to say who I am" (*EH-WKtr*, p. 217). This "I" is situated somewhere between the self and the text. But how is the "I" (first person singular) the writing of Nietzsche's own life? He could be deceiving himself or his reader. The word could be a poor representative of the self in question. The word could be a mask or impoverished version of the self. This debate could go on without end—with the possible conclusion falling on one side or the other, on the side of the subject or on the side of the object, on the side of the self or on the side of the text. Yet the writing of the "I" is the writing of a fragment—not as a representational unit, nor as a substitutional entity. The writing of the fragment is the trace or supplement at which the autobiographical textuality of Nietzsche's *Ecce Homo* is situated. Hence a textualized self announces its obligation to say who it is. This saying of a particular sort—one which links its own imperative with its own identity—leaves something unthematized. In the transition from the imperative to the identity the autobiographical textuality is left over in the text. The remainder in the transition indicates a problematic: that a particular self, whom we can call Nietzsche, needs to account for itself. When realized, if realized, this need for the self to account for itself, to write itself as text, could result in an autobiography. If unsuccessful, it would at least leave the traces of an autobiographical textuality.

Continuing, the text reads: "This ought really to be known already: for I have not neglected to 'bear witness' about myself" (*EH-RHtr*, p. 33). The remark would be curious if it were to be supposed that there is no connection between the author of the remark and its effect. By the remark, a relationship between this written self and some reputation is affirmed. The text takes itself outside itself. It refers—or better still, establishes a connection—between this particular textualized self and the author of other works. The connection is not established as some sort of revelation to the reading public as in Kierkegaard's *The Point of View of My Work as an Author*, where he indicates that he is the author of all those pseudonymously published works. Whereas Kierkegaard announces an obligation to affirm an identity between himself as author of *The Point of View* and Constantine Constantius, Johannes de Silentio, Victor Ermita, and all the others, Nietzsche points out that the self in question in *Ecce Homo* already has a reputation. His identity is already known. There is already testimony of who he is. This textualized self is already on record as having an identity.

At bottom, one should know *(Im Grunde dürfte man's wissen...)* who this self is. But *who* should know who this self is? Can it be the same "one" who is specified in the subtitle of the work: "*Ecce Homo*: How One Becomes What One Is" *(Wie Man Wird—Was Man Ist)?* Surely the "one" who should have come across Nietzsche as a testimony will not always be identical with the "one" who becomes what one is if *Ecce Homo* is a successful demonstration. The "one" who should have encountered Nietzsche as a text can be called Nietzsche's "reader." This "one" who is his "reader" is different from Montaigne's reader, mentioned at the outset of his *Essays*, because Nietzsche—the author—does not name this "one" as a reader. *This* "one" is only the one who should already know. And what this "one" should know is something about Nietzsche's corpus. In the section entitled "Why I Write Such Excellent Books" there is some mention of his readers. If we take his claims to the letter, then he has readers everywhere except among Germans. His readers are "nothing but first-rate intellectuals and proven characters, trained in high positions and duties." He writes: "I even have real geniuses among my readers. In Vienna, in St. Petersburg, in Stockholm, in Copenhagen, in Paris, in New York—everywhere I have been discovered; but not in the shallows of Europe, Germany" (*EH-WKtr*, p. 262). These non-Germans, then, could well satisfy the conditions of the "one" who is announced as having already some acquaintance with the self in question. But what of his non-readers—those who are mentioned in the passage which says: "And let me confess that my non-readers delight me even more—those who have never heard my name, nor the word 'philosophy'" (*EH-WKtr*, p. 262). Although these non-readers are surely excluded from the "one" who is already witness to his textualized self, they are given credit for recognizing a lived self who meets them on the street and in the markets.

Yet it still must be asked whether any of these readers or non-readers qualify as the "one" who is announced in "How One Becomes What One Is." If, as readers, they are restricted to those familiar with other books by Nietzsche, then surely they are excluded as are his non-readers who do not have *Ecce Homo* available to them. This exclusion, however, is operative only if these readers and non-readers can become who they are only by reading *Ecce Homo*. In a certain sense, this is indeed the condition announced, for the very title "How One Becomes What One Is" suggests that *Ecce Homo* is a manual, from the tradition of Ovid's *The Art of Love*, Capellanus's *The Art of Courtly Love*, Alberti's *The Art of Painting*, Erasmus's *The Education of a Christian Prince*, Machiavelli's *The Prince*, etc., to the many articles in *Popular Mechanics* where one learns how to build bookshelves, transformers, and woodsheds. Since Emily Post's and Amy Vanderbilt's volumes on etiquette, Alex Comfort's *The Joy of Sex*, and Hans Küng's *On Being a Christian* also qualify as "how to" books, they can be incorporated into the field in which "*Ecce Homo*: How One Becomes What One Is" is situated. But if *Ecce Homo* is simply a "how to" book, a manual on the art of living, then surely the "one" in question is realized only in the reading of it. If, however, the "one" in "How One Becomes What One Is" is only another way of saying "How I Have Become What I Am," then the substitution of the "I" for the "One" reverts even more directly to the textualized self who can be called Nietzsche. But is *Ecce Homo* simply an account of how Nietzsche has become what he is? If that were true in its strictest sense, then there could be no doubt that *Ecce Homo* is an autobiography, for it would thereby be Nietzsche's own life as written and not a manual at all. But doubt has already been placed upon *Ecce Homo* as autobiography in the narrowest sense. The third alternative is that "How One Becomes What One Is" constitutes a maxim according to which Nietzsche himself has or would like to have lived and according to which others might live—whether they be his readers or not. Why, though, does Nietzsche write "How One Becomes What One Is" and not "How One Becomes Who One Is?" Why not: *Wie Man Wird—Wer Man Ist?* In considering this self which is to become what it is, the question of *personal* identity is evaded. The question of identity remains, but the "who" is not at issue. In this respect, the problem as to whether the "one" is Nietzsche's non-readers, his readers, or himself is less pressing. The particular person—as a unity or a multiplicity—is not raised as a concern. The "what" rather than the "who" prevails.

Can one become what one is? Is this a task for the overman (the *Übermensch*)—a task which we all-too-human mortals could not achieve without great effort? Could even Nietzsche himself become what he is? Surely an element of the textuality of *Ecce Homo* is that Nietzsche sees himself as no longer announcing the eternal return and *amor fati* through his spokesman Zarathustra but that at last Nietzsche has placed himself in question. But Nietzsche is not in question as a person. He does not appear in person in the text. Rather what appears is a textualized self—the "what" in "how one becomes what one is." This "what," this textualized self, is in a sense more real than the "I" which appears as a unit in *Ecce Homo* or the living Nietzsche whom we can read about in biographies such as the one offered by Walter Kaufmann. To become what one is is doubtless not an easy enterprise. Hence the passage: "I live on my own credit; it is perhaps a mere prejudice that I live" (*EH-WKtr*, p. 217). The other books, each of which is assessed in a separate section of *Ecce Homo*, establish themselves as a kind of credit, an advance on Nietzsche's own life such that his life itself is borrowed—not borrowed time, but borrowed autobiographical textuality. Without the writing of *Ecce Homo*, Nietzsche's autobiographical textuality would remain fragmentary, disjointed, and dismembered like Orpheus on the shores of Lesbos. But *Ecce Homo* inscribes itself as the account of Nietzsche's own life, as the identity which has been concealed behind so many clever and excellent books. Yet all those books are a kind of credit which has allowed Nietzsche to live. On the other hand, like a manuscript for which one is given an advance before it is submitted, like a car for which one is given credit before one has the money to pay for it, Nietzsche announces that he lives on the credit which he has given himself by writing his "other" books. For this reason, it could be doubted whether he lives at all, whether he is what he is, whether it is a prejudgment that he lives, that there is an author who gives unity and identity to all those books. He must become what he is by writing *Ecce Homo*. But this claim is already the writing of *Ecce Homo*, is already the writing of his own life, is already the establishment of his autobiographical textuality.

In becoming what he is, Nietzsche also announces a duty. He must say: "Hear me. For I am such and such a person. Above all, do not mistake me for someone else" (*EH-WKtr*, p. 217). There are specific characteristics to his identity. His autobiographical textuality could be given definite descriptions. He does not give them, except as self-justification: why I am so wise, why I am so clever, why I write such excellent books…. What is important is that these features and characteristics of his identity could be given and if they were given then the textualized self would not be mistaken for someone else. The problem is that when one lives on credit, not only is there some question as to whether the bill will be paid, the manuscript submitted, the life lived, but also if not done appropriately someone else might supply the funds, the book, or the life. And since the goods are not already on hand, a mistake could be made. If someone else paid the bill, that would be fine. If someone else submitted the manuscript, that would be disconcerting. But if someone else lived the life, that would be intolerable. And mistaking someone else for what one is would leave one without an identity—or at best with a sense of fragmentation. For this reason, Nietzsche needs to say what he is or, even more significantly, he needs to become what he is by writing *Ecce Homo*. Hence the writing of *Ecce Homo* is the place of his autobiographical textuality. For in it, he can and does say what he is and what he is not. In the writing of *Ecce Homo* he becomes what he is and he distinguishes himself from what he is not.

"I am a *Doppelgänger*," he writes (*EH-WKtr*, p. 225). A *Doppelgänger* comes and goes as a double. Sometimes it is regarded as a ghost after the person has died. Sometimes it is simply a double: a Dr. Jekyll and Mr. Hyde, a Golyadkin, Sr., and Golyadkin, Jr., in Dostoevsky's *The Double*, an alter ego in Conrad's *Secret Sharer*, an ego ideal in the Freudian account. In *Ecce Homo*, the *Doppelgänger* is the self and its text. The self is a kind of ghost which seeks its own form, its identity, its realization so that no one will mistake it for someone else. The autobiographical text is its form, identity, realization. The statement "I am a *Doppelgänger*" indicates that this dichotomy is not real, is not lived. What is lived is the textuality which announces itself as autobiographical, as writing one's own life, as appropriate to the authorship specifically at the intersection of the self and the text, at the stroke or slash between one and the other, between the "I" of the authorship and its textualization. At this juncture, Nietzsche's autobiographical textuality establishes its place.

EVENT/WRITING

Ecce Homo is divided into a variety of sections. The foreword introduces the text with four subsections. This foreword is signed "Friedrich Nietzsche." Then there is a series of sections with a justificatory tone: "Why I Am So Wise," "Why I Am So Clever," "Why I Write Such Excellent Books." Following, there are ten separate sections in which he discusses in turn ten of his books. The final section is entitled: "Why I Am a Destiny."

Apart from the title page, I have omitted one item in my accounting. Situated between the foreword and the main body of the text, which begins with the section entitled "Why I Am So Wise," one finds an inconspicuous half-page single paragraph text. This fragment has no title, no subsection number—in short, no regular place within the text as a whole. One might even say that it is out of place in the order of things. Since the foreword is signed, we may be sure that Nietzsche names—as his own—the autobiographical textuality which arises at the intersection of self and text. This textuality then opens the space in which the remainder of *Ecce Homo* is situated. But what of the curiously placed fragment? Situated *after* the announcement of an autobiographical textuality in which the self/text is set as a pre-text, and *before* the main body of the text, the fragment occurs as an index of the juncture between the event and the writing of Nietzsche's own life.

A further remark is required concerning the placement of the fragment. Not only is it untitled, unnumbered, and unidentified, but in the German text,[3] it is printed on a single page with nothing on the back. In both the Hollingdale and Kaufmann translations, this supplementary feature is lost, for on the back page is printed the beginning of "Why I Am So Clever." In the German text, then, the page could simply be torn out, and except for the gap in sequential page numbering, its absence would not be noticed. This tear-page, this interleaf, is thus a marker of a textual difference established in the interstices of *Ecce Homo*. But it is an extremely important marker. It marks an event of Nietzsche's life written at the border of the foreword, on the one hand, and at the beginning of the principal text, on the other. It occurs at the limits of Nietzsche's signature and of the "I" which is so clever.

The event which the fragment marks is the moment of Nietzsche's writing of his own life. It is Nietzsche's appropriation of the gate of the moment (which he describes in *Thus Spoke Zarathustra*) as his own. The gate of the moment loses its status as a theory, as Zarathustra's proclamation, and as an account of how one might live. In this event, the gate of the moment becomes proper to Nietzsche himself. It establishes an autobiographical textuality appropriate to Nietzsche himself.

The fragment reads:

> On this perfect day, when everything is ripening and not only the grape turns brown, the eye of the sun just fell upon my life: I looked back, I looked forward, and never saw so many and such good things at once. It was not for nothing that I buried my forty-fourth year today; I had the *right* to bury it; whatever was life in it has been saved, is immortal. The first book of the *Revaluation of All Values*, the Songs of Zarathustra, the *Twilight of the Idols*, my attempt to philosophize with a hammer all presents of this year, indeed of its last quarter. *How could I fail to be grateful to my whole life?* and so I tell my life to myself (*EH-WKtr*, p. 221).

The perfect day is Nietzsche's forty-fourth birthday. This is surely a momentous event in that—if he is accurate and the date is October 15, 1888—Nietzsche completes his last work: *Ecce Homo*. Thenceforth he no longer writes any more books. Thenceforth he goes mad and collapses in the Piazza Carlo Alberto in Torino (on January 3, 1889). Although he continues to live until 1900—what could equally well be a momentous event—he no longer produces anything. Thus the momentous event is his birthday—forty-four. Christ is said to have been crucified at the age of thirty-three—for Nietzsche it is a factor of four instead of three. The day is "perfect"—the sun is at its height. Ripeness is a transitory time which will soon pass and on this perfect day, everything is ripening. Grapes turn brown as they tip from ripeness to overripeness. On this day, the eye of the sun falls upon Nietzsche's life. Just as the blazing sun beat down upon Van Gogh as he furiously painted whirling cypress trees and fields of bright yellow corn at the verge of his own insanity, so too the burning eye of the sun provided Nietzsche with the brilliance and luminosity which accompanied the production of *Ecce Homo*. Thenceforth Nietzsche passed beyond sanity. In the intensity of the sun, he became overripe. When the sun is at its height there are no shadows, no lines on the map of one's life. As in the interposed fragment, at a prior moment, the account is written as a foreword, a moment later it is the text of his writings. Since the sun casts no shadow at its apex, it gives only the place where the self stands, it gives the self as it is—what it is. It marks the place where one becomes what one is.

The self looks backward and forward. On each side, one finds writing: the writing of a life as pre-text on the one hand, as main text on the other. At the interface, however, the past and the future are entered as a moment, as the present, as the place where the eternal return is realized for the time being. Since the future would announce and affirm all that Nietzsche had written—treating each of his already published books one by one, and the past would announce the place of his autobiographical textuality as what is to be read as his own, the fragment itself is where Nietzsche returns eternally. Whatever is eternal or immortal about his life is identified, preserved, saved. But *we* cannot save Nietzsche. We cannot simply follow what he says and claim it to be eternal. He must save himself—just as he has the right to bury himself on this day. He has the right to go mad, to stop writing, to become what he is. As he cites in the passage from *Thus Spoke Zarathustra* just before he signs his foreword, "Now I bid you lose me and find yourselves; and only *When you have all denied me* will I return to you" (*EH-WKtr*, p. 220). By losing him, we find ourselves. We cannot find ourselves in him, in reading him, in seeking to make his eternal return our own. And yet we can read his perfect day; we can find his special event; we can see where he writes his own life as his own, as his own choice, as his own right. Just as Christ told Peter that he would deny him three times before the cock crowed at dawn and that he would also found Christ's Church on the rock, similarly Nietzsche can only live, can only become what he is, if we deny him, let him be, and become our own. In this sense, his autobiographical textuality belongs to him alone. He can and must present to himself the four books which he completed in the last quarter of 1888. As gifts, he must be grateful for them. But since he has given them to himself, the delight is his own. He is of course grateful not only for these presents, his gifts, but also for his whole life—a life which he lives and makes his own, a life which he writes in *Ecce Homo* and tells to himself. *Ecce Homo* is his narrative written to himself and the place at which the self enters the narrative as event is the limit-text or fragment in which he announces a "perfect day."

DESTINY/UNDERSTANDING

In many of his writings, Nietzsche appeals to his notion of *amor fati*—the love of fate which one must enact in order to go beyond and become oneself. The last section of *Ecce Homo* is entitled "Why I Am a Destiny." Nietzsche begins by writing: "I know my fate" (*EH-WKtr*, p. 126). He knows what lies before him—his testimony is clear as he writes it in his last testament. Yet he asks again and again: "Have I been understood?" He asks it three times at the outset of the last three subsections of "Why I Am a Destiny." Is there any doubt? For him to be understood would be for all the contradictions, reversals, and paradoxes to be resolved. For him to be understood, his destiny would have to be understood, his destiny would have to be clear to others. Yet his destiny is filled with misunderstandings. And if he is a destiny, then he must love, accept, and take on as his own whatever understanding ensues. Can he possess these consequences? Can he own them? To appropriate them as his own is itself his destiny. He has no other alternative. The effects of his writing returns him to his writing itself. He cannot deny these effects because he has written them as his own—they are as much his autobiographical textuality as the life he announces on that perfect day. To be true to his principles, he must will to live his destiny over and over again. But even if he were to deny his principles, he writes his own life as a destiny, as an autobiographical textuality which cannot be denied—only noted and remarked.

In becoming a destiny, he situates his textuality at the intersection between his self and his writings. At the opening of "Why I Write Such Excellent Books," we find the following passage: "I am one thing, my writings are another.—Here, before I speak of these writings themselves, I shall touch on the question of their being understood or *not* understood. I shall do so as perfunctorily as is fitting: for the time for this question has certainly not yet come. My time has not yet come, some are born posthumously" (*EH-RHtr*, p. 69; *EH-WKtr*, p. 259). The disjunction between his writings and his self is the place in which his autobiographical textuality inscribes itself—but it need not be accepted or even understood that a life is written in this interface. The disjunction itself however does establish the space for such an understanding to occur. The interface is the place of his birth (day) and as a "posthumous birth," it is his destiny.

He writes: "I do not want to be taken for what I am not—and that requires that I do not take myself for what I am not" (*EH-RHtr*, p. 69; *EH-WKtr*, p. 259). In order to avoid taking himself for what he is not, he narrates his own life as an autobiographical textuality at the intersection of self/text, event/writing, destiny/understanding. He situates himself at the time of the apex of the sun where he marks himself without a trace of shadow. Yet along the way there are shadows. Looking backward, he writes that he is "a disciple of the philosopher Dionysus" (*EH-RHtr*, p. 33; *EH-WKtr*, p. 217). Looking forward, he presents his spokesman Zarathustra. Nietzsche stands somewhere between. But he also stands opposed to "the Crucified." The last words of the text are "Dionysus versus the Crucified...". His philosopher is opposed to Christ. Dionysus is therefore the anti-Christ. But Dionysus is not a philosopher, he is a Greek god.

And Christ is not a philosopher any more than Dionysus. Yet in the *Birth of Tragedy*, Nietzsche claimed that a new god had entered the scene of classical Greek life—destroying the tragic beauty of works such as that of Aeschylus. This new god infected Greek tragedy (especially that of Euripides) with rationality. Socrates opposed himself to the Greek Dionysian (which represented the harnessed passion of the Apollonian tendency) and to that of the barbarian Dionysian. This new god Socrates opposed Dionysus; he opposed Nietzsche's philosopher. Just as Socrates was an anti-Dionysian, Nietzsche's Zarathustra announces the will to power which will take the overman beyond pity, beyond the herd morality, beyond good and evil—beyond Christian values in a revaluation of values. But where does Nietzsche stand if the one he follows is opposed by Socrates and the one he espouses opposes himself to Christian values? Nietzsche—as autobiographical textuality—stands between Dionysus and Zarathustra, but against the followers of Socrates and of Christ.

It will be remembered that the book is entitled *Ecce Homo*—the words uttered by Pontius Pilate as he had his soldiers bring Christ before the Jews. "Behold the man," Pilate said. In order to become his own destiny, Nietzsche applies this appellation to himself: behold the man. But the man—and particularly his identity—does not appear. He is the anti-Christ and yet we have only the text of his position. The man is nowhere to be found. He is born posthumously. He cannot be understood except by being whatever his destiny may become. He must be the autobiographical textuality in which his own life is written as *Ecce Homo*.

11

THE TIME OF AUTOBIOGRAPHY
Lévi-Strauss's *Tristes Tropiques*

At a crucial moment in his autobiographical text, provocatively entitled *Tristes Tropiques*, Claude Lévi-Strauss writes: "Time, in an unexpected way, has extended its isthmus between life and myself."[1] This crucial moment at which "time" is given a distinctive location occurs in the last sentence of the first part under the heading "An End to Journeying" *(La Fin des voyages)*. Since the body of the narrative begins where an end is announced, one might not expect an elaborate account of his travels in the remainder of the text. By situating a report about time at the place of juncture between the writing of the end and the beginning of the account of Lévi-Strauss's journeys, the notion of time is thematized as neither the starting point nor the place of conclusion. Time, in this view, is in-between. Time is in between the self and the life that the self narrates. Time is therefore situated in the place of narrative, at the conjuncture of a self and the life which it claims as its own. This time is what will be called the time of autobiography as it structures and delimits the autobiographical textuality of *Tristes Tropiques*.

Autobiographizing is the writing of one's own life. The writing enacts the life as a text. The enactment of the life as a text is the autobiographical narrative. When Lévi-Strauss identifies the relation between the self and life as time extending an isthmus, he is situating time in the same place as the autobiographical narrative. In this sense, the autobiographical temporality of *Tristes Tropiques* occurs where the writing of one's own life occurs—not as text but as the textuality of the text. The autobiographical textuality of *Tristes Tropiques* manifests an ordering or structuring, namely, the autobiographical temporality of the text.[2]

In elaborating the autobiographical temporality of *Tristes Tropiques*, the self which Lévi-Strauss identifies in relation to the life that is narrated is a cultural fiction. As a cultural fiction, the self is literally incorporated into the autobiographical textuality of the text and thereby into that which structures its textuality. To clarify how autobiographical temporality gives meaning to the narration of a life, I shall explore four respects in which the time of autobiography occurs in the writing of one's own life, that is, in autobiographical texts and, specifically, in *Tristes Tropiques*. These four considerations are as follows: (1) the historical time of autobiography; (2) the personal chronological time of autobiography; (3) the marking of autobiographical time; and (4) the re-marking or reformulating of lived time, i.e., the autobiographical temporality itself.

THE HISTORICAL TIME OF AUTOBIOGRAPHICAL TEXTUALITY

The practice of writing one's own life—at least in the Western world—began in Roman times. Marcus Aurelius, second-century Roman emperor, writing in Greek—the cultured language of his epoch—composed a work nominally addressed to himself. The text which has come to be known as the *Meditations*, is an account of the values and virtues that Marcus acquired from others and from his own philosophical considerations. As an autobiographical text, the *Meditations* inaugurates a mode of writing one's own life without appeal to dates and years, segments and slices, moments and periods. Nevertheless the *Meditations* does offer an account of Marcus's moral, philosophical, and spiritual life as recounted to himself. The absence of autobiography as a literary genre in classical Greece, its origination in late classical Roman times, and its further development as *Confessions* in the patristic period, situates Marcus's text at the beginnings of the historical time or framework in which autobiography achieved accepted status.

However autobiography as the full-scale writing of one's own life—rather than as the project of addressing some circumscribed dimension of a singular life—does not come into "its own" until the early nineteenth century. Even the very word "autobiography" cannot be found prior to the eighteenth century. Augustine, for instance, operating during epistemological spaces many centuries prior to the establishment of autobiography per se, concerns himself with the avowal and acknowledgment of his sins. He thereby recounts his moral and religious development. About eight centuries later, Dante—in the *Vita Nuova*—offers an allegorical picture of the spiritual turn in his life as figured by and through his love for Beatrice. The self in this world is matched against one engulfed by divine love. The Renaissance narratives of Cellini, Montaigne, and Loyola each offer up the self as *all there:* Cellini in terms of his adventures as a musician, goldsmith, sculptor, warrior, etc.; Montaigne in a self-portrait which conveys the fullness of his natural being; and Loyola in the recounted formation of a spiritual leader. The theory of self that is presumed in each of these three cases is one of a natural self available for anyone who cares to hear the story. The self-disclosure is purportedly complete and full. Descartes's *Discourse on Method* raises the possibility of a self which is both singular and universal in that he provides an account of the human mind with his own instance as a model. Although Dante's text also carries a feature of universality, it does so without locating the self entirely in the place of the mind. With Rousseau's *Confessions*, the rational, centered self which is fundamental to Descartes's account yields to an affective domain of passions, all the while remaining open to an Enlightenment appeal to experience. The *Confessions* establishes the modern conception of autobiography as a sincere and honest report (or so the claim goes.) The report characterizes a life from its origins up to the time of writing with all the details and dimensions that the autobiographer can muster. In these respects, Rousseau stands at the threshold of a new way of writing one's own life. Goethe's *Poetry and Truth*, Ben Franklin's *Autobiography*, and Henry Adams's *Education* are only a few of the many versions which follow Rousseau's model of self-expression. By the twentieth century, autobiography becomes a commonplace replete with self-narratives by novelists, poets, philosophers, psychologists, painters, athletes, military generals, and movie stars. Some portray a fragmented, divided self, some find the self decentered and dispersed, some postulate an unconscious inaccessible domain, some claim that the self is located in its verbal or textual articulations, and some regard it as a multiplicity of behaviors. Each particular historical time of autobiography operates within the wider scope in which the writing of one's own life can and does occur. Each particular epoch is conditioned by a conceptual framework which renders it possible to account for the life in a determinate range of ways and which incorporates a specific view of what constitutes the self.

The particular account of mind offered by Descartes in the *Discourse on Method* would have been out of place in ancient Greece. Rousseau's *Confessions* as a self-defense and an attempt at rectifying the wrongs perpetrated against him could not substitute for Augustine's reverent *Confessions*, even though both texts bear the same title. Cellini's adventures fighting for Renaissance popes and receiving the attention of the "divine Michelangelo" would hardly belong to the context of Simone de Beauvoir's mid-twentieth-century wartime situations and the burgeoning experiences of freedom that she and Sartre described philosophically. Similarly, *Tristes Tropiques*, published in 1955, would make little sense in a world inhabited by an Augustine, Cellini, Descartes, or Rousseau. Lévi-Strauss sets out on an account of his travels and explorations. He does not journey to Rome or Carthage, Florence or Pisa, Paris or Stockholm, Frankfurt or Strasbourg. Rather he goes to New York and São Paolo, Karachi, and Calcutta—markedly distant places for a resident of Paris. Moreover, Lévi-Strauss travels to such cities in order to conduct anthropological research.[3] Instead of a confession, self-portrait, account of adventures, demonstration of a mind ordering itself, self-defense, or the like, Lévi-Strauss offers a story of his expeditions:

> It is now fifteen years since I left Brazil for the last time and all during this period I have often planned to undertake the present work, but on each occasion a sort of shame and repugnance prevented me from making a start. Why, I asked myself, should I give a detailed account of so many trivial circumstances and insignificant happenings? Adventure has no place in the anthropologist's profession; it is merely one of those unavoid-

able drawbacks, which detract from his effective work through the incidental loss of weeks or months; there are hours of inaction when the
informant is not available; periods of hunger, exhaustion, sickness perhaps; and always the thousand and one dreary tasks which eat away the
days to no purpose and reduce dangerous living in the heart of the virgin
forest to an imitation of military service...(*TT*, p. 17).

The time of Lévi-Strauss's autobiography is characterized by extensive scientific
research and investigation, with emphasis on the researcher's extraordinary effort
and suffering. All this is ostensibly presented for the sake of ethnographic
knowledge about how a distant people live in terms of their customs, kinship
relations, attitudes, and social organization. Although Montaigne reflects upon
cannibals and Montesquieu writes his *Persian Letters* in order to explore alternative societies, they both operate according to a Euro-centric model.
Lévi-Strauss's structural formulation allows for the analysis of various societies
by examining repeatable transformational structures. In principle, Europe is no
longer the measure for the understanding of other social groups and their practices.

Underlying Lévi-Strauss's autobiographical account is the basic view that
anthropological investigation has come into its own and that a narrative can be
built upon it. The time of travel notes was especially popular in the mid-1950s:

This kind of narrative enjoys a vogue which I, for my part, find incom-
prehensible. Amazonia, Tibet, and Africa fill the bookshops in the form of
travelogues, accounts of expeditions and collections of photographs, in all
of which the desire to impress is so dominant as to make it impossible for
the reader to assess the value of the evidence put before him (*TT*, p. 17).

Lévi-Strauss goes to great efforts to make it clear that *Tristes Tropiques* does not
simply assemble travelogue material. Rather it takes its timeliness seriously—not
just reporting ethnographic data but structuring it, ordering it, placing it within a
theoretical framework, and retaining all the while its autobiographical textuality.

Because *Tristes Tropiques* is timely, it cannot be replaced by other texts such
as Augustine's *Confessions* or Stendhal's *Life of Henri Brulard*. This radical non-
substitutability of texts from another era suggests that what counts as a "life"
(according to Lévi-Strauss's text) would not even be appropriate in a different
historical context. Although some texts written at the same time would probably
also not be substitutable, it would be for a different reason. Contemporaneous
autobiographies might incorporate different theoretical, disciplinary, or professional traditions, or they might simply develop features which are unique and
individual—all of which would establish differences in the text produced. In
each case, however, the historical time of autobiography establishes a preliminary condition of difference.[4] The life is the life of a self as recounted at a
particular historical epoch. Indeed the life is as it is narrated and as it is situated
in a determinate *Weltanschauung* (both individual and social.)

THE PERSONAL, CHRONOLOGICAL TIME OF
AUTOBIOGRAPHICAL TEXTUALITY

Many autobiographies begin with, or cite near the opening of the text, the day and year of the narrator's birth. In the case of autobiography, the narrator's birth is naturally the same as that of the autobiographer. The personal chronological time of autobiography is the moment or moments when the autobiographer engages in a narrative of his/her own life. The framed duration of the autobiographed, spanning from the time of composition to the autobiographer's date of birth, or the segment when the narrative begins, constitutes "the life" in question. The autobiographical text is therefore delimited temporally in terms of the life narrated. The text *qua* narrative frame sets an outer temporal limit to the portion of the life that is narrated (or autobiographized.) The text determines the space of time described in relation to the space of time lived. Although predictions, hopes, and aspirations can be announced for the time outside (i.e., after) the writing of the autobiography, the time beyond the limits of the writing cannot be incorporated as such. The dissymmetry on the other side is noteworthy. Although the date of birth sets a limit to the autobiographical narrative, the autobiographer can report events, occurrences, views, lives, etc. which took place before he/she was born. Indeed, Marcus Aurelius devotes the whole first book of his *Meditations* to a report of what he learned from others, Sartre describes with much detail the outlines of his ancestor's careers, and Lévi-Strauss records the arrival of Villegiagnon from Geneva at the bay of Rio de Janeiro almost 378 years before his own landing there. But the stretches of time beyond the limits circumscribing the beginning of the life and the conclusion of the narrative moment are not what predominate or prevail in the autobiographical text nor are they what characterize the autobiographical temporality.

The personal chronological time of autobiography is the period (or periods) when one writes one's own life.[5] Cellini, for example, reports that "no matter what sort he is, everyone who has to his credit what are or really seem great achievements, if he cares for truth and goodness, ought to write the story of his own life in his own hand; but no one should venture on such a splendid undertaking before he is over forty." He adds: "Now that I am leaving the age of fifty-eight behind me and find myself in my native place Florence my thoughts naturally turn to such a task."[6] In spite of self-aggrandizement, Cellini articulates a prejudice that there is a time for the writing of one's own life. One must be ripe enough. He offers "forty" as the magical age. After that, sufficient experience, knowledge, understanding, or the like will have accrued such that a writing of one's own life is possible.[7] To learn that *Tristes Tropiques* was written fifteen years after Lévi-Strauss last left Brazil and at the age of forty-seven is not at all surprising. Its timeliness comes at a period when perspective, distance, judgment, and assessment are possible attitudes with respect to one's own life. However, such qualities require time—time one must live before the life can be written, and time for a determinate character to form. Memory is the retention and revival of the life. Narrated memory is the material for the autobiographical text. The autobiographical text organizes memory just as much as memory gives content to the autobiographical text. Memory is the instrument by which the autobiographer shapes his or her writing—but this shaping can only occur when remembering is transformed into writing, at the time of autobiography.

When one writes one's own life, one writes what one remembers. Yeats writes, in the preface to his *Reveries over Childhood and Youth* (1914):

> I have changed nothing to my knowledge; and yet it must be that I have changed many things without my knowledge; for I am writing after many years and have consulted neither friend, nor letter, nor old newspaper, and describe what comes oftenest into my memory.[8]

Remembering is fundamental to the task of writing one's own life. When set off against imagining, it establishes the place of autobiographical textuality. Though perhaps not willfully or knowingly changed from what actually occurred, what is remembered is surely a reformulation. Attempts at replication in the writing of what transpired in experience are bound to fail. Remembering only sets up the condition for the reconstruction of the life as narrative. It does not assure accuracy. However, the appropriation of what occurred as what is remembered does establish the autobiographical text. Appropriation in this sense is the gathering together of relevant details and data into an integrated whole such that the account organizes itself into a reasonable story. Appropriation also involves appropriateness: the autobiographical text is not only concerned with how the details are brought together but also with what details are relevant. In concert with Yeats, Lévi-Strauss states:

> What has happened is that time has passed. Forgetfulness, by rolling my memories along in its tide, has done more than merely wear them down or consign them to oblivion. The profound structure it has created out of the fragments allows me to achieve a more stable equilibrium, and to see a clearer pattern. One order has been replaced by another. Between these two cliffs, which preserve the distance between my gaze and its object, time, the destroyer, has begun to pile up rubble. Sharp edges have been blunted and whole sections have collapsed: periods and places collide, are juxtaposed or are inverted, like strata displaced by the tremors on the crust of an ageing planet. Some insignificant detail belonging to the distant past may now stand out like a peak, while whole layers of my past have disappeared without trace. Events without any apparent connection, and originating from incongruous periods and places, slide one over the other and suddenly crystallize into a sort of edifice which seems to have been conceived by an architect wiser than my personal history (*TT*, p. 44).

Forgetfulness transforms memories such that they no longer have the shape of what occurred. This misshaping of events is the basis for the reformation that constitutes the narrated life. The reforming is a forming which establishes the autobiographical text. Reforming is remembering and remembering is what makes the time of autobiography possible. The writing of a personal history is the link between remembering and the chronological time of autobiography.

A fourth feature of the time when one writes one's own life—in addition to the aforementioned: (a) delimiting factors; (b) the period in one's life when the text is written; and (c) what is specifically recalled—is the determination of what is relevant. Autobiographical texts offer at most fragments of the life. The life may be narrated as a whole because it is whole, but the narrative itself can at most bring together those fragments which are relevant to the account. What is relevant will most likely differ from time to time in one's life, and from individual to individual, whether of the same historical epoch or not. The moment in the life when the autobiography is written will play a role in what constitutes the autobiographical text. The moment may even determine which particular fragments are incorporated and the manner in which they form the text of the life.

What is relevant to an autobiographer at forty is not necessarily relevant to the same person at fifty. By writing at several stages in their lives, Rousseau, Mill, and Yeats, for example, are able to demonstrate some variations in their primary preoccupations—though their fundamental concerns tend to persist. Without considerable continuity, the texts are more likely to be separate works rather than parts of the narrated life. Virginia Woolf's *Diaries,* for instance, are highly fragmented and disunified in concern, theme, and project, while Simone de Beauvoir's multivolume autobiographies are very much a singular enterprise. Furthermore, what is significant for one person is not necessarily significant for another. Different aspects or features are given a kind of temporal prominence and magnitude by different autobiographers: Descartes offers only an account of the mind; Rousseau, of reason, feelings, and experiences; Mill, of his mental life and progress; Henry Adams, of his education; Sartre, of his choice to become a writer; and Lévi-Strauss, of his personal discoveries at the juncture between nature and culture. The personal time of autobiography has a uniqueness to its origination and a selectivity to its actualization.

THE MARKING OF AUTOBIOGRAPHICAL TIME

Time often appears in autobiographical narratives as a marked item. Typically such markings occur throughout the autobiographical text. They indicate temporal moments in the life that is written. They range from the specification of dates, hours, and minutes to the identification backwards or forwards of moments other than those under description to the occurrence of an experience to the comparison of one moment with another. The marking of autobiographical time is the specification of a determinate unit or set of units which involve an ordering or disordering, a connecting or a disconnecting, of the life as it is written. In this respect, marked time has a status similar to the marking of places or climates. Marked time has no special status over against other sets of marked elements within the text.

Lévi-Strauss marks time in a wide range of ways, extending from the descriptive to the valuative. He registers dates and hours: "My career was decided one day in the autumn of 1934 at nine o'clock in the morning, by a telephone call from Célestin Bouglé who was then head of the École Normale Supérieure" (*TT*, p. 47). He juxtaposes past with present:

> In 1918, the maps of the state of São Paolo, which is as big as France, showed it as being two-thirds "unknown territory inhabited only by Indians;" by the time I arrived in 1935, there was not a single Indian left, apart from a few families who used to come to the Santos beaches on Sundays to sell so-called curios (*TT*, p. 49).

He employs the flash-forward technique to characterize his pre-experiential images of Brazil. He imagines clumps of twisted palm trees concealing bizarrely designed kiosks and pavilions. He conjures up an atmosphere permeated with the smell of burning perfumes. And he explains:

> Considered in retrospect, these images no longer seem so arbitrary. I have learnt that the truth of a situation is to be found not in day-to-day observation but in that patient and piecemeal process of distillation which the linguistic ambiguity suggesting the idea of perfume perhaps encouraged me to practice in the form of a spontaneous pun, the vehicle of a symbolic interpretation that I was not yet in a position to formulate clearly (*TT*, p. 47).

He identifies "*firsts*": "The first contact with Rio was different. For the first time in my life, I was on the other side of the Equator in the tropics, in the New World" (*TT*, p. 85); and, "My first impression of Rio was of an open-air reconstruction of the Gallerias of Milan, the Galerij of Amsterdam, the Passage des Panoramas, or the concourse of the Gare Saint-Lazare" (*TT*, p. 85). He marks associative coincidences from different experiential moments:

> Today, the memory of that big hotel in Goiania coincides with my recollections of other hotels which, at the opposite poles of luxury and poverty, bear witness to the absurdity of the relationships which man consents to have with the world, or rather, which are increasingly formed upon him. (*TT*, p. 127).

And he compares his judgment of the time of the European world with that of other regions:

> What frightens me in Asia is the vision of our own future which it is already experiencing. In the America of the Indians, I cherish the reflec-

tion, however fleeting it may have now become, of an era when the human species was in proportion to the world it occupied, and when there was still a valid relationship between the enjoyment of freedom and the symbols denoting it (*TT*, p. 150).

In each of these cases, time is marked in a different way. These markings of time could also occur in a biography, a novel, or a history book. Yet marking them as specifically part of the autobiographical narrative indicates their incorporation into autobiographical time. Since most such markings are written with reference to the larger autobiographical space of the text, they enter into the autobiographical textuality as traces of autobiographical temporality.

Each of these markings establishes a particular temporal location within the narrative as a whole. They serve as landmarks in the mapping out of the autobiographical terrain. Each occupies an assigned position in the narrative and serves a specific function in relation to other positions. Together these temporal elements set up the framework in which the time of the autobiography can be rendered determinate. As such they are indices of the historical and personal time in which the text is written, but, even more specifically, they are indices of the relationships among the various events or minimal narrative units in the text. The marking of autobiographical time makes it possible for a reading of the text to sort out the chronology of the life.

AUTOBIOGRAPHICAL TEMPORALITY, OR THE RE-MARKING OF LIVED TIME

Autobiographical temporality is the structuring or ordering of autobiographical textuality in terms of the development of the life that is written. The particular way that the life is textualized in the autobiographical text constitutes its structuring or ordering. Hence the lived time of the autobiographer is formulated as text and the formulation as text establishes a narrative. The narrative carries a textuality which is autobiographical in nature and an essential feature of that autobiographical textuality is its autobiographical temporality.

Instead of simply marking time in the autobiographical text, autobiographical temporality re-marks or re-formulates lived time in one of many possible ways. The time as actually lived by the autobiographer is written as remembered/imagined. The remembering/imagining is a re-formulating as text. The autobiographed or narrated life and its temporal accountings are marked along the way, but the text is structured, ordered, and acquires meaning through the re-marking of lived time in the autobiographical text as narrative.

There are many ways to narrate one's own lived time. The traditional procedure is to offer a text with a diachronic narrative. Augustine, Cellini, Rousseau, Goethe, Adams, and de Beauvoir—to cite some examples—all write their own lives in a temporal sequence which attempts to reproduce the order in which the events took place as they occurred in relation to one another. Since, as indicated in terms of the personal chronological time of autobiography, one cannot narrate the whole life in its every aspect, the narrative with respect to the life is at most fragmentary. Only fragments, segments, selected portions of the life are recounted. Certain aspects are stressed—for instance, conversion in Augustine, virtuosity in Cellini, and rectification of wrongs in Rousseau. Autobiographical temporality is an ordering or structuring of the life by a coordination of the various fragments that are offered and emphasized. When given in a diachronic fashion, what is offered is a semblance or representation of the life as lived.

But semblances and representations are not the life as such: hence, there is no compelling reason why the writing of the life must reproduce the sequence in a diachronic order. Since the autobiographical text is other than the life, it need not replicate the life. The temporality of the writing as text or as narrative has its own rules and structuring principles. Both are inaugurated in the writing itself. They establish and delimit the autobiographical textuality. For John Stuart Mill to produce an extensive examination of his childhood and early development, his education, and the crisis in his mental history, followed by his close friendship with Harriet Taylor, and then simply to conclude "the remainder" of his life (i.e., the subsequent thirteen years) with a single chapter is to rewrite the temporal sequence of life as a whole. In *Walden*, Thoreau reports only one of his two years at Walden Pond. He does not narrate the second year since, he claims, it repeats approximately the same pattern as the first. Thoreau's view is that a year is a cycle and that to recount one sequence of seasons is to recount the next. In this way, the writer produces a textual ordering that establishes the autobiographical temporality in a nonlinear, *non-diachronic* way—at least once a full cycle has been achieved. Sartre as well need not report more than the first decade or so of his life. The fundamental project to become a writer has already been initiated. He had chosen who he would be—the rest (i.e. the subsequent forty-five or so years) was just a filling out of his choice of being. *Roland Barthes* by Roland Barthes breaks with the chronological account altogether. The text establishes an autobiographical temporality that is ordered according to the alphabet with captioned photographs, and even various charts, cartoons, and diagrams to supplement the account. One could, by contrast, extract a diachronic ordering from Barthes's text. In fact, a one and a half page "biography" or chronology is offered as an appendix. However in Barthes's case, the listing of dates and events in a linear sequence is quite inessential to the autobiographical textuality and therefore to the autobiographical temporality.

Although Lévi-Strauss's text is framed by a "setting out" and a "return," with an arrival in the New World and a departure from it, the journey is not single. There were many trips to the New World—to Brazil in particular, but also to North America. Then there were trips to Buddhist and Muslim cultures. These various trips are all integrated into the autobiographical narrative of his journey to Brazil in the 1930s and to the United States during the Second World War. Hotels in Goiania are juxtaposed with hotels in Karachi. The enormity of America is found in various places: "I have experienced it along the coast and on the plateaux of central Brazil, in the Bolivian Andes and the Colorado Rockies, in the suburbs of Rio, the outskirts of Chicago and the streets of New York" (*TT*, pp. 78–79). The juxtaposition of different places which were experienced at different times are narrated as systematically related. The association of one hotel with another, one enormous place with another, establishes a synchronicity to the autobiographical temporality of *Tristes Tropiques*. Sometimes the association is not one of identity but of difference:

> Once, during my first teaching post in the Landes area, I had visited poultry yards specially adapted for the cramming of geese: each bird was confined to a narrow box and reduced to the status of a mere digestive tube. In this Indian setting, the situation was the same, apart from two differences: instead of geese, it was men and women I was looking at, and instead of being fattened up, they were, if anything, being slimmed down. But in both instances, the breeder only allowed his charges one form of activity, which was desirable in the case of the geese, and inevitable in the case of the Indians (*TT*, p. 129).

The autobiographical temporality of the autobiographical text need not be ordered in any predetermined way, but each autobiographical text carries its own appropriate determination. If there is a time of autobiography in its fullest sense, whatever ordering and structuring takes place is re-marked in the autobiographical textuality. Lévi-Strauss, one will recall, describes time as extending its isthmus between life and himself. By situating the autobiographical temporality in the place between life and the self, as the place where the text is read as a narrative, Lévi-Strauss offers an account of where the time of autobiography is located.

But if the self is a cultural fiction and life is at most a reality narrated as text, then autobiographical temporality is not *my* time or *his*, rather it is the social space of a narrated life that is practiced in the autobiographical text. Lévi-Strauss describes this narrated social space as the personally chosen place between life and the self. Accordingly he concludes *Tristes Tropiques* with the following passage:

> The self is not only hateful: there is no place for it between us [*un nous*] and nothing [*un rien*]. And if, in the last resort, I opt for us, even though it is no more than a semblance [*une apparence*], the reason is that, unless I destroy myself—an act which would obliterate the conditions of the option—I have only one possible choice between the semblance and nothing. I only have to choose for the choice itself to signify my unreserved acceptance of the human condition…(*TT*, p. 414).

In choosing the choice between "us" and "nothing," he selects the place in-between and that place is where the autobiographical text delineates its temporality and where a version of the self is offered. The self in question is reported only in the text. The text is its formulation. The formulation establishes its identity. Its identity is a cultural fiction—cultural because it is characterized by a particular historical time in a circumscribed social context, and fiction because it depends upon the narrative or personal account to bring it into its own. As a cultural fiction, the self has features similar to those of other members in the society. Such a self achieves its determinateness in the textualization of the autobiographical narrative. But since the textuality embodies real life (nonfiction) in its formulation, the version offered is as valid (and unique) as any. Its temporality is as full and complete as can be.

The task here has been to establish the status of autobiographical temporality. As a feature of autobiographical textuality, autobiographical temporality sets the particular way in which the positions or markings of time are ordered or structured. It provides the manner and design in which the various temporal marks are related to each other. It incorporates the historical time and social spaces in which the text is written and the moment in the autobiographer's life when the narrative is animated. The historical time, the personal chronological time, and the temporal markings are not, however, constitutive of autobiographical temporality. Autobiographical temporality contributes to the production of an authorized version of the self and organizes a narrative of the life. The narrative gives particular weight to isolated elements or marks, events or changes, persons or places. It thereby selects, de-emphasizes, omits, or denies other features. Autobiographical temporality gathers together the dispersed aspects of a life and gives them a shape. The shaping or recounting of a life establishes it as this life and not that one. The narrated life is structured so as to render a particular character determinate in accordance with its unique qualities. The writing of one's own life involves a re-marking of its most significant features. The remarking of that which develops or lives as a life is the autobiographical textuality understood temporally in terms of the autobiographical text. While the historical time of autobiography puts something into the text, autobiographical textuality in its temporal dimension is what the text puts into history.

12

THE SELF-INSCRIPTIONS OF
SARTRE AND BARTHES

Autobiography is the *writing* of one's own life. Autobiographical *works* are particular entities, created objects, in time and space. Autobiographical *texts* have no space per se; they have only a differential or juxtapositional relation to other texts (autobiographical and otherwise). *Autobiographizing* occurs in the zone of this relation. As a topic—for discussion and examination—*autobiographizing* operates at the limits of non-autobiographical texts. In this sense, autobiographizing accomplishes the shift from the non-autobiographical to the autobiographical, from what is outside an autobiographical text to what constitutes the autobiographical text per se. Hence, *autobiographical textuality* as a *topos* (space, domain, topic) in which autobiographizing occurs is a discursive space. A discursive space is a region of discourse (actual or potential) in which a text defines itself in particular ways, with determinate features and specifiable characteristics. A text establishes these ways, features, and characteristics by calling into question aspects of the text that spill over its limits, that supersede its own qualifications, that exceed its expectations. The juxtaposition of a text with one or more other texts opens up a unique space of textuality that accounts for the text's excesses and superfluities, that motivates readings, interpretations, or critiques which would not have been otherwise accessible. Hence the discursive space of autobiographical textuality and the effects of the decentered autobiographical self-inscription are disclosed—at least in part and in the instance—by the juxtaposition of Sartre's *Les Mots* [1] and Barthes's *Roland Barthes* [2].

Sartre devoted his life to the writing of philosophy, on the one hand, and to literature, on the other. And, as a supplement to the chasm between philosophy and literature, he produced biographies, political theory, art and literary criticism, and (of course) autobiography. The space between philosophy and literature is constituted with reference to the very boundaries set by Sartre's philosophy (notably, in *Being and Nothingness*, the *Critique of Dialectical Reason*) and by his literature (*Nausea*, *The Roads to Freedom* novels, *No Exit*, *Dirty Hands*, *The Devil and the Good Lord*, *The Condemned of Altona*, etc.). Hence, in relation to Sartre's written production in general, *Words* is neither philosophy nor literature, neither fiction, nor nonfiction. As text, *Words* occupies a definitive space between philosophy and literature. The autobiographical textuality of *Words* operates at the limits of the Sartrian text. It establishes its identity in relation to a variety of considerations including the spatiality and temporality of the text: it transgresses the distinction between fiction and nonfiction, serves as a metaphorical expression as opposed to a literal function, demonstrates the effects of imagination and memory, and enacts the relation between autobiographer and autobiographed.

Roland Barthes by Roland Barthes occupies a similar frame. It too can be understood as the inscription of a text whose autobiographical space is opened up by a reading of its textualities. As text, *Roland Barthes* is located between criticism and theory in the same way that Sartre's autobiography is situated between his philosophy and his literature. *Roland Barthes*—the text—has elements of criticism and elements of theory. It indicates, on the one hand, affinities with *Writing Degree Zero*, *Elements of Semiology*, and *The Pleasure of the Text*, and, on the other hand, with *On Racine*, *Critical Essays*, *Mythologies*, *S/Z*, and *Sade/Fourier/Loyola*. However, just as Sartre's autobiographical textuality occurs at the symmetrical limits of temporality/spatiality, fiction/nonfiction, metaphoricity/literality, imagination/memory, and autobiographer/autobiographed, Barthes's text invokes a similar "map" of delimitation and articulation. Furthermore, an interfacing of philosophy/literature and theory/criticism needs to be identified, for while Sartre and Barthes can be opposed in many respects, the theory/criticism relation operates between the limits of philosophy and the limits of literature. Hence, the space opened up by the philosophy/literature relation is filled not only by Sartre's *Baudelaire*, *Mallarmé*, *What Is Literature?*, *Saint Genet*, and *The Family Idiot*, but also by the whole Barthesian enterprise. Setting *Les Mots* off against *Roland Barthes* by Roland Barthes is therefore an opposition within an inclusion. The inclusion defines a space, the opposition announces the limits to a space, and the limits to the space establish a *topos*—namely, in this case, the autobiographical textuality of Sartre and Barthes.

The elaboration of autobiographical textuality out of the Sartre/Barthes opposition establishes its own parameters. They include: (1) image/text, (2) diachronicity/synchronicity, and (3) reading/writing. The further specification of these oppositional constituents will indicate the field of the *topos* of autobiographical textuality at the place where utopia and atopia intersect.

IMAGE/TEXT

The image/text opposition would have no validity if only Sartre's *Words* were at issue. As his title suggests, *Les Mots* is an examination of the significance that words have for Sartre's development. His own insertion into language is the assimilation and the subsequent active production of words. Almost as a prefiguration of Foucault's *Les Mots et les choses*, Sartre reviews the epistemological frameworks that account not only for his inscription of self between words and things but also for the shift that takes place in his own personal itinerary.

It is not unusual to say that Sartre's text is an entirely verbal text. *Words*—published in 1963—is circumscribed by a beginning ("Around 1850, in Alsace, a schoolteacher with more children than he could afford was willing to become a grocer" [*Words*, p. 5]) and an ending ("A whole man [*tout un homme*] composed of all men and as good as all of them and no better than any" [*Words*, p. 160]). A larger picture appears, however, if one adds to the corpus the original 1953 version of *Words*, the 1975 "Sartre at Seventy" interview (which first appeared in *Le Nouvel Observateur* and then in English in *Life/Situations*) as well as a variety of other transcribed oral reports of his life[3] including even the 1972 film *Sartre, un film réalisé par Alexandre Astruc et Michel Contat*[4] and Francis Jeanson's *Sartre dans sa vie* (1974).[5] Even in the film Sartre offers his own narrative—as he sits at his desk with friends and colleagues distributed around his apartment room or cluttering Simone de Beauvoir's Paris flat. All of these personal accounts would extend far beyond the specific domain of the 1963 autobiographical text. This disclosure of the realm of textuality introduces a feature which has implications for its counterpart in Barthes's text. In the film *Sartre*, images, photographs, and footage of Sartre in context fill out the picture of his life. These images are at the horizon of Sartrian words; they announce a lifetime of activity and constitute a historical documentation which assists in the identification of a particular autobiographical self. To this network of Sartrian self-portraits, one could also add what is not offered by Sartre himself and yet which complements the words presented in *Les Mots*, the interviews, and the film: namely, a volume of photographs by Liliane Sendyk-Siegel entitled *Sartre: Images d'une vie*.[6] The text—Sartre's autobiographical text—is enhanced by images. Thereby Lessing's bias in favor of the textual over the pictorial—established in the *Laocoön* but recalling Horace's *ut pictura poesis*—is strongly maintained: images (what Lessing calls "painting" in general) are marginalized since they lack the flexibility and diversity provided by words.

For Barthes, by contrast, images occupy an important place in the autobiographical text. With the exception of a simple statement at the outset, Barthes remarks:

> To begin with, some images: they are the author's treat to himself, for finishing his book. His pleasure is a matter of fascination (and thereby quite selfish). I have kept only the images which enthrall me, *without my knowing why* (such ignorance is the very nature of fascination, and what I shall say about each image will never be anything but...imaginary) (*RB*, p. 3).

Images, in this case, are essential because the pleasure of the text is essential. The author's pleasure is continually at issue—in both word and image. In *The Pleasure of the Text* (1973), Barthes had already established that the reader's pleasure is derived from both an enjoyment in the text and a distance from the text.

This self-distance invokes the classic problem for self-portraiture and self-narrative. How does one obtain distance from oneself? The Husserlian conception of a transcendental ego is one way: it proposed to make transcendental reflection possible. But as Sartre has himself shown, the ego cannot capture itself in the act of reflection. Reflective consciousness will always produce an object which is other than consciousness, other than the knowing—or in this case, the enjoying self. Barthes as well would have no appreciation for a self that can know itself in the act of knowing. Yet the self-narrative that takes the author's pleasure as an issue can, for Barthes, be inscribed in the autobiographical text. As I shall indicate, however, self-narrative is not merely a matter of ex-static pleasure (or the *jouissance* which Barthes takes to be the proper place of reading and presumably "self-knowledge"). The pleasure in images, then, is a special kind of pleasure. It is the pleasure of Narcissus—seeing oneself there revealed to oneself and thereby, potentially, to others. The pleasure in images is nothing other than the *imaginary* at work. By *the imaginary*, Barthes implies something more like an "image-system" (as opposed to Sartre's notion of *l'imaginaire*, whereby imaginative consciousness constitutes things in an imaginative way as the concrete analogue of what is experienced imaginatively). In contrast with what occurs in Sartre's *Words*, images and image-systems (*l'imaginaire*) in Barthes play a significant role in the constitution of the autobiographical text and its textuality.

For Barthes, the image is where the body is pictured—even though the language here is the language of the body. The language of the image is the body of the text, at least for the first 43 pages in the English version (46 pages in the French). Because imagination and fictionalization are at work in the text, the images are the imaginary given identifiable form. The "image-repertoire" enters into an erotic discourse with textual desire, called *jouissance*, which Barthes cannot forget. The pleasure of the textual image is repeated throughout the book. Except for the group photo with members of his seminar (which is the only photograph beyond the opening segment of the text), the verbal body of the text is interspersed with images from painting, music, cartoons, writing, and diagrams. Situated under the heading of "The Image-System" (*l'imaginaire*) is the following claim: "The vital effort of this book is to state an image-system" (*RB*, p. 109). In human life, the image-system does not consume (everything). By the same token, the projection of images does permeate the autobiographical textuality of Barthes's *Roland Barthes*.

As Lacan shows, the mirror-stage is that moment when the child recognizes him- or herself as other. It follows the stage in which the mother acquires alterity. Within his text, Barthes includes, along with a variety of images of his mother at various ages, one image in which she is holding a young child. Both mother and child seem to be looking into a mirror. The caption reads: "The mirror stage: 'That's you.'" Images of Barthes as a baby, as a young boy, as a young man, as a teacher, as a lecturer, as a panel participant, and as a writer in his Paris apartment—each supplement the horizons of Barthes's autobiographical textuality. Yet do these pictures actually contribute to the autobiographical textuality? While they would more appropriately be characterized as "photobiographical textuality,"[7] incorporated into the autobiographical text, the photo-graphic images take on new meaning, a meaning relevant to the authorial mode inscribing itself in both words and pictures.

DIACHRONICITY / SYNCHRONICITY

Sartre's text is constructed under the guise of diachronicity. The autobiograph-er/autobiographed passed from the stage of reading to that of writing. While this theme of reading/writing is to be developed in the next section, what is rele-vant here is the abrupt shift from the first part, entitled *Lire* (Reading), to the second part, entitled *Écrire* (Writing). Given that the text narrates only the first eleven years of the boy's life, the division of the book into two parts—on the one hand, "Reading," and, on the other, "Writing"—marks a significant shift in his early experience. This marking of a threshold between the two halves of his boyhood corresponds quite markedly to the account Sartre gives of the transi-tion in Flaubert from "poet" to "artist."[8] In a similar way, it can be said of Flaubert, once he has accomplished the epistemological break between the activ-ity of reading and the activity of writing, that he has in effect achieved his "fundamental project". As Sartre reports in his own "existential psychoanalysis" (in *Being and Nothingness*), once one makes an original choice early on, that option constitutes one's freely chosen fundamental project thereafter. Once the young Sartre has entered into writing, the rest is just a postscript. He is simply carrying out the fundamental project of a writer (of philosophy and literature).

The initiation into writing occurs between the ages of seven and eight. Hence the first half of the narrative actually covers almost three quarters of the age span in question. The concern with his initiation into writing focuses on three to four years of his life—from seven or eight to eleven years old. The next break occurs when his mother remarries and they move to La Rochelle as he reaches the age of twelve. This new break accompanies his mother's 1917 "liber-ation" (though Sartre would have difficulty understanding it in these terms) from the chains to which she was returned when Sartre's father died in 1906. The new break is Sartre's "tragedy"—his personal despair—which, strangely enough, is concomitant with his mother's escape from the stifling atmosphere of his maternal grandparents' home. This new mark in the diachronic line is one of significance. It is enough to interrupt the narrative altogether. However, that he has already become a writer is much more important.

From the perspective of a "*Jean sans terre*" (the title of the 1953 version), a middle-aged man of forty-eight reflects upon his childhood. The absence of something—anything—of his own is of special concern. Furthermore, in *Saint Genet*, which he had just published in 1952, Sartre reads into Genet's experience the sense of *propertylessness*—the condition of having nothing of one's own. His name, his parents, his home were all given to him. Genet did not choose them. It was not until he chose to be the thief "that others made of him" that Genet was able to affirm an identity of his own. Correspondingly, Sartre interprets his own life in a parallel fashion. With the death of his father, his mother became more like his older sister in her parents' home. In this sense, like Genet, he had neither a father nor a mother. He lived in the Schweitzer household—not a Sartre home, and permission always depended on the good graces of his mother's parents. Just as Genet became a saint by making himself into a thief, Sartre becomes—in his self-narrative—a sort of saint by acquiring the identity of a writer. And from the standpoint of a fifty-eight year old (in 1963), Sartre is able to also incorporate the progressive-regressive method, which he had first introduced six years earlier in *Search for a Method* (1957). In *Les Mots*, he offers not only the progressive (diachronic) movement toward the writer that he will be but also the regressive account of his experiences in relation to those of family, friends, acquaintances, as well as to the social and political events of the time. This latter movement bears the characteristics of a synchronic reading as Sartre insists in his debate with Lévi-Strauss.[9]

Sartre's progressive-regressive method, however, hardly matches up to the synchronic reading that Barthes offers in reporting his own life. With Barthes, the diachronic account is kept in reserve until the final two pages in which a short biographical chronology is provided. In this chronology, like the twelve-page account offered in an English critical edition of Sartre's *Les Mots*,[10] the listing begins with the author's date of birth. Perhaps Barthes's shorter life (he was sixty-five when he died in 1980—the same year as Sartre, who was seventy-five at the time) will account for the difference.

Apart from the two-page chronology, however, Barthes's autobiographical text, assuming that it is indeed one, interrupts the normal expectations for an autobiographical text. The set of photographic images that open the text are hardly organized in anything like a chronological order. Views of Barthes as a young man (lying by himself on the beach) are juxtaposed with him standing "among friends" as an older man; scenes of a child sitting Humpty-Dumpty-like on a wall are juxtaposed with pictures of him looking thoroughly bored (at a panel discussion) or animated (while lecturing); and a 1942 portrait is placed above one from 1970. Similarly, the narrative (not the captions accompanying the pictures) does not follow a chronological, diachronic line. Rather the organizing principle is the alphabet. The whole self-portrait is motivated not by the "arbitrary" succession of dates, but rather by the sequential order provided by the alphabet.

Barthes had been familiar with the Seuil series of critics on writers, for he had himself published a study of Michelet in the series many years earlier.[11] Presumably the possibility of writing a study—not this time about someone else, but about himself—must have intrigued him. Indeed, *Roland Barthes* by Barthes is the only self-written study in the whole series (which includes many illustrious figures such as Racine, Shakespeare, and Cervantes). The judgment that Barthes ranks among the great writers is certainly merited—and, despite the self-inscription implied by its authorship, the selection of his contribution marks this interest. The intrigue,however, did not end with the publication of the book. When it came time for the *Quinzaine Littéraire* to publish a critical review of the book, the editors sought after the most renowned critic around. Since this happened to be Barthes himself, it was (perhaps) not all that unusual that Barthes should have been asked to write the review. The magazine gave the essay the title "Barthes, à Trois Puissances" ("Barthes to the third power" or "Barthes with three powers").[12]

The text *Roland Barthes* is a collection of *fragments*—reflections in the tradition of Pascal's *Pensées*. Instead of grouping them together with a number system, it operates with an alphabet system. The first heading is entitled "*Actif/réactif,*" the last "*Le monstre de la Totalité.*" One can only suppose that there were no further fragments beginning with U to Z. To place the dates "August 6, 1973—September 3, 1974" seems a bit incongruous and yet the dates serve as the frame for the whole synchronic slice rather than as markers along the way. The inclusion of the alphabetically arranged fragments provides an ordering to what might otherwise be simply disparate "thoughts"—by Barthes—about a range of topics related to the body, experiences, reflections, and the writings of one Roland Barthes. If Barthes were reading these fragments rather than writing them, one would think him the already paradigmatic *autodidact* (the self-taught man) from Sartre's 1938 *Nausea*. The *autodidact* teaches himself by reading everything written in the library by an author whose name begins with "A", then "B", etc. For Barthes, however, the self-portrayal is in terms of alphabetically arranged fragments where, for example, "atopia" is followed by "autonomy." The alphabetical system constitutes the order of *lexias* (as Barthes called the lexical entries or items marking his reading of Balzac's *Sarrasine* in *S/Z*).

Synchronicity in Barthes is the counter to diachronicity in Sartre. The interface between synchronicity (as marked by the alphabet, lexias, and as image system) and diachronicity (as highlighted by a series of events and the significant or minor breaks between them) is the place of temporality for the autobiographical self—a self which is neither Sartre nor Barthes but the *topos*, as cultural fiction, opened up by their unique textual formations.

READING/WRITING

Who reads and who writes? The young Sartre reads in order to play the role of the little adult. He has no father to provide him with a Superego: "… I readily subscribe to the verdict of an eminent psychoanalyst: I have no Superego" (*Words*, p. 11). His father dies only a year or so after Sartre is born, leaving him without a natural father. For Sartre, the paternal role was one of absence: "I left behind me a young man who did not have time to be my father and who could now be my son" (*Words*, p. 11). And although Sartre claims that his father's death "sent my mother back to her chains and gave me freedom" (*Les Mots*, p. 11), the role of his grandfather, Charles Schweitzer, seems to occupy the paternal position quite effectively: as both grandfather and father. Nevertheless Sartre asserts that this absence of a Superego makes it possible for him to construct the

"I" however he wishes. Yet the self that reads—the activator of words—is already in the words that he reads. He only needs to transform the words which he has read in popular gazettes into short stories or novels of his own. This transformation is the formation of the self. Many years later this self will be transformed into another self through the ongoing activity of autobiographizing per se. This narrative self—which is also a narrated self—takes shape out of the early reading by which Sartre transformed himself. This narrative self, or autobiographizing, contrives the myth of the word and gives the narrative self a place in which it can become what it will be. From the self as reader to the self as writer, words stand as the gate between reading and writing, for they are given a place in the general field of writing. Words are read and words are written. Sartre narrates the function of difference between reading and writing. Originally, the words were to a large degree the same—words in reading and in writing were an effect of early learning, but also an early acquisition of writerhood. That Sartre continued both to incorporate and to make something new out of what he read is part of the record: the biographies, for instance, are detailed retranscriptions of his readings. Consider *Saint Genet*, which closely follows and interprets *The Thief's Journal* (including Sartre's account of Genet's ultimate theft, and the subsequent "derivative" prison poem entitled "The Condemned Man," which plagiarizes the lines of many well-known poets). These same traits can also be found in his early philosophy, most notably *Being and Nothingness*, which in many respects is a synthetic reinscription of Husserlian and Heideggerian phenomenology in Sartrian terms.

The place of the self is in the writing of the self who writes. Barthes describes this transformation in terms of the writerly text *(le scriptible)*, which is reconstructed, rather than the readerly text *(le lisible)*, which is read uncritically and without interpretation. *Roland Barthes* by Barthes is *scriptible*—a writerly text. It reconstructs the autobiographical self into a set of images. Together with the photographic images, the rewriting of the self forms what is neither the "I" nor the "me" (terms which Sartre explored in considerable detail in *The Transcendence of the Ego*). In Barthes's text, the self operates on the level of the mirroring, in the place where the viewer (having achieved the mirror-stage) states: "that's me." This autobiographical self has no center. It writes its own identity by writing with words, but the words are only one among various vehicles whereby the autobiographical self becomes an autobiographical textuality—at the intersection of reader and writer, I and me, image and text, philosophy and literature, theory and criticism.

Autobiographizing is an interface activity whose condition as pure limit is situated between the non-space of atopia and the ideal space of utopia.[13] This autobiographical *topos* is the inscription of a self at the juncture between reading and writing—in Barthes as well as Sartre. Barthes describes "atopia" in the following terms:

> Pigeonholed: I am pigeonholed, assigned to an (intellectual) site, to residence in a caste (if not in a class). Against which there is only one internal

doctrine: that of *atopia* (of a drifting habitation). Atopia is superior to utopia (utopia is reactive, tactical, literary, it proceeds from meaning and governs it) (*RB*, p. 49).

The drifting is the movement of self-decentering. Responding to the pigeonholing, the self writes itself in a narrative that accounts for caste/class, status/position, identity/stereotype. Each formation is a constitution of the autobiographed in the mode of autobiographizing. Its place is neither here nor there. This autobiographical *topos* is the discursive space which identifies, singularizes, appropriates, personalizes, and decenters. Autobiographizing is writing a space which cannot be a space: it must remain active as it moves close to its self-defining limits at the self-inscription of Sartre and Barthes.

13

THE AUTOBIOGRAPHICAL TEXTUALITY OF HEIDEGGER'S SHOES

...perhaps it is only in the picture that we notice all this about the shoes. The peasant woman, on the other hand, simply wears them. If only this simple wearing were so simple. When she takes off her shoes late in the evening, in deep but healthy fatigue, and reaches out for them again in the still dim dawn, or passes them by on the day of rest, she knows all this without noticing or reflecting. The equipmental quality of equipment consists indeed in its usefulness...

—Heidegger, "The Origin of the Work of Art"

The "truth" of the useful is not useful, the "truth" of the product is not a product. The truth of the product "shoe" is not a shoe [*une chaussure*]—
—But one could think the difference between Being and a being like the shoe, through it in its step. And likewise the ontological difference: shod in painting/a pathway in painting [*chausser en peinture*].

—Derrida, *La Vérité en peinture*

When Jacques Derrida first published his essay on the "exchange" between Heidegger and Meyer Schapiro in the art journal *Macula* (no. 3), it bore the title "La Vérité en pointure." The title could be rendered in English as "Truth in Shoe Size." The essay was then republished in the "book" entitled *La Vérité en peinture* (1978), and translated into English as *The Truth in Painting* (1987), including as the fourth of four essays—the one called a "*polylogue*", an expanded version of "La Vérité en pointure." The new title for the essay—or "poly-logue"—is given as "Restitutions de la verité en pointure." An English translation of the first part of the essay was published in the 1978 issue of *Research in Phenomenology*. Hence there are three linked titles that accompany this essay: "Truth in Shoe Sizes," "Truth in Painting," and "Restitutions." What links these three titles—provisional and permanent at the same time—will be the topic of what follows. In other words, what brings together the questions of shoes and shoe sizes, the question of painting, and the problem of restitution will constitute the fabric of my own contribution.

To be more precise, Derrida's essay (in its various versions and translations) is concerned with Heidegger's essay "The Origin of the Work of Art" (*Der Ursprung des Kunstwerkes*), originally presented—also in several versions—in 1935 and 1936, and finally published in the 1950 volume entitled *Holzwege*, then again in the 1960 Reclam edition, and ultimately in the more recent *Gesamtausgabe*.[1] But Derrida's essay is also concerned with an article by the art historian Meyer Schapiro first published in a memorial volume for Kurt Goldstein entitled *The Reach of Mind* (1968). Derrida's essay—in its multiple versions—is not *about* Heidegger's "Origin of the Work of Art" but *about* an exchange or a correspondence between Heidegger and Schapiro—one in German, the other in English, and the third (Derrida's) in French. In this way, Derrida enters into the exchange and contributes to its movement. The *topos* of the exchange—if *topos* is understood as a rhetorical topic and not so much an actual place in which the exchange occurs—centers around shoe sizes: not shoe sizes per se, not even the dimensions of actual shoes, but rather the role and status of the question of shoes in one or more Van Gogh paintings, in one or more paintings in which shoes appear, in one or more texts (Heideggerian, Derridean, etc.) in which shoes are discussed.

SUBJECT/BELONGING TOGETHER

Is this a question of things—of shoes in particular? Surely not. No one asks about the shoes Heidegger was wearing when he delivered his lectures in November 1935 in Freiburg, in January 1936 in Zürich, and later in 1936 in Frankfurt. No one asks what size they were. No one asks what shoes Meyer Schapiro, the Columbia professor of Art, was wearing when preparing his article "The Still Life as a Personal Object" for publication in 1968. No one asks what shoes Derrida was wearing when completing his essay for its initial publication in *Macula*,—nor are the shoes I am currently wearing of any importance whatsoever. These shoes are all out of the question, outside the discussion. And similarly Heidegger would not have found any interest in the shoes that Van Gogh himself was wearing when painting a picture of shoes at the end of 1886—specifically "Old Shoes with Laces" ("*Vieux Souliers aux lacets*") or just "*Les Souliers*" as they are identified in the French translation [*Tout l'Oeuvre peint*] of the 1971 *Tutti le Opere* edition by Paolo Le Caldano.[2] The shoes that Van Gogh was himself wearing would not be a matter for question, for study, for concern. And even the shoes that Van Gogh had before him as the *subject* of his study—assuming, of course, that there was indeed such an object—would be of questionable interest (but not without interest!)

In the first section of the "Origin of the Work of Art," after the introduction, Heidegger asks about the relation between "Work" and "Thing." Here he chooses as an example "a common sort of equipment" ["*Wir wählen als Beispiel*] *ein gewöhnliches Zeug*," says Heidegger—"*ein Paar Bauernschuhe*"]—"a pair of peasant shoes" (*PLT-OWA*, p. 32; *Holz* p. 22). But which peasant shoes? Actual peasant shoes that Van Gogh was to have placed before him in 1886?—shoes that he would have used as a model for his work, his *Arbeit*? Were these peasant shoes actual things—entities, or beings *(Seiendes)* that are present, that present themselves for questioning, for concern, for thinking—or in this case, for painting? Let us presume that Van Gogh was indeed painting some peasant shoes—"a pair of peasant shoes" as Heidegger calls them. And these peasant shoes are "things" according to Heidegger, things that one might encounter in everyday life, in everyday experience. And yet these are not just things: they are an example of *Zeug* (equipment), for the case in point—the example of "a pair of peasant shoes"—comes in *only* to illustrate Heidegger's discussion of equipment *(Zeug)*, and further, *das Zeugsein des Zeuges* ("the equipmentality of equipment").

The things—the pair of peasant shoes—are not just things: they are also "equipment." And what is equipment? Heidegger makes it clear that equipment is that which has a certain serviceability *(Dienlichkeit)*. But what serviceability is in question here? It is certainly *not* that these peasant shoes serve Van Gogh as a painter, serve him in his painterly activities, serve him as a model. Heidegger makes no such allusion. The peasant shoes in question do not serve Van Gogh at all. Rather they serve the peasant woman whom Heidegger goes on to describe in some detail. Heidegger offers a narrative about the shoes and the context in which they are worn:

> From the dark opening of the worn insides of the shoes the toilsome tread of the worker stares forth. In the stiffly rugged heaviness of the shoes there is the accumulated tenacity of her slow trudge through the far-spreading and ever uniform furrows of the field swept by a raw wind. On the leather lie the dampness and richness of the soil. Under the soles slides the loneliness of the field-path as evening falls. In the shoes vibrates the silent call of the earth, its quiet gift of the ripening grain and its unexplained self-refusal in the fallow desolation of the wintry field. This equipment is pervaded by uncomplaining anxiety as to the certainty of bread, the wordless joy of having once more withstood want, the trembling before the impending childbed and shivering at the surrounding menace of death. This equipment belongs to the *earth*, and it is protected in the *world* of the peasant woman. From out of this protected belonging the equipment itself rises to its resting-within-itself (*PLT-OWA*, pp. 33–34; *Holz*, pp. 22–23).

Heidegger waxes poetical in his account of the envisioned peasant woman: her world, her experience, her hopes, her fears, her daily toil, her needs, her care, her anxiety, and her wonder. Heidegger's interpretation is indeed an interpretation. He offers a hermeneutic of the visible thing—the pair of peasant shoes in Van Gogh's painting. He invokes the world that they disclose. He describes the meaning that is imbedded in the painting and that opens up a clearing (a *Lichtung* as he later calls it) that reveals a world and that sets a horizon for that world.

This hermeneutic of the picture of peasant shoes is not only convincing, it is even instilling. Heidegger is able to bring out a world which he himself understood well. His peasant background made it possible for him to understand the world of the peasant woman. His early years were spent in Messkirch (Baden) and his later pastoral moments in Todtnauberg (Schwarzwald) where he could observe, speak with, and even blend into the world of peasant life in the Germany of the 1930's.

But Van Gogh's painting was painted toward the end of 1886—while he was living in Paris. Indeed, he had traveled to Paris early in 1886 from Anvers, Belgium (where he had spent a few months in the late autumn 1885 just after leaving Holland.) He remained in Paris until the beginning of 1888. And during this two year period Van Gogh painted a number of scenes of Paris—rooftops, scenes of city life, windmills integrated into the city view (at Montmartre and elsewhere), still lifes, some portraits of Parisian women, paintings from sculpted busts of women, and a good number of self-portraits. He also painted a few pictures of shoes. Le Caldano reports three paintings of shoes dating from the end of 1886 through the winter of 1886–87, and then two more during the first semester of 1887.[3] During this 1886–88 period in Paris, Van Gogh would have had very little contact with peasant women. He was discovering a whole new world of light and color that had been hidden from him during his earlier years in Holland. Even in Anvers and up until early 1887, he still painted with darkening colors, somber backgrounds, and quasi-depressing scenes. His paintings of shoes are situated precisely at this juncture between the earlier style that marked his work in Holland, and the bright, colorful, even brilliant tones that followed upon his acquaintance with the work of some of the reigning impressionist painters in Paris. The painting of "Old Shoes with Laces" from 1886 is still quite dark and somber. It could accompany those of his earlier years—except that it bears a somewhat brightening yellow in the background, a yellow that was largely absent from the Dutch period. As Heidegger reports in response to a letter from Meyer Schapiro, he saw this painting in a show in Amsterdam in March 1930. Situated alongside other paintings from Van Gogh's earlier 1882–86 period, as might have been the case during the reported 1930 Amsterdam exhibit, Heidegger might have associated the painting of the shoes with paintings of the earlier years when Van Gogh often drew his subject matter from peasant scenes (see, for instance, "Peasants in the Fields" [1883], "Work in the Fields" [1885], or even the famous "Potato-Eaters" [1885]). There is even a painting of wooden shoes—a "Still Life with Wooden Shoes" ("*Nature Morte aux Sabots*") from Spring-Summer 1885 which could satisfy a portion of the description that Heidegger offers. (However, as a still life included with a covered jar and a bottle on a table, it escapes the full sense of world that Heidegger evokes.)

Returning to the question of the subject of the painting, what of those things that Van Gogh had before him as he painted? What of the equipmentality of these shoes? And is it at all important what shoes Van Gogh himself was wearing when he painted "Old Shoes with Laces"? Had Heidegger seen one of the later 1887 paintings of shoes—most notably the one identified as residing in the Baltimore Museum of Art, he might have provided a different account of the equipmentality at hand. This 1887 painting portrays two shoes, one overturned, with the bottom visible, but again with laces from the upright shoe untied and partially escaping from the scene. These shoes are a deep brown, except that the bottom of the overturned shoe is almost illuminated and the extending nails are a distinctive white, making them stand out quite markedly. What is especially remarkable is the blue floor upon which the shoes rest—it is patched with streaks of white that make it almost come alive with energy, almost like the waves of a blue sea. And the "Vincent 87" signature in the lower right corner is almost a pink—in the style of some of his very late paintings, but even more flamboyant and more distinctively inscribed. Had Heidegger considered this painting of shoes, he might have varied his description. But why?

The shoes in the painting that Heidegger discusses are—as he says—without any definite location. The ambiguity of the context allows the interpreter some freedom in the description. But how much? Surely it is not important what shoes Van Gogh was wearing when he painted "Old Shoes with Laces." Nor would it matter what shoes Heidegger was wearing when he wrote about the painting. But given that Heidegger is concerned—in the example at hand—with the relation between "thing" and "work," the shoes that were "actually painted" may not be irrelevant.

But what is this relation between thing and work? Not all works of art have the same relation to those things that are represented, imitated, reproduced, or even interpreted. Kandinsky, Mondrian, Pollack—they all have a relation to things, but the things do not generally appear as represented objects. The subject is not so easily identifiable as in the Van Gogh painting of "Old Shoes with Laces." Except, perhaps, for Mondrian's "Broadway Boogie Woogie," it would be quite difficult to find a thing whose equipmentality is in question in the paintings of Kandinsky, Mondrian, or Pollack—except to the extent that the whole painting might serve a decorative or ambience-producing function. But then the painting itself, rather than the thing represented, provides the equipmental character.

To return to our shoes—and to the question of what shoes Van Gogh had available when he painted "Old Shoes with Laces"—Meyer Schapiro is concerned about the subject: whose shoes are these? There is a question that the shoes might not be those of a peasant woman as Heidegger supposes. But if they are not "*ein Paar Bauernschuhe,*" then presumably they would not disclose a "*Welt der Bäuerin.*" Whose shoes, then, are they? Given that Van Gogh was living in Paris at the time, it is not likely that they are even peasant shoes. Van Gogh was very poor. He had just arrived from Anvers, and before that from the kind of context that Heidegger does, in fact, offer as the world of the peasant woman. Van Gogh was often writing to his brother Theo for money to help him pay for his paints and supplies. He certainly had no money to pay models to sit for him. So he painted landscapes, cityscapes, and objects that were readily available. There is a long tradition, going back to Fillipo Lippi, Leonardo, Rembrandt, and Dürer where the most available subject is oneself—the painter's own body, the painter's torso. The self-portrait has for centuries been the solution to the poor painter's economic limitations. Only a mirror is required, and a model is immediately available. Like Cézanne and other contemporaries, Van Gogh painted many self-portraits. Upon arriving in Paris (early in 1886) he painted himself with a pipe and, indeed quite elegantly dressed—the reddish beard is unmistakable. In the summer of 1887, and again in early 1888, he returned to the self-portrait—sometimes wearing a hat, sometimes not. And many will be familiar with the later self-portraits after he cut off part of his ear—bandaged, yet still intense.

Schapiro's thesis is that Van Gogh was not painting the shoes of a peasant woman but rather his own shoes—shoes that he had perhaps brought with him from the North, shoes that were really boots, with at least eight lace holes on each side. These were substantial boots, boots that were made to last—nothing delicate here—these are shoes that would get one through the cold winters in Paris, as well as most anywhere else. These are rugged boots, made for walking, made for heavy-duty work—characteristics that are all linked to the equipmentality of the shoes or boots. So what if they are not the shoes of a peasant woman, but those of Van Gogh himself?

But then how many shoes did Van Gogh have? Another of the five paintings of shoes that he painted during his two years in Paris portrays no fewer than six shoes—three pairs, one might suppose. Are any of these the same shoes as those in the painting Heidegger discusses? Careful examination shows that there is one "pair" that has no shoe laces—they are boots to be pulled on. These shoes resemble the "pair" that is portrayed in the fifth painting of shoes—the one which is included along with Derrida's essay. As to the other two "pairs," one could easily be the same as in the Baltimore Museum of Art painting. The last set (where one is turned over, as in the Baltimore version) lacks the large protruding nails in the soles.

Can one suppose that Van Gogh made it through that winter of 1886–87 with three pairs of shoes (or boots)? If he had others, he was not telling. Surely the tendency to do self-portraits, to paint his room, to choose fruits and bottles, etc. for his still-lifes suggest that Van Gogh tended to paint whatever was readily available—"personal objects," as Schapiro calls them. The subject then is a personal object—a fetishized object, according to a certain psychoanalysis. Why did Van Gogh paint so many shoes? And assuming that they are indeed his own shoes, what of their equipmentality?

Surely they served a purpose. They might have gotten him through the winter—they would doubtless have been too warm for the summer. But their purposiveness is not Heidegger's concern. He wants to suggest that they are equipment—things that serve, things that can be counted on, that are reliable, that have *Verläßlichkeit*. Do these shoes accomplish that end—even if they are not those of a peasant woman? No doubt they served him well as something to paint. But that is not Heidegger's point. Shall we then transform Heidegger's description to that of a poor painter who arrives in the big city, in Paris, who struggles to find the needed sustenance so that he can rise each day to return to his canvases, who cannot afford a new pair of shoes, who must wear whatever he brought with him, who cannot afford something stylish?

Here is another interpretation than that which Heidegger offers. The hermeneutic brings a set of meanings to life: it sets the shoes—these beings—in relation to Being *(Sein)*. Only the world of the painter has been substituted for that of the peasant woman. The set has changed, the location has changed, the context (city instead of countryside) has changed—but the shoes remain the same. If the world has changed, if the equipmentality has changed, is the thing still the same? The substitution has resulted in a very different object. But where is the difference? Assuming that the *Dienlichkeit* is that of shoes, they serve a very different function in relation to the one who wears them, when they are worn, and where they are worn. And the work of art, is it different?

According to Heidegger, the work of art requires its origination from an artist—just as the artist gains his or her identity from the work. But the thingliness of the work doubtless affects the character of the work. The thingliness of the thing is not in question here. It is the thingliness of the work that is under scrutiny—for there is a problem of a sex change, a place change, and a world change. Van Gogh's shoes are not the same as the peasant woman's shoes. How can the truth of a work which discloses a world be the same truth if it discloses something different?

Leaving the question of the distinction between change and difference here, let us follow Derrida at least one step along the way from the subject matter (the shoes themselves as things which disclose, indecidably, either a peasant woman's world or the painter's world) to a further problem. The problem is again that of Meyer Schapiro: it is possible that the shoes in "Old Shoes with Laces" are not *a pair*. It is not only possible that what Heidegger calls "*ein Paar Bauernschuhe*" are *not* the shoes of a peasant woman but also that they are not a pair either. Indeed two of the six shoes appearing in the painting entitled "Three Pairs of Shoes" could constitute the two in question. The belonging togetherness (the *Zusammengehörigkeit*) of these two shoes may only be that of contiguity or juxtaposition—they may not actually constitute "a pair" at all. They are laced differently; they may be of different height; and so forth.

Belonging togetherness *(Zusammengehörigkeit)* is a formulation which Heidegger employs most particularly in connection with the pairing of Being and beings. If there is a question of the belonging togetherness of the two shoes, as Schapiro wants to show—in honor of Kurt Goldstein, who lasted through a very difficult year in Amsterdam in the late 1930s—could it be that the belonging togetherness of Being and beings should also be questioned? As Derrida points out,[4] another place where Heidegger cites Van Gogh is in the *Introduction to Metaphysics*.[5] There Heidegger is working on the relation of beings to Being. The Van Gogh painting is an example of "what is there" *(Da)*, a being, the what is, the "that"which is present, namely, *Da*—here or there [*Da/Fort - Fort/Da*]. Beings in their relation to Being—a relation that *belongs*

together, that establishes difference, the ontico-ontological difference—is a relation that is repeated in the aesthetic hermeneutic circle: namely, the relation of
the work to the artist and the artist to the work.

But while wanting to separate Heidegger from his interpretation of the Van
Gogh painting, it could be claimed that Schapiro has accomplished just the
opposite. For if indeed the shoes in question are in fact those of the artist and
not those of a peasant woman, in painting his own shoes (even if they are different shoes, not a pair of shoes), Van Gogh the artist (who belongs together with
his work) and the artwork itself are brought together in the difference established by the *Zusammengehörigkeit*. And the bringing together of artist and
artwork is the place where Art (which is the origin of both) discloses, brings out
of concealment, establishes itself in the place of difference. Hence the nonpair-
ing of the shoes, like the sex change of their subjecthood, marks a difference and
prepares the being together.

IDENTITY/APPROPRIATION

The difficulty here is that the difference in question is not the same difference.
The difference—or better, the distinction *(die Unterscheidung)*—between the
peasant woman's shoes and the artist's shoes is not the same difference as the
ontico-ontological difference *(die ontisch-ontologische Differenz)*. Repeated in the
case of the work of art in its relation to the artist as Art, the difference (as
Differenz) is marked by the truth *(aletheia)* of the work of art. Art is the disclosure of the work as *Differenz*.

This *Differenz* is also the identity of Art. So we return to our question, asked
in another way. What is the identity of the two shoes as a work of art? The
answer will have to reside—for Heidegger—in the relation of the painting of
the two shoes to that with which it is paired, namely Van Gogh. By showing
that the two shoes are most likely those of the artist, the disclosure in the
belonging together of artwork and artist brings out the identity of the shoes. In
this sense, Art (at least with respect to the Van Gogh painting of two shoes
called "Old Shoes with Laces") is not a matter of peasant life, not a matter of the
truth or disclosure of this ponderous life that Heidegger describes, but more
specifically a question of the truth in shoe sizes. Out of the difference between
the peasant woman's experience and the artist's experience comes the truth in
shoe size. Surely the peasant woman's shoe size will not be the same as that of
Van Gogh the artist. The difference *(Unterscheidung)* is marked at the place of
Art, at the place of *Differenz*, at the place where—as Derrida has shown elsewhere—the difference is also a sexual difference, a question of *Geschlecht*.

The disclosure of sexual difference is inscribed in the place of ontological difference. Male shoes are not the same as female shoes. But the difference is a
matter of distinction, a question of *Unterschied*. The difference itself, however,
raises the question of the relation to Being, and that relation to Being is a matter
of ontological *Differenz*. Hence the dislocation of the shoes as things; and the

dis-pairing of the two shoes in fact inscribes ontological difference out of sexual difference.

And what of the sex of these shoes? Derrida cites a 1916 study by Ferenczi entitled *Sinnreiche Variante des Schuhsymbols der Vagina* (*Verité*, p. 305; *TP*, p. 267). Reading shoes as a vagina, the convex shape of the shoe is linked up with the concave shape of the foot. The shoe envelops the foot, says Derrida. Not only is the difference marked by the differing activities of the peasant woman and the artist, but also there is a sexual difference to be noted here. The belonging together, not of the two shoes, but of the shoe and the foot is duly noted. But as Freud has pointed out, and as Derrida remarks, *the* shoe is no more the penis than the vagina. The outer shape of the shoe corresponds with its inner shape. This bisexuality of the shoe—to which Derrida returns at intervals—brings out a tendency in childhood to ignore sexual difference. Freud adds that most dreams are bisexual and can be linked to the organs of both sexes (*Verité*, p. 306, *TP*, p. 268). Hence the shoe (like the umbrella in Derrida's account of Nietzsche's "I have forgotten my umbrella")[6] read as a sexual indecidable—as either male or female or both—discloses the shoe as the paradigmatic place of sexual difference. Like the "pair" (?) of gloves which Van Gogh painted in January 1889, the inside also carries with it the outside. While the foot fits in the appropriate shoe, Derrida demonstrates that the shoe itself—a personal object like the glove—is both concave and convex. The truth of the shoe, then, is its bisexuality and its identity of indecidable sexual difference.

The identity of the subject of the shoes is outside the work—a *parergon*. The work, the *ergon*, marks an otherness in relation to the shoes as *parergon*. The shoes are marginal to the identity of the work. In order for the work to establish its identity, in order for it to appropriate what is indeed its own, it will have to entertain its relation to the artist—or so the hermeneutic move goes. A deconstruction of the work "Old Shoes with Laces" will distinguish the work from its *parergon*. And the indecidability of that difference—the difference in shoe size, shoe sex, shoe space—expropriates the relation of shoes as "things" to shoes as "work" to the place of "Art," namely, the relation of the artwork to artist.

The laces of the shoes are supposed to have, as their primary function, as what is readily available, the tying together of what is separate. But the shoes themselves are unlaced—and so too is the relation of thing to work, the relation of work to truth, and the relation of truth to Art. This tripartite set of relations constitutes the three main sections of the "Origin of the Work of Art." Heidegger's task is to tie them together, to weave the three sections, to tie the knot, and to close the discussion. The shoes—the painting of "Old Shoes with Laces"—is the metaphor for the task of the essay itself: to tie together, to weave together, what would otherwise remain separate. For this reason as well it is appropriate to substitute the artist's shoes for those of the peasant woman.

The laces pass through the lace holes—*oeillets* as they are called in French—that is, the "eyelets." Passing the laces through the eyelets brings the whole thing together. It is perhaps not insignificant that Van Gogh, during his two years in Paris, painted a number of "Still Lifes" (*Nature Mortes*) of flowers, and especially the *Oeillet*—bouquets of *oeillets*. The synecdoche of the eyelets for the *nature mortes* in general indicates that Van Gogh's whole enterprise was not only to identify the paintings as separate studies, but also to open the possibility of tying them together, linking them—as Heidegger does with the sections of the "Origin of the Work of Art."

"Around this pair of peasant shoes (*souliers de paysan*) there is nothing to which they could belong [*wozu und wohin sie gehören könnten*]—only an indefinite space" (*Verité*, p. 385; *TP*, p. 337). The belonging of the shoes is indeed a concern. To what do they belong? They belong to an indefinite space. This belonging is repeated in the relation of belonging of artwork and artist. Heidegger names this belonging, this appropriateness, this tying together—Art. Art is the place of disclosure of what is appropriate—as appropriate of artwork to artist as of thing to artwork. This repetition, or doubling, even *Doppelgänger* (writes Derrida), is the place of belonging, of what is proper, of what is the artwork's own: its identity in the truth of shoe size. The working of origin (artwork/artist/Art) is the tying together, or the belonging together in the truth in the painting—in this case, the truth in shoe size.

EXCHANGE/RESTITUTION

Heideggerian hermeneutics wants to interpret the Van Gogh painting—which Derrida calls "Old Shoes with Laces"—in relation to the equipmentality (*Zeugsein*) of actual shoes. The project of understanding the work in relation to the thing makes it possible to tell a story about the thing, to show that it evokes or discloses a world—for Heidegger, the world of a peasant woman. The world disclosed is the truth, not of the shoes but of the work, of the work in relation to the artist. But in Heidegger's account of the peasant woman, the artist is absent. In the 1968 correspondence between Meyer Schapiro and Martin Heidegger, the evidence is offered by Heidegger, gathered by Schapiro, and returned to Heidegger in that Schapiro demonstrates Heidegger's misreading of the shoes in the painting. By disclosing the misreading, Schapiro makes Heidegger's point even more effectively.

These shoes (or boots, really) belong to, are appropriate to, provide an event (an *Ereignis*) for the disclosure of the relation of the artwork to the artist—and hence an uncovering of Art. Heidegger's dislocation of "origin" to the place of difference is rendered particularly effective as a result of the correspondence and ultimate exchange which Schapiro provides. The interpretation of shoes, replaced by a deconstructive reading of shoe sizes—literally "shoe points" (although these are hardly "pointed" shoes)—identifies the place of what Heidegger calls "Art." The shoes have become an instance of a text whose textuality is not just a matter of truth but of the specific shape, size, and belonging of the shoes that are disclosed.

Out of the correspondence which becomes an exchange—a substitution of peasant woman shoes, the shoes of someone from the country, with "the shoes

of the artist, by that time a man of the town and city" (Schapiro's expression)—
Schapiro provides the evidence with which the deconstruction operates to
produce a reading of the Heidegger text, now tied to the Schapiro text, that
brings out "even more clearly" the truth of the Heidegger text. Just as the shoes
are a *parergon* in relation to the artwork, so the Schapiro text is a *parergon*—a
context—for Heidegger's "Origin." Schapiro's text dislocates Heidegger's origin
one step further: the critical philosophical correspondence turned into a shoe
exchange discloses, gives truth to, the Heideggerian hermeneutic—in spite of
both correspondents. The *parergon* enframes, traps (in its detective-like procedure), but in the process opens up the textual space, namely the textuality of the
ousia: Art as an ontico-ontological difference.

The correspondence between Heidegger and Schapiro accomplishes an
exchange, a substitution of a woman's shoes for a man's shoes—those of the
artist—which had "originally" been substituted (by Heidegger) for the artist's
shoes in the first place. In the grand rhetorical tradition from Aristotle and
Quintillian and on, metaphor involves an operation of substitution. Is the substitution of the peasant woman's shoes for the artist's shoes a metaphorical
operation? Is Heidegger really trying to talk about the artist's self-constitution in
Art by replacing the artist's shoes with those of a peasant woman? Heidegger,
with his peasant background, sees in these shoes his own experience. Is it not
really an effort at substituting his own biographical circumstances for those of
the artist? Does he not see himself, the philosopher, the thinker, on a *Denkweg*
which is closely associated with a *Feldweg?* Is not the philosopher associated—as
in Hegel—with the artist: the philosopher as a kind of thought-artist? The substitution of the peasant woman's shoes for the artist's shoes arises in the context
of the philosopher's "personal" experience, his "personal" acquaintance with
fields, soil, earth, the "silent call of the earth," the "quiet gift of the ripening
grain," and the "unexplained self-refusal in the fallow desolation of the wintry
field" (*PLT-OWA*, p. 34; *Holz*, p. 23). Gadamer, for instance, who edited the
essay "The Origin of the Work of Art" for the 1960 Reclam edition—himself,
the son of a university professor in Marburg, a "man of the town and city"—
would not slip into the substitution that Heidegger offers. And Schapiro, also a
man of the town and the city—especially "*the*" city, New York City—would be
careful to note the attribution of shoes, to detect differences in "style." After all,
Schapiro's famous essay on the "concept of style" is well known among art theorists and critics. Neither Gadamer nor Schapiro would permit a substitution
such as the one that Heidegger makes; they would be too attentive to those sub-
tle ontic distinctions, distinctions that one of discernment, one of taste, one of
bürgerliche Gespräch would want to notice.

But what does this substitution accomplish? Heidegger ties together the peasant world with the world of the artist. He does so by replacing the artist's shoes
with the peasant woman's shoes. He makes a *pair* out of two *disparate* worlds.
Supposing that the shoes in the painting are not even a pair, but two left shoes,
can it not be said that Heidegger twice makes a pair out of what is not—on the
surface—a pair at all. He shows the belonging togetherness of two disparate

worlds—the world of the peasant and the world of the artist. And not any artist, but Vincent Van Gogh, who from 1888 to 1890, after leaving Paris, paints intensely—out of a kind of madness—during his final two years. The mid-1930s were also the years when Heidegger was lecturing and writing books about Nietzsche—who also went mad in 1888, writing (as Van Gogh painted) madly for his final year, leading into the year 1889. Nietzsche survived until 1900, while Van Gogh, confined to an Auvers sanitorium, died in 1890. These years of intensity were not insignificant for Heidegger. For instance, Heidegger himself was born in 1889. Would Heidegger have simply ignored this coincidence, his birth year corresponding to the years of crisis and even madness for Van Gogh, for Nietzsche—Van Gogh with his shoes, Nietzsche with (or without) his umbrella—objects which, for Derrida, are charged with sexual indecidability, *loci* of deconstructive intrigue?

Heidegger's substitution of the peasant shoes—perhaps recalling his own shoes, putting himself in the peasant woman's shoes, trying them on, testing them to see if they fit—accomplishes not only a substitution of one set of things for another, but a transformation in the meaning of the artwork. And the transformation in the meaning of the artwork is accomplished by a transformation in the artist as well—the philosopher or thinker as artist. Heidegger was interested in writing poetry. He wrote some. He was an artist of words (thinking and poetizing) rather than an artist of paint (painting). Hence when it comes to an account of the nature of art, he names it poetry *(Dichtung)*: "The nature of art is poetry. The nature of poetry in turn is the founding of truth" (*PLT-OWA*, p. 75; *Holz*, p. 62). Heidegger the poet, the philosopher, the thinker sees the nature of Art as poetry, as *Dichtung*. Indeed, Heidegger's account of the peasant woman's world resembles some of his own poetry. The poetry is pastoral, imbedded in a world tied to nature:

> When through a rent in the rain-clouded
> sky a ray of the sun suddenly glides
> over the gloom of the meadows… (*PLT*, p. 6).

And again:

> or when the mountain brook in night's
> stillness tells of its plunging
> over the boulders… (*PLT*, p. 10).

These poems link the pastoral with the philosophical:

> when the cowbells leap tinkling from
> the slopes of the mountain valley
> where the herds wander slowly….
> The poetic character of thinking is
> still veiled over (*PLT*, p. 12).

Although written in 1947, these poems from *Aus der Erfahrung des Denkens*[7] show the persistent link that Heidegger makes between the pastoral elements in his experience with the path of the thinker. As poet, as artist, Heidegger would substitute poetry for painting (a theme that recurs from Horace to Lessing to Sartre, who also in 1947 takes up the topic). But the poet—taking the place of the artist as painter—in this case tries to wear the shoes of the painter. Do they fit?

In researching the question, Meyer Schapiro makes explicit that the substitution has taken place—at least with respect to the shoes. But while Schapiro is attempting to tie up the loose ends, to bring together what seems not to fit in the story, instead of tying a rope around Heidegger's neck, the *piège* does not work. Heidegger has escaped; because indeed he is "really" substituting himself—the interpreter, for Van Gogh the artist, the painter. Hence the relation between artist and artwork, its mutuality and *Zusammengehörigkeit* has been accomplished.

But what of Art, the third term in this relation? If the shoes in question are really Heidegger's shoes, and the artist in question is really Heidegger, then what he is calling Art *(die Kunst)* is really a self-portrait—or more specifically, self-portraiture. The experience of the thinker is the textuality of the self-portrait; Heidegger himself is the text in question, and Art *(die Kunst)* is its textuality.

And I return to Derrida, who writes:

> I suggest we come back to the passage in which, with the frame [*le cadre*] playing discretely [inaudible moment of the lace], the event, which is keeping us here with its police, political, historical, psychoanalytical stakes, happens [*se produit en silence l'événement qui nous retient ici avec ces enjeux policiers, politiques, psychoanalytiques*]. The border [*la bordure*] between this text (in the usual and supposedly strict sense of a thing printed in a book) and a general textuality with no absolute edge [*sans bord absolu*] here comes away [*s'y enlève*].

> *S'y enlève* (comes away): in the sense of a Gestalt appearing against a background? Or else of something that is effaced and lost?

> Perhaps both: Both can be "at work" [*à l'oeuvre*] (*Verité*, p. 373; *TP*, p. 327).

As one learns from the 1960 addendum to the "Origin of the Work of Art," not only the work of art but also Art itself is enframed, given shape, put into a form [*ge-stellt*]. *Stellen*—the setting-into-frame—is not only the demarcation of a border [*une bordure*] for the work but a delimiting of its frame: what is to be included and what is to be excluded, what belongs inside and what is outside, what fits and what does not fit. The work of art is like a shoe—not every description fits. The task of the art critic—the task of hermeneutics—is to determine what fits and what does not, to outline and posit (*stellen*) the meaning or meanings *(Sinne)* of the work of art. A deconstruction of the artwork will understand it in its textuality in the place demarcated by what Heidegger calls Art, in the place where truth happens, in the place of difference, in the event of the textualizing of the work. That the invocation of "Old Shoes with Laces" demonstrates a textuality that can be characterized as philosophical self-portraiture—namely, Heidegger's own experience as text—is brought to the fore through the correspondence and the exchange that Schapiro introduces. The extent to which Derrida enters into the exchange—as I do as well—is another illustration of a SARL: a *société anonyme à responsabilité limité* [S.A., Co., INC., Ltd.],[8] a speech act in which the exchange brings about the content, at the same time, in the same event….

But what is actually accomplished by this exchange? Derrida suggests that it is a kind of restitution, a debt paid back. But to whom? To Heidegger? To Van Gogh? To Schapiro? To Goldstein? To Lebensztejn? To Derrida? To us, the readers of Heidegger, Derrida, *et al?* Or to…?

Restitution is a rebuilding of what was undone, a moment of restoration, a giving back, not just a giving (as in Heidegger's *es gibt.*) Is Derrida, then, restoring to Heidegger what Schapiro has taken away? Is Schapiro restoring to Kurt Goldstein what he lost in 1933 when he escaped Nazi Germany, spending a year in Amsterdam and finally becoming a faculty member at Columbia University from 1936 to 1940? Schapiro, who spoke at the memorial service for Goldstein in 1965, may have been returning to the memory of his friend once again by his essay. Is Derrida restoring to J. C. Lebensztejn (a Polish painter and friend in Paris, whose name is rendered only as "J.C….sztejn") both the metonymy of his name with that of Goldstein or of his profession with that of Van Gogh? Am I by this essay restoring to Jacques Derrida the debt I owe him since June 1972 in Paris when I first met him upon the occasion of a weekend seminar in which a small group of mostly American philosophers (including Marjorie Grene, Hubert Dreyfus, Arthur Danto, Marx Wartofsky, Victor Gourevitch, Charles Rosen, Hélène Cixous, Jeffrey Mehlman, and Kathleen McLaughlin) was led through his deconstructive paces for the full three days? The debts are many— and they are all surely worthy.

Painters render things or objects. For example, a painter such as Van Gogh will render *(rendre)* shoes in a particular way. The French word *rendre* however, also means "to render," "to give back," "to restore," "to give restitution." Is Van Gogh, then, restoring to the shoes their "essence" (*Wesen*) by rendering them in his painting? Is Heidegger taking that essence away when he gives them to a peasant woman? Is Schapiro giving the shoes' essence back when he demonstrates that the shoes "actually belong" to Van Gogh as "personal" objects? Is Derrida returning the essence of the shoes to Heidegger when he tries to "render justice to Heidegger, restitute what is his due, his truth, the possibility of his own gait and progress" [*rendre justice à Heidegger, de lui restituer son dû, sa verité, la possibilité de sa marche et de son cheminement propre?*]" (*Verité*, p. 343; *TP*, p. 301). And am I restoring the picture that Derrida paints of the correspondence by proposing that the "Art" that Heidegger describes in "The Origin of the

Work of Art" is itself a text whose textuality is that of Heideggerian self-portraiture? The shoes that Heidegger reads are ultimately *his own*.

"*Je vous dois la verité en peinture*" is derived from a letter (a correspondence)
between Cézanne and the painter Émile Bernard in 1905. The debt is also that
of Heidegger. He is concerned to show how truth—*aletheia*—discloses, operates
in the relation of the painting to the artist and on the relation of the painting as
work along with the artist to Art. For Heidegger the movement from work and
artist to Art and back again to the work opens up a space—a space for truth, a
space for *Dichtung*, the essence of Art, the disclosure of the textuality of
Heidegger's whole "personal" enterprise. Heidegger as well owes truth in painting—just as banks in the United States have an obligation called "truth in
lending," a "financial disclosure," as it is called—a disclosure in which all debts
and assets are to be made explicit. Here truth in painting has become truth in
shoe sizes. But truth in shoe sizes is in turn returned to truth in painting, truth
in Art, truth in thinking, truth in textuality.

I shall end the exchange, the movement, this chapter, with a passage from
Derrida:

> Let us admit that in this way we have just reconstituted, resituated, a cer-
> tain trajectory of *The Origin*, by interpreting it, by negotiating with it. Let
> us admit that this trajectory had to pass *via* the very uselessness of the
> shoes *and* of the painting, of the product and the work; that it needed to
> speculate on this out-of-service lacing across the line in both directions,
> making come back, making go away, making come back again, inside,
> outside, down there, here, *fort, da*. (Heidegger holds the thing, the shoes,
> by the lace and plays with the bobbin
>
> —which is, for Schapiro, playing in the same way, that of Van Gogh, "a
> piece of his own life," "facing us."
>
> —drawing it toward him and then making it go away thanks to the relia-
> bility of the lace) (*Verité*, pp. 407–8; *TP* p. 357).

IV

Visible/Scriptive
Textualities

14

THE PHOTOBIOGRAPHICAL TEXTUALITY OF
THE PHILOSOPHER'S BODY
Sartre/Heidegger

The philosophical text presents itself as a monument. It stands sturdy and stead-fast. It requires a world to make it plausible. It requires a philosopher to animate it. Readings of a philosophical text proliferate—they are multiplied and dissemi-nated. Explications, commentaries, analyses, justifications, objections, criticisms, developments...elaborate the philosophical text, rendering it philo-sophically valid, significant—respectable. Even when such texts address themselves to the problem of the body they are not thereby concerned with the philosopher's body. They remain disincarnate. The philosopher's body is some-thing other. It does not enter into the movement, action, argument, or position of the text. Even if the philosopher's intentions are incorporated into the philo-sophical text, the philosopher's body is left aside. The philosopher's body remains something other.

When, however, the text in question is not a philosophical text per se with its disquisitions, propositions, and interrogations, but rather a photograph of the philosopher, then the philosopher's body itself becomes the *topos*. The body in the photograph is not embodied there. The face, the expression, the gait, the place of the hands, the relationship to other people, even the context are there in the photograph. Yet they do not produce a philosophy. They do not consti-tute a life. They do not enact an experience. The philosopher's body announces itself in the body of the photograph. But the body *of* the photograph is not the body *in* the photograph. The body of the photograph is the text and context in which the philosopher's body appears. The body in the photograph is what is inscribed there.

Two philosophers (Martin Heidegger and Jean-Paul Sartre)—perhaps the most celebrated of this century in their respective countries—independently occasioned the 1978 publication of two separate volumes of photographs.[1] With the deaths of these two philosophers (Heidegger in 1976, Sartre in 1980), what remains is the body of their work, the memory of their vitality, and the photographs of moments captured during their lifetimes. Despite enormous differences in the environments, periods, and situations which mark these two volumes, the photographs themselves incorporate the philosophies, attitudes, and above all the bodies of the two philosophers. Like the philosophies produced by the two men, these volumes have a life of their own. The photographs survive the deaths of the philosophers. They animate bodies which can no longer speak for themselves. They give expression to what is not expressed in words and to what is not dreamed of in their philosophies. In the photographs Heidegger's body and Sartre's body are not philosophical bodies—except as they represent the body philosophizing. They are bodies—caught in the act—like any of us who might have been captured for reasons of posterity, personal recollection, or even official documentation. Yet they are not just any body; they are the philosopher's body—and a specific body in each case. The life that rendered the photographs possible is specified in the documentation. The philosopher's body philosophizes without speaking, and like the philosophical text, the body in the photograph acquires a renown of its own. For those who never met either philosopher personally, because they were not fortunate enough or because they did not desire it, the body of the photograph constitutes another dimension, another experience...another text.

At the end of the book entitled *Roland Barthes* (1975), Roland Barthes offers the following statement: "To write the body. Neither the skin, nor the bones, nor the nerves, but the rest: an awkward, fibrous, shaggy, ravelled thing, a clown's coat" (*RB*, pp. 180–81). The statement accompanies an eighteenth-century anatomical sketch of the stems and branches of the *Vena cava* dissected in an adult body. How does one "write the body"—not with sketches, caricatures, drawings, or even paintings—but with photographs? Before beginning the written text of this "autobiography," Barthes provides a series of photographs. For each of these photographs, he offers a short commentary. Thus we have not only the photographs of the body in question, but also the words of the self which accompanies them. He contrasts the photographs of himself—his body— with a photograph of a doctor's chart indicating the recurrence of tuberculosis, with the remark: "Every month, a new sheet was pasted on the bottom of the old one; at the end, there were yards of them: a farcical way of writing one's body within time" (*RB*, p. 35). Like someone looking at a series of photographs of himself just back from the developers, the commentary turns into a narrative—as if the body in the photograph were someone else—perhaps an action in a film, perhaps some famous personage in a magazine, perhaps a clown in the circus, but in any case, "not me." Yet there is also a familiarity, an understanding, an interest. What Barthes says about himself lighting a cigarette with his left hand—"Left-handed" (*RB*, p. 42)—does not strike the reader as an idle, informative, even plausible commentary by someone else. The autobiographical features of the remark situate themselves somewhere at the interface between the photograph and the description. "That's my body," he might have said, announcing the place of an embodied self between the image and the word

"Left-handed." Indeed, the words repeat the photograph a number of pages earlier in which his mother is seated holding the baby Roland Barthes in her arms. The older Barthes comments: "The mirror stage: 'That's you'" (*RB*, p. 21). In appealing to this Lacanian formulation, Barthes identifies himself with the photograph of what seems to demonstrate a stage of infantile development. The body in the photograph is like one's own image in a mirror—the eyes are directed straight ahead. "Is that me whom I see there?" one might ask. The "me" one sees is one's own body. Yet the body that is presented can only be a picture. It is not the lived body.

Merleau-Ponty's contribution to an understanding of the body was to have interpreted the body as lived. The body is not animated like a pilot in a ship nor is it a prison for the soul as Plato suggested. The body is not a functional unity in concert with the soul as Aristotle argued. Nor is the body extension as in Descartes, or a machine as La Mettrie proposed. For Merleau-Ponty, the body is lived through in an intentional arc. Where Husserl distinguished between the physical body *(Körper)* and the phenomenologically reduced transcendental living body *(Leib)*,[2] Merleau-Ponty understood all physical human body as already lived through, incarnate, expressive, perceptual, and free. As he noted in his last writings, the body is a visible which sees, a visibility which bridges a gap *(un écart)*, a seeing which renders the invisible visible through a "perceptual faith." The photograph of a body is thus a visible that marks the place of a visibility which remains virtual. The photograph cannot fulfill all the expectations one might have of it were it a living body. Yet the photograph renders visible what is unavailable to memory, imagination, and even construction. The body in the photograph cannot—does not—see, yet its textuality is a visibility. The visibility of a living body—seeing and seen, touching and touched—appears as a text in the photograph. The picture of the body is a picturing which holds in abeyance the impossibility of it seeing as it is seen. Yet the possibility that the body in the photograph might see, touch, hear, smell, and taste is never realized. The visibility of the body in the photograph is an unrealized possibility which becomes a text. The philosopher's body in the photograph offers a philosophizing body as a textuality—even when a philosophical stance is not represented. Whatever picture of Sartre or Heidegger may be offered up to the public will embody the textuality of a philosophical presence. The interest in a photograph of Sartre or Heidegger—whether he be standing before an audience at a conference, sitting at his desk, attending to a manuscript, walking in the woods, lighting a cigarette, eating dinner, or brushing his teeth—is an interest in a celebrated philosopher, thinker, or writer. The very same positions held by just anyone would not suffice. The textuality of the philosopher's body is not the textuality of just any body. The textuality of the philosopher's body enhances, informs, and perhaps even incarnates the philosophy itself.

The two volumes of photographic studies—one of Heidegger, the other of Sartre—were occasioned by different conditions. Although both were published in 1978, Heidegger requested specifically that the photographs taken of him not be published until after his death. They record a series of pictures taken at his house in Freiburg and at his hut in Todtnauberg on September 23, 1966, and again at the Todtnauberg hut and at his house in Freiburg on the 17th and 18th of June, 1968. The photography was realized by Digne Meller Marcovicz. Heidegger was 86 years old when he died in Freiburg on May 26, 1976. Thus the photographs, produced within a span of two years, were at least a decade old when they appeared. They are a record of a thinking reed—as Pascal called us— inscribed in a book as the trace of a thought which also reappears in the form of printed words, disciples, commentators, and dissidents. These photographs serve as an archive of an ontological questioning which speaks only as ontic outlines on a glossy page. The situations were apparently selected in a predetermined way—and although Heidegger is shown with wife, colleagues, and friends, he is also posing for a camera.

By contrast, the photographs of Sartre trace a life from that of a very young child to that of a man nearing his death on April 15, 1980. The photographs of Sartre were taken by a number of different photographers—each catching him and his bodily presence—in situations which could best be characterized as impromptu. They show Sartre *en situation* and often not quite prepared to be recorded for posterity. Unlike the long 1972 film production entitled *Sartre*,[3] which shows him holding forth in his flat (or sometimes in that of Simone de Beauvoir) and which is interspersed with scenes out of his life, the volume gathered together by his friend Liliane Sendyk-Siegel captures some of the diversity of his contexts, experiences, and commitments. It shows him at home in Paris, traversing the dunes of Lithuania, discoursing with French soldiers in Portugal, sitting beside a statue of a pharaoh in Egypt, photographing a house in Japan, standing under an arch with Simone de Beauvoir and some friends in China, conversing with Castro in Cuba, meeting with Tito in Vienna, walking with Simone de Beauvoir in Stockholm, and so on. The contexts multiply and Sartre is clearly at home in all of them. Published during his lifetime, he might not have actually seen some of the more recent photos due to the blindness which afflicted him in later years. In a certain respect, although he continued his personal enterprise—even appearing on television less than a year before he died—the case of Jean-Paul Sartre was already in the hands of others at the time of his death. Friends, colleagues, and commentators were hard at work rounding out his contribution—interviews were produced, unpublished manuscripts were manicured, a major colloquium on his work was held at Cerisy-la-Salle in Normandy (during the summer of 1979), a large volume of the review *Obliques* was devoted entirely to Sartre, and a special issue of *Critique* on the "Sartre Effect" was announced. Although the man now no longer lives, the dossier is hardly closed. Yet while his record will be read, studied, analyzed, critiqued, and continued, the record of his bodily presence is conserved in the series of photographs.

The two separate volumes represent very different yet related philosophical lives. The sets of photographs indicate, on the one hand, a contemplative life grounded and elaborated in the Black Forest and, on the other hand, an active life devoted to the establishment of human freedom throughout the world.

They are related in that the two philosophers were well aware of each other's work on the existentialization of Husserl's transcendental phenomenology. Heidegger's enterprise was already under way when Sartre went to Germany in the early 1930s—thus *Being and Nothingness* (1943) doubles *Being and Time* (1927) in its Gestalt if not also in its detail. To insist upon some sort of influence has no value here. Rather the repetition of a textuality—which has often gone under the name of "existential phenomenology"—is far more significant. Yet in juxtaposing the two volumes of photographs *Martin Heidegger: Photos* and *Sartre: Images d'une vie*, the textuality in question is not the same as that arising out of the juxtaposition of *Sein und Zeit* and *L'Etre et le néant*. Although, by the present juxtapositional reading, both photographic studies contain the opposition Heidegger/Sartre, one elaborates a phenomenological ontology (as Sartre called it) and the other a contextualized corporeality. This second type of textually contextualized corporeality can be called photobiographical textuality. It recounts a life by writing it in pictures. Lodged somewhere between the self-portrait and the official portrait (in painting), between autobiography and biography (in the domain of letters), between my life and that of another (in human experience), photobiographical textuality stresses the corporeality of Sartre and Heidegger. Photobiographical textuality "interprets" the philosopher's body somewhere between thought and action. Although the body is represented statically, it is nevertheless in the middle of something—tending toward an expression which remains incomplete and unattainable. The body is about to speak, about to light a cigarette, about to smile, about to write, about to object.... The movement will never be fulfilled, the words never pronounced, and the thought never realized. Yet the corporeality of the photobiographical textuality is distinctively that of Heidegger or of Sartre. No confusion arises. There is no doubt—particularly with all the photographs incorporated into one volume. It is Heidegger there in the mountains with his walking stick or Sartre seated there in the cafe with pen in hand. The photobiographical textuality of these pictures inscribes the bodily life of the philosopher as a text. Since the text is a photograph, its textuality is visual. The body is to be seen. Touching it, smelling it, listening to it, tasting it, will be disconcerting, for the expectations created by the usual image will be unfulfilled in the other senses. The photo is not a *trompe l'oeil* but it is *trompeur* for the other senses. The black-and-white photos have depth, contrast, and luminosity. These are not the sombre, even sinister, portraits of a New York Times article reporting the philosopher's death. These photographs have a vitality and animation with their own expression, their own voice, their own being. The bodies which they incorporate have a life of their own—even in the photograph. The bodies originate in the photograph and signify their expressivity and contextuality.

Published in the same year—one in France, the other in Germany, the two volumes of photos are approximately the same size and length (less than 120 pages). The principal similarities stop there. The Heidegger volume is primarily synchronic. Heidegger is shown at the ages of 77 to 79. His renown and achievements are already accomplished. Photographed in his years of retirement,

Heidegger exhibits an authority, complacency, and wisdom worthy of a recognized philosopher. The Sartre volume is primarily diachronic. It begins with a little boy of about four years old standing on a boat with a sail in one hand and a staff in the other. The caption—by Simone de Beauvoir, who is responsible for the commentaries—echoes the title of a Gauguin painting: "A child set off into life. Where is he going? Where did he come from? This album answers your questions. The child's name is Jean-Paul Sartre" (*Sartre: Images*, p. 7). And the volume ends with Sartre seated beside Dr. Michael Stern who wished him a happy seventy-second birthday and who expressed his gratitude for Sartre's concerted efforts in favor of human freedom. Photographed throughout his life, Sartre is presented according to his development from youth to old age, from a young boy in the arms of his mother to one of the most celebrated personalities in French intellectual life. The genesis of a writer, thinker, and activist is followed through its various stages of achievement.

The Heidegger volume is officially divided into three parts: (1) Freiburg and Todtnauberg (1966); (2) Todtnauberg (1968); and (3) Freiburg (1968). The two domiciles are the places where Heidegger made his home and in which he was most his own. The passage between the two houses is like a country path between two poles of his being. In fact, the volume is divided further. The first part includes: (1) Heidegger in his Freiburg study talking with three house guests (a fourth guest—the photographer—remains absent from the scene); (2) Heidegger with his guests at the mountain hut; and (3) in-between: the walk up and arrival at the door of the hut. The second part shows the mountain hut and then Heidegger (1) alone inside and outside his hut; (2) with his wife Elfride in the kitchen, dining room, bedroom, and again outside sitting, talking, and walking on the mountainside; and (3) with István Klempa walking through a field. The third part begins and ends with a picture of Heidegger outside the Freiburg house surveying his garden. Most of the photos show him in his study with a couple of views in the dining room.

The book cover is the only color photo in the two volumes—Heidegger is standing at a window in the Todtnauberg cabin. Three strips each with five uncut color views of the same subject are displayed on the back cover. Heidegger's body is divided by the window frame. His hand and arm hang out beyond the frame. His wry quasi-smile tends to project itself from out of the chiaroscuro behind. His eagle eyes peer out of the darkness—and yet his face is illuminated with light and color. His comfortable-looking pullover sweater is partially inside the hut, partially outside. The arm and hand are separated off from the remainder of the body. And yet the hand and the face are linked by color as well—fragmented by the sweater, shirt, and tie. The fragmentation occurs along different lines—here cut by the window frame, there by the sweater. One could imagine André Breton describing this scene when, in his *Manifesto of Surrealism*, he writes: "There is a man cut in two by a window."[4] The fragmentation is not physical mutilation. It is accomplished by an act of photographic expertise. Heidegger is enframed—the window is a kind of *Ge-stell*, so too is the sweater; but the ultimate *Ge-stell* is the camera itself. The instrument accomplishes the fragmentation of the body. Like a statue made of cement and clay, divided into various parts so as to facilitate transportation, Heidegger's body is segmented by a photo-grammatological act. The division is further accomplished by a reproduced Ektachrome negative: Heidegger squared off by the window frame. He looks down, he looks up, he looks to the right, he looks to the left, he even looks upward. In the first group, his one hand still hangs out the window; in the second, his other hand—and even his head—take position on the other side. He is enframed; he is fragmented; he is divided from himself.

Like the Heidegger volume, *Sartre: Images d 'une vie* is divided into a number of official parts: (1) the preliminaries: Sartre as a youth, his family, and well-known relative Albert Schweitzer; (2) the professor: from his years at the École Normale Supérieure to 1939 when Sartre was mobilized in the meteorological corps and dressed in military uniform; (3) the writer: not entirely chronological, these photos span the period from as early as 1934 and as late as 1967; (4) the traveler: from 1946 after the war to 1975 and including visits to Italy, Austria, China, Cuba, Brazil, Greece, Russia, Japan, Egypt, Israel, and Portugal; (5) *On a raison de se révolter* (we are right to rebel): the title of Sartre's book of discussions with Pierre Victor and Philippe Gavi[5]—including scenes of Sartre during the 1968 May-June events in France, his visits to Stockholm and Denmark for the Bertrand Russell Tribunal on U.S. War Crimes in Vietnam, his participation in various demonstrations, and his actual arrest connected with the publication of *La Cause du Peuple* in the early 1970s; and (6) seventy years old: Sartre on location for the 1972 film on his life and with his friends for his seventieth birthday. Although largely chronological, the groupings are more explicitly arranged according to the categories officially proposed—though the family scenes at the beginning and the celebrations at the end provide a more rigorously diachronic form. Since Sartre ceased his role as teacher by the end of the Second World War, the section devoted to that topic is limited in its period of selection. He remained however a writer ("*nulla dies sine linea,*" he wrote in *Les Mots*), a world traveler (with an international conscience), and a kind of revolutionary throughout most of his adult life.

While the Heidegger study includes a list of his publications, there are very few captions—only enough to identify the six people who appear in the volume. The Sartre book, however, includes a caption for each of the wide variety of friends and acquaintances who followed him at the various stages of his itinerary. Naturally his fifty-year companion Simone de Beauvoir reappears often in the pictures. In both volumes, however, the philosopher's body is given prominence over the philosopher's words (which are noticeably absent) and even over the captions. What speaks, what announces itself most distinctly is the philosopher's body itself.

But what sort of bodies are these? Sartre has big feet, big hands and big ears, all of which extend oddly from his small body. He is noticeably short and wall-eyed. From his last years in the *lycée*, he wears glasses. Until 1968, he is usually seen wearing a suit or jacket with a tie. From 1968 on, the tie disappears completely from his attire. He is often smoking—usually a pipe, but in later years more regularly a cigarette. Only by 1960 at the age of 55 does his hair begin to thin out. He is often smiling, except when writing, discussing, or posing for a camera. Heidegger, by contrast, is there with his familiar brush-like moustache, his piercing eyes, and his controlled smile. He is balding slightly for a man of 77–79—some five to ten years older than the last pictures of Sartre. Heidegger seems to gesture more with his hands than Sartre—sometimes raising his right pointing finger, sometimes holding a large imaginary balloon, and sometimes clasping his hands in front of him. Both men walk upright, but when sitting, they demonstrate years of shoulders bent over a manuscript. Both have multiple circles under their eyes—indices of many hours spent writing. Both have pro- duced a second chin in later years. Heidegger's nose is larger and more fallen than that of Sartre. Except for glasses, a watch, and a pipe or cigarette, Sartre's body is without ornamentation. He is never seen with a hat—except in 1939 when in uniform. Heidegger, however, has several hats for outside or inside his mountain cabin. He always has a tie on—even if he is only wearing a sweater or house jacket. (But then it must be remembered that the period of the Heidegger photos is brief and motivated while Sartre's photos span many years and are often unexpected. Also since Heidegger was sixteen years older than Sartre, he is marked by a different generation and different fashions as well as a different context.) Heidegger wears a watch, and unlike Sartre who never married, Heidegger's gold band wedding ring is distinctively evident on his right hand.

When Sartre is shown at his desk, it is filled with papers sprawled every- where. Piles of reprints are on one side; books, letters, cigarette boxes, and a large Martini ashtray filled with cigarette butts and ashes are strewn elsewhere. The overflowing wastepaper basket is noticeable underneath the desk. Only the books on the shelves are relatively well organized. Heidegger, by contrast, is markedly neat. Books—all upright—line the walls of his large Freiburg study. The desk itself is quite spacious compared to Sartre's. Everything on Heidegger's desk is in its proper place: pencils, pens, papers, books, pentray, calendar, plants, pictures, etc., are all carefully arranged. Even the books in his mountain cabin have their own place on a high shelf in the dining room. Empty shelves adjoin his relatively empty desktop. Papers carefully placed on the shelves are either manuscript pages just completed or paper ready for writing. Is this the differ- ence between a life-long professor (and hence civil servant)—except during the years following the war when he was prohibited from teaching, and in his years of retirement—and a man who gave up the functions of a teacher in order to become a writer (who sets his own hours and his own schedule)?

The philosophy of the body that supports these two forms of bodily presence is also significantly different. The photobiographical textuality that distinguishes Sartre and Heidegger is reproduced in their theories (or interpretations) of the body. With Heidegger, it is most markedly present in its absence. Only on rare occasions in *Sein und Zeit* does he even mention our bodily nature. He specifies however that the Cartesian split between a spiritual and a bodily nature does not pertain—and hence photographs of the body should not be regarded as representations of things. Spatiality is a fundamental characteristic of Dasein's Being-in-the-world. The body is not an ontic correlate of Dasein's Being. Rather the body exhibits a spatiality that is most appropriately situated in the ontological difference between Being and beings. Spatiality is bodily and its manner of being present is the body. The body's equipment, such as eyeglasses, a watch, or a pipe, indicates a directionality for Dasein's spatiality.

When understood in terms of photographs of the body only the ontic—that which is present—appears. Yet the photograph is the ontic manifestation of a bodily presence with its spatiality and equipment. The directionality of bodily spatiality is only indicated in the photograph. Even in those instances where the expression is equivocal, a polyvalent directionality appears in the picture. For instance, in one photo of Heidegger—the fifth from the beginning—he raises his right hand index finger upward. Is he enumerating, objecting, asking for his turn to speak, making a point, indicating something, or simply gesticulating? The spatiality is the same—yet its directionality is variable. Reading the photograph, a possible conflict of interpretations becomes evident. Yet there is no need to resolve the multiplicity or variability. The bodily expression in the photograph indicates Heidegger's Being-in-the-world, but as ontically determined. The multiplicity in the expression emerges in the interpretation. Heidegger's own experience, which allowed the production of the photograph and which is itself situated in the ontological difference, is other than the interpretational multiplicity which arises out of a reading of the photograph per se. The body in the photograph is the present of a bodily presence turned into a static (and sometimes fragmented) image whose possibilities are interpretive rather than lived, whose vitality enters into its photobiographical textuality.

The case of Sartre is again different. Although not as phenomenologically appropriate as the position taken by his former friend and colleague Maurice Merleau-Ponty, Sartre's account of the body is well-developed. What needs to be asked is whether Sartre's philosophy of the body is confirmed by the textuality of the man in the photographs. Although Sartre returns to the question of the body on a number of occasions—often when providing a philosophico-biographical account, as in his studies of Baudelaire, Genet, Flaubert, and even his own childhood experience—his basic formulation occurs in the second chapter of the third part of *L'Être et le néant*. In distinguishing three ontological dimensions of the body, Sartre offers a justification for the position occupied by the photographs. Although he relegates his own treatment of photographs to his earlier study of the imagination, he could well describe the body in the photograph as indicative of the second ontological dimension. The body in the photograph can no longer be for-itself (the first dimension); it has been objectified in the photograph. Its consciousness of itself as body no longer functions. Similarly the body in the photograph cannot be for-itself as an object for others (the third dimension)—since it is no longer for-itself. Thus if one were to interpret the body in the photograph as one of the three dimensions, it is most likely to be the body for others *(pour autrui)* as, without noticing, sitting in a restaurant, that someone else is watching. Looking at the body in the photograph then is like being caught in the act, captured in the middle of something—objectified in the process. But the body in the photograph was caught in the act only once—not like the young Jean Genet caught stealing and thereby continuously becoming the criminal that others made of him. Someone could take the photograph as a point of departure for his or her own experience, but this would be a subsequent feature of the body of the photograph and not a reading per se of the photographic text.

The body in the photograph, however, cannot simply be a body for others; it is an analogue of the three-dimensional being of Sartre's body. The body, reduced to a body for others, operates as an image of the body. For example, in the photograph of Sartre writing at a table outside the cafe Le Dôme, his eyes are oriented downward toward the paper on the table (*Sartre: Images*, p. 43). He does not notice that he is photographed. Yet the textuality of Sartre pictured sitting there is one of a writer writing. His whole being is oriented toward what he is writing—he is the consciousness (of) what he is writing, he is *for* the photographer who has captured him there, and he is *for* the subsequent viewer of the photograph. But his orientation toward writing is not writing itself—it is the *analogon* of writing.

The body in the photograph is a textualized presence. As the correlate of a lived bodily experience, it is inscribed in a visual text. The text—the photograph—had a body of its own. What is appropriate to the body of the photograph is not always appropriate to the body of the philosopher. The philosopher—such as Heidegger—perhaps does not want to be shown talking to colleagues with his hand flat on his head, to be mistaken for someone playing the game of "Simon Says." Or Sartre may not be happy shown walking alongside Simone de Beauvoir indicating that he is much shorter than she. Yet the body of the photograph gives signification and contextualization to the philosopher's body as the body in the photograph. The photobiographical textuality of the photograph inscribes a corporeality (sometimes unified, sometimes segmented, sometimes cut off from itself, as in the postmodern body). The photographic corporeality enhances and correlates with the philosopher's words. The image stands at the limit of the philosopher's words, and the philosopher's words are just beyond the horizon of the photographs.

The body as text signifies. Its textualization elaborates a body whose multiplicity cannot fulfill a philosophy nor respond to the philosophy of another. This body cannot develop from the views of others nor can it account for its own experience. Yet it signifies as the philosopher's body, as a textuality which explains itself, sustains itself, and contains itself. It sets its own limits as a philosophizing text. The philosopher in the photograph can still exemplify a philosophical position, demonstrate the applicability of the philosophy as if it were an illustrated story, or it can present the contradictions of thought and picture. It can show what cannot be realized in words and it can indicate where the philosopher's body has no relevance whatsoever to the philosophy itself. The body in the photograph demonstrates the inappropriateness of biography for the understanding of a philosophy. Yet the photobiographical, as a textuality, raises the question of the philosopher's body—not the philosopher's ideas and arguments. Photobiographical textuality does not resolve the unanswered questions in the philosophy. Rather it demonstrates—in relation to the philosophy—the correlative and juxtapositional function of the philosopher's body. More particularly, it raises the question of the body in a different way from that announced in a philosophy or in a personal encounter. Photobiographical textuality signifies precisely in this difference.

15

THE VISIBILITY OF SELF-PORTRAITURE
Merleau-Ponty/Cézanne

Self-portraiture is the hidden agenda of Maurice Merleau-Ponty's last essay: *Eye and Mind* (1961).[1] Although he does not mention any particular self-portraits nor does he cite the activity that produces them, the question of self-portraiture serves as the organizing feature of the whole essay. The text is permeated by discussions of painting, the eye, the painter's hands, mirrors, the specular image, and my body as both seeing *(le voyant)* and seen *(le visible)*. All the necessary elements of self-portraiture are available in Merleau-Ponty's account of the relation between eye and mind. Although the text can be (and has been) read without ever raising the question of self-portraiture, the complex workings of the essay become clearer once this feature is uncovered.[2] And for an understanding of the meaning and practice of self-portraiture, Merleau-Ponty has a great deal to offer.

A self-portrait is produced in the activity of self-portraiture. The self-portrait results from the painter's practice. The self seeks to render itself visible by painting a picture of itself with the use of a mirror. What appears, what is made visible, is the painted self. Working directly from a single mirror without applying any correction in the rendering of what is seen, the painter will appear to be painting with the left hand if the actual procedure was done with the right. Although many self-portraits show only the head and shoulders, the specular image still produces a left-right inversion which is understood only when the function of the mirror is taken into account. Van Gogh's severed ear is indeed on the left side as one might expect for a right-handed person who might be inclined to cut off an ear. However in the various self-portraits which were produced after the self-mutilation took place, it seems as though Van Gogh has lost his right ear. Specific self-portraits of Dürer, Rembrandt, Corot, Pissarro, and De Chirico show them to be painting with their left hand—indicating that they are each in fact right-handed. Other Dürers and Rembrandts, a Reynolds, and a Kokoschka show that the hands and arms have been readjusted to look as though they were not engaged in the act of painting at all. In these cases, both hands are occupied with some other function. A 1917 self-portrait of Max

Beckmann shows him painting with his right hand while a 1937 version is inde-terminate. What must be noticed however is that the eye is coordinated with the hands. In both Beckmanns the eyes are directed away from the frontal view—suggesting that two mirrors were used. Although some painters have no objection to portraying themselves as holding a brush and palette, most present themselves as if they were a statue bust or as if sitting for a court painter. Often rectifying the self to look like the pose of another, self-portraiture offers a pictor-ial account of the self. In self-portraiture, the self constitutes itself as other—slightly modifying Rimbaud's dictum: *le "je" est un autre.*

Selbstbildnis—autoportrait—autoritratto—autoretrato—self-portrait. A self-made portrait of oneself—a drawing, picture, image, painting, or some sort of delineation of oneself by oneself. The German term stresses the self's production of an image or likeness of itself. The Romance language locutions pick up the Greek prefix *auto-*, meaning "of itself" or, more specifically, "of oneself"—what is done independently, naturally, and just exactly so, not with the help of others. Understood as an *auto*portrait, by contrast with what is "natural" in a "*nature morte*" (a dead nature or still life), the self-portrait draws out precisely what is alive. One's self is alive. The reflexive pronoun *autos* appeals to one's true self, but the self in the Greek (Orphic-Platonic) view that one's true self is the soul and not the body is rendered impossible in the case of an *autoportrait.* The *auto-portrait* is precisely a rendition of the painter's body by the very one whose image appears in the painting. Leonardo, Dürer, Rembrandt, Chardin, Delacroix, Cézanne, Van Gogh, Miró, Picasso, and so forth all paint their own bodies. The *autoportrait* offers a plan or an image (*protractus* in Medieval Latin) of the self. The plan offered is corporeal. The body is what is seen in the paint-ing. Although the self renders itself—the true self, the very one (*autos*)—it is distinctively embodied, visible, seen. The Italian version provides another fea-ture: the self—the very one—is not simply given there in the painting, on the canvas; in an *autoritratto* there is a drawing out (*ritrarre*), an extracting. On the one hand, the self draws itself out, extracts itself; on the other hand, the self is what is drawn out or extracted. In the Spanish word *autoretrato*, there is an ambiguity as to whether the prefix is to be understood as *auto-* or *autor-*. If the latter, then the *autor* or author is portraying-portrayed. The author is agent and patient. The author portrays and is portrayed. To the Spanish way of speaking, the self is an author—the direct connection with autobiography is established—the self originates the painting, the self produces its own picture of itself as a writer might write about his or her own life, as an autobiographer might write his or her own life.

In self-portraiture, the self offers a plan of itself; in painting oneself, one draws oneself out. The self-portrait cannot be a drawing or image of the self understood only as soul (*psychē* or *anima*); it must also involve the body. In the self-portrait, the self is necessarily represented as embodied. Traits of the self—traces of the self—constitute the self-portrait. The traces are bodily shapes, expressions, and glances. The self traces itself and leaves traces of itself in the painting of the self-portrait. Self-portraiture is the self establishing a likeness of itself as a painting. The likeness is a visible trace, extract, sketch, plan, outline of the self. As such, it is not the self. As such, the self-portrait is inadequate as a rendering of the self. Nevertheless, something is appropriated; the trace or extract or image is complete—it delimits itself as self-portraiture and fulfills its task even though it does not capture the self.

THE VISIBILITY OF PAINTING

Self-portraiture is painting. Merleau-Ponty distinguishes painting from science and philosophy. The three activities intersect in crucial ways. By following Merleau-Ponty's account it will become evident that what painting accomplishes is different—not separate—from the workings of science and philosophy. More particularly, the status of visibility as that which arises in the activity of painting and which is articulated in philosophical interrogation establishes the space in which self-portraiture can and does occur.

Eye and Mind opens with the statement "*La science manipule les choses et renonce à les habiter*" (*OE*, p. 9). Science takes knowing as its enterprise. Scientific activity according to Merleau-Ponty attempts to manipulate things and gives up trying to inhabit or live in them. Science keeps its distance from things in their particularity. It offers models for understanding things as objects in general. Variables and indicators provide the mechanisms according to which things are manipulated. Even when science treats forces, fields of energy, chemical reactions, and biological instincts, scientific activity concerns itself with the natural world of things but at a distance. The project of knowing, in which science engages, refuses to enter into the texture of things, to live the things it studies. The thinking which science involves places great weight upon the various techniques for grasping and obtaining the knowledge of the things which it seeks. It introduces experimental conditions according to which things are operated upon, worked over, and transformed. But the specific thing or things in question could be substituted by others. Indeed they lose their interest and significance when they acquire a uniqueness and individuality which does not allow for substitutability and generality. The activity of science is an activity of mind *(l'esprit)*. Scientific thought does not want to enter into the visible. It wants to stand back from the visible in order to provide rules, regularities, and models for understanding it.

Descartes's *Dioptrique* offers an example of thinking which gives itself a model and then tries to reconstruct the visible according to that model. Descartes seeks to eliminate the equivocal and the ambiguous in vision. When a Cartesian looks in a mirror, he does not see himself; he sees only a mannequin, an exterior, an outside. For Descartes, scientific thought deals with extension. If a Cartesian were to try to paint, he would offer only a representation of that extended thing. Painting would thereby be only an artificial device for representing extension. In another way, but with similar difficulties, the Renaissance theory of perspective tries to account for every point in space. The famous Dürer woodcut of the painter looking through a grid in order to paint what he sees in each of the little squares provides an example of how a technique can be employed to reproduce the thing scientifically in its spatial multiplicity. In both procedures, the painter makes a science of painting and stands back from the things that are painted. Colors are de-emphasized and perhaps even rendered incidental to the representation of, or perspective on, the object. Scientific thinking in general involves what Merleau-Ponty calls a *pensée de survol*. This overview thinking or bird's eye view of things tries to grasp the totality from a distance. However, something in space escapes our efforts at *survol* (*OE*, p. 50). What escapes is precisely what a painter such as Cézanne makes visible in painting.

In distinguishing painting from scientific activity, Merleau-Ponty appeals to a certain type of modern painting which the eye *(l'oeil)* symbolically signifies more than mind *(l'esprit)*. Cézanne is paradigmatic; but in the 1964 Gallimard edition of *L'Oeil et l'esprit,* one also finds reproductions of work by Giacometti, Matisse, Klee, Nicholas de Stael, Richier, and Rodin. Although a few other artists are cited, including Robert Delaunay, Duchamps, Rouault, and Dubuffet, together they constitute the type of painters and sculptors whom Merleau-Ponty regards as stressing the eye as opposed to the mind. They serve as exemplary of what is in question when he speaks of painting.

Painting dips into the net of brute sense ["*la peinture puise à cette nappe de sens brut dont l'activisme ne veut rien savoir*" (*OE*, p. 13)]. Where science stands back from things in order to make sense of them, painting dips into the very texture of the sense of things. Where science (under the Cartesian model) succeeds in a particular domain and tries to apply its achievement to all others, painting enters into the field of sense in its specificity. Painting limits itself to the visible of the here and now. As Merleau-Ponty puts it, "*l'oeil habite comme l'homme sa maison*" [the eye inhabits as one lives in one's house (*OE*, p. 27).] And earlier in the text: "*l'oeil voit le monde, et ce qui manque au monde pour être tableau, et ce qui manque au tableau pour être lui-même, et, sur la palette, la couleur que le tableau attend, et il voit, une fois fait, le tableau qui répond à tous ces manques, et il voit les tableaux des autres, les réponses autres à d'autres manques*" [The eye sees the world and what is lacking in the world in order to be a painting; the eye sees what is lacking in the painting in order to be itself, and once achieved, the eye sees the painting which answers to all these lacks and it sees other people's paintings as other responses to other lacks] (*OE*, pp. 25–26). The eye sees lacks and rectifies them in painting because the painter enters into the texture of the world with its multiplicity of sense. The painter can fulfill these lacks because he notices them as precisely that which is to be made visible on the canvas. To everyday seeing, the lacks remain invisible. The painter makes them visible by painting them. "Painting gives visible existence to what profane vision believes to be invisible" (*OE*, p. 27). Painting establishes what Merleau-Ponty calls "visibility." Visibility arises out of the conjuncture of the visible and the invisible, out of the making visible of what is invisible to everyday seeing. The thing seen is situated in a relation to the seer. It is not quite the same to the painter's eye as it is to everyday seeing. The thing embodies a network of brute sense (or meaning), a sensuousness which is invisible to everyday seeing and which is unimportant to scientific thought. To the painter, the primary task is to make the network of brute sense visible as the visibility of the painting.

In Merleau-Ponty's later ontology, visibility arises out of the seeing-seen *(voyant-visible)*. In everyday experience, the locus of this visibility is the body. The crossing over (back and again)—*recroisement*—of touching touched, seeing seen, one eye and the other, one hand and the other establishes the intertwining, chiasm, or bodily space. Merleau-Ponty, the philosopher, calls this intertwining visibility. He speaks of the body as a "curious system of exchanges" *(OE,* p. 21). He cites Valéry as claiming that the painter "brings along his body." "In lending his body to the world, the painter changes the world into painting" *(OE,* p. 16). By establishing the visibility that delineates the space of his body and by lending that visibility to the world of things, the painter is able to translate his own visibility into a new visibility—the visibility of the painting. By directing his mobile body into the visible world, the painter transforms that visibility into a painting.

Visible things and my body double each other with a secret visibility *(OE,* p. 22). The secret visibility involves a tracing *(un tracé)* which arises out of the concatenation of things and my body. This tracing is what is left over in the double crossing of the inside and the outside, the outside and the inside. The tracing is a marking out of the secret visibility which is neither outside nor inside, neither thing nor body, neither visible nor invisible. This tracing is what makes painting possible. The tracing of the secret visibility is rendered in a particular way on a particular canvas. It could have been otherwise. When the secret visibility is rendered in a particular way in a particular painting, a transubstantiation has taken place. The visibility is no longer the visibility of a painter's body confronting a mountain or a bowl of fruit. The visibility is now the visibility of a visible painting. The mountain or the bowl of fruit is no longer visibly there; it has been replaced by the painting of a mountain or a bowl of fruit as what is visibly there. The substance of the visibility has been radically transformed: transubstantiated. The tracing of the painter lending his body to the mountain or to the bowl of fruit has become the tracing of the viewer looking at a painting of the mountain or bowl of fruit. The new tracing is indeed a tracing of the old. The secret visibility of the painter's body given over to the mountain is not the same secret visibility as that of the viewer looking at the painting. The tracing continues; the visibility is continually reborn. The painterly seeing-seen *(voyant-visible)* is transformed for the viewer. Painting celebrates the enigma of visibility and offers a restitution of the visible while scientific thought provides a model for the control and transformation of the things themselves. The only way science can accomplish its task is by ignoring visibility and by providing an intelligible construction of what is there—visible or not.

The task of the philosopher is to interrogate. The philosopher can interrogate the relation between eye and mind, body and things, science and painting. Interrogation for Merleau-Ponty is an asking in the between *(inter-rogare)*. By situating the inquiry between body and things, the philosopher can articulate the character and meaning of visibility. By interrogating the relation between science and painting, the philosopher can establish the place of philosophy itself. By interrogating painting, the philosopher asks about the particular type of visibility that arises in the practice of painting. The philosopher delineates the single network of Being and particularly its various "branches" as manifested in painting, notably: depth, color, form, line, movement, contour, and physiognomy. These "branches of Being" constitute the special visibility of painting and give it its specificity. The philosopher does not provide an account of how these branches or ramifications of Being are produced, nor does the philosopher *qua* philosopher engage in the producing of them. The philosopher does not offer a history of their occurrence in particular paintings nor does the philosopher analyze how the various branches interrelate in a particular painting. The philosopher remarks them as branches of Being and interrogates their function, meaning, status, and location in the production of the visibility of painting.

THE DOUBLE VISIBILITY OF SELF-PORTRAITURE

Self-portraiture is a kind of painting—a rather special kind. To interrogate the differences in the thing painted is to ask about painting itself. When the thing painted is a mountain, a mirror, or oneself, fundamental differences occur in the type of visibility produced. Consider the case of Paul Cézanne.

During the last nine years of his life, Cézanne often painted the Montagne Sainte-Victoire near Aix-en-Provence. In 1894, after the death of his mother, Cézanne decided definitely to abandon his special sites near Estaque on the Mediterranean. Although he continued to spend some of his time in Paris, he returned to his natal city of Aix-en-Provence perhaps with the idea that he would find a new subject to paint. The Montagne Sainte-Victoire served his purposes admirably. He painted the mountain from the quarry in Bibemus, from the north of Aix, from the Tholonet road, from the Château-Noir terrace, from the Lauves heights, from Saint-Marc, from Gardanne, from Beaurecueil, and so on. Each constituted a different view of the mountain. He would paint the mountain at different times of day (perhaps not with the meticulousness with which Monet rendered versions of the Rouen cathedral, but nevertheless with extensive variety). He chose different seasons. He used oil on canvas, and some watercolors on white paper. He painted the mountain year in and year out during his later life. Again and again he brought his body to a site from which he could see the mountain. The last time he went out to paint it in 1906, he was caught in a storm and died soon thereafter. He regularly lent his body to the mountain in the act of painting it. Visible, ominous, "imperious and melancholy" (he described it in his youth), the Montagne Sainte Victoire was as invisible to the inhabitants of Aix as the Eiffel Tower is to Parisians and the Empire State Building is to New Yorkers: always there, but hardly noticed. Even today driving along the Autoroute du Sud, if it were not for a landmark sign along the road, many automobile drivers would find the mountain invisible to their everyday gaze. By lending his body to it, standing before it with his easel and palette, Cézanne would lean forward toward his canvas and render visible what the profane eye would not see. Through both vision and movement, Cézanne would transpose the visibility of his own body in its relation to the mountain into the secret visibility of his canvas. The tracing of the invisible in the visible mountain would be inscribed onto the canvas and the new visibility would appear. Painting with his eyes and his hands, he attends to the depth of Being there in the mountain; he establishes that depth along with color, form, line, movement, and contour in the painting.

It would not suffice for Cézanne simply to reproduce external forms. He would have to paint pure forms which follow their own internal laws of construction. His practice was to paint traces or slices of things by attending to the solidity of Being, on the one hand, and its diversity, on the other. The domain in which he operates is the space of difference between Being as a fullness and Being as sheer multiplicity. What he paints specifically are the traces of the difference—the network of sense. In order to paint the traces, he paints color. But there is no recipe for painting the visible. No predeterminations are available as to *which* colors are to be used. Indeed, the vast array of colors used to render the mountain at different times and from different views is quite extraordinary. Yet in each case, the Montagne Sainte-Victoire is distinctively visible in the painting; the tracings of the actual mountain are carried into the visibility of the painting.

The painter does not paint a world displayed before him as in the representation of things. The representational account no longer holds. The painting becomes "autofigurative" in that it establishes its own figuration—through the ramifications of Being. The painting determines itself as a trace, fabric, cloth, texture. This network constitutes the field of difference in which visibility arises.

Although the painter must stand back a considerable distance from the mountain in order to paint it, Cézanne paints the Montagne Sainte-Victoire in its particularity. He is interested in *this* very mountain. And the visibility of his painted mountain is that of this specific mountain in the painting. As Cézanne says, "the painter thinks in paint." Rendering the visible as visibility is thinking in paint. Thinking in paint is not an activity of mind *(l'esprit)* as it is for scientific thought. Oddly the geologist, botanist, or zoologist must move much closer to the mountain than Cézanne does. However, what the scientist who is concerned with rock formation, vegetation, and animal life wants is not this particular case of the thing, but this particular one as an instance of many (for which other examples would probably be equally suitable). The scientist's thinking is calculative and generalizing. The thinking the painter engages in is interpretive and specifying. As Merleau-Ponty remarks in "Cézanne's Doubt,"[3] the painter interprets. However, "this interpretation must not be thought *(une pensée)* separate from vision" (*Doute*, p. 27). The thinking in which the painter engages is noncalculative, but as Cézanne said, "a painter is not an imbecile" (*Doute*, p. 27). "The mountain makes itself seen by the painter and the painter interrogates it with his gaze" (*OE*, p. 28). The painter thinks in paint—utilizing but transforming the activity of the scientist. The painter interrogates with his gaze—employing the activity of the philosopher but charging it with the sensuous. Although Cézanne stands back from the Montagne Sainte-Victoire, he also makes it visible—each time with a novel visibility as he interrogates, thinks, and interprets it.

Suppose now that the thing in question, the object to be painted is no longer a mountain, but rather a mirror—a mirror placed in front of the painter so that the same sort of triangle that occurs when painting the mountain is reproduced, i.e., the painter, the canvas, and the thing. This time, however, the thing—the mirror—incorporates an image of the painter painting. The object is not just the mountain over there, but the mirror with the painter's image right here. What is visible is not the mountain, but rather the painter's image. Usually the frame of the mirror is omitted in the painting—only the image of the painter is rendered visible. In painting the mountain, Cézanne renders visible what is invisible to the profane eye. In self-portraiture, he makes the mirror invisible and his specular image visible. Unlike the Montagne Sainte-Victoire which became a motif in Cézanne's later years, he produced self-portraits throughout his lifetime. In 1858–61, he is young clean-shaven (except for a trim moustache), short-haired and scowling. In 1865–68, he is bearded, balding at the forehead, and looking back from his apparent right with a somewhat pensive air. In 1873–75, he is wearing a cap with a long full beard, has hair falling over his ears, and a drawn look. At about the same time, another self-portrait shows him quite bald with a trimmed beard and what Rilke called "an incredible intensity." In 1877–79, his beard is shorter, more carefully cut, and he is wearing a white malleable folding hat. His look is that of a storekeeper caught unaware that someone is looking at him. And so the self-portraits go: his hair and beard length change, usually he directs his attention off to his apparent left suggesting that he painted with his actual right hand. In a couple of paintings, he has a melon hat. Once in 1885–87, he portrays himself holding a palette in his apparent right hand facing an easel concealing his apparent left hand, indicating that he was in fact painting with his right hand. In 1898–1900, the last of the available self-portraits, he is wearing a beret, a goatee, and a moustache with a rather concentrated look. This time, although still facing toward his apparent left, if one covers the lower arms, it is evident that the painting was performed with the apparent right. But then if one looks at the eyes, unlike the earlier self-portraits, they are oriented off to the apparent left. Coordinating the hand and the eyes in reading the painting, it is now clear that two mirrors were employed. The apparent right is the actual right—the double mirroring corrects the inversion.

Unless two mirrors are employed, the eyes in the self-portrait are centered—oriented directly forward. The viewer has the sense of being caught in a face-to-face stare. The eyes are looking at "me," one might think. It is as if he is trying to tell "me" something. Yet he is only looking at himself in the mirror. The viewer who is duped into believing that a staring match is under way is in fact an intruder. Cézanne is simply looking at himself in the mirror. But the mirror is invisible. Cézanne the *voyant-visible* produces a visible self with an invisible mirror. Visibility, in the case of the Cézanne self-portrait, is traced in the visible of the self-portrait producing a new visibility as it is seen by a viewer.

When Cézanne sees himself in the mirror, a single visibility is produced. When Cézanne looks at his own self-portrait a double visibility occurs. The new visibility becomes equivocal to Cézanne's gaze and unequivocal to that of another viewer. For Cézanne, the self-portrait is the self as other reflecting itself as the same. What is invisible to Cézanne the man is made visible in the visibility of the self-portrait and offered as posterity in the painting. What is now visible in the painted self, like the painted mountain, is a new visibility tracing out the old. Cézanne's many self-portraits offer a chronicle of his self-images but they will always leave behind the *voyant-visible* of Cézanne's actual life. They are at most the traces of that life made visible in paint.

CÉZANNE'S MIRROR STAGE

Jacques Lacan reintroduced his conception of the "mirror stage" in 1949 at the Sixteenth International Congress of Psychoanalysis under the title "Le stade du miroir comme formateur de la fonction du Je."[4] In that same year, Merleau-Ponty gave his lectures on *Consciousness and the Acquisition of Language*[5] as Professor of Child Psychology and Pedagogy at the Sorbonne. In those lectures, he cites Lacan's notion of "prematuration" in the child's psychological development. Although Lacan was seven years Merleau-Ponty's senior, they knew each other's work and were acquainted personally. Lacan, for instance, provided an article for the special number of *Les Temps modernes* devoted to Merleau-Ponty after his death in 1961. The notion of "prematuration" arises particularly in the "Mirror Stage" essay, which had been presented in earlier form at the Fourteenth International Congress of Psychoanalysis in 1936.

The mirror stage, which apparently occurs anywhere between the ages of six months and eighteen months, involves basically three levels. At the first level, the child reacts to the image presented by the mirror as a reality or at least as the image of someone else. Then the child stops treating the image as a real object, and no longer tries to take possession of the other hiding behind the mirror. But subsequently the child sees this other as the child's own image. At this last level, identification begins to take place: the child progressively takes on the identity of the subject. Identification with the specular image only occurs after the child has treated the image as an image of another and after that assumption of alterity breaks down and a radical distancing from the image as other takes place. Thus when the child sees the image as an image of him- or herself, it is not so much that it is the self as that it is *not other*. The "I" ("*je*") is formed out of a dialectic in which the image is postulated as other, denied, and then affirmed as the self. One could say that it is a process of incorporation of otherness into the self. Naturally this occurs only in the case of the recognition of self in the mirror. Objects and other people remain other.

For Lacan, the mirror stage involves the self or subject becoming a subject. When the child assumes an image of him- or herself as other, a transformation in the self takes place. The mirror catalyzes a discordance between the self (*le "je"*) and its own reality. The mirror stage accomplishes a relation between the organism and its reality or between the *Innenwelt* (inner or personal world) and the *Umwelt* (environment). Thus "the specular image seems to be the threshold onto the visible world."[6] The mirror itself brings about the recognition of otherness in order to identify with the image it sees. What is other in the mirror is determined at the third level as precisely the same as the self (and not, in fact, "other").

In Merleau-Ponty's account, the mirror in what is here called Cézanne's mirror stage reverses the transformations Lacan describes. When painting the mountain, Cézanne stands back from it in order to lend his body to it (unlike the scientist who moves closer to it in order to stand back from it). When painting the mirror, Cézanne knows that the specular image is himself. Cézanne identifies with the image in the mirror; but in self-portraiture he undertakes to make himself other, to paint a portrait of himself as other than himself. Indeed, as Lacan claims, the specular image seems to be the threshold onto the visible world. But in the case of Cézanne, the door opens the other way: the specular image is a threshold onto the visible world of the painting and not the world from which the painting arises. The specular image is a threshold onto the visible world of the self-portrait and its visibility. With the help of the mirror, the tracings of the relation between the *Innenwelt* (inner world) and the *Außenwelt* (external world) established from childhood are transposed by an inversion of the intertwining. The effect is to produce tracings of the *Innenwelt* in the *Außenwelt* of the self-portrait.

Instead of painting the mountain, Cézanne is painting himself, making himself other, making his body visible. In this case, he literally lends his body to the world of things in order to transform them into paint. Cézanne takes the visibility of his body as the visibility of a *voyant-visible* and transposes it onto the canvas. In the case of self-portraiture, Cézanne doubles the invisible. When looking at a mountain, one does not see oneself seeing; one sees only the visible. When painting the mountain, the painter makes visible what is invisible in his experience of the mountain. When looking at himself in the mirror, Cézanne sees what is typically invisible to him: he sees his nose, his eyes, his chin, his beard, etc. The mirror makes what is invisible visible. When painting himself from the image in the mirror, Cézanne takes what is typically invisible to him and brings another invisible—the one that accompanies all his seeing—and produces another visible, which is the self-portrait. The self-displaying visibility of the mirror is reproduced in the self-displaying visibility of the self-portrait. But self-portraiture is not representational any more than painting the Montagne Sainte-Victoire is representational. The self-displaying visibility of the mirror is not duplicated in the self-displaying visibility of the self-portrait. They are not identical, although there is a tracing of one onto the other. Cézanne produces the self-portrait by bringing out (making visible) what would be invisible to someone else looking at Cézanne and painting a portrait of him (as Pissarro did in 1874 and Renoir in 1880). Hence in painting the visible specular image, Cézanne doubles both the invisible of the self and the image and the visibility of the image and the painting. Cézanne's seeing fills in the visible of the specular image with a plan *(protractus)*. The visible is filled in with the invisible which Cézanne makes visible in paint. Cézanne draws out or extracts features of himself and renders them visible by means of what Merleau-Ponty calls the branches of Being—the tools of painting. The self-portrait leaves traces of the specular image and hence of the self. But the traces are not the visible self. The traces are the self as other, as self-portrait.

Self-portraiture almost invariably requires a special tool: the mirror. This everyday instrument establishes the painter's visibility in its most salient respects. The mirror locates the place of the eye *(l'oeil)*—the very feature which Merleau-Ponty symbolically associates with the painter. The mirror pinpoints the *voyant-visible* as visibility, as the place of freeplay *(Spielraum* or *enjeu)*, as the repeated tracing, and marking out of, the difference between visible and invisible, seer and seen. The place of the freeplay, the visibility, the difference, is the place of the "*je*," the place of the self, the "I"—centered where the eye is located. Self-portraiture appropriates what is appropriate to the visibility of the painter, makes visible what is invisible in the specular image, and appropriates the canvas producing a new visibility. The mirror stage makes the new visibility of the self-portrait possible.

The mirror makes it possible for the self which paints itself to disclose the flesh *(la chaire)* of the painter. The mirror functions as an instrument of disclosure *(dévoilement)*. It uncovers the painter's painterly embodiment. Since, according to Merleau-Ponty, every technique is a technique of the body, the mirror also operates in that way. In this case, rather than concealing its function as a technique, the mirror discloses itself. The mirror operates as a dispositive. It discloses itself because of the orientation of the subject's eyes and because of the tending toward painting that one arm indicates. But at the same time, it conceals its identity as a mirror in all of Cézanne's self-portraits. Because the mirror acts as a dispositive, the visibility that arises in self-portraiture both discloses and conceals, makes visible and invisible at the same time. The mirror marks the ambiguity of the painterly experience while also structuring that experience according to depth, color, form, line, movement, contour, and physiognomy— the branches of Being *(les rameaux de l'Être)*.

Although the mirror is always hidden in Cézanne's self-portraits, not all painters require that the mirror be invisible. A 1787 Gainsborough shows the painter looking forward, elegantly attired, with an oval shape around the bust-like pose that could well be the frame of a mirror. Furthermore, not all painters use only one mirror. A 1917 Max Beckmann shows him painting himself. His eyes are directed away from the frontal view and he is painting with his right hand. Similarly, a 1484 Albrecht Dürer has the young man looking off to the left. A view of his right cheek is provided. Only the right hand is seen and it could well be holding a brush. Once again, it is quite plain that both Beckmann and Dürer in these instances made use of two mirrors in order to correct the mirror image effect. Only Beckmann would have had access to photography, whereby the appropriate double impression effect could be produced. A 1980

Francis Bacon triptych entitled "Three Studies for Self-Portrait" discloses three views of his face in Bacon's habitually distorted fashion. In the center view, the eyes face forward as in traditional self-portraits. The two side panels are oriented about 45 degrees toward the center, indicating that he painted from three mirrors with the two side ones angled inward about the same on each side. Thus the one on the right shows his apparent left cheek and the one on the left shows his apparent right cheek. Since only the head is displayed, it would be difficult to determine whether the actual sides or their mirror images are seen. And the distorted visibility accentuates the difficulty of such a determination.

Some self-portraits conceal not only the mirror, but also the sense of the painter painting. When only the head or bust is shown, the question of deception does not arise. But when Dürer in 1493 holds a plant in both hands or in 1498 sits with his hands folded on a table in front of him; when a later Rembrandt shows the artist plumply and ornately seated holding a scepter in his apparent left and his apparent right placed firmly on a hazy chair arm; when Reynolds in 1780 grasps a document in one hand and places the other at his hip; or when Max Beckmann in 1937 holds both of his hands in front of him encircled with prisoner's chains, the painter orients the visibility of the painting away from its status as a mirrored self-portrait in order to establish the self in an alternative role. Many painters have no objection to portraying themselves with brush and palette in hand. They disclose their painterly embodiment as visible, but the differences in the particular manner and style of Henri Rousseau, Corot, Monet, Kokoschka, Modigliani, and Picasso—to cite some examples—are quite extreme. In each case, the mirror operates as a dispositive (as the locus of visibility with its concomitant ambiguity) establishing its uniqueness and vitality of function.

SELF-PORTRAITURE AS AUTOBIOGRAPHICAL VISIBILITY

Many autobiographers have characterized their enterprise as self-portraiture. The celebrated report by Montaigne to his reader in the *Essais* is indicative: "I want to be seen here in my simple, natural, ordinary fashion, without pose or artifice; for it is myself that I portray."[7] Montaigne understands his writing project as self-portrayal. Almost two centuries later, Rousseau begins his *Confessions* with the statement: "*Voici le seul portrait d'homme, peint exactement d'après nature et dans toute sa verité, qui existe et qui probablement existera jamais.*"[8] (Here is the only portrait of a man painted exactly according to nature and in the fullest truth that exists or will probably ever exist.) Montaigne and Rousseau borrow from painting what they seek to accomplish with words. In writing their own lives, they offer a verbal picture of who they are and what they have done. Their picture is in fact a narrative. With respect to self-portraiture, the traces are not visible tracings but rather the writing of their lives as text. The intertwining that produces visibility results in textuality in the case of autobiography.[9] Visibility is perceptual textuality and textuality is written visibility.

Because of the mirror stage, in self-portraiture the eye is centered. When a single mirror is employed, the eye is oriented in a directly frontal view. The forces of the painting tend to draw toward and concentrate upon the place of the eyes. In autobiography, the self is dispersed, disseminated throughout the narrative. The eye is substituted typically by a first-person singular "I" which speaks and narrates its own life. The eye in self-portraiture is coordinated with the hand, for both are instruments of visibility. In the autobiographical text, the self speaks and is spoken in terms of the "I," but the hand that writes remains invisible.[10]

The case of photographic self-portraiture more closely approximates painting because it is visual and also involves vision. However, the differences are notable. Just as there is no mirror in autobiography—the brush corresponds to the pen, the paper to the canvas, the ink to the paint—in photographic self-portraiture, the camera forces the elimination of the mirror stage. In self-portraiture, there are two moments of self-displaying visibility: that of the specular image and that of the painting. The painter lends his body to the mirror which provides a self-displaying visibility. The painter reiterates that self-displaying visibility by tracing it in paint and thereby providing another self-displaying visibility. In the case of photography, where the photographer takes the picture of him or herself with a cable, the camera does not operate like the mirror—it is a type of non-self-displaying visibility. Unlike the painter who sees what he or she paints and hence paints from the visible, the photographer has to set the scene with him- or herself as markedly invisible. The context is arranged and the photographer must look through the camera in order to determine where to sit or stand when the picture is taken. Hence before and while the picture is taken, a specifically non-self-displaying visibility is at work. The photographer lends his body to the photographical procedure by placing it before the camera. The painter is situated in front of the mirror, but what is painted is the specular image. The photographer takes a picture of the actual body and not an image of it. The photograph itself is a kind of fixed image of the self and its body.[11] Hence although the photographer lends his body to the photographic procedure, only the photograph itself offers a self-displaying visibility.

In self-portraiture, the self is displayed, made visible, drawn out, extracted, projected, and rendered as a version of itself. The mirror stage offers a unique feature to the activity of portraying oneself. The traces of the portrayal constitute the frame out of which the self in its corporeality is rendered visible. The painter's visibility is the painter's identity as other. The painter's life—captured at a moment, in a phase—is identified in the space of difference that the mirror as dispositive marks in its visibility. This specular self-displaying visibility is appropriated and reiterated in the self-portrait. Self-portraiture forms an enterprise in which a new self-displaying visibility comes into being by tracing the ex(ap)propriated self of the mirror into the texture of painting.

16

THE TEXT OF THE SPEAKING SUBJECT
Merleau-Ponty/Kristeva

The speaking subject speaks—but not always. The speaking subject is embodied, but that embodiment can be read as a text. Dividing itself and yet also bringing together difference, the speaking subject is embedded in a difference between the semiotic and the symbolic or between indirect language and a pure language. These characteristics of the speaking subject link together two philosophical enterprises that might on the surface appear to be radically different, namely, those of Julia Kristeva and Maurice Merleau-Ponty.

Julia Kristeva entered the philosophical scene in a significant way in 1969 with a volume of essays entitled *Semiotikē*. This was only two years after Derrida's initial contribution in *Writing and Difference, Of Grammatology*, and *Speech and Phenomena*; and yet it was also only eight years after the death of Merleau-Ponty. Kristeva's major theoretical statement, however, came in 1974 with her *Revolution in Poetic Language*. While portions of *Semiotikē* along with essays from a later volume *Polylogue* (1977) were collected together in English as *Desire in Language*, the English translation of *La Révolution du langage poétique* did not appear until 1984 (ten years after its initial publication). As a *thèse d'état*, it was crucial that the volume be comprehensive, theoretically well-formulated, and embellished adequately with practical implications—and indeed the French version is precisely that. What was translated into English (and much earlier into German) is only the first (theoretical) portion of the book. Hence all the "practical" readings of particular texts are left for a future translation.

What I propose to develop here is the role of the "speaking subject" as articulated by Merleau-Ponty from the time of *Phenomenology of Perception* (1945), carried through *Consciousness and the Acquisition of Language* (1948–49), reformulated in *The Prose of the World* (1952), and, subsequently, elaborated in Kristeva's theoretical writings. Despite the commonality of concern with the "speaking subject," it would appear that the two discourses lack a common domain. Indeed Merleau-Ponty does not appear in the bibliographies of

Kristeva's theoretical writings while the figures of Husserl, Freud, Saussure, and Lacan are all fully represented. One would expect that her treatment of the latter would have also traversed the thought of Merleau-Ponty, implicitly if not explicitly. And since the role of the "speaking subject" in Kristeva's writings is rather crucial, she has admitted that further examination of the particular relation between her own notion of the "speaking subject" and that of Merleau-Ponty is called for.[1] Here I shall explore what brings the two discourses into potential dialogue and exchange despite their obvious divergences.

This reading of the speaking subject in Merleau-Ponty and Kristeva will focus on: (1) relationship between Kristeva's semiotic/ symbolic distinction and Merleau-Ponty's account of indirect language versus pure language, and (2) the signifying process in relation to the text of the speaking subject as the subject *en procès* ("in process" and "on trial").

SEMIOTIC/SYMBOLIC: INDIRECT/PURE LANGUAGE

According to Julia Kristeva, the "semiotic" and the "symbolic" are two modalities of the same signifying process. Language is formed by a signifying process. The type of discourse in question is determined by the particular modality operative at a given time. Whether it is theory, narrative, poetry, metalanguage, or some other form of discourse will be determined by the specific functioning of the semiotic or the symbolic. Kristeva characterizes the relation between the two as a "dialectic." The nature of the dialectic itself needs clarification. Although there may be dominance of the one or the other (the semiotic or the symbolic) at any particular moment, they never operate in isolation of one another. They are never exclusive in the sense of being totally independent of one another.

These terms "semiotic" and "symbolic" have long and complex histories. Kristeva wants to understand them after her own fashion. For Kristeva, the *symbolic* is tied up in the signifier (a word)/signified (a concept) relation. Although one might expect this signifying relation to be associated with the semiotic as in Saussure, Kristeva sees it as largely symbolic. Saussure calls this relation the "sign" and characterizes it as "arbitrary." However, he leaves room for the bringing together of a word and a concept as "motivated." Kristeva suggests that the motivated aspect of the relation lies in the unconscious drives (or *pulsions*) and the primary processes (of displacement and condensation) that underlie the arbitrary conjunction of a particular signifier with a particular signified. The association of the primary processes of "displacement" and "condensation" with "metonymy" and "metaphor" is already suggested in Lacan's reading of Jakobson and Freud.[2] "Displacement" involves a veering off to a contiguous signifier. Hence: metonymy. "Condensation" involves an overdetermination of the signified in its relation to the signifier. This crowding of signifieds onto a particular signifier is offered as a version of metaphor. Both metaphor and metonymy operate as symbolic elements in language. Thus the linking of the signifier and the signified in one of these ways interrupts the purely arbitrary account. They also bring out the syntactic and semantic aspects of language, aspects which Kristeva calls *symbolic*.

The symbolic—namely, "the syntactic and linguistic categories of a signifying process"—is, according to Kristeva, "a social effect of the relation to the other, established through the objective constraints of biological (including sexual) differences and concrete, historical family structures."[3] The symbolic, then, is an effect of how one relates to other people as limited by differences that are set biologically, genetically, and within a determinate family context. The symbolic accounts for what arises within certain social and linguistic frameworks. Yet there is only so much that the symbolic can accomplish within these frameworks. The symbolic is limited in what it can formulate, limited by its own structures, determinations, and motivations.

Furthermore, the symbolic operates as a scientific language in which the structures of discourse are rigidly defined, bounded, and set. The symbolic is the authoritative, assertive, definitive mode. It operates—and here Kristeva agrees with Lacan—by way of the paternal negation: the law of the Father (*le nom/non du père*). The symbolic posits the subject. The subject does not (as Husserl would have claimed) constitute the symbolic. For instance, and this is one of Kristeva's major theses, when the phallic function becomes *the* symbolic function, speaking begins to take hold. Before the law of the father is introduced, the mother occupies the place of the phallic function. And when the phallic function becomes the symbolic function, the mother loses her special status. Prior to that time, "her replete body, the receptacle and guarantor of demands, takes the place of all narcissistic, hence imaginary, effects and gratifications; she is, in other words, the phallus" (*RPL*, p. 47). However, with the "discovery of castration," she loses her special status: the subject is detached from its dependence on the mother, "and the perception of this lack [*manque*] makes the phallic function a symbolic function" (*RPL*, p. 47). Since the phallus is itself a signifier it motivates a particular set of relations to gravitate toward a particular signified (or particular set of signifieds). In this way, the symbolic achieves its own particular formation.

Certain elements of the semiotic permeate the symbolic. The symbolic wants to affirm itself, define itself, give itself its own name. However, the semiotic irrupts into the symbolic while at the same time maintaining its autonomy, thus the subject's position is retained as always in process/on trial [*en procès*]. The layer of "semiosis" that underlies the symbolic relation of the signifier to the signified is typically relegated to a pragmatics and semantics of language. Kristeva takes as her task to show that the semiotic has other dimensions.

Kristeva points out—in careful symbolic form—that there is, along with the ordering, law-like functions of the symbolic, another modality, namely that of "the Freudian *facilitation* and structuring *disposition* of drives, and also the primary processes which displace and condense both energies and their inscription" (*RPL*, p. 25). These drives are described as "energy" charges and "psychical" marks. As such, they articulate what Kristeva calls a "*chora*." This key idea for Kristeva characterizes notably a "nonexpressive totality formed by the drives and their stases in a motility that is as full of movement as it is regulated" (*RPL*, p. 25). The *chora* designates what is "mobile" and "an extremely provisional articu lation constituted by movements and their ephemeral stases." The *chora*, "as rupture articulations (rhythm), precedes evidence, verisimilitude, spatiality, and temporality" (*RPL*, p. 26). Further, she states that "the *chora* is a modality of sig nificance in which the linguistic sign is not yet articulated as the absence of an object and as the distinction between real and symbolic" (*RPL*, p. 26). Hence the *chora* is more fundamental than—or underlies—the basic relation between the signifier and the signified. With the semiotic *chora*, difference and identity are not yet present. Hence certain differentiations do not yet pertain. For instance, one feature of the sign is that the signified does not necessarily desig nate an object that is present. The *chora* precedes this sense that the object is absent. The differentiation is not part of the semiotic functioning, for that itself would be a symbolic matter. Even the Lacanian distinction between the real and the symbolic remains unspecified. This also means that the formation or estab lishment of the sign follows from the semiotic and its functioning.

What does it mean to say that the semiotic is more basic than the sign itself? For Kristeva, the semiotic is characterized by "flow and marks, by facilitation, energy transfers, the cutting up of a corporeal and social continuum as well as that of signifying material." And the *chora* is a "pulsating, rhythmic, nonexpres sive totality" (*RPL*, p. 40). Further descriptions of the semiotic include: "indifferent to language, enigmatic and feminine,...unfettered, irreducible to its verbal translation...musical, anterior to judgement, but restrained by a single guarantee: syntax" (*RPL*, p. 29). Understood metaphorically here, "syntax" structures the flow, channels experience, and gives shape to the symbolic content but does not determine it.

Just as sign and syntax are features of the symbolic function, so correspond ingly flow, energy, musicality, maternity, receptivity—in short, poetic language—can be ascribed to the semiotic. The semiotic practice of language highlights "nondisjunction" and continuity. It brings the bodily, material aspects of language in conjunction with the cognitive and formal aspects. The semiotic, therefore, does not necessarily stand apart from the symbolic but rather acts in occasional concert with it.

The correspondence between Kristeva's account of the relationships between the symbolic and the semiotic and Merleau-Ponty's descriptions of pure lan guage in relation to indirect language are striking. While Merleau-Ponty's notion of indirect language was offered in two published essays in *Signs*: "Indirect Language and the Voices of Silence" and "On the Phenomenology of Language" (both originally from *Les Temps modernes* in 1952), it is most fully developed in the posthumously published study (from those same years): *Prose of the World*.[4]

In "Indirect Language and the Voices of Silence," Merleau-Ponty writes: "...if we rid our minds of the idea that our language is the translation or cipher of an original text, we shall see that the idea of *complete* expression is nonsensi cal, and that all language is indirect or allusive—that is, if you wish, silence."[5]

And further: "If we want to understand language as an originating operation, we must pretend to have never spoken, submit language to a reduction without which it would once more escape us by referring us to what it signifies for us, *look* at it as deaf people look at those who are speaking, compare the art of language to other arts of expression, and try to see it as one of these mute arts" (*Signs*, p. 46). And from *The Prose of the World*: "We may say that there are two languages. First there is language after the fact, or language as an institution, which effaces itself in order to yield the meaning which it conveys. Second, there is the language which creates itself in its expressive acts, which sweeps one on from the signs toward meaning—sedimented language *(langage parlé)* and speaking language *(langage parlant)*" (*Prose*, p. 10).

Merleau-Ponty is claiming here that there are effectively two types of language.[6] One *(le langage parlé)* is "sedimented" and "spoken" once it is already established—something like an already motivated relation between the signifier and the signified—even though, in the Saussurian understanding, the relation is purely arbitrary. It is as though this one type of language were a transformation and limitation placed upon language by language itself. The other type *(le langage parlant)* makes itself in its practice. It is not bounded by the established, sedimented elements of an already constituted language—one in which there is a "stock of accepted relations between signs and familiar significations" (*Prose*, p. 13). In this second type of language, the set "arrangement of already available signs and significations alters and then transfigures each of them, so that in the end a new signification is created" (*Prose*, p. 13). In other words, this second type of language is not bounded by laws, conventions, and established understanding. It corresponds to Kristeva's *semiotic* which is not limited, circumscribed, and constrained by the *symbolic* paternal law, by the set of semantic prescriptions that are carried in language.

For Merleau-Ponty, the two types of language: the "sedimented" and the creative, revolutionary, indirect—operate in opposition to one another. The tendency of sedimented language *(le langage parlé)* is to consolidate, to formalize, and to regulate established meaning, while speech *(le langage parlant)* or speaking language is actively breaking out of these controlled, limiting circumstances. Merleau-Ponty asks: "How are we to understand this fruitful moment of language in which an accident is transformed into reason and there suddenly arises, from a mode of speech that is becoming extinct, a new, more effective and expressive mode—in the way the ebb of the sea after a wave excites and enlarges the next wave?" (*Prose*, p. 34). His point is that novelty and creativity in language have no place in sedimented language, in the already established, formed, and confirmed mode of speech. What breaks out from the bounded is another form of expressivity, another type of communication, an indirect language that has not yet become codified and solidified and which often appeals to alternative modes of expressivity. Often Merleau-Ponty appeals to painting as a paradigm. Although painting for Kristeva is to be read in terms of underlying meanings, she does not find to the same degree the emerging sense of newness and revolutionary creativity that Merleau-Ponty discovers there. With

Merleau-Ponty, painting demonstrates the powers of indirect language—a language that is expressive, that speaks without always turning into what Kristeva calls the symbolic. Yet for Merleau-Ponty, poetry—but more often literary language in general—is capable of enacting this indirect language, this language of silence, in which what speaks is not the established meaning but rather another order of sense and expression. For Kristeva, poetic language (as in Mallarmé and Lautréamont) exhibits features of the semiotic as they work in concert with and in dialectical opposition to the symbolic. What is relevant here is that both Merleau-Ponty and Kristeva understand indirect language or the semiotic respectively as a poetic or pictoral function, a function in which the positing, assertive, formal, or systematic features of a language are not determinative.

In Merleau-Ponty there is more of a worry that the specter of a pure language will predominate in some important way, that the algorithm will take over and stifle all possibility of expressivity and fullness of sense. By contrast, in choosing the term *semiotic* to characterize the undifferentiated, revolutionary, unbounded mode of language, Kristeva is indicating that the use of sign systems does not negate these special conditions for language. Yet Merleau-Ponty's sympathetic reading of Saussure's account of signs and signifiers in the mid-1940s is hardly reducible to what he is calling a "pure language." He deplores only the scientifizing of language into a metalanguage devoid of accident, flexibility, and ambiguity.

Merleau-Ponty's "inventions of style" carry as much weight as Kristeva's notion of "significance"—namely, the unlimited and unbounded process of meaning production. Yet, while Merleau-Ponty remains committed to the practice of dialectic, especially throughout the 1950s, he does not emphasize the particular dialectic between indirect language and pure language. By contrast, in opposing the two, and in stressing the difference between spoken language and speaking language, he implicitly maintains both kinds of language in a potentially creative, dialectical tension. For Kristeva, however, the dialectic between the symbolic and the semiotic is an active and crucial one. Indeed, her whole notion of the signifying process depends upon it.

THE SIGNIFYING PROCESS AND THE TEXT OF THE SPEAKING SUBJECT

The semiotic and the symbolic are two modalities of the same signifying process. For Kristeva, they are in dialectical relation. *Significance* is this unlimited and unbounded generating, heterogeneous process. It is both a bringing together of the divergent orientations and a separating of them at the same time. As Kristeva puts it: "This heterogeneous process, neither anarchic, fragmented foundation, nor schizophrenic blockage, is a structuring and de-structuring *practice*, a passage to the outer *boundaries* of the subject and society. Then—and only then—can it be *jouissance* and revolution" (*RPL*, p. 14).

This radical and yet also consolidative reading of language allows for the multiple dimensions of the signifying process. What remains to be explored is the role of the speaking subject in this process.

The signifying process, for Kristeva, involves three elements: the semiotic, the symbolic, and significance. The differentiated unity of these three elements is the process of the subject. The symbolic is able to posit the subject, but as absent, while the semiotic offers drives—as demonstrated through psychoanalysis—of the subject in process/on trial *(en procès)*. The *thetic* element of signification occurs during the signifying process in such a way that the subject is constituted without being reduced to the process—for the subject is "the threshold of language." In this area, the subject is neither reduced to a phenomenological foundational ego, which would function as center and source of all knowing acts, nor denied the thetic phase by which signification comes about. Hence, in Kristeva, the subject is neither a posited entity, a centered self, nor is it devoid of significance. The self-decentering effected here makes it possible to posit the subject, but always as an aspect of the signifying process itself. As we have learned from a long itinerary (which includes not only Sartre's transcendence of the ego, Derrida's self-decentering deconstruction, and Foucault's archaeology of the absent subject, but also Merleau-Ponty's embodied subject), the subject cannot have a centered existence: the subject cannot posit itself as positing itself or anything else. To posit the subject is to posit an object which is discrete and identifiable. And the subject in identifying itself as an object opens up regions of desire (in language) that are determinate and specifiable.

For instance, and most notably, for Kristeva, the text is a signifying practice. It is distinguishable from the "drifting-into-non-sense" that characterizes neurotic discourse. As a signifying practice, the text incorporates the subject, but as distributed throughout the text semiotically or as posited at relevant places symbolically (*RPL*, p. 51). The sociohistorical function of the signifying practice is to insert itself into everyday discourses such that it will irrupt at relevant places out of the material *chora* and as a posited symbolic formation.

For Kristeva, the speaking subject is itself a text. It is inscribed within the signifying process—not as a posited entity but as the semiotic, symbolic, and signifiable features of the signifying process. Yet the speaking subject is also not simply identical with the signifying process. It is rather the absent element in the syntax of what is spoken, what is said, what is articulated. When the subject reemerges as object, it is symbolically constituted as speaking, as holding a position, as being an object. The reemergence of the subject involves a disturbance in the syntactical relation as well. Hence Kristeva allows for various ways in which the passage from one sign system to another *(transposition)*, and the specific articulation of the semiotic and the thetic for a sign system *(representability)*, can account for some of these disturbances in the relation between the semiotic and the symbolic. What is especially important here is that the motility of the speaking subject is at once the flexibility of the signifying process.

For Kristeva, a speaking subject is already dispersed into an intersubjective world. This world is understood in terms of an intertextuality in which the text of the speaking subject inscribes itself with significance both semiotically and symbolically. For Merleau-Ponty, the speaking subject is set off against the thinking subject.[7] Merleau-Ponty's earlier move to the "tacit cogito" is transformed into an account of indirect language. And the transformation is a shift from an account of the speaking subject as that which is experienced, that with which one communicates, and that which speaks gesturally and through the body, to an expressivity in which signification is the essential ingredient. What is crucial here is that in speaking, the subject is *not* speaking, acting, or being *from a standpoint*, but rather as an *embodied*, *historical*, and *social* being. As such, it is the incorporation, insertion, and inscription of the self in the intersubjective world.

Between Merleau-Ponty and Kristeva, where the semiotic is informed by the symbolic and where speaking speech and spoken speech delimit an embodied experience, the speaking subject speaks but at the same time places pure, scientific, controlled, strong language in question. At the margins of this symbolic-pure language is a semiotic-indirect language, one that displaces the self in its centered being, one that marginalizes language itself into the expression of either "poetic language" or the language of the "neurotic" (filled with melancholy or depression).[8] When the speaking subject is not fulfilling the ideals of the culture (inaugurated by the Greeks, codified by the Romans, and carried on in the Western tradition), it provides a place for these ideals by marginalizing them, by delimiting them, by controlling spaces of expression—either indirectly or semiotically. This is not the romantic creation of a "natural," individual, pastoral idyll. Rather it is a delimitation, weakening, dissemination of the self's identity into an undifferentiated, yet not inarticulate space of self-textualization. The text of the speaking subject then is both its direct, symbolic modality and its edges, borders, and margins in the indirect, semiotic dimensions of language. This alternative space of language is a revolutionary, abnormal, non-dominant form of expression—one in which speaking takes place but where the subject is already a displaced self, a marginalized mode of expression—as in that of women, poets, neurotics, and unconventional philosophers.

17

WRITING ON WRITING
Merleau-Ponty/Derrida

What is writing on writing? Who writes on writing? What writing writes about writing? Is writing an act or an effect? In phenomenology, writing is an act. In semiology, writing is an effect. In interrogation, writing is placed in question in an act of inquiry. In deconstruction, writing is the inscription of a differential space.

For Merleau-Ponty, interrogation asks about writing. It announces that writing is neither an entity, nor a product, nor a result. For Merleau-Ponty, writing is style. For Derrida, writing is difference: it is neither speaking nor the graphic effect of speech.

Style in Merleau-Ponty is expression. Writing for Derrida is the inscription of signature. Expression for Merleau-Ponty results in signification. Signature for Derrida results in traces. The elaboration of the place of difference is the marking off of a textuality—scriptive textuality—in which writing is neither act nor effect but in which writing operates at the conjuncture of style and inscription, expression and signature, signification and trace. The task here is to elucidate this place where writing makes a difference.

STYLE/WRITING

What's in a style? The question echoes the Shakespearean: what's in a name? The answer is not inconsequential. Merleau-Ponty writes:

> Style is what makes all signification possible. Before signs or emblems become for everyone, even the artist, the simple index of already given significations, there must be that fruitful moment when signs have *given form* to experience or when an operant and latent meaning finds the emblems which should liberate it, making it manageable for the artist and accessible to others. If we really want to understand the origin of signification—and unless we do, we shall not understand any other creation or

any other culture, for we shall fall back upon the supposition of an intelligible world in which everything is signified in advance—we must give up every signification that is already institutionalized and return to the starting point of a non-signifying world. This is always what faces the creator, at least with respect to what he is about to say (*Prose*, p. 58).

"Style is what makes all signification possible." Style is at "the origin of signification." Style is not just *a* style; it is that which conditions all signification. Style—whether in painting or writing—is not "a certain number of ideas or tics that [the painter or writer] can inventory but a manner of formulation that is just as recognizable for others and just as little visible to [the painter or writer] as his [or her] silhouette or his [or her] everyday gestures" (*Prose*, p. 58). While literary or art historians attempt to offer a list of the elements that constitute a writer's or painter's style—Proust is ponderous, penetrating, thoughtful, subjective, whereas Monet is light, airy, glimmering, pastel-like, etc.—these are not what *constitutes* style itself. They are rather an itemization of some features of an artistic result, pieces of an endless list which is necessarily reformulated and reformulatable in what Foucault would describe as new *discursive frameworks*.[1] These descriptive units—collectable, presentable, and impressive as they may be *still* do not account for style. They are at best indicators of a style at work in a particular aesthetic object or set of objects. They hardly constitute style per se. Rather style per se makes each of these particular significations possible. Style for Merleau-Ponty partakes of a "non-signifying world," a condition that anticipates signification but which itself is not differentiated into specific determinations. Style is not an emanation of the writer or artist, nor is it an effect of the written or painted product. Style is located at that place where signs "give form to" the world of experience, where signification becomes possible.

In order for style to be the very possibility of signification, it must be pre-significatory. This does not mean that style is pre-objective nor even pre-subjective. And yet in a sense, style is neither objective nor subjective. Earlier in Merleau-Ponty's writings, the interweaving of subjective and objective would have been called "ambiguity."[2] In *The Visible and the Invisible* (1964), it takes shape as the chiasmatic intertwining of visible and invisible. Style inserts itself in the ambiguous domain, in the place of the intertwining, where differentiation has not yet resolved itself into the objective or the subjective, where specifications are not yet relevant and where a distinct position cannot be found, asserted, or offered. Style is the in-forming, the giving form to what is not yet formed, not yet specified, not yet shaped. The writer's style is not a determinate form, yet it is the forming of the formation of writing. The writer writes. In writing, style is enacted. The enactment of style is not the production of an object nor the invocation of a concept. The enactment of style is the bringing into being of a whole orientation toward the world, toward culture, toward persons, and toward one's own experience of the world, culture, and other people.

Style is the "stylizing" of language. Language is shaped, articulated, brought into being, by way of style. Style is the rendering specifiable of what remains unspecified in language. Style is not the set of specifications themselves, but rather that through which determination and specification are brought about. The style of a writer is the style of the writer's language. An analysis of—or even an algorithm for—a writer's language will not render a full account of the writer's style. The style of writing is for Merleau-Ponty *an indirect language*, a language that is neither produced nor accessed directly. Although Merleau-Ponty often characterizes style with respect to painting, style in writing plays a similar role. The style of writing "claims to retrieve things as they are" (*Prose*, p. 101). This is not the direct language of everyday speech and conventional discourse. The style of writing seeks to retrieve everything in its narrative grasp. Writers writing can only conceive of themselves "in an established language" (painters by contrast are able to refashion language) (*Prose*, p. 100). Painting is not the sole proprietor of indirect language. Indirect language also operates in writers' writing. Writers' writing however must enact style by reincorporating it into a language that is already there, already imbued with a past, already recognizable despite the transformations introduced by the new writing. Style shapes new writing, it does not create a new object. Robbe-Grillet's novelty does not lie in a refashioning of language as in Mondrian's painting: his novels speak language as a retrieval of language such that it speaks differently. Writing in Robbe-Grillet is a reincorporation of language such that the descriptive repetitions, geometrical constructions, and perceptual constatations are still language, still French or English translation. However *what* it says recasts the body of language such that its past is reintegrated in a new way. The past of the writer's language is "not just a dominated past but also an understood past" (*Prose*, p. 101), a past that is not only controlled in a new way but is also recognizable by those who might not yet know it. Writing then is shaped out of its past, returned to its past, and augmented by its past for the present of its readership. Style makes it possible for language to speak in a particular way. Style makes the past speak in a recognizable shape—even after the writer is gone.

For another language, a language which is critical, philosophical, and universal, Merleau-Ponty states, it is "essential to pursue self-possession, to master through criticism the secret of its own inventions of style, to talk about speech instead of only using it. In a word, the spirit of language is or pretends to be spirit for itself, to have nothing that does not come from itself" (*Prose*, p. 101). Critical language, critical writing, seeks to explore how style introduces novelty, how style serves as the precondition for the reincorporation of language, and even tries to specify how style forms its own preconditions. The task of a critical language is to show how style could be the style of a writer writing, a literary movement affirming itself in a variety of writings, or a period forming itself as a kind of *Zeitgeist*. But a critical language also has a revolutionary task, one of interrogating writing, understanding style and styles, allowing the indirect language of writing to speak for itself.

Merleau-Ponty's account of style is itself located in the context of the early 1950s when it was most fully formulated. His understanding is often set off against Malraux's views, most notably in *La Création artistique*. Merleau-Ponty's account of style is thereby located in a time when a certain style of thinking was prevalent. Developing out of a phenomenological tradition, his thought moved beyond it and was limited by it. His own style picked up the relevant pieces of that tradition and reincorporated them into a philosophical writing that was distinctively his own. Yet he was limited by the style of his time; his language—as he admits—was recognizable albeit difficult. It forged ahead while at the same time reintegrating its phenomenological past.

By contrast, Derrida's style—equally difficult, effectively perplexing to some, becoming eminently familiar to others—mobilizes a new language, a new writing. This new writing, inscribing itself in the late 1960s (and in the two decades thereafter) cannot claim to speak as Merleau-Ponty's own philosophical language does. Yet it cannot dissociate itself entirely from Merleau-Ponty's writing. The Derridean mode of writing is not simply a style—though in one of the more restricted senses of style, it certainly has identifiable characteristics. As already indicated, for Merleau-Ponty, style is not a specifiable set of features: indirect language is the pre-condition for writing itself. With Derrida, however, writing itself occupies a place analogous to that of style in Merleau-Ponty. Indeed, "analogous" is too weak: there is a distinct juxtapositional relation between the Merleau-Pontean account of style and the Derridean formulation of writing.

One would expect that style and writing are not the same. As is evident in Merleau-Ponty, style is the precondition for writing. Yet in Derrida, writing is not simply the product nor the correlate of speech. Derridean writing, or *écriture,* is not the opposite of speech, just as style for Merleau-Ponty is not the opposite of language. For Merleau-Ponty style is an indirect language that conditions writing itself. For Derrida writing is the inscription of difference between speech and writing, between word and concept, between the sensible and the intelligible. Just as style for Merleau-Ponty is chiasmatic (bringing about the intertwining of the visible and the invisible, the spoken and the unspoken, the specifiable and the unspecified indirect language of writing), similarly *l'écriture* for Derrida is inscribed in a place of difference, marking off the inside and the outside of written language, setting the margins of text and context, delimiting what is one's own and what is not one's own.

For Derrida writing *(l'écriture)* is difference (or more specifically *différance*). *Différance* is neither a word nor a concept, neither *phonē* nor *graphē,* neither the signifier nor the signified. *Différance* is spacing *(espacement)* and spacing is the opening up of a space where the indecidability of *différance*—as neither deferral nor differing, neither the temporal putting off nor the spatial distanciation—can establish itself as having priority, as resolving itself on one side of the opposition or the other. *Différance* is hardly identical with Merleau-Ponty's "ambiguity" in the early writings and "chiasm" at the end of his career, yet the indecidability of *différance* certainly marks a similar if not corresponding place in the Merleau-Pontean enterprise. *Différance* is also the *pharmakon:* neither a poison nor a remedy, neither what kills nor what cures—it is a medicine that could produce either result: too much could be fatal, whereas the right amount could cure. Writing is a *pharmakon.* Too much can make us forget, lose the need to keep in memory; too little and we cannot hold it all in memory. Derrida suggests that writing is a "dangerous supplement," corresponding to Rousseau's account of masturbation, which—as Rousseau confesses—can enhance sexual relations with the other, or replace them even to the extent of suspending any mutual involvement. Yet writing for Derrida has no determinate effect: its determination is to be indecidable just as style for Merleau-Ponty remains chiasmatic.

What of style for Derrida? In "Qual Quelle," Derrida writes:

> But, if there is a timbre and a style, will it be concluded that here the source *presents itself?*
>
> *Point.* And this is why *I* loses itself here, or in any event exposes itself in the operation of mastery. The timbre of my voice, the style of my writing are that which for (a) me never will have been present. I neither hear nor recognize the timbre of my voice. If my style marks itself, it is only on a surface which remains invisible and illegible for me (*Margins*, p. 296).

Speaking of Valéry, Derrida writes, "*if there is* one literary event, it is inscribed by style" (*Margins*, p. 296). This one literary event—Heidegger's *Ereignis* (namely: appropriation, happening, en-own-ment, advent)—is the inscription of a style: a marking of what is one's own, a proclamation of ownness. Style inscribes ownness—not as *I* but as appropriation. Style for Derrida marks an event: not a momentary event but the persistence of event in writing. Style is not the prose of the world but the inscription of ownness in writing. And writing, as we have remarked, is differential and "spacing" in its places of origination.

Style is also the stylus, the writing instrument, the tool for the marking of words, lines, margins. The stylus, the pen, the pointed thing writes, inscribes, delineates. As Derrida elaborates in *Spurs* (1973), Nietzsche's style—his styles— are manifold. Yet each involves the use of the writing tool, the male instrument. Truth, by contrast, is associated with woman. Woman is the disclosure that *aletheia* portends. Woman is the veil and unveiling of truth, the *Unverborgenheit* that Heidegger offers as an account of truth. The truth in writing, the truth of writing, is not in the style. Its truth resides in the writing, but the writing takes place—as a literary event, as style.

The inscription of the difference at the juncture of Merleau-Pontean style and Derridean writing is their inverse: namely Merleau-Pontean writing and Derridean style. While style, for Merleau-Ponty, is a way of being-in-the-world, writing, for Derrida, is the differential space in which readings must necessarily take place. The *scriptive* textuality that results from this juxtaposition becomes even more evident in the intersection of Merleau-Pontean expression and Derridean signature.

EXPRESSION/SIGNATURE

Merleau-Ponty writes: "expression always goes beyond what it transforms" (*Prose*, p. 69). And Derrida asks: "does the absolute singularity of an event of the signature ever occur?" (*Margins*, p. 328). For Merleau-Ponty, expression enters into his basic understanding of language and its activities. As early as *Phenomenology of Perception*, speech *(la parole)* is characterized in terms of expression and gesture. The gestural, the embodied orientation toward not only objects but also articulation, is linked to anthropological studies—particularly those of Leroi-Gouran—which show the direct correlation between types of gesture and speech itself. With Merleau-Ponty, as with a long tradition, speech is not writing, speaking is not written language. Yet writing or written language carries with it what he calls *speaking speech* and *spoken speech*. "Speaking speech" *(parole parlante)* is the direct articulation of sense through words and gesture and general bodily comportment. "Spoken speech" *(parole parlée)* is the produced cultural artifact which enters into literary and other aesthetic forms such as painting, writing, sculpture, etc. But "spoken speech" need not be exclusively high culture. Grocery lists, course descriptions, and legal documents are also "spoken speech." However even for Merleau-Ponty, the distinction between spoken speech and speaking speech is not so simple. "Spoken speech" is already imbued with "speaking speech." An orientation toward expression, as a result, is already implied by "speaking speech." "Speaking speech" wants to say something. What it wants to say is not only speech itself but also meaning. And it wants to say it in "spoken speech." The wanting-to-say in spoken speech by speaking speech is expression. Gesture is one form of expression—one way in which our embodied Being-in-the-world takes shape in the speaking of and into spoken speech. The interlacing of speaking speech and spoken speech is crucial here. Expression is that interlacing such that the writing of writing, for instance, is not just the production of new reincorporated cultural artifacts but also—and even more important—the speaking of speech.

In *Prose of the World*, writing (like painting and other forms of indirect language) is expression—the speaking of spoken speech. What is crucial here is that expression is an orientation toward the world through language. The expressive language of writing is not the same as that of painting, for instance. During the eighteenth century, Lessing (in the *Laocoön*) affirmed that the distinction between the plastic arts and poetry is indeed decisive. But even the Roman poet Horace had called attention to the difference as well as the relation between them. For Lessing, however, it was "expression" that marked the difference. Painting expresses differently than poetry: the plastic arts do not express feeling, emotion, and intensity in the same way as do poetry or writing. Many nineteenth-century writers (including Peacock and Shelley) were preoccupied with the debate over the distinction between poetry and prose. And even a century later Sartre's *What Is Literature?* prompts a divergent response in Barthes's *Writing Degree Zero*, but also in Merleau-Ponty's *Prose of the World*. Here, however, expression is not just an effect or feature of writing, but rather an intricate link with style. Expression "always goes beyond what it transforms." Expression cannot be located simply in writing but takes writing beyond itself: it transforms writing and brings writing to an understanding that goes beyond it. Expression, then, for Merleau-Ponty is both an activity of writing and an effect that transforms it.

The correlation between Merleau-Pontean expression and Derridean signature is not obvious. One would expect that expression (as a phenomenological activity) operates in opposition to meaning or content. And indeed Derrida at times offers such an account of expression—as just one more of those binary oppositions that partake of the text of metaphysics and that are available for a deconstructive reading. Expression—one might suggest—is active, noetic, and experiential. Content is objective, noematic, and analyzable. Yet for Merleau-Ponty, expression is not just a correlate of content. Expression is a characteristic of a whole orientation of thought and being. Writing as expression is both productive and transformative. Derridean signature is an inscription of identity, an indecidable marking of ownness, an indication and expression of what is one's own in writing. Derridean signature marks difference in writing—*différance* as writing. It marks the authorial inscription of writing. Signature is not just a sign or indicator; it is also the making of the particular signs of a particular text: this text (and not any other), this text with this context and not another, this text bounded and limited in these ways.

As Derrida remarks in "Signature Event Context" (*Margins*, pp. 307–330,) communication is a "signature event." Communication—writing—is not just an object that is passed around, read, and accepted or rejected. Communication is also an event, an event not of presence but of presentation. Communication, building upon both the hermeneutic and semiotic models, is both event and message. Communication is a paper delivered at a conference, a message transmitted, and a bringing in of what was previously not said. Communication is a "signature event" made into a text—or "texted" (a *signature événement qu'on texte*). But what is it "to text" a "signature event"? To text a "signature event" is to delimit an expression in such a way that it is authorially marked, to enter into the differential space of style and expression (as Merleau-Ponty would understand them) and to inscribe a particularity to replace the singularity of the person who signed with the signature. The signature takes the place of the actual person. A comparison of signatures on a bank check will suffice to determine identity. The signature communicates.

To the question "does the absolute singularity of an event of the signature ever occur?" the answer cannot be other than equivocal. "Signature events" are supposed to be individual and singular. Counterfeits and mistaken identities do occur. But the "signature event" itself is an occurrence that marks what is unique. Is the signature that can be reproduced—like Derrida's at the end of the last essay in *Margins of Philosophy*—the same as *the* signature event? To the extent that the graphic marks are reproduced with each copy of the book, the signature is reproduced—counterfeited in a way. But there could be no legal case against the publishers. The signature has not been stolen—not a letter of it. The signature has been reproduced in a book published under Derrida's authorship. Hence Derrida's signature is authorized. But does a new version of the text emerge every time his signature is replicated? Or is the authority of each reproduction a concession that Derrida makes—a concession that need not be licensed each time? Surely it must have been licensed (or authorized) at least once—by way of a contract signed by Jacques Derrida. But would the singulari-ty of *that* signature event authorize all the others? In a sense, the answer must surely be yes. In another sense, the signature is not the signing, the making of a sign. The signing, the production of signification or at least the traces thereof, are reproducible without prejudice to the publisher—indeed the publisher seems to be benefiting quite nicely as a result. But what is communicated in the signature event is a reading of communication, the expression—as Merleau-Ponty would call it—of a positionality as text, as writing.

The signature marks writing as correlative with a style that is one's own. The scriptural textuality of signature/expression inscribes an authorial place in which writing takes shape, in which writing not only takes on style, but in which and by which it *has* style. The style of writing is the signature event of expression. The writing of style is the differential marking of expression as "signature event."

SIGNIFICATION/TRACE

The question of signification preoccupied Merleau-Ponty from the earliest stages of his philosophical career. His account of writing continually alludes to the intersection of *signification* with style and expression. Signification is not reducible either to "meaning" or "sense." The sense of expression or the sense of style is the orientation of writing—the direction of its articulation, the path it sets for itself. On the other hand, the meaning of expression and the meaning of style concerns the elaboration of conceptual specificities. What characterizes sig-nification is marked out where meaning and sense meet one another, where the indirect language of style and expression seems to constitute a determinate semi-otic identity: Kafka's style, as expressed in *The Trial (Der Prozeß)*, or Wordsworth's style expressed in his "Lines Composed above Tintern Abbey." Its signification is the unique formulation of a given sign system—Kafka's sign sys-tem, Wordsworth's sign system—each animated by a particular vitality and expression of meaning.

To the extent that Derridean traces mark off the differential spaces left open in a signifying system, writing takes style to its limits. To the extent that Derridean traces permeate writing, they iterate the very signatures that consti-tute a style. Traces are left by a style that seeks to impose itself, to make a mark, to achieve an identity, to affirm a set of conditions that places limits on a partic-ular type of formulation. Style not only produces traces, it also uses them:

> Style would seem to advance in the manner of a *spur* of sorts *(éperon)*...
> style also uses its spur *(éperon)* as a means of protection against the terrify-ing, blinding, mortal threat (of that) which *presents* itself, which obstinately thrusts itself into view. And style thereby protects the pres-ence, the content, the thing itself, meaning, truth—on the condition at least that it should not *already (déjà)* be that gaping chasm which has been

deflowered in the unveiling of the difference. *Already (déjà)* such is the name for what has been effaced or subtracted beforehand, but which has nevertheless left behind a mark, a signature which is retracted in that very thing from which it is withdrawn (*Spurs*, p. 39).

Style then advances, proceeds from wherever it is. It goes ahead, carrying on with its task, presenting itself as what needs to be presented. Style is not a position of its own. Rather style goes forth in order to establish a position. It establishes a position by forming a set of identities not as positivities but as marks of what is no longer, what has been erased from the surfaces, what is other than what has been thematized. In this sense, the traces are not even identities. Rather they are marks, signatures, inscriptions, which account for neither the absence of that which forms the style nor the presence of some sort of meaning, truth, thing itself, which is described, narrated, identified, clarified, articulated, or even expressed. The marks or signatures are neither the marking of a style nor the style that is marked in an inscription. In the unveiling of difference, one would expect there to be truth. This may have been the Heideggerian expectation, but with Derrida the unveiling, the disclosure, the opening, is not the appearance of truth but rather the mark of the truth that has been styled by "a stroke of the pen."

As already noted, the pen is a stylus, a writing instrument, ready to mark out whatever writing is prescribed. What it marks out is the truth of what is said; it marks out a disclosure, which reveals something other than itself. What is other than itself is that which is disclosed. Marking the disclosure, marking the difference, marking the marking does not amount to the founding of a context, or anything upon which to base anything else. The marking of the difference for Derrida is writing itself. Style marks the difference. The stylus writes—and the trace of writing continually evokes the dimension of style. Thus Derrida notes:

The *éperon*, which is translated *sporo* in Frankish or High German, *spor* in Gaelic, is pronounced *spur* in English. In *Les mots anglais* Mallarmé relates it to the verb *to spurn*, that is to disdain, to rebuff, to reject scornfully. Although this may not be a particularly fascinating homonym, there is still a necessary historic and semantic operation from one language to the other evident in the fact that the English *spur*, the *éperon*, is the "same word" as the German *Spur:* or, in other words, trace, wake, indication, mark (*Spurs*, p. 41).

All this etymological and translinguistic magic is pertinent to the extent that it indicates the link between *stylus, style,* and *trace*. The trace, which Heidegger sometimes identifies with the gods who have fled, leaving an abyss (*ein Abgrund*) in the place of some sure ground *(Grund)*, is not that which is marked, nor is it the marking. It is neither the active agent nor the passive patient. The mark, along with the signature or the writing, remains differential. And the movement from "spur" to "trace" is itself a differential movement.

What, one might ask, does the trace have to do with Merleau-Pontean signification? The question is particularly acute when one remembers that
signification—understood as meaning—is associated with truth in Derrida, and
truth or meaning are surely other than the writing of difference that the trace
identifies. Yet in Merleau-Ponty, the project of signification is not a result, nor is
it an agent. Signification arises out of the expression of a style through the indirect language of the body, of painting, of architecture, etc. Signification is not
the effect of signifying, nor is it the signifier. Signification is that chiasmatic
domain in which neither expressing nor expressed have any priority, where neither the visible nor the invisible takes precedence. Signification is itself a fabric
of perceptual and experiential relationality. Formed by indirect as well as direct
language, signification is styled in writing and expressed in the enactment of an
embodied Being-in-the-world. Like the trace, signification is neither an agent
nor a result, neither a producer nor a produced, neither an initiation nor an
effect. Like the trace, signification is differential. Signification has no identity
other than the stylizing activity which produces that which signifies.
Signification is not what is written, nor is it the writer. Similarly, the trace is neither the stylus nor the thing that is given style. The trace is neither that which is
true nor the writing of what is true. The trace is the marking off of what is disclosed in the being true of any particular thing or content. The trace like
signification has no positive identity. The being of the trace is a matter of *différance*, just as the place of signification is a site of ambiguity (or the chiasmatic).

Writing, then, for Derrida is a dispersed network of traces. The traces are
given style by the stylus that writes them. Writing is the tracing out and delimiting of its own network, its own text. Writing for Derrida marks out the domain
of a textuality that sets itself off from Merleau-Pontean style. Merleau-Pontean
style could achieve the "prose of the world." Yet it can do so only by its achievement of expression and enactment of signification. Merleau-Pontean style
cannot be a private, individual activity. It must enter into the texture of the
world. In that way and only in that way can it fulfill its political necessity—
which is to be style, expression, and signification in a social context where
communication, understanding, and action are not only valued but also indispensable features of writing and its realization of itself as an indirect language.
Correspondingly, Derridean writing, signature, and traces hardly occupy an isolated, independent, solitary space. Writing, signature, and trace operate in the
formation of a fabric of meaning, truth, and reality that are constituted textually
as institutions, social formations, and communicative constructions. Textually,
they could have been otherwise. The looming presence of alterity marks the difference in which Derridean writing operates, where it sets limits to itself as
identity and outlines the frame that keeps it from becoming fully other. Hence
Derridean writing marks its own limits, identifies its outside, its externality, and
thereby makes itself difference. Writing as difference—even the difference that
sets Derridean writing off from Merleau-Pontean style—is the mark of a scriptive textuality that will have been expressed even if only as a dispersed complex
of traces here in the present—which I mark off at this juncture.

V

The Institution(s) of Philosophy as Textualities

18

ON THE UNIVERSITY
Nietzsche/Schopenhauer

> It seems most important to me that there be a higher tribunal outside the
> universities to supervise and judge these institutions in respect to the cul-
> ture which they promote; and as soon as philosophy withdraws from the
> universities and cleanses itself of all unworthy considerations and obscuri-
> ties, it will necessarily become such a tribunal.
>
> —F. Nietzsche, *Schopenhauer as Educator*

What is supposed to go on inside the university? The university is at least in
principle a universe of studies. Can one even say: *the* universe of studies? But
then if the university is a whole universe of studies—the universe of studies—
what is supposed to go on in it? Indeed is there anything that is not legitimately
its province—within, in any case, the general field of studies, or more specifically, academic studies? In other words, what is proper to the university and what is
not proper to it? Or better still is there anything in the way of academic work,
intellectual study, theoretical research which does not officially and practically
belong to the university? What we are asking here is, what constitutes the university as whatever it is? What defines it as whatever it is? How does it
determine itself as what it is? How does it delimit itself or set its own boundaries? And concomitantly, is there anything in the realm of study that can be
said to belong outside the university? Or to put it another way, what sort of fabric, network, texture, or simply "text" is it that establishes the domain or
domains of the university?

When Nietzsche claims that "it is important that there be a higher tribunal
outside the universities,"[1] one is led to wonder what this could really mean. Are
we to suspect that there is some sort of university-like function that needs to
operate outside the university? Or is it simply a matter of something else, something that really has nothing to do with the university and is therefore irrelevant
to it? But if this idea of a "higher tribunal, were really irrelevant to the university, there would be no point in offering it as a "tribunal," that is, as an institution

of arbitration and adjudication. As a *tribunal,* a higher (or at least *other*) social form, it must certainly operate *in relation to* the very institution for which it is the "tribunal." Thus to be and to occupy a place outside the university—at least, if it is to be a tribunal—this second institution will have to both distinguish itself from the university and at the same time affirm and delineate the inside of that "primary" institution.

The difficulty is that, upon inspection, (i.e., upon careful consideration) of Nietzsche's account, it is not clear that the university really is the "primary" institution. Indeed, it seems to be that the "tribunal" is the more fundamental, more basic, more primary institution. Nietzsche goes on to indicate that this "tribunal" will "supervise and judge these institutions in respect to the culture which they promote." To "supervise" and "judge" is not simply to stand back and watch or even to examine and speculate. Nietzsche suggests a function which is much more effective, much more significant, much more powerful. This tribunal will "supervise" and "judge." This means that whatever goes on within the university will be subject to the evaluation and viewpoint of the tribunal. Whatever happens within the university will depend upon a verdict and assessment *from the outside.* The concern of the tribunal—if it is to perform its tasks from the outside—is not necessarily everything that transpires within the university. Nietzsche says that it is to "supervise" and "judge" with respect to the culture which these institutions "promote." Nietzsche specifies that the principal activity which is to be the province of such a tribunal is quite specifically the "culture" *(die Bildung)* which the universities promote. But what is this culture, this *Bildung,* which universities engage in? At this juncture Nietzsche does not say "*Kultur.*" When he refers to "*Kultur*" a bit further on, he speaks of a "so-called Culture." To the extent that *Bildung* is what Nietzsche wants to encourage, he is really talking about the whole set of images and ideals of the society. He is referring to the general education which a person of high standards is to manifest. He is speaking of self-development: personal enhancement through knowledge of the picture that the society gives to itself. In effect, he is referring to something like what the Greeks called *aretē.* Universities concern themselves with this sort of general education into the values and standards maintained by the society in question. What is promoted therefore is not simply culture in the sense of the artifacts, works, products, and ideas of knowledge but also (and much more important) the whole set of features which give shape to and constitute the society as it is. In fact, universities—in Nietzsche's view—have become one of the primary *loci* for the establishment and development of precisely those respects in which people are to think, act, and express themselves. As long as universities are allowed to operate on their own without any external evaluators, without any outside perspective, without any alternative point of view, they limit themselves to the values, aspirations, and aesthetic judgments which they set for themselves. Or, if they are not fully able to set these valuative conditions for themselves, they simply follow those which have been instituted by what Nietzsche calls the "State." In either case, whether self-determined or imposed by the State, there will be no external point of view from which and by which these values can be made available to scrutiny.

What is needed then is some outside perspective with respect to the very culture which the universities promote. The *Bildung* that is offered, espoused, and even generated by the universities is not the same as the *Kultur* that Nietzsche envisions. *Kultur* is given form and life by the individual—not by the State and not by the self-production of the universities in their sterility. Culture is both a reaction against the *Bildung* or education that universities constitute as their mission and a determination or affirmation of what is to be sought after, what is called for, what is required—whether the universities and those who administrate them know it or not. The difficulty that poses itself at this juncture is that of a dilemma: is it possible for those whose task and function it is to propagate the *Bildung* of the society also to provide a context for the culture by which and through which a proper evaluation can take place? In other words, is there a space within the university for the criticism and self-determination which are essential to culture but not necessarily compatible with *Kultur* as postulated and proffered by the university? Is there a domain inside the university by which the university and its ideals can be assessed?

Nietzsche characterizes culture as "the child of every individual's self-knowledge and inadequacy" (*SE*, p. 61; *UB*, p. 96). It is not sufficient for one who possesses or acknowledges (*sich bekennen*) culture to operate simply on the basis of what he or she knows; it is also essential to recognize that of which there is not enough. The person who possesses culture knows limits: knows what is within his or her sphere of knowledge and also knows what needs to be fulfilled and completed beyond it. To avow culture is to recognize one's own inadequacies, to be aware of what is still to be done, to take into account what is incomplete in itself. Nietzsche recounts the self-narrative of the person of culture. Such a person says: "I see something higher and more human than myself above me. Help me all of you to reach it as I will help every person who recognizes the same thing and suffers from the same thing so that finally the man may again come into being who feels himself infinite in knowing and loving in seeing and ability and who with all his being is a part of nature as Judge and criterion of things" (*SE*, p. 61; *UB*, p. 96). The person of culture knows his or her limits: both those that constitute the inside and those that constitute the outside of one's knowledge. The person of culture prays that what is beyond his or her knowledge can be brought within it; but there is also the recognition of what cannot be brought within that sphere.

"Culture," Nietzsche states, "demands action" (*Die Kultur verlangt... die Tat*) (*SE*, p. 62; *UB*, p. 98). The person of culture cannot just sit back and let things happen, cannot simply accept whatever is offered, cannot merely follow what others say. The person of culture must act. "This means fighting for culture and being hostile to the influences, laws and institutions in which he does not recognize his goal: the production of genius" (*SE*, p. 62; *UB*, p. 98). The person of culture must work on the production of genius. Genius does not simply happen. It must be encouraged, stimulated, and animated. The person of genius must make genius happen. There is no need to wonder whose genius is in question. It is clearly that of the person of culture. But once again the question arises: can this sort of genius be produced within the university or is it condemned to operate outside the boundaries of the hallowed academic halls? Does genius—of the sort that Nietzsche describes—have a place in the university? Can one fight for culture from within the university? Are universities suitable to the goals that the person of culture recognizes as what needs to be fulfilled? Or do universities stifle genius, prohibit its production, inhibit the very core and source of culture?

Part of the answer to this last question lies in the distinction Nietzsche offers between *Kultur* and "*Kulturstaat*" ("the cultural tasks of the State" or, simply, "State culture"). What needs to be promoted is "culture." What one typically finds especially in universities is "State culture" *(Kulturstaat)*. State culture "serves the existing institutions and is useful to them" (*SE*, p. 65; *UB*, p. 102). State culture reiterates and repeats the values and ideals that the State and its institutions produce for it. As Nietzsche puts it, State culture derives from the "selfishness of the State" *(die Selbstsucht des Staates)*. This "selfishness of the State" "desires both maximum extension and generalization of culture and has the most effective tools in its hands to satisfy its wishes" (*SE*, p. 65; *UB*, p. 102). To the extent that the university is an instrument of the State it participates in the extension and generalization of culture in accordance with the interests of the State. And those interests are without any doubt selfish interests—they serve the needs and goals of the State. To the extent that the university promotes and develops—through *Bildung*—preoccupations of the State, it is the handmaiden of that broadest of social edifices. Thus when the picture that the university has of itself, and the culture that it seeks to generalize, derives from the State, the culture that it proliferates is fundamentally a State culture. And as a State culture it makes the production of genius practically impossible. It radically undermines any chance for the development of ideas and interests that are not for the benefit of the State. In truth, such ideas and interests need not be opposed to the aspirations of the State; they need only *lie outside* the advantage of the State. But if there is no place for what Nietzsche calls the production of genius then there is no place for what he also calls "culture." And if there is no place for "culture" *(Kultur)* within the university, then there is no place for those who render it, generate it, extol it, and make it proliferate. But once again the question must be asked: is the university completely and entirely devoid of any possibility of the kind of activity—"action" as Nietzsche calls it—that will generate culture? Is there no place within the university for thinking, for interrogation, for judgment, for the production of genius?

Nietzsche's thoroughgoing doubt and despair with respect to the viability of what is typically received as "German culture" leads him to claim quite definitively that he would not himself want to have anything to do with it. "German culture" as he understood it was overwrought with an interest in "beautiful form." He thought of German culture as above all trying to disguise "ugly or boring content" (*SE*, p. 66; *UB*, p. 104). The idea was to "make life prettier" (*SE*, p. 67; *UB*, p. 106). And while he was still willing to agree with Richard Wagner (*Schopenhauer as Educator* was published in 1874 when Nietzsche was thirty years old), Nietzsche quotes Wagner as saying, "The German is awkward and uncouth when he wants to behave in a genteel manner; but he is divine and superior to all when he catches fire" (*SE*, p. 68; *UB*, p. 106). He then points out that this German fire is quite deadly and all-consuming when it catches on. It was Wagner's atypicality that attracted Nietzsche, that led him to appeal to Wagner's wisdom. The "abnormal" ones—like Hölderlin and Kleist—"could not endure the climate of so-called German culture; only iron constitutions like Beethoven, Goethe, Schopenhauer, and Wagner (were) able to hold out" (*SE*, p. 20; *UB*, p. 40). He also cites Lessing as particularly un-German even though his prose style is most seductive (*SE*, p. 14; *UB*, P. 34). The point is that, although Nietzsche's examples stress the exceptions, and he hardly cites "typically" German writers or artists, nevertheless the predominantly canonical figures who were taught and discussed in the *gymnasium* and in the universities were the primary target of his concern. However, if whatever was taught in the universities was to be identical with "German culture" (and therefore "State culture") then indeed it is quite reasonable that there is no place for Culture in the universities. It would also be reasonable for Nietzsche to claim that some position, some tribunal, outside the university would be necessary in order to "judge" and "supervise" the education *(Bildung)* that would give rise to such "German" or "State" culture. But we have yet to examine what constitutes the university, in what respect the university constitutes itself as a kind of text—a text which Nietzsche identifies with State culture and which is bordered and delimited by that which is taught, promoted, and generated within it.

To what extent then is the university a kind of text whose content is whatever is taught, promoted, and generated within it? To what extent is this universe of studies—this diversity of disciplines—a fabric, texture, or network of topics, concerns, and styles of writing? To what extent is the university at once both text and context, both a complex of fields of inquiry and the container for those fields of inquiry?

To what extent is the university both the culture that is promoted—whatever it may be—and the practice of educating students into the ideals and values of the culture? As a set of fields and disciplines and matters of study the university sets limits to what is acceptable and what is not acceptable as the complex of domains forming the university. Naturally there will be some variations from one university to another but on the whole certain fields or topics are included and others are excluded from the academy. But the university is also a set of educational practices, enactments which determine what is viable, what is good, what is valuable (and what is not). These practices or enactments establish the *Bildung* that constitutes the university. The university as *Bildung* is the educational institution in its teaching function. Together as *Bildung* and as culture (or more typically *Kulturstaat*), the university constitutes itself as text.

But what sort of text is it? The university inscribes itself in a particular society. The university fulfills the ideals of that society (or at least it aspires to that end) by enacting those ideals through an educational performance and by delimiting those disciplines that are appropriate and worthy. But it is the society—what Nietzsche calls "the State"—that determines the nature of the *Bildung* and the form of *Kultur*. The university is rife with the authorial traces of State invocation, State inculcation, and even State intervention. The university in its performance and in its self-determination is an instrument of the society—and its State—with its self-interpretation of excellence, its culture, and its morality. The university both inscribes and delimits itself as an institution, as an instaurating practice, and as an organon that is different from other features of society.

Understood as a text the university is a paragon of both unity and diversity. In its diversity, it makes way for the development of many different disciplines of study from chemistry to psychology to philosophy, from medicine to law to music. It even allows for the development and incorporation of new fields such as biochemistry, sociology, anthropology, and comparative literature—fields which would not have known separate status in Nietzsche's time. Similarly, in our own time, departments of genetics, linguistics, and literary theory are beginning to make their mark on Western universities. But all these disciplines are *inside* the university or are brought inside the university. This is, of course, to suggest that: (1) they were originally *outside* the universities; or (2) they were prohibited from inclusion in the universities; or (3) they arose *ex nihilo*; or (4) they appeared with the development of new research; or (5) they came into being because of a reorganization within the universities. To a certain extent all or most of these reasons can be offered. Studio art at one time belonged only to art schools—now it is often part of the "Arts" curriculum in universities. It was brought in from the outside. Psychoanalysis is rigorously excluded from many psychology departments in the English-speaking world. Continental philosophy was for a long time kept out of analytically oriented philosophy departments in England and America. Although comparative literature and now literary theory do not arise *ex nihilo*, and they even tend to find a place alongside more traditional literature departments, they do not supplant them. Biochemistry and environmental studies have found a place beside existing fields because of new needs for research in these areas. In some universities a reorganization will account for the combination of disciplines as seemingly diverse as physical anthropology and anatomy. Or more obviously related fields are brought together: such as theater and national literatures into dramaturgy programs, or Japanese history, Chinese literature, and Korean religion into Asian studies departments.

Out of all this diversity, the university is to be a universe of studies, a framework for the unity of the variety of disciplines. So the question returns: what brings them all together? Or perhaps more important: what *should* bring them all together? In Nietzsche's view—and there is good evidence that the situation has not changed in the past century—what brings them all together is very much like what he calls the State. According to Nietzsche, "If a man appeared who really looked as though he intended to operate on everything, including the State, with the scalpel of truth, then the State, because it affirms above all its own existence, is justified in excluding such a man from it and treating him as an enemy" (*SE*, pp. 95–96; *UB*, p. 146). The *Kulturstaat* sets the conditions of inclusion and exclusion with respect to the university as a social inscription, as a narrative of the society itself, in short, as an institution. The State would exclude the individual whose position taking would run counter to the values and ideals of the State. But here we return to the coordinate formulation of the university, namely, as *Bildung*, as a practice in which certain activities or kinds of activities go on. The university is a performative: at the same time that it says that this is what needs to be learned, studied, researched, theorized, it is also the very bringing into being of this learning, studying, researching, and theorizing. The university is not a set of buildings—with ivy, stone, red brick, concrete, or pane glass. The university is not a whole list of statistics which includes the number of students, the area of the campus, the geographical location of the administration, the list of jobs acquired by students, the degrees of deans and vice-presidents, etc. The university is the fields of inquiry, the content of such research, and the teaching of it. The university is the performance of educational practices in which a certain culture is taught. This circumscribed binary function—namely, the "what" that is investigated (whether it be truth or just the prescribed version) and the instilling of educational ideals (whether they be truly valuable or just those espoused by the State and its administrators)—is what constitutes the text of the university.

This textuality of the university places the philosopher in an awkward position. Philosophy is one of the disciplines typically included within the university. Philosophy is—in the contemporary university—sometimes grouped along with other humanities and sometimes along with the social sciences. Philosophy is typically taught as a body of information with its so-called "areas" such as epistemology, metaphysics, philosophy of language with its "history" and with its officially sanctioned "methods," "styles," or "orientations." Often these latter considerations—specifically, how philosophy is done—are given shape in terms of what counts as "logic." What counts as logic permeates the so-called "areas of philosophy" and even, to a certain extent, the "history of philosophy." Advanced research into particular logics often sets the pattern for the other types of work that are conducted under the name of philosophy. By separating logic from the "methods," "styles," or "orientations" of philosophy, it becomes possible to introduce various philosophical practices and teachings without arguing over what is to count as "logic." One way to reduce these styles, methods, or orientations, to render them tame or nonthreatening, is to determine different methods, styles, and orientations as "areas" or as "history" of philosophy. The operations of power within the discipline often move to exclude by disarming, by determining what counts as "logic," by transposing different "ways" of doing philosophy into "areas" or "historical periods" which are no longer current, contemporary, or therefore threatening. The operations of exclusion within philosophy as a discipline within the university can be performed irrespective of particular personnel, particular individual philosophers. The operations of exclusion can take place simply through the practice of certain types of administration and organization of courses of study. But these are the manifestations of what Nietzsche calls *Kulturstaat* as they are performed within the university. From within, one must submit to being a "State philosopher," namely, one who reiterates the ideals and values of the State. Thus if medical ethics or business ethics, set theory or argumentation are appreciated and valued by the State, then the task of the State philosopher is to teach and conduct research on these topics and in these ways. As Nietzsche writes: "If anyone can bear to be a State philosopher, he must also be content with being looked upon as if he had given up pursuing truth into all its secret retreats. At any rate as long as he is favored and provided with a position, he must recognize something higher than truth—the State" (*SE*, p. 86; *UB*, p. 146). Accepting the authority of the State—the infusion of State culture into the activities of the university—is to trade off the proper functions of philosophy for authorized philosophical research.

In Nietzsche's day, many of the activities of the university philosophy professor—particularly in Germany and Switzerland—were different; and yet the positionality continues even today. It was the historians of philosophy—like Ritter, Brandis, and Zeller—who, for Nietzsche, cast a cloud of dullness over Greek philosophy. Nietzsche indicates that he would prefer to read Diogenes Laertius to Zeller. For Nietzsche, academic or "professional" philosophy has its limits—as does any form of textualization. His objection to university philosophers, however—especially those who were "philologists, antiquarians, linguists, historians"—was that they did not really count as "philosophers." They were performing a State function—the *Bildung* which they promoted had little to do with actual philosophizing. And those who could be called philosophers—Herbartians and others—would in effect "make philosophy something ridiculous" (*SE*, p. 103; *UB*, p. 158). In this respect they were actually harmful. Philosophy is not one of those disciplines that the State would like to encourage. As Nietzsche puts it: "I believe in all seriousness that it is more useful to the State not to concern itself with philosophy, to desire nothing from it, and as long as it is possible to treat it as something indifferent. Without this indifference it becomes dangerous to the State and the State may persecute it . . . the State can have no further interest in the university than to educate devoted and useful citizens" (*SE*, p. 105; *UB*, p. 160). Hegelizers—as Nietzsche calls them—might have filled the barns with a function useful to the State. But now—he says—the Hegelizers *have* the power. In Hegel's time they *wanted* it. The difference is significant. Now, according to Nietzsche, philosophy has become scrupulous. The State no longer has need of (so many) philosophy professors.

But it is not that the State no longer needs philosophy professors. There would still be the discipline of philosophy in the universities—it is just that they would be linguists or journalists and not really philosophers. And as to the real role and position of philosophers—that would have to be something other. The philosopher's real role and position would have to be—Nietzsche claims—something *outside* the university. The position of the philosophers would have to be a kind of *tribunal* for the university—a "higher tribunal" which would "supervise and judge these institutions in respect to the culture which they promote." In this way, the philosopher need not become enmeshed in the compromising, self-limiting conditions of university life. In this way, the philosopher need not be subjected to the will of the State or society or even the philosophical conventions of his/her own day. In this way, the philosopher need not become contaminated with the interests and values of those who may not even do philosophy themselves but who are responsible for the type, character, and extent of philosophical investigation that can be tolerated within the State. In this way, philosophy can "withdraw from the universities and cleanse itself of all unworthy considerations and obscurities." In this way, philosophy can truly come into its own, affirm itself on its own, be on its own. In this way, philosophy can reflect upon, think about, even contemplate, the woeful condition of philosophy and, notably, not philosophy as it is practiced in the university, but as it *might* be, *ought* to be, *must* be, if it is to have any significant life.

But what sort of philosophy would it be that stands outside the university, that reflects upon the practices of the university, that "supervises and judges" the *Bildung* that is promoted in the universities? What sort of philosophy would it be that seeks to abstract itself entirely from universities so that it can be a tribunal for the universities? What sort of philosophy would it be that remains untainted by any of the worries of university life, of teaching, educating, dialoguing with colleagues, arguing over appointments, and setting courses of study? Is it not in fact the task of philosophy to know its own limits—to look to the outside of the university so as to know the inside, to look to the inside so as to know the outside? The practice of philosophy cannot be simply that of what Nietzsche calls "the Schopenhauerian man"—who "voluntarily takes the pain of truthfulness upon himself," whose "suffering serves to kill his individual will so as to prepare the complete revolution and reversal of his being, the attainment of which is the actual meaning of life" (*SE*, p. 105; *UB*, p. 160). This sort of self-inscribed otherness, self-inflicted wildness, self-imposed exile—the loneliness of a Zarathustra at the top of a mountain—can at best offer what Merleau-Ponty calls a *pensée de survol.* But this kind of reflection from above—bird's eye thinking—cannot see very well from a distance. It can only know the limits from the outside—just as the philosophy professor can only know the limits of university philosophy from the inside. The task then for philosophy will be to place itself at the margins of both the inside and the outside, at the place where the inside and the outside inscribe a border, a slash, an edge—where the place of difference makes a difference: the difference between the *Bildung* based on State culture and that which is able to make sense of *Kultur,* a culture free of State-instituted, administratively governed constraints. At the interface between philosophy on the inside and philosophy on the outside an activity can take place. That activity will be—perhaps with luck, and a bit of industry—an appropriate sense and proper style of philosophical practice—a marginal philosophical practice—a philosophical politics of a different sort.

19

ON PHILOSOPHICAL DISCOURSE
Merleau-Ponty/Blanchot

Blanchot's reading of philosophical discourse[1] is at once a concern with what philosophical discourse ought to be and an account of how he understands Merleau-Ponty's project. Blanchot's assessment in 1971 was published ten years after Merleau-Ponty's death. Blanchot assigns to Merleau-Ponty a special status. He is described as "a certain contemporary philosopher"—just as Dante throughout the *Divine Comedy* speaks of Aristotle as "the Philosopher." For Blanchot, what is significant in Merleau-Ponty is exemplary of philosophy in general.

"Le 'Discours Philosophique'" is hardly an extended philosophical disquisition. Blanchot does not himself engage in long philosophical disquisitions. Indeed one might wonder whether Blanchot ever writes philosophy. On the other hand, his texts are obsessed with the philosophical. But what are his texts? Sometimes they are clearly short stories, tales, or brief narratives, sometimes they are books comprised of essays. But what sort of essays? Critical essays, literary essays, or philosophical essays? Unquestionably philosophical themes arise, mark off, or characterize the essays themselves. The essays are philosophically informed—imbued with the French philosophical tradition, a tradition that takes Heidegger seriously. But they are not themselves "philosophical discourse."

What is at issue, however, in the essay "Philosophical Discourse" is philosophical discourse itself. Merleau-Ponty's exemplarity provides an instance. Just as Blanchot—writing about writing—elucidates philosophical discourse by writing about it, Merleau-Ponty is often concerned with style, philosophical practice, and even literary language. Yet Blanchot is preoccupied with Merleau-Ponty's philosophical enterprise. He asks about—"interrogates" to use Merleau-Ponty's term—the language of philosophy. In following this path of inquiry, thinking, and interrogation, I shall consider: (1) the theme of what philosophical discourse seeks to say, (2) the matter of authorship—the necessity of naming, and (3) the status of the discourse that enters into the general domain as philosophical discourse—as transgression.

204

SAYING THE STILL TO BE SAID

Philosophy is its discourse. Blanchot's claim identifies the whole project of philosophy with what is says. Could philosophy be anything other than what it says? One might suggest that there is nothing else for philosophy to be than what it says. Could philosophy be what it does not say? Surely not. Could philosophy be what it has not yet said? or what it cannot say? or what it has no hope of being able to say? or what it refuses to say? Philosophy, we must agree with Blanchot, cannot be anything other than what it says.

The crucial question, however, remains: what does philosophy say? Does what philosophy says depend upon *how* it says what it says? Does it matter if philosophy is said poetically, interpretively, theoretically, mathematically, analytically, speculatively, hypothetically, and so forth? In a certain sense of course it matters how it is said. Who will read it, hear it, or understand it; who will appreciate it, respect it, comment upon it, repeat it, or compare it to other philosophies; who will make sense of it, incorporate it into a history, respond to it, or react to it—will all depend upon how it is said. What philosophy says, however, is only shaped, formed, and transformed by how it is said. The ultimate consideration continues to be a matter of *what is said.*

A philosophy might be "coherent, historically linked, conceptually unified, system forming, and accomplishing its task" (*DP*, p. 1). By contrast, it might be "not only multiple and interrupted, but also lacunary, marginal, rhapsodic, resifted [*ressassant*], harking back to the same old story, and dissociated from all right to be spoken" (*DP*, p. 1). It might bring knowledge together in a collective, cooperative, cohesive fashion. Or it might assess knowledge in a dispersive, dissociative, dislocative manner. Philosophy might be systematic or it might be differential, analytic or interpretative, respectful or combative, hopeful or despairing, conceptual or practical, radical or conservative, narrow or broadsweeping, impulsive or meditative, international or xenophobic, creative or plodding, absolutist or relativist, direct or circuitous, and so on. But again the point returns: no matter how philosophy says what it says, it must still say what it says.

But what does philosophy say? One might say that there is so much that philosophy says that it would be futile even to attempt to say anything about it—except perhaps in the most detailed, historical, and comprehensive terms. There is so much that philosophy needs to say, wants to say, has to say, that to even attempt a formulation of what it says would seem almost futile. And yet Blanchot forges ahead. Again he takes Merleau-Ponty as exemplary. With Merleau-Ponty, philosophy has much to say. What it says, however, cannot have been said already. Philosophy cannot say what has already been said. Philosophy cannot be simple repetition, reiteration, restatement. The task of philosophy is to say what is still to be said.

Une parole encore à dire. Philosophy is speech that is still to be said. Philosophy must engage, describe, offer, discourse upon, what is yet to be said. To say what is already said is to say nothing new. To say what is not new is to repeat, reiterate, restate, what has already been established, affirmed, and made evident. This concept of philosophy as setting for itself the articulation of what is still to be said is not simply the modernist program. For the modernist (the modern philosopher to be precise) the task of philosophy is to break with the past, to interrupt the past, to say something new, to build upon, what has already been said, to accumulate further what has already been accumulated.

But there *is* something new in this idea that philosophy says what-is-still-to-be-said. Here philosophy's task is not to add on, to provide what has not yet been provided, to advance beyond where things now stand, to travel where no person has yet traveled. Rather philosophy must say what-is-still-to-be-said. Once said, there remains what is still to be said. Philosophy's task is to say what-is-still-to-be-said.

What is to be said is not lost, yet one can lose oneself in it. In the silence of what is still not said, the philosopher brings thought. The philosopher interrogates the silence that pervades what is still to be said. With that interrogation, the philosopher produces a discourse. The philosopher's discourse attempts to bring out of silence what cannot affirm itself as anything other than silence. Once it is given voice, that which is still to be said is given a name, requires a name, and establishes itself as discourse under a name.

THE NECESSITY OF NAMING

In attempting to speak the still unsaid, the philosopher tries to grasp what does not yet have a name. The still-to-be-said has not yet been said. It does not yet have a name. It is not nameless nor unnameable. It is not beyond the bounds of nameability. The philosopher wants to give it a name, wants to identify it, wants to bring it in under a particular philosophical grasp. Yet it remains still unsaid, still without a name.

With a name comes an identity, a definition, a determination, a specification, a characterization of what had none. The production of philosophical discourse is the production of a name. The name belongs to that which is now said. The name also belongs to the philosopher who names it. What is now said was previously unsaid. What is now said is said by this philosopher or that. This philosopher or that says it with a particular style, a particular method, a particular approach, a particular way of philosophizing. Thus not only is that which was previously unsaid now named in a specific way, but also the philosopher gains a name in the naming. It may not bring a Nobel Prize, but in the naming, the philosopher's prestige is genuinely enhanced. If the philosopher simply names what has already been named, there is no prestige in it. If the philosopher produces a discourse that has been previously unnamed, unspecified, unarticulated, then the philosopher's status cannot remain anonymous.

Anonymity describes that which is still not said; anonymity characterizes the philosopher who has not yet said it. Philosophical discourse, however, is not permitted anonymity: it is necessarily named. Philosophical discourse bears a name; it carries the aegis under which it says what it says. The naming is a performance of the philosophical discourse itself. The discourse names what it names, states what it states, elaborates what it elaborates, instaurates what it instaurates. The philosophical discourse gives shape to the philosophical enterprise, gives form to the philosopher's project, and gives an identity to what has been produced. The philosopher can remain anonymous; that which is still not said must remain anonymous; but the philosophical discourse is denied anonymity.

What is anonymity? Blanchot suggests that it is simply a game for hiding a name and ultimately giving it value. In anonymity, a name is not given: it is concealed, covered over, kept in the dark. In anonymity, a kind of oblivion prevails. This may be the oblivion of the philosopher; it may also be the still-not-said of what the philosopher wants to say. It cannot be the oblivion of philosophical discourse itself. Read in a Heideggerian way, the still-to-be-said is in a state of forgetfulness (*Vergessenheit*). The production of philosophical discourse is the bringing out of concealedness of what-is-still-to-be-said. Read in a Merleau-Pontean way, the hiddenness of what-is-still-to-be-said is the wildness of brute Being, the freedom of non-philosophy, the expression of indirect language. Philosophical discourse renders what is brute, non-philosophical and indirect as explicit, named, and identified. The value of anonymity is to make it possible for its denial to take place. Philosophical discourse makes use of the denial of anonymity. In its denial, it speaks what-is-still-to-be-said.

TRANSGRESSIVE DISCOURSE

The solitude of anonymity that the philosopher can presume is analogous to the dread of the writer whose writing has not yet become writing. The philosopher's speech brings the concealedness of what-is-still-to-be-said into disclosure. The philosopher's speech interrogates. What it interrogates remains anonymous. As the philosopher interrogates, the philosopher remains anonymous. With philosophical discourse itself, the anonymity of the interrogation is removed. With philosophical discourse, the philosopher's own name is given and his or her identity is established. This means, however, that the silence and solitude of the philosopher's inquiry are gone. They can no longer be preserved. The philosophical discourse takes them away. Yet in taking them away, philosophical discourse also affirms itself as speaking with authority. Hence philosophical discourse cannot be anonymous.

But philosophical discourse per se cannot by its very practice enter into the canon of philosophy. Philosophical discourse is itself transgressive. "*Le discours philosophique est d'abord sans droit*" (*DP*, p. 1). Without a right, without the benefits of the establishment, without even any traditional authority, philosophical discourse enters the scene with an identity. Philosophical discourse transgresses the line of anonymity, cuts across the silence, and discloses from out of the still-to-be-said. Philosophical discourse also transgresses what has already been said. It interrupts the established, confirmed, and authorized versions of what counts as philosophy. Philosophical discourse by its very practice both denies anonymity and becomes an outlaw. Philosophical discourse both gives itself authority and loses its sovereignty. Philosophical discourse enters the domain of philosophy by affirming itself and by denying what has called itself philosophy up to that time. Hence philosophical discourse is both denial and affirmation, affirmation and denial. Philosophical discourse transgresses by denying and affirming, affirming and denying.

Philosophical discourse produces itself as text. Philosophical discourse establishes a difference between what was not yet said and what is now said, between what was silence and what is spoken, between what had no name and what is now named, between what was sovereign but without authority and what has authority but is no longer sovereign, between what affirms itself and what is confirmed or disconfirmed by the establishment. Philosophical discourse transgresses by crossing the place of difference, by constituting itself as both apart from the establishment and as part of it, by becoming its own textuality.

Philosophical discourse begins in speech and ends in writing. The lessons of Socrates and Plato need not follow such a tidy division of labor. The philosopher—like Merleau-Ponty—lectures, speaks, teaches, then writes. With writing, philosophical discourse attempts to say what is still to be said as a text. The saying is the production of a textuality that is in its own right. Out of difference, the text circumscribes itself, gives itself a distinctive character, acquires a name. Its name is its textuality. As a textuality, philosophical discourse effaces the solitary philosopher, it affirms itself in its particularity, it calls for a precedence, it opens itself to criticism and review, study and examination, historicizing and anthologizing. The study of philosophical discourse is the study of its difference as transgression and as textuality.

Philosophical discourse then is transgressive discourse. It removes the secure, serene, solitary thought from its silence. It enters into discourse; it becomes discourse by its very performance; it is its own illocutionary speech act. In becoming discourse, however, philosophical discourse transgresses from both sides. It transgresses its own solitude and it transgresses the assurance of accepted, traditional, conventional, established philosophy. Philosophical discourse operates in a space of difference—the difference between the solitary and the public, the silent and the spoken, the closed realm of the "*je*" and the accessible context of the "*il*." For Blanchot philosophical discourse is difference itself. It dif-fers. It establishes a dis-tance—not now of literature but certainly that too. Dis-course dif-fers in the space of dis-tance. Discourse trans-gresses, runs across, opens up a *Lichtung*, a clearing where philosophical activity takes place.

Philosophical discourse dis-closes. Heidegger calls it *a-letheia*; Merleau-Ponty calls it the origin of truth. Naming the disclosure is naming the *écart* in which disclosure takes place. What is said is what-is-still-to-be-said. Yet what-is-still-to-be-said is not yet said. Once said, once turned into philosophical discourse, once textualized, once rendered text, once institutionalized, the still-to-be-said must be read otherwise. The still-to-be-said has been transgressed, named, given an identity. Its identity is in the difference, distance, discourse, but its reality differs, distances itself, runs away from the still-to-be-said. The still-to-be-said is invisible, inaudible, inaccessible. Philosophical discourse is the still-to-be-said becoming visible, audible, accessible. As Derrida demonstrates, philosophical discourse is a passage, a moving across, an *Übersetzung*, a trans-lation, trans-fer, trans-mission. Philosophical discourse travels across a space of difference, a textual distance whose space becomes a metaphor, a new name for an old thing, a very old thing in Heidegger's eyes: namely, philosophy itself, that which has been forgotten, that which most merits being thought. Philosophical discourse is the still-to-be-said at a place where there is no lack of words, where the still-to-be-said has lost its innocence, where the still-to-be-said is the about-to-be-said-and-done, now said and done—but not without more to say and do.

20

ON THE TIME OF THE LINE
Derrida/Heidegger

Die Zeit der Linie
Le Temps de la ligne
The Time of the Line

What time is it in New York? What time is it in Paris? What time is it in Vienna? A line links three cities—perhaps not a straight line, but surely a straight*er* line than New York-Paris-Rome. But even if the line is straight, there is a difference in time. New York is not the same time as Paris, but Paris is the same time as Vienna. Noon in New York; six o'clock in Paris and Vienna. But the more or less straight line that New York-Paris-Vienna makes does not make the same difference in time. And even though Paris and Vienna are the same time, it still takes another two hours (by plane) to get there. Yet again, one might say that New York, Paris, and Vienna—in the 1990's—are of the *same* time. But what time? *Welche Zeit? Eine Neu-Zeit*—no longer simply modern but distinctly postmodern. What sort of time is this new time that calls itself postmodern? The Renaissance of the fifteenth and sixteenth centuries had to wait for Burkhardt in the nineteenth century to receive its full self-understanding as the "Renaissance." So there must be something peculiar about a time which can name itself. To name itself *post*-anything (post-impressionist, post-industrial, post-capitalist, post-structuralist, post-phenomenological, post-analytic, post-partum, post-historical, post-critical, post-modern, etc.) announces that the previous time is at an end, that a new time is on the rise, and that it is self-consciously *avant garde*. This new time is a time of *difference*—direct difference from what went before. This difference does not occur by traversing different time lines, different time zones, different countries and cities. This historical time is rather the time of periods and moments, epochs and centuries, then and now. This marking off of a difference in historical time itself partitions off the past from what is no longer past, establishing a threshold, a gap, or an end which has become a beginning.

But my purpose here is to speak of another time—the time of the line. But what line? Not the line between past and present, not the line from New York to Paris to Vienna, not the line of the tramway or underground, not the line *behind which* one stands for an eye test or when waiting for passport control, not the line *on* which one must walk for an alcohol test, not even a police line-up, or a line (that is a *queue*) *in* which (or, if one is from New York, *on* which) one stands when waiting with devoted seriality for the bus, and furthermore not even the artist's line or drawing. The issue at hand is not even the line on which one signs one's name, the line of an argument, a line of reasoning, or a line of thought.

The line in question—not the line of questioning—is the line about which Heidegger discourses with Ernst Jünger (in *The Question of Being*)[1] and which Derrida inscribes in his memorial to Jacques Ehrmann (that is, his celebration of Shelley's *Triumph of Life* in "Living On: Border Lines.")[2]

But here too, the line is not the same. Both Heidegger and Derrida mark out a line of difference while also differing in their respective accounts (and at the same time approximating each other). This inscription of a difference at the juncture between Heidegger and Derrida is a *philosophical* line of difference—and not a historical, artistic, geographical, chronological, or linguistic line. But what is the meaning of the inscription of a philosophical line of difference? Such a difference is marked out by two philosophical enterprises that are brought into conjunction—particularly when both formulations are established by another text in which the line itself is in question.

Here the time of the line is a reading of two philosophical texts: one by Heidegger, the other by Derrida. They each delimit themselves in terms of a rather unique philosophical *Weltanschauung*, a set of strategies, and a specific complex of questions. Yet there are some common themes, not held in common, only like common land—terrain in which both Heidegger and Derrida graze, in which both the Heideggerian text and the Derridean text participate, in which both operate at the limits of their own proper territory. This ground—which is hardly foundational—is a differential space, a domain without identity, a line of difference: difference at the line where the line as *topos* is placed on the line in a reading of the line.

HEIDEGGER

In *Zur Seinsfrage* (1955), Heidegger writes to Ernst Jünger concerning his essay "Über die Linie." *Über die Linie* could be understood as either *de linea* or *trans lineam*. The division itself between these two understandings of *Über die Linie* is crucial for an account of Heidegger's concern when examining Jünger's title.

De linea—concerning the line—is the investigation or inquiry about the line. The line is *in question*. Here the line is in question in the same way that "experience" is in question for Montaigne in the last of his essays,[3] or "studies" are under consideration in Francis Bacon's *Essays*,[4] or "grammatology" is at issue for Derrida in the book of that title.[5] Archaic in form, discursive and essayistic in practice, the preposition *de* or *peri* designates a discourse on a topic that is to follow. Aristotle uses this form when speaking *about* interpretation *(peri hermeneia)*.

Trans lineam is the "going across," passing from one side to the other, or the transport across. "Crossing over" the line is getting safely to the other side. The line then separates two sides: it is a kind of obstacle or division between the here and the there. Like the "Trans-Europe-Express" (TEE, for short) or a Trans-Atlantic flight, it gets the traveler from one place to another. Such transports are not simply a crossing over from one side to the other as in border disputes or in choosing up teams or determining one's affiliation. But then *trans lineam* is of another order when understood as a transportation line (viz. the London "Circle Line," the Paris RER, or the Vienna U-Bahn).

Über die Linie can also be understood as "above" the line: *meta-linea*. When Aristotle wanted to speak *about physics*—not purely as nature—but as the study of first principles ("metaphysics"), he found it necessary to go *above* nature, to discuss nature *from above*, from a *higher* point of view, from a perspective that takes into account the *causes* and *conditions* of nature. But to be *above* nature and to be *above* the line are not the same. To be above the line is to hover over it, to *examine* (or *think about*) it, but also to be *superior* to it, to take a position of greater authority, greater power, greater strength in relation to it. Machiavelli's counsel to the Prince was to manipulate one's circumstances so as always to retain the upper hand. To be above the line then—and *above all* in general *(überhaupt)*—is to have an overview of it, to see its perfections and imperfections, its advantages and disadvantages. Merleau-Ponty characterized this sort of "overview thinking" as *la pensée de survol* and correspondingly expressed his dismay at its employment as a philosophical strategy.[6]

When Nietzsche's Zarathustra[7] comes down from the mountain, he finds—in many instances—that he has come too early. He thereby goes *over (über)*, *above, back up* the mountain—for from the heights he can see afar. However, from above, Zarathustra cannot communicate. He must go under *(untergehen)* in order to speak, in order to address the people. If they do not wish to hear of the *over*man (the *Übermensch*), they will not hear and Zarathustra will, once again, be obliged to return—again to *go over, above*, back up the mountain, over the line, even above the tree line.

Hence *Über die Linie* is: (1) to discourse *on* the line; (2) to *go across* the line; and (3) to *stand above* or oversee the line. Heidegger is less certain of this third sense—and yet only by "standing above" (making itself different from) can the relation to itself be made thoroughly clear. Heidegger also wants to say that these different senses of *Über die Linie* belong together. They are all understood in the response to Jünger.

But what Heidegger is after is not just a reflection on the different senses of *Über die Linie*. There is a special line that concerns him—a line in which all three senses are raised. This line is the one that differentiates Being from beings. The Being of beings *(das Sein des Seienden)*—the is-ness of that which is—establishes a line of difference between what is and its Being. This line of difference is not anything—Heidegger reaffirms that it is nothing of content or even of substance—and yet there is a difference between Being and beings, a difference in the relation beings have to Being. This line of difference is marked by a genitive, the "of"—what Heidegger elsewhere calls the ontological genitive (the Being of beings). Like the "time of the line," the difference between "time" and "the line" is that the genitive designates the non-sameness of the two.

Heidegger claims that the Being of beings, the line of difference, designates the "essence of man." The "essence of man" *(Das Wesen des Menschen)* is the nothingness designated by the line of difference. In the 1920s, Heidegger called the affirmation of this difference *Dasein.* By now announcing it as the *Menschenwesen,* he reaffirms the place of difference without reifying it. But what is the Being of beings? Why does the "essence of man" *(Menschenwesen)* constitute this place? And how does Heidegger propose to designate it?

The Being of beings marks a line. Heidegger proposes to inscribe this line by writing this relation of a being to Being as B̶e̶i̶n̶g̶ . In effect, then, Being is a double line—a crossing *(trans, über)* and a crossing over (and out) of two lines. Not only is the line traversed once but it is also crossed a second time. This double crossing is the *trans* rendered twice. To speak about this double line is to speak about *(de, peri, über)* the line—but in this case in its doubleness. And further the crossing of the line designates the respect in which Being stands *above (über)* beings in their particularity. Being, Heidegger says, is always at the horizon of beings, just above or beyond beings (or any particular being). Being then designates the *über* as "concerning" Being *(de Sein)*, as "across" Being *(trans Sein)*, and Being as "above" or "over" *(Sein als über)*. Being as *Übersicht* cannot be understood as *pensée de survol,* hence it is crossed out, marked off as what cannot have a transcendental position, as what cannot stand apart, cannot be—on its own—without the Being of beings. Being, then, is a crossed word, a puzzle of sorts, whose enigmatic character is designated by B̶e̶i̶n̶g̶ . The question of Being (the *Seinsfrage*) then marks the "of" as the line between Being and beings: as difference—not overview; as crossing out—not separating off; as a matter of concern *(Sache des Denkens)*—not some auxiliary interest. But what sort of line is it that becomes polysemous, that has the many senses of *über,* proliferated in the space of difference, and marked out by a cross, a sign, a *chi?* The difference as essence of man, as line, as polysemous, as multiple otherness, as not the same, and as crossed out, constitutes a space that is not a space, not a concrete line, not a mark of what is—but rather a mark of what *is not.* Between Being and beings, the ontico-ontological difference cannot be, it cannot constitute a positive entity. Hence Heidegger calls this line of difference—nothingness. Nothingness here is not a vacuum, not a chaotic emptiness. Rather it is what *is* not—for both Being and beings *are* and B̶e̶i̶n̶g̶ is *between* yet neither one nor the other.

The Being of beings is also—particularly in the later Heidegger—an event. The event of the relating of beings and Being is an event of significance. This event is not some everyday occurrence, some ontic occasion that will pass into another event perhaps without even notice or remark. This event is of major importance, for it marks the very call of Being, the accounting for any being's relation to Being, the happening of the ontico-ontological difference, the mark of temporality itself.

In the Heideggerian formulation, this happening is ecstatico-ontological. This means that the ontico-ontological difference is not simply a difference constituted for all eternity. Rather this difference is precisely the event or happening of a being going outside itself. The event of the relating of beings to Being occurs in time, it is ecstatic in that it goes outside itself. *Ex-stasis* departs from the static, the stable, the eternally unmovable. In so doing, it brings about an occurrence of otherness, an alterity with respect to a being's identity. But again, this alterity is not simply otherness; it is also the happening of the otherness, the coming to pass of otherness, the passage from identity to difference. Heidegger calls this event of difference: *Ereignis*.[8] *Ereignis* is the ecstatic happening of a being's difference from itself, namely, the time of its relation to Being.

Just as *Eigentlichkeit* is the condition of being most one's own, namely, "authenticity," so *Ereignis* is the happening of what is most one's own. The *Eigen* is what is one's own; the *Eigentlich* is the description of a being—a human being, for instance—which is most its own; and *Eigentlichkeit* is the condition of being most one's own. Albert Hofstadter would translate it as "ownliness." Similarly *Er-eignis* is the coming-to-be of what is one's own.[9] And what is most one's own for a being is its relation to Being. Hence what is most one's own is its difference from itself, its marking of a line between what is itself, its own, and what is other—not just distinct from it (a mere *Unterscheidung*) but a difference *(Differenz)* of the highest order, namely the ontico-ontological difference, the difference that traces its relation to Being. For the relation to Being is no everyday relation. It is also not a relation to just any otherness. Rather it is a relation to *its own* otherness, a relation to that otherness that is most its own, most authentic, most the particular relation to itself. Hence, the event of otherness in the ontico-ontological difference is the event of crossing over the line that a being sets for itself, not necessarily actively but simply by defining itself as what it is, that is, by *being* what it is. The line between what it is and what it is not, between its being and its relation to Being is the very line of difference, the line whose event of occurrence is *Ereignis* itself.

What does it mean for difference to happen? And how is it marked? In "The Origin of the Work of Art," Heidegger demonstrates that the difference marked in the happening of the artwork is a difference that is best called (by) "poetizing" (*PLT-OWA*, pp. 72–78). "Poetizing" is not only the naming of the relation to Being in terms of the artwork, whether it be a poem, painting, or building, but it is also the "calling" of Being. For Heidegger, Being is not simply in relation to beings. Rather it is also called *to* Being and called *by* Being. The *Ruf des Seins* is the "call of Being" in that beings are drawn to Being. Beings are marked by their very alterity—and this alterity is the "call of Being." This is to say that the identity of a being includes its relation to the is-ness that all beings have in common. This is the "call of Being." Being is even "heard" by beings. That is, there is a "belonging-togetherness" of beings and Being. This *Zusammengehörigkeit* of Being and beings is the hearing *(hören)* of the relation of beings to Being. All these marks of the relation of beings to Being: "naming," "calling," "hearing," and "belonging" are the very features of the line between beings and Being, the traces of the difference that is already inscribed in beings themselves. "Poetizing" is the saying of the ontico-ontological difference in the event of the truth of an artwork, in the disclosure of a painting, in the bringing out of concealedness of a poem, in the making open of a temple. "Poetizing," then, for Heidegger is the saying of the time of the line.

The saying of the time of the line can also occur from one poem to another, from the time of one poet to another. This is Heidegger's point in "*Wozu Dichter?*" (1946).[10] Hölderlin writes of "the destitute time" of the nineteenth-century age in which he lives. He remarks in his elegy "Bread and Wine"—and with characteristic romantic despair—that there seems to be no way out of this unfortunate time, and therefore asks: "What are poets for in a destitute time?"

He is speaking of the age in general. For Hölderlin, it is an age in which the gods "have fled" leaving only their "traces" *(Spuren)*. In this time, Hölderlin remarks on the abyss *(Ab-grund)* in which he finds himself. The time of the abyss is a falling away from the ground *(Grund)*. It is a sense of being cast off, broken away from the ground, the foundation, the solid mooring. By contrast, Heidegger notes, Rilke detected that in his time—a number of decades later—the possibility of falling back to the ground is in evidence. Poets may be able to fill the gap, the line of difference, between ground and abyss, between definitive assurance and hopelessness. Poets may be able to offer some solace, some disclosure, some opening up of what seemed closed off. The truth of poetry, according to Heidegger, is this disclosure, this opening of a clearing *(Lichtung)* in the space of difference, in the event of the Being of beings, in the happening *(Ereignis)* of the line—not only in Rilke's time, but also in the time that is distinguished, marked off, separated from the destitute time that Hölderlin identifies.

DERRIDA

And what of the line between Derrida and Heidegger? Has its time come? Has its time come into its own? What time is it that marks the line of difference between Derrida and Heidegger? In some respects, the reading of Heidegger offered here is already a Derridean reading, already a thinking that situates itself in the line between Heidegger and Derrida. And yet where Heidegger's text inscribes the *crossing* of Being, the *crossing out* of Being, the naming and thinking of Being, Derrida's text—and particularly "Living On: Border-lines" (published in French as *Survivre*)[11]—formulates another line of difference. The thematization of the line of difference itself will make it possible for an inquiry into the line between Heidegger and Derrida. However without understanding how the line operates in Derrida, it will not be possible to formulate the place between the Derridean "line" and the Heideggerian double-crossing of Being (i.e., B̶e̶i̶n̶g̶), what Derrida will call Being *sous rature*.

Derrida's line of difference—also multiple—designates not a relation to Being, not a generality for a particularity, not the *essence of man*, but rather the relation between Shelley's "Triumph of Life" and a memorial to Jacques

Ehrmann. Just as Heidegger is addressing Ernst Jünger and his *Über die Linie*, Derrida is also addressing a person (now and then passed away)—a professor of French at Yale (in the context of other colleagues all at the time still at Yale, including Geoffrey Hartman, Harold Bloom, and J. Hillis Miller). The topic is not the "question of Being" but rather the "triumph of life"—or one might simply say: "*living itself*." With Derrida, *living* is not a *topos* which is given centrality in his text. "Living" permeates Derrida's text while "living on" moves to the edge of his text. Indeed, as the text is constructed, there are in fact two texts: the main text (the *Haupttext*) and a second long running footnote that *under-lies* the main text. The second text—not really a *secondary* text—goes *unter* (not *über*). This second *Unter-text* serves as a memorial with dates and other chronological marks referring to Jacques Ehrmann—whose initials would name the self or subject le *"je,"* which is not other. What then is the relation between sub-text—or under-text—and the over-text (*Übertext*)?

The over-text is concerned with Shelley's poem—written in Italy during a journey, in fact, his *last* journey. Shelley's poem remains unfinished: life is triumphant in the poem but not in the author. The poem's unfinished character gives it the quality of a cliff whose edge marks off a limit. At its limit, the poem calls for an abyss. In fact, Shelley drowned. For Derrida, the abyss is not as it is for Heidegger an *Ab-grund*—a falling away from the ground (*Grund* or *Sein*), a marking of the ontico-ontological difference as event. For Derrida, the abyss is the margin, the edge, or end of Shelley's poem—incomplete and unfinished.

At the edge of Shelley's poem, Derrida juxtaposes another text—this time Blanchot's *L'Arrêt de mort* (translated as *Death Sentence*).[12] More than half a century separates these two texts. Yet, by juxtaposing the two, Derrida inserts a new line. The Blanchot narrative (short story or *récit*) comes after the Shelley poem. Derrida places them side by side—just as Heidegger's *Zur Seinsfrage* and Derrida's *Survivre* are juxtaposed here. Shelley's text (in English) announces the prevalence and achievement of life. In its placement, the poem is also Shelley's very death-knell (his *glas*). Hence the "Triumph of Life" is a triumphing *over* life—namely *death*. Correspondingly, Blanchot's *L'Arrêt de mort* is a proclamation of death to come, to be executed by an edict of the judicial system. But literally an *arrêt de mort* is a stopping or interruption of death—hence: life. So Blanchot's text is formulated as at once the stopping of death and the proclamation of death—a kind of annunciation: birth and crucifixion, death and resurrection. Shelley's poem pronounces at once the affirmation of life and the success of death over life. At the juncture of the two texts there arise the very basic questions of life and death, living and dying, survival in life and the coming of death. The line "between" marks the achievement of life or death as a question. On the line—here: the line between *The Triumph of Life* and *L'Arrêt de mort*, and there: the borderline between the main text "Living On" and the subtext "Border-lines" (written under the line)—the inscription of living itself is turned into a *speech act*. The borderline marks the place of living—not toward death (*zum Tod*), as in the early Heidegger—but as marked out in the text, as indicated between the *Übertext* and the *Untertext*, the vitality of living itself. Living itself can only be a theme in a text—but between the texts, like Heidegger's ontico-ontological difference, the disclosure of living itself comes alive.

To keep in mind all that Derrida says about Heidegger would be an enormous, if not infinite, task. Yet there are some key moments such as "Ousia and Grammé" (1968) in *Margins* (1972) and the recent *De l'esprit* (1987),[13] where Derrida comments directly upon Heidegger's texts. Often there is the concern for what Heidegger has omitted or left out. In *De l'esprit*, for instance, Derrida remarks that Heidegger continually sought to avoid (*éviter* or *vermeiden*) anything that has to do with "mind" or "spirit" (*Geist* or *geistige*). He seemed to want to keep the matter of mind or spirit apart from the rest, beyond the pale, outside the corpus of his work. Hence for Heidegger, the mind would be, it seems, another matter, other even than the very matter of the Being of beings. In this sense, the mind—a concern that preoccupied the whole intellectual lineage from Descartes to Hegel to Freud—has been absented from Heidegger's inquiry into the meaning of the Being of beings. Hence, just as Sartre rejects the Husserlian transcendental ego, so too Heidegger rejects the preoccupation with mind (*Geist*). In this way, he leaves aside the matter of a mind-body distinction, the concern with a self-world relation, the fear of the psycho-somatic, the obsession with the empirico-transcendental doublet. Derrida's reading of Heidegger as placing to one side the dimensions of mind or spirit marks a line along the edge of the Heideggerian enterprise.

If there is no place for mind in Heidegger, then can Heidegger himself, or at least his writings, be kept in mind? As Derrida shows in his reading of Plato's pharmacy, such an action would require "*memory*." For Heidegger, memory is not a mental event. Rather its opposite (forgetting, oblivion, concealedness) is invoked in order to give an account of truth, for truth is the disclosure, revealing, bringing out of concealedness, the denial of what has been forgotten. The task of thinking, then, is a kind of memorial activity, remembering what has been forgotten, disclosing what has been hidden or buried within the Western philosophical tradition itself.

But even as a mental activity, memory is itself limited. One cannot keep so much in memory. Hence the need to "write it down." Writing an account of Heidegger (or of anything for that matter) obviates the necessity to hold it all in memory. However, just as memory is limited, writing is also limited. The limits of writing show that there is always more to be written down. Yet to note down all the memory traces would not only produce a massive result but would also leave an indecipherable mess. At the border between memory and writing is the line that separates the two. An epitaph is a writing down of what is to be remembered—most notably, the person. How is Heidegger to be remembered? For his philosophical writings, for his teaching of students, for his political (or nonpolitical) activities, for his party affiliations, for his familial relations, etc.? Biographies will tell. Subsequent disclosures will reveal. But what they tell or reveal are what is presumed to be known about Heidegger—the man. Remarks he made, effects on others, views expressed, statements written, writings published, etc.—all inscribe the life, constitute the memory, mark off the line between the man and the memory, the difference between the life and the life story (the life as written).

One might ask then: what is the bottom line? The answer cannot be other than: living, living on, and living on in memory, disclosing (in the ontico-ontological difference) what must not be forgotten. This is doubtless why Derrida has taken on the task of writing, *in memoriam*, of Jacques Ehrmann, Roland Barthes, and Paul de Man. In each case, the memories are real.[14] They mark the life as relived in memory, memory that when narrated—as in Plutarch's *Lives*, Dante's *Vita Nuova*, Vasari's *Lives of the Artists*, Boswell's *Johnson*, and Derrida's own account of Plato or even Heidegger—makes the life "come alive" again. In each case, memory as narrated is written. The writing of memory, memory of one no longer with us, is a writing sometimes without a "by" line—just an obituary, a remembering of one no longer living. The bottom line then is living on—in writing, in narrated memory, in philosophy—on the line.

Derrida's pro-gramme is not to offer biographies, critical studies, or analyses of texts. Rather his task is to offer readings of texts, to work through a text or network of texts such that the boundaries and limits are respected, the borders marked off, and the margins carefully delineated. Derridean readings mark edges, barriers, or obstructions to the smooth passage through the text(s) in question. They also highlight places of indecidability: hinge elements that separate off and bring together at the same time. In short, Derridean readings mark lines, membranes, hymens, bars, and borders. There is no attempt to claim itself as an alternative philosophy, nor is it an effort at analyzing or offering arguments implicit in what is read. Derridean deconstruction moves to the line between synthesis and analysis, between system building and critical breaking down, between construction and destruction. In Heideggerian terms, it does not operate at the ontic level of beings, nor does it attempt to give an account of Being. Rather it is performed or enacted at the very place of difference in what Heidegger would call the Being of beings, the place of truth, of unconcealment, of disclosure. For Derrida, the place of difference is a line, a line between, a pairing and separating. For Derrida, deconstruction will provide an accounting of the very textualities of a text, its lines of demarcation and its lines of contrition, its lines of marginality and its lines of delimitation. The textualities of the text are differential considerations, features that identify and mark as different, that present and postpone the meaning(s) of the text, that clarify and obscure what is happening in the text.

THE BETWEEN-LINE

In conclusion—so that it will not be necessary to read between the lines—consider the juxtaposition of Heidegger's text and Derrida's text. Mark off the relation between the difference in the Being of beings and the difference in the living on (surviving) and the being overcome by death (by drowning), between the "essence of man" *(Menschenwesen)* and living on *(Sur-vivre)*. Together, juxtaposed at the place of difference—between Derrida and Heidegger—is the time of the line, the time of difference, the time of the inscription of living as marked out in a reading of the two texts, in short, the time of textuality. But what are the characteristics of this line between Heidegger and Derrida, this line between, which marks off the two in their respective regions of discourse and philosophical practice? In order to provide something like an answer, consider Jacques Lacan's account of the line between the signifier and the signified. In Lacan, reading Saussure with his obsession for anagrams, the very bar between the two aspects of the sign is telling. Lacan shows that in distinguishing and bringing together the binary pair of signifier and signified, word and concept, Saussure offers an example. He wants to demonstrate not only the binary character of the sign but also its arbitrary nature. Saussure's example is that of *l'arbre* or "tree." For the signifier, he offers the word "*arbre.*" For the signified, he draws a picture of a tree. But the anagram of "arbre" is *barre*. Saussure's unconscious is at work selecting the very example of that word which distinguishes itself from its concept by designating the line between, the "barre" between the signifier and the signified. Hence the sign, a unit which gets its identity only from its *difference* from all other signs, is itself compromised by Saussure's very example. For not only does the word for "tree" in French designate that which separates that word from its concept, but also *l'arbre* becomes *l'arbitraire*—the arbitrary nature of the sign itself. The tree proliferates and also designates the place between the word and its concept: it marks the bar or barrier between and calls that relation "arbitrary." The tree, then, becomes the sign that makes the difference, that marks the line between, that is alive with multiplicity: it branches off and is disseminated in many directions—all at the place of difference.

Hence like the difference between the signifier and the signified, which together constitute the oppositional sign unit, the difference between Heidegger and Derrida itself marks the bar, the limit, the barrier between the German tradition and the French tradition, and yet these are two traditions whose common border both establishes difference and builds a common market, economic strategy, and intellectual collaboration. Identity and difference—elements of the line, the signifier and the signified of the between line, which cannot be other than their respective texts brought into juxtaposition, brought into confrontation with one another at the line, the Rhine, the river between, the place where they meet, the place where their respective philosophies come alive. The line therefore is not only a theoretical line, a critical line, a philosophical line, but also a political and textual line, a line that marks all sorts of differences between Heidegger and Derrida while at the same time bringing them together into a vital relation.

The reading of the line that inscribes particular living is also the mark of the line that inscribes the remembering of living. Living that was, living that should be remembered or that cannot be forgotten, living that mattered, living that meant something, living that is distinctly not mine but not unrelated to mine, living that lives on in remembering. The reading of the line of difference marks not just living, but also remembering. Living is not dying. Dying distinguishes itself from living. Dying makes remembering possible. Remembering another is retrieving the other from obscurity, making the other live again—in memory. Marking that memory not only with a memorial, a tombstone, an epitaph, an obituary, a biography, a testimonial, a recollection, or a prayer but also with a reinscription of the line of difference between living and dying as the line of difference between dying and remembering.

The line of difference between Derrida and Heidegger marks other lines of difference. This one line proliferates other lines of difference. If the bottom line is difference and "living on"—and living marks off dying, and dying marks off remembering, and remembering overcomes forgetting, and forgetting makes way for truth as disclosure, and truth as disclosure occurs along political lines, and political lines are set according to different ways of thinking, then the bottom line for the line of difference is repeated differently, repeated between philosophy and non-philosophy, between thematic and theoretical practice, between the text and its textualities. The bottom line is a shifting line, a line drawn in many places for the purpose of distinction, specification, clarification, identity. As a shifting line, the bottom line is repeatable, unfathomable, without end. Others will live on, others will die, others will be remembered, others will write, others will frame texts. Inscribing the line of difference is not only the marking off of a philosophy of the text, but also a philosophy of life. Like a palmist reading the lines in a client's hand, the text is both a fortune and fortunate. Without it, the lines could not be read. With it, one can, must, will live on—if not in life, then in the differences marked by the text.

And thus the final line of each text—*and now there are three:* two from Derrida: (1) "I take this unhappiness on myself and I am immeasurably glad of it and to that thought I say eternally, 'Come,' and eternally it is there" (*DC*, p. 176); *and* (2) "Not without repeating it, and that goes without saying" (*DC*, p. 176); and one from Heidegger: (3) this time it is the time with which he ends his letter, whose last line reads: "I send you my hearty greetings" (*Question of Being*, p. 8). The time of the letter has become *literally* the time of the line— with greetings that will return eternally.

21

ON THE ORIGIN(S) OF HISTORY
Foucault/Derrida

What is found at the historical beginning of things is not the inviolable identity of their origin: it is the dissention of other things. It is disparity.
—Foucault, "Nietzsche, Genealogy, History"

The phenomenon of "crisis," as forgetfulness of origins, has precisely the sense of this type of "reversal."
—Derrida, *Introduction to the Origin of Geometry*

The theme of origins has plagued history and historians since time immemorial. Indeed, the very immemoriality of time points to a time before memory. What memory could be before the beginning of time? That memory which would be before the beginning of time surely cannot be human memory. Augustine had a view of divine memory as somehow before time, outside time, different from time. But what of that time that is "before memory"—at the very origins of history? What of the time that is before human memory, before the time when time could be marked by memory, in memory, from a remembering point of view? Are there many such original times, or is there just one? Is there any point in speaking of an origin that marks the beginning of time itself? Or are there different times with different origins? This theme of origins has marked the discourse of both Foucault and Derrida in different ways and at different times. However, what origin means for Foucault and Derrida, what "origin" means for a theory of history, what origin means for their respective textual practices itself operates at the very place where the theory of origins becomes most explicit. Let us begin then with the theory of origins.

Foucault's reading of origins is marked off by his reading of discursive practices. As he demonstrates in *Les Mots et les choses* (1966), [1] history does not begin at a certain moment and then continue—in linear fashion—from then on. Rather, moments of dominance of certain discursive practices prevail for a time and are then succeeded by a new set of discursive practices. Where a particular practice ends, a new one is about to begin. Origin then will occur where a new discursive practice starts to take place. But where and when do such new practices begin to take place? They clearly do not occur at a determinate moment in time such as a date or year. Certain discursive practices pertinent to a particular epistemological space, as Foucault calls it, continue into a new epistemological space, while others die out.

But what is a discursive practice? For Foucault, a discursive practice is a whole set of documents produced within a broadly general period of time in which common themes or ideas occur across that period in a wide variety of disciplines and areas of human knowledge production. For instance, in the nineteenth century the relations between biology, economics, and philology would seem to be entirely unrelated. However Foucault has shown that they all consolidate in terms of a relatively singular conceptual unity, or what Foucault calls an *epistemē*. For the broad space of the nineteenth century, Foucault identifies the theme in question with what he calls an "anthropology," that is, the theory of "man" as defined by the "empirico-transcendental doublet."[2] The particular Kantian idea that empirical (objective) considerations must always be understood in connection with a transcendental (subjective) set of conditions permeates the discursive practices of the nineteenth century. The theme of subjectivity in relation to objectivity pervades the nineteenth-century understanding of life, labor, and language. Thus the discursive practices of the nineteenth century repeat themselves in a variety of contexts—all explicitly unrelated to each other. These differences then form an *epistemē*.

The *epistemē* of the nineteenth century succeeds the *epistemē* of the "classical age." This prior epistemological space is marked by another set of discursive practices. These include the classification of species, the analysis of wealth, and natural grammar. What one would take to be entirely unrelated concerns are here brought into relation to one another in that they each exhibit features of the "classical age" *epistemē* namely "representation." As Foucault reads the general period of the seventeenth century and first half of the eighteenth century, the idea of "representation"—the projection or postulate of ideas before the mind—formed the frame for a distinctly "classical" way of thinking. The relation between this classical *epistemē* and the nineteenth-century *epistemē* is much less significant than the relation between the various practices at each of these respective time-slices.

And what of origins? The origin of the *epistemē* is not the beginning of the *epistemē*. A particular *epistemē* is marked by a certain dominance. The place where the *epistemē* dominates is the place of the *epistemē*'s origin. The place of dominance for the empirico-transcendental doublet is the place of origin within that epistemological framework. Similarly the place of dominance of *representation* in the classical age is the place of origin within that epistemological framework. However, where is this place of origin in each case? Dispersed throughout the epistemological space, the place of origin occurs wherever there is a discursive practice that exhibits it. Hence the origin is in many places: reappearing in many locations throughout the epistemological space itself. In the nineteenth century, one can find the empirico-transcendental doublet not only in Hegel and Hölderlin, but also in biologists such as Cuvier (whose "fixism" is set off against the backdrop of human historicity), economists such as Ricardo (for whom history is a vast compensating mechanism), and philologists such as Schlegel (with his 1808 essay on the language and philosophy of the Indians), Grimm (most notably the 1818 *Deutsche Grammatik*), and Bopp (whose 1816 study of the Sanskrit conjugation system became an object of study). Each of these places constitutes itself as an origin, as a locus in which the concept of "man" as a subject-object is brought into discourse production itself. No longer does language, for instance, operate between words and things resulting in an operation of representation. And in the nineteenth century, words are objects themselves, objects for scrutiny and study by a scientific practice that hopes to judge them and their interrelationships.

Origin, then, for Foucault is not a source from which all historical events follow. Origin is not the beginning from which history begins to unfold. Origin is not the inception from which development ensues. Origin does not establish the moment before which nothing else will have occurred. Rather origin springs up in many places within a broad, general, historical time-frame. Origins occur in various discourses, scarring them with marks of a common practice that is unaware of its own commonality.

Jacques Derrida, in his first significant publication [*IOG*], the introduction to his translation of Husserl's 1936 *Origin of Geometry* [*Der Ursprung der Geometrie*],[3] takes up the question of origins. In his accounting of Husserl's enterprise, Derrida reviews three main considerations with respect to history (as understood within the Husserlian purview). These include the views:

(1) that history, as empirical science, was, like all empirical sciences, dependent on phenomenology;

(2) that history—whose own content was, by virtue of its sense of being, always marked by oneness and irreversibility—still lent itself to imaginary variations and eidetic intuitions;

(3) that, in addition to the empirical and non-exemplary content of history, certain eidetic content (for example, that of geometry as the eidetic analysis of spatial nature) had itself been produced or revealed in a history which irreducibly inhabits its being sense (*IOG*, p. 30).

And Derrida continues:

[For] if, as Husserl affirms, the history of the geometrical eidetic is exemplary, then history in general no longer risks being a distinct and dependent sector of a more radical phenomenology. By remaining completely within a determined relativity, history in general no less completely engages phenomenology with all its possibilities and responsibilities, its original techniques and attitudes (*IOG*, p. 30).

Derrida speaks of these three considerations as "ambitions which animate" the *Crisis of the European Sciences and Transcendental Phenomenology*, which was not actually published until 1954, years after Husserl's death in the late 1930s. The time of its writing, however, is coordinate with *The Origin of Geometry*. What Derrida is addressing in 1962 is the very possibility of a "phenomenological history," what such an enterprise would mean and how it would establish itself in relation to the "development" of history itself. Derrida is concerned with the *sense* in which history, as an empirical science, occupies itself with origins and addresses the problem of origins as objects of study, while also depending upon a *phenomenology* that will make sense of them. Husserl's problem is that although history is unique and irreversible, it is also available for "imaginary variations" and "eidetic intuitions," including phenomenological devices that allow the phenomenologist to study history as a whole, as a circumscribed phenomenon, whose sense can be described transcendentally. Furthermore, while Husserlian phenomenology takes as its task the study of history as a phenomenon, Husserlian phenomenology itself must necessarily take place or have been produced within that history. The problem, then, is that origins can be considered as part of history, and yet history itself (as well as the phenomenology that studies it) is also located in relation to a whole set of origins.

Derrida writes: "to meditate on or investigate the sense *(besinnen)* of origins is at the same time to make oneself responsible *(verantworten)* for this sense *(Sinn)* of science and philosophy" *(IOG*, p. 31). In what sense is the phenomenologist "answerable" or "responsible" for the "sense" of science or philosophy? Phenomenology offers itself as a "rigorous science." Yet phenomenology is also a philosophy. Husserl develops what he takes to be the meaning or "sense" of phenomenology as a philosophy that is also a rigorous science. Its "sense" *(Sinn)* is not itself located in historical time. Presumably it was always there. It is simply instantiated in each act of intuition in which a phenomenon is to be described. Phenomenology itself, however, came into being, historically, at a particular time: first in protean form in Hegel, then developed in connection with a theory of intentionality in Brentano, and finally full-blown at the beginning of the twentieth century in Husserl's own teachings and writings. Hence when phenomenology attempts to give an account of history, it will have to also take account of the fact that it is itself located in history. The problem then is: how does a science of history account for itself as itself occurring in history? Can it account for origins that happened before its own beginning? And if so, then what is the status of its own origins with respect to history, most notably when history itself is taken as that phenomenon which is to be described phenomenologically. Phenomenologically speaking, transcendental description must occur after that which is to be studied has been bracketed and reduced to its eidetic conditions. But if history itself is to be so bracketed and reduced, what of those features which suggest that history not only makes phenomenology possible, but also indicates that the sense of history (understood phenomenologically) includes the origin of phenomenology itself? Understanding this "sense" of phenomenology as both concerned with history and historically marked still leaves the problem that the place of those origins operates precisely at the intersection of a phenomenology of history and the history of phenomenology.

With respect to the origin of geometry, at issue is the inception of a science that treats of eternal objects existing prior to the beginning of that science. Similarly, phenomenology—when concerned with history—will also have to confront the problem of origins. But what is the origin of such origins? Such origins are themselves located in history. They mark off what claims to have access to that which occurred before their time. Hence what will be historical, temporal, and "in time," marks off what is ahistorical, atemporal, and "out of time." For Derrida, the origin that intersects the historical beginning and the atemporal inscription is the origin that needs to be investigated. Yet to investigate such origins, which will be many and which will occur wherever a science confronts its own history, is to inscribe an indecidable marker dispersed into the broad frame of scientific inquiries and their historicities.

What is the relation, then, between Foucault's multiple origins (dispersed throughout a discursive practice) and Derrida's origins (also multiple and also dispersed throughout scientific practices but which appeal specifically to eternal and universal objects of study)? For such an answer, we must look further into Foucault's account of origins and Derrida's "archaeology."

Derrida`s *Introduction to the Origin of Geometry* was published in 1962, almost three decades after Husserl wrote it. Foucault's essay "Nietzsche, Genealogy, History"[4] in homage to Jean Hippolyte was published in 1971 only two years after the appearance of *The Archaeology of Knowledge*. "Nietzsche, Genealogy, History" could serve as a kind of introduction to *The Archaeology of Knowledge*—much in the way Foucault's inaugural lecture at the Collège de France[5] is offered as an afterword to *The Archaeology of Knowledge*. Furthermore, "Nietzsche, Genealogy, History" (1971) is also a kind of introduction to Nietzsche's *Genealogy of Morals*, since it discusses that text and its formulation of the problem of origins. Correspondingly, although Foucault is most known for and associated with the method of "archaeology," Derrida publishes (in 1973) his introduction to another text—this time not German, but French, not nineteenth century but eighteenth—namely *The Archeology of the Frivolous*, a reading of Condillac's *Essay on the Origin of Human Knowledge*. How are we to understand all these essays, introductions, and afterwords—these crossovers and correspondences? And how do they help to sort out the problem of origins as now dispersed in the texts of Foucault and Derrida?

First, it will be recognized that just as Derrida's *Introduction to the Origin of Geometry* (1962) is both an *ex post facto* introduction and a study of the problem of origins, so too Foucault's "Nietzsche, Genealogy, History" is an *ex post facto* introduction to *The Genealogy of Morals* (1887).[6] While Foucault's *Archaeology of Knowledge* is offered as an account of his own archaeological method, it is already on the way to a genealogy. Similarly, Derrida's *Archeology of the Frivolous* (published four years later in 1973) is *both* a reading of Condillac's study of the origin of knowledge *and* a counterpart to Foucault's *Archaeology of Knowledge*. Furthermore, it accounts for Derrida's shift from grammatology (1967) to deconstruction (1974). What then is to be said of these differing methods, knowledge claims, and original studies?

Foucault's "introductory" essay "Nietzsche, Genealogy, History" is concerned with the problem of the different senses of "origin" in Nietzsche's *Genealogy*. The term in question is *Ursprung*: one is unstressed, the other stressed (*NGH*, p. 140). "Unstressed" is the multiple use of *Ursprung* dispersed discursively into a variety of alternative terms for "origin." These include: *Entstehung, Herkunft, Abkunft,* and *Geburt*. As Foucault points out, in Nietzsche's *Genealogy of Morals,* "*Entstehung* or *Ursprung* denote the origin of duty or guilty conscience" (p. 140), while in *The Gay Science, Ursprung, Entstehung,* or *Herkunft* are "used indiscriminately" (p. 140). By contrast, when *Ursprung* is stressed, Nietzsche distinguishes the analyses of historical philosophy "*über Herkunft und Anfang*" from the miraculous origin *(Wunderursprung)* by metaphysics (p. 140). *Ursprung* is typically translated as "origin," *Herkunft* as "descent" or "extraction," *Anfang* as "beginning," and *Entstehung* as "emergence." This dispersal of "origin" into a wider variety of discursive formulations is itself a kind of performative. It demonstrates the dissemination (as Derrida would call it) of the very idea of origin.

Since the *Genealogy of Morals* is concerned with the origin of moral preconceptions, the problem for Foucault is how Nietzsche articulates this tracing of origins. "Genealogy" designates a series of successive derivations, one producing another in a continuous chain. So the issue of origin—one would think—has to do with the source, beginning, or origination of the whole genealogical line. One would think that it involves going back to where it all started. And in a sense, Nietzsche *can* be read as going back to where it all began—to where good and evil were first formulated as good versus bad. But Nietzsche undermines this reading of successive development by showing that the very sense of origin is itself multiple, dispersed, spread out throughout his own narrative. For Nietzsche, then, at least as Foucault reads the text, "origin" is at once emergence, descent, birth, beginning, etc. It has been said that in the beginning was the word *(Verbum)* or in the beginning was the act *(die Tat)*, but with Foucault, one might say, in the beginning was multiplicity and dispersal. In Foucault's words: "What is found at the historical beginning of things is not the inviolable identity of their origin; it is the dissention of other things. It is disparity" (*NGH*, p. 142). In the beginning, then, Foucault might say, was discursive practice (in all its multiplicity). And Nietzsche's account—with its own discursive practices—demonstrates this very dispersal. For Nietzsche, the birth of tragedy already bears the marks of its decline, the emergence of morality undermines its affirmation, for it postulates only difference: good/bad, good/evil, noble/slave, *Übermensch*/herd morality.

The Nietzschean problem of the "site of truth" also enters this context of origins. The traditional linear account of history—from Hesiod through St. Augustine, and on—places the site of truth in the moment of origin, beginning, creation, birth. Nietzsche reports on the history of an error—the error we call truth. As Foucault puts it: "truth, and its original reign, has had a history within history from which we are barely emerging in the time of the shortest shadow, when light no longer seems to flow from the depths of the sky or to arise from the first moments of the day" (*NGH*, p. 144). Foucault's reading of Nietzsche shows "origin" to be dispersed throughout history's discursive practices and to rely upon an error (namely, a concept of truth) in order to affirm origin as identity.

Derrida, by contrast, in *The Archeology of the Frivolous* shows that Condillac, who was fervently seeking to formulate a first philosophy, a metaphysics that would found, ground, and originate all philosophy that is to come, is not first (or originary) after all. Rather, this first philosophy will—as a consequence—have to *follow upon* the Aristotelian first philosophy (which itself claims to go back to the first mover, to the originary cause or *aitia*). Derrida writes:

> What Condillac denounces in Aristotle's first philosophy is as well an unconscious empiricism, one that takes derived generalities for premises, products for seeds or origins [*germes*]: as a second philosophy incapable of establishing itself as such, it is an irresponsible empiricism. Through a chiasmus effect, the new meta-physics, by advancing itself as second philosophy, will methodically reconstitute the generative principles, the primordial production of the general—starting from real singularities. The new metaphysics will be metaphysics only by analogy...and will be properly named *analysis*, or analytic method. By retracing the true generation of knowledge, by going back to the principles, an actually inaugural practice of analysis can finally dissolve, destroy, decompose the first philosophy. That means, in the end: replace the first first philosophy while inheriting its name (*AF*, pp. 35–36).

First philosophy can only be offered by Condillac as an *analogy*, a repetition, a supplementation, a retracing of the *first* first philosophy. Thus Derrida demonstrates that while Condillac seeks after, even *desires* to be original, to offer a first philosophy, what he in fact produces is an *after-effect*, that which follows, that which is supplementary—perhaps even derivative. Hence Victor Cousin claims that Condillac "sacrifices everything for the frivolous benefit of reducing everything to a unique principle" (*AF*, p. 29). The idea then that philosophy can have a "unique principle," a single origin, a central idea, a point from which all else is derived, either conceptually or historically, is quite simply "frivolous," not serious, not plausible—*an error* (as Nietzsche would say). To think that there can be a single truth, a unitary principle, can at best be laughable—and that again is how Nietzsche would have regarded such attempts at excessive "seriousness." The postulate of an origin can at best be a postulate of an idea—not derived from experience or sensation as Condillac would have hoped (and fervently desired), but rather from the mistaken idea that one can *originate* a first philosophy, that one can *derive* an origin from a sense-experience. The Lockean plan, transformed into its French analogue in Condillac, is once again a repetition of a repetition—not unlike the Platonic artwork which is a copy of a copy.

And since first philosophy must be derived from experience, its origins will also have to be regarded as suspect, for they are also derivative—derivative of each sense-experience as well. It is therefore not surprising that "Condillac multiplies the considerations of history in his own discourse. He does not hold them as marginal" (*AF*, p. 85). Hence history—which might trace a path back to an origin—is also dispersed throughout Condillac's discourse, decentering its possibilities of origin as well. Another frivolity. That *history* might provide an origin is held in check. History has no access to the answer, for it too cannot serve up a first philosophy. So either history is too frivolous for Condillac and unable to provide first principles, or history is serious and first principles can be inserted into history at the appropriate moments. In the first case, Condillac is too serious, i.e., according to Cousin "too frivolous"; in the second case, history is too serious, providing origins and therefore undermining Condillac's whole project—leaving him without the true first philosophy he sought after.

Returning to the juxtapositions of Foucault's essay on origins ("Nietzsche, Genealogy, History") and to Derrida's essay on origins *(The Introduction to the Origin of Geometry)*, we find that origins themselves have been displaced in the search for origins. The need for a singular origination is deviated, diverted, and passed over as not located in any place—neither in history nor in the interpretation of history.

What remains unspoken in the account of origins, of *Ursprung* in its many facets, is another text—a kind of intertext—one that was almost contemporaneous with Husserl's *Origin of Geometry*. The text—marked off *in* history in 1935–36—is Heidegger's *Origin of the Work of Art.*[7] Heidegger's essay accounts for another formulation of "origin"—origin with respect to the work of art—and yet, in the end, the same understanding of origin.

For Heidegger, the attempt to articulate origin as singular, unitary, and located in a determinate place in time simply fails. It becomes clear that each time one cites origin as singular and particular, it turns out to be multiple and repeatable. Heidegger begins the essay by asking about the origin of the work of art. He then proposes—according to the common view—that the artist is the origin of the work of art. The artist is the one who generates the work. The artist produces the painting, the novel, or the sculpture—so why not say that the artist is the origin of the artwork? But then Heidegger notes that the artist as well has an origin. And it turns out that the origin of the artist is the artwork itself. That is, there would be no artist if the person did not create works or produce objects for enjoyment, scrutiny, and criticism. The artist acquires his or her special status as artist from the works that can be ascribed to that particular artist. Similarly, both the artist and the artwork *together* have *another* origin. This origin is neither the artist nor the artwork but rather the very "Art" that occupies the general domain in which the artist and artwork operate. Hence the artist would not be an artist were there not some general conception of Art, or at least some general understanding as to what constitutes Art and what does not.

Given that the very notion of origin has been divided into three origins: namely, the artist, the artwork, and Art, one might think that Heidegger would stop there. But he does not. Indeed, he then goes on to ask about the origin of Art. In this case, however, the answer is that the origin of Art is the artwork itself. This means that Heidegger has returned to the place where he began. Returning to the beginning means that the beginning is where one of the origins is located. However, that beginning is (and was) only temporary since the whole process of inquiry developed from that beginning was only to show that it is not really a beginning but rather a step along the way in an ongoing circuit of investigation. Heidegger calls this movement a "circle." Whether it is a circle is not crucial here. What is crucial is that it is a multiplication of the very notion of origin. And furthermore, the multiplicity of origins indicates quite clearly that for Heidegger, origin is not in one place but in many.

What is even more significant is that this multiple origination or proliferation of origins does nevertheless set up a domain in which the process of origination operates. This domain or space is the space of disclosure, *Lichtung*, but also *aletheia*, bringing out of concealment, truth. What in Nietzsche is an error, in Heidegger is the appearance of that which would seem to be foundational. Yet, if one follows the Heideggerian formulation carefully, it becomes evident that truth, for Heidegger, is not simply a ground, a foundation, a place from which other knowledge or understanding is derived. Truth is also not that to which all investigation or seeking is oriented as end. Rather truth is disclosed in a differential space, in an Open, in a clearing, in a place in which neither the artwork, nor the artist, nor Art itself can be found. Truth, by contrast, is precisely where there is no origin, where there is no ground, no source, no basis for understanding. This means that truth discloses only by difference, only by negation, only by being non-originary. Or to put it another way, truth is that space or place which arises out of the very multiplication and proliferation of origins. Hence truth depends upon a poly-origination and a dispersal of origin such that a discourse of poetizing or artistic disclosure can take place. With respect to aesthetic matters, then, artistic understanding or a discourse in which the aesthetic and aesthetic textuality is in question arises only out of the multiplicity and repetition of origins.

To situate this Heideggerian conception of origin in relation to the Foucauldian and Derridean juxtaposition will result in a reformulation of the very concept of origin. What an archaeology uncovers is a multiplicity of discursive practices. What a deconstruction of origin produces is an iteration and repetition such that origin is not a beginning and not even a decent start. Rather it is only a limit, a margin that is not achieved and wholly inscribed as such in history. What the Heideggerian discovery produces is an inscription of the differential space, marked off by a whole sequence of origins—a space in which what is disclosed is the denial of origin in art, in literature, in philosophy, and, for that matter, in history. In that differential space, the non-originary demarcation of origins produces a multiplicity of discourses—each at a historically designated time, and each designating the historical as that which is to be read in a variety of places, with a variety of markings, and in terms of a delimited chain or non-linked grouping of narrated events, texts, and situations. No event, text, or situation is substitutable for another—and yet no disclosed complex of discursive practices can achieve hegemony over those that they have replaced. The inscription of a set or complex of enunciated occurrences follows a crisis. As such it has no other origin than its own disclosure and no other achievement than its own prevalence in a determinate context and at a delimited moment in time.

22

PHILOSOPHY HAS ITS REASONS…

If there cannot be a pure concept of the university, if there cannot be a pure and purely rational concept of the university on the inside of the university, it is simply because the university is *founded*. An event of foundation cannot be simply understood within the logic of that which it founds.

—Derrida, "Mochlos ou le conflit des facultés"

As far as I know, nobody has ever founded a university *against* reason. So we may reasonably suppose that the University's reason for being has always been reason itself, and some essential connection of reason to being. But what is called the principle of reason is not simply reason. We cannot for now plunge into the history of reason, its words and concepts, into the puzzling scene of translation which has shifted *logos* to *ratio* to *raison*, reason, *Grund*, ground, *Vernunft*, and so on.

—Derrida, "The Principle of Reason:
The University in the Eyes of Its Pupils"

Beware of the abysses and the gorges, but also of the bridges and barriers. Beware of what opens the university to the outside and the bottomless, but also of what, closing it in on itself would create only an illusion of closure, would make the university available to any sort of interest, or else render it perfectly useless. Beware of ends; but what would a university be without ends?

—Derrida, "The Principle of Reason:
The University in the Eyes of Its Pupils"

Whence the necessity, for a deconstruction, not to abandon the terrain of the University at the very moment at which it is taking responsibility for its most powerful foundations. Whence the necessity not to abandon the terrain to empiricism and therefore to whatever force comes along.

—Derrida, "L'Age de Hegel,"
Qui a peur de la philosophie?

231

At a time when the European university was already established and even renowned in certain key centers, Blaise Pascal delivered an outline of his collected thoughts to the gentlemen of Port Royal. When he died in the mid-seventeenth century, he left the text of his "apology" for Christianity in the form of "thoughts" [*pensées*]. Among them is the celebrated *pensée* that states: *le coeur a ses raisons que la raison ne connait point: on le sait en mille choses.* (The heart has its reasons which reason doesn't know at all; a thousand things declare it.)[1] By a simple substitution, this maxim might well read: philosophy has its reasons which reason doesn't know at all. It would then go on to state: "a thousand things declare it." And furthermore: philosophy "loves the universal Being, and itself naturally, according to its obedience to either; and it hardens against one or the other, as it pleases."[2] The replacement of the "heart" with "philosophy" is not terribly outlandish considering that the heart is a kind of metonymy in which love is at issue. The heart stands for love. And love has access to domains that are inaccessible to reason. But philosophy is love *(philia)* not *caritas:* a love of wisdom. Even Socrates in the *Symposium* goes out of his way to report the Diotimian claim that the path from *eros* to *philia* (the love of wisdom) is a series of steps. The passions of the body can become the passions of the soul. The soul, when properly directed—by its own passions—can come to love and know the ideal forms according to which all things are fashioned. As the love of the heart replaces the love of wisdom, philosophy takes over the affairs of the heart. Pascal's heart is a heart of devotion, wagered conviction, subtlety in the face of the infinite. Pascal's heart has perspectives, justifications, conditions of understanding that are inaccessible to reason, that are outside the competence of reason, that reason cannot know. Philosophy—as another kind of love—bears these same characteristics. But this is curious since the very concern of philosophy has to do with the affairs of reason. The simple seventeenth-century dichotomy between reason and passion is not so easily constructed. In that philosophy is both a love or passion and the proper employment of reason, philosophy itself becomes indecidable.

Philosophy is an indecidable just as *pharmakon* is both a remedy and a poison, communication is a message and an action, difference is meaning and expression, trace is the present mark and the designated absence, and so forth. Jacques Derrida has gone to lengths to demonstrate that the indecidable is neither conjunction nor disjunction, neither the unity of a duality nor the duality of a unity. The indecidable affirms and negates, brings together and separates, posits connection and disconnection, establishes a difference without decidability. The indecidable is left with the indecision.[3]

Now what of philosophy? In *Archeology of the Frivolous* (1973), Derrida demonstrates that metaphysics is (in good Aristotelian language) first philosophy. But when Condillac (following Locke if not Aristotle) practices metaphysics, he is certainly concerned with it much later than Aristotle. And even Aristotle places metaphysics *after* physics. Metaphysics is at best *alongside* physics—first philosophy in second place. Metaphysics requires that physics (the concern with nature) be displayed before metaphysics so that metaphysics (as philosophy) might comment upon it, discourse about it, render judgment on it. But these are only the beginnings of philosophy. Philosophy begins in wonder, for it has to have something to wonder about. At the other extreme, much has been said about the end of philosophy—by Hegel, by Heidegger, by Derrida, and so on (endlessly one might suspect). Yet the beginning and the end are not the respects in which philosophy is an indecidable—at least not for the present inquiry. Inserting philosophy, it would seem, at some place between the discourse of beginnings (first philosophy) and ends (where it all comes together for the one and final time) is the substitution of philosophy for the heart. With Pascal, one might say, philosophy can't decide whether it is first or last, whether it is finite or infinite, whether it appeals to the *esprit de géometrie* (as it did for Descartes) or the *esprit de finesse* (as Montaigne might have seen it). With Pascal the difference is to be clear (perhaps not so distinct—for both are of the *esprit*). The heart knows what reason does not, reason knows what doesn't belong to the heart. Philosophy knows (has its reasons) and reason has nothing to say about it. Like the heart, philosophy can stand outside reason while at the same time having its own reasons for being rational and employing reason. As long as philosophy is a love, it cannot be reason itself. But can it be the principle of reason?

To the extent that philosophy is at once passion (love or heart) and reason, it is a poor substitute for the heart as such. Yet as a poor substitute, it is also a good substitute in that it demonstrates the indecidability of philosophy itself. Philosophy is that which sets reason in motion. Philosophy gives weight and force to reason. Its very energy and enthusiasm is what takes it beyond what is simply accepted knowledge *(scientia)*. In this sense, philosophy both generates and regulates reason. It is the principle of reason and the passionate exercise of reason. Here reason is both a power and a human faculty. As a power, reason can bring order, sequence, continuity, justification, support, and even understanding. As a human faculty, reason can overcome the passions, desire, aimlessness, confusion, and even ignorance. As a power, reason can persuade, deceive, cloud over, cover up, and even overpower. As a human faculty, reason can dry up emotion, enthusiasm, excitement, decisiveness, and even action. To the extent that philosophy is above all that, it can prevent itself from submitting to the desiccation of passion and the deceits of reasonableness. It is not that philosophy (like Nietzsche's *musikē* which is neither the excessive passion of the barbarian Dionysian nor the overwhelming discipline of Apollonian individuality) is a harnessed frenzy, an opposition held in tension. Rather philosophy is quite straightforwardly indecidable.

There is no *Aufhebung, dépassement,* superseding, surpassing, uplifting, conserving, or preserving here. Whatever is uplifting about philosophy—like the puffing up of leavening in bread—is deflated by the indecision. If only the love, the passion, the heart of philosophy could be unequivocally uplifting, the work would no longer be like work. It would be a *par-ergon.* And besides, something that ought to be like work (and isn't) should surely be suspect. And there are those who suspect philosophy. Philosophy is suspect because it looks like fun. It requires leisure *(scholē).* But what is leisurely can't be scholarly, for what is scholarly is hard work. And those who practice the scholarly work that has been associated with philosophy since medieval times are charged with overlooking intuition—the kind of clear and distinct apprehension that Descartes associated with the rendering of absolute ideas. But if Descartes is right, such apprehensions cannot be the direct product of work. Work will ultimately bring about the passage (or bridge) from relative ideas to absolute ideas. The work is not in the intuition—this was Plato's view of *noesis* as it was Descartes's impression of the *intuitio*. Intuition comes only at the end of work (education, dialectic, method). Philosophical intuition occurs—if it is to happen—when all the work is done, energy expended, exercise and practice maintained. Philosophical intuition *(Anschauung)* is neither scholarly (the meticulous exercise of reason) nor available to those who make sport of it (philosophizing with a golf club). If only Nietzsche could philosophize with a hammer. If only Wagner's hammering against an anvil could fashion more than a magical Rheingold ring. But such *Leitmotive* typically just pass into cultural history— and some are even too loud and tempestuous to hear in one's leisure. Heidegger tried to philosophize with a hammer—because paradigmatically and pragmatically *zuhanden*. To construct with a hammer is hard work. Destruction with a sledge hammer goes a bit more easily. Neither can be done leisurely—they must both be done out of school.

But what kind of philosophizing can be—should be—done in school, in the academy, in the university? The question of the nature and essence *(Wesen)* of philosophy has now become a matter of the ethics of philosophy. What it means to philosophize—when, where, and how it can be done—also has implications for what it ought to do. The problem for philosophy is to deal with its own indecidability. Philosophy cannot simply speak from the heart. At the same time, reason is not the heart of philosophy. Philosophy has its reasons which reason does not know at all. There are domains of philosophy which are not simply translated into reason. Philosophy is neither reason nor passion. Philosophy has its own reasons. That which is philosophy's own seeks to define itself, to delimit itself, to say what it is, to produce a discourse about itself that it finds comfortable—that fits into its system, that is consistent with its style of practice, that articulates its very principles, that undoes its very presuppositions, that opens up a space in which it might operate, that offers hope and sometimes the revelation (apocalypse) of despair. Philosophy's own has many shapes. To presume to catalog them would be futile. Its aspiration is to be grounded in some sort of principle of reason—it wants passionately to achieve such an end. It would be so uplifting, elevating, and—if the sun is right—enlightening for it to be grounded in some sort of principle of reason. It is not that philosophy— like metaphor, is heliotropic, though it may well be that the ethics of philosophy—as Plato's allegory of the sun would show—will require an identification of the good with the sun. But then if we could only see what philosophy sees, or what it ought to see, or what it would love to see...imagine the light it would bring. The light would illuminate the ground—like a medieval manuscript—while some principle of reason might stand in the clearing, unveiled, disclosed, and available for the sort of careful reading that it would require. Such a principle of reason would have its own rules—as Kant claimed, properly it would be "only a rule." Opening up at the ground, what sort of gathering would the principle of reason be able to achieve? What range of regulation could it achieve from the ground? Leonardo had the idea long before Kant: wouldn't some *"pensée de survol"* be more effective? One can see so much more from a flying machine, an airplane, or even a missile. But Merleau-Ponty's warnings about thinking from on high ought to be heeded. Bird's-eye thinking sees far, extends to the very horizons of sight, and surveys the breadth of the terrain, but it relies upon reflection. It is so far from the ground. And if philosophy is to operate in terms of a principle of reason, it must be grounded. Too much high-flying, "highfalluting" philosophy will go nowhere. The reasonable place within which to ground philosophy—for centuries the chosen place—is the university.

Inside the university, standing solidly on the university grounds, keeping out of the clouds and off the ivory towers, philosophy can do its work. Philosophy is comfortable within the university. It is sometimes so comfortable that it can and has become—in some instances—its own technology. Its reason for being (sometimes its sole *raison d'être*) is to provide tools for critical reasoning—and the hammer is rarely among them. Critical skills depend upon argumentation and the proper application of rules for "clear thinking." But logical tools have little to do with *logos*. To *serve* the academic community, philosophy need not involve thinking. To understand discourse, to read texts, to examine the unexamined limits of *what is* requires thinking, illuminating, grounding. Derrida has elaborated upon the groundedness of "basic" research. "Fundamental" research has foundations—even some which are below the ground. "Oriented" research is applied. When philosophy becomes "oriented" research, it reaches out beyond its ground. It thereby extends out beyond the comfortable zone. It performs its services, but it loses the comfort that comes from playing with its tools. Basic research in philosophy sticks close to the base. Theory, criticism, and history— the pillars of its *domus*—need to stand firmly on the ground. These pillars of philosophy need to speak from the ground, they need to shine in the light, they need to dispel the shadows—so that a peripatetic stroll through the *stoa*, around the quad, from one building to another, will be both pleasant and productive. Philosophical production demands that it be derived from a ground, that it speak from the ground, that it be a *Satz vom Grund*. Without the *Satz vom Grund*, theory, criticism, and history remain in the dark. The university is the "natural" place for the establishment of a ground for basic research in philosophy, for the university is purely a *cultural* institution.

The university's foundations are cultural. In Europe, they derive from the State. In America, they are more varied. Their funding *(les fonds)* may be church-related, privately endowed, or legislature-dependent. The success or failure of the American university may depend upon the virtues of its financial base. Whether its authority comes from church coffers (derived from one sect or another, one order or another), from granted land and legislative whim, or from successful alumni and friends, the achievement or failure of philosophy may remain substantially independent. Philosophy may be instituted by the Church or it may be a component of a general education requirement. There may even be endowed chairs that support a philosophy program. But the practice of philosophy will generate itself in accordance with the power struggles at work among its practitioners. On occasion, its achievement may be related to the virtues of enrollment, the popularity of its subject-matter, and, albeit more rarely, the integrity of its thinking. But these concerns—financial and political—barely touch the principles upon which philosophy is based. From an administrative point of view, any philosophy will do. The content is irrelevant. Within the university, it is important that there be philosophy, because philosophy has always been *in* the university. The normal review processes will be invoked to ensure "quality"—whatever the content, whatever the practice, whatever the production. The standards are those set by the reviewers and the reviewers are chosen in accordance with recommendations from those who seek to be confirmed—or by those who seek to disconfirm. But all this is like rafts tied to one another in the middle of the sea. There is no ground, no mooring, no principle of reason, no base from which to speak, no foundation upon which to build. How can philosophy build itself in the university when the building must be without ground? Philosophy has its reasons which reason does not know at all. If reason can't do the job, philosophy must appeal to its *own* reasons.

What must philosophy do when founded upon an abyss? In "What Are Poets For?" (*Wozu Dichter?* 1946), Heidegger writes:

> Because of this default, there fails to appear for the world the ground that grounds it. The word for abyss—*Abgrund*—originally means the soil and ground toward which, because it *is* undermost, a thing tends downward. But in what follows we shall think of the *Ab-* as the complete absence of the ground. The ground is the soil in which to strike root and to stand. The age for which the ground fails to come, hangs in the abyss. Assuming that a turn still remains open for this destitute time at all, it can come some day only if the world turns about fundamentally—and that now means, unequivocally: if it turns away from the abyss. In the age of the world's night, the abyss of the world must be experienced and endured. But for this it is necessary that there be those who reach into the abyss.[4]

Heidegger is speaking (philosophically) about the poet who might reach into the abyss, who might call for the need to establish or reestablish a ground. But will it not, of necessity, be the philosopher who must reach into the abyss to find the ground? The sea is a kind of fathomless abyss. Derrida's reading of Cornell University as situated on the edge of an abyss (a gorge, whose grounding remains unthought) points to the place at which the ground *(Grund)* meets the abyss *(Abgrund)*. The abyss is away from the ground. The task of philosophy is to found the principle which founds the ground. Just as the university needs to be founded, erected, instituted on solid terrain, it needs to appeal to philosophy in order to found itself—to establish itself on a firm footing. It needs a theory of the university.

For the philosopher to reach into the abyss, into the *Ab-grund*, the philosopher must nevertheless stand somewhere. There must be some standpoint. A full-scale foundation is not necessarily called for, although foundations sometimes make philosophical activity possible. Just as the Renaissance goldsmith or the court painter drew strength from the support of a patron, so too the philosopher can often make good use of a grant or fellowship offered by a foundation to conduct the sort of research that will establish another ground outside of the abyss. But is it necessary for the philosopher to form a base from which to work? Must the philosopher speak or write from a ground? If not, what sort of standpoint is possible? Temporary supports like grants and fellowships only call attention to the need to speak from a ground *(Satz vom Grund)*. They fill a gap, a leave, a sabbatical. But then they are a ground away from home. The *Stiftung* constitutes a building or erecting of an institute. What is instituted is not a full-scale institution, but rather a permanent impermanence, a granting agency that allows for the development of many different perspectives, different studies, different inquiries. The foundation as granting agency (private or public) establishes the principle of continual substitution of points of view. A new investigator will receive the grant the next year. However, the philosopher as investigator still requires a ground. Even the very principle of application requires that one apply *from an institution* and, once funds are granted, that they be placed in the institution's research foundation. It seems then that foundations are "all over the place." But like the sea for Coleridge's ancient mariner, there are foundations everywhere, but "not a drop to drink." Even when philosophers are able to benefit from foundations, there are few *real* foundations for thought.

The philosopher seeks principles of reason just as the scientist seeks grants. But when *on* a "foundation grant," the philosopher is still looking for foundations. And so the philosopher is always operating at the edge of an abyss—not quite able to fall in and not quite able to stand on solid ground. The philosopher's responsibility is to survey the abyss, to seek after *terra firma*, and to operate in those places which are most the philosopher's own. These are the places in which the abyss looms ahead and the ground stretches out behind. The hope is for a bridge—*faire le pont*—it would clearly be the most effective way. Derrida says of the bridge at Cornell:

A matter of life and death. The question arose . . . when the university administration proposed to erect protective railings on the Collegetown bridge and the Fall Creek suspension bridge to check thoughts of suicide inspired by the view of the gorge. "Barriers" was the term used; we could say "diaphragm," borrowing a word which in Greek literally means "partitioning fence." Beneath the bridges linking the university to its surroundings, connecting its inside to its outside, lies the abyss. In testimony before the Campus Council, one member of the faculty did not hesitate to express his opposition to the barriers, those diaphragmatic eyelids, on the grounds that blocking the view would mean, to use his words, "destroying the essence of the university." What did he mean? What *is* the essence of the university?[5].

The bridge is a linking function. It brings together elements that are different—at least spatially, if not in kind. But a bridge over an abyss is a dangerous crossing. Nietzsche's "man" is a rope stretched between beast and overman. The bridge is not stable ground. It is not a place to stay. Rather a bridge is an *on the way (unterwegs)* to another place—a transport or a transition, an interruption of location, passing from an old place to a new one. Indeed the very metaphor for the metaphor of transportation is already a bridge between two places. The philosopher's responsibility is *to be a bridge*, to link ideas, concepts, points of view, practices, and so on, and to show how and that they are different. The philosopher as bridge is a passage, or link between differences. When it is most its *own*, philosophy practices differencing. The bridge crosses over the pit. It names difference; it even inscribes difference. At Stony Brook, when the main campus was being developed, there was a bridge, built from the union toward the library. But it was never completed. It passed over a road which leads in and out of the campus. At many universities, the union—in principle the gathering place for students and campus activities—is centrally located and sometimes even includes (as at Iowa and Indiana for instance) a hotel and many restaurants. The union is the center of life on campus. At Stony Brook, the bridge leading out from this center was commonly called "the bridge to nowhere." For a campus beginning its second decade in the early seventies, this appellation designated a sort of uncertainty that comes with a young but rapidly growing university. By the end of the seventies, a Fine Arts center had been constructed and the bridge was extended so as to link this new edifice with the library. With its completion the "bridge to nowhere" became a "bridge to somewhere." Psychological services on campus were then called "the bridge to somewhere"—the bridge no longer simply traversed a road that passed in and out of campus. Now the bridge itself, along with the university and its students, was finally going somewhere. The bridge to somewhere was the hope that the university itself was not an abyss, but rather a groundwork for a determinate direction. The bridge became the symbol of a *vita nuova* for the university, a new vitality, a new reason to be. The bridge to somewhere was not a passage to anywhere in particular, but simply a bridge to somewhere.

Philosophy as a bridge does not necessarily bring the outside in relation to the inside and vice versa. By setting apart and marking off the ground from the abyss, philosophy may well establish its principle of reason at the limits or borders of the university—where the university defines itself as a system of disciplines and practices in relation to one another. The statement from the ground can at best be a statement in relation to the non-ground. The philosopher's responsibility is to establish the bridge between them.

Some bridges identify *internal* relations (the Hertford College bridge at Oxford, the Memorial Bridge linking Harvard Square with the Business School in Cambridge, Massachusetts, the passageway between Lewis Tower and the Marquette Center at the Loyola Water Tower Campus). Others make the connection between the two different campuses of the same university—a bus links the old SUNY/Buffalo campus with the Amherst site, the University of California/Santa Cruz with University of California/Berkeley, and the Chicago Loyola Water Tower campus with the Lake Shore location. Some bridges are tunnels like those that permeate the University of Alberta and Brown University. Some bridge-tunnels connect the outside with the inside, such as the one linking the British Rail station with the university at Sussex, ascending right up through the heart of the campus resembling as well the ascent up the Faculté des Lettres at the Université de Nice in Southern France. In such cases, the impression of steps leading upward is itself inspiring. The universities of San Diego, San Francisco, Duquesne, Montreal, Tübingen, and Perugia are even built on a hill. Those which aspire to the heights of church steeples (like Pittsburgh, Stanford, and Essex) offer no illusions about the expectations of their cathedrals of learning. But to turn bridges into towers is to entertain the often dreaded conflict in which the philosophy faculties must distinguish (and defend) themselves from aspiring theological (not to mention legal and medical) faculties. But what is philosophy's role in all this? Is there a bridge within philosophy, as philosophy might be the bridge within the university, and as the sciences might be a link with the world at large? Philosophy has a responsibility to speak from the bridge. Philosophy has a responsibility to straddle the various intellectual concerns within the university *and* to provide an overarching view of them—without encouraging a sense of ultimate detachment. Philosophy has a responsibility to provide a set of views on literature, the arts, science, the individual, and society. It must also devise its own methods, styles, and modes of self-expression, self-representation, self-articulation, and self-understanding. Philosophy has a responsibility. It is most its own (most *eigentlich*) when it both looks out and looks in on itself. It needs to look *out* onto the spectrum of disciplines and concerns that constitute our world. And it needs to look *in* on its own essence, meaning, structures, and activities. It needs to look into the *logos* of the universe and its own *logos*, the passion to know (*la volonté de savoir*) and its own reasons for being (*raison d'être*), the commitment to search out the nature of things and the obligation to "check itself out," to assess its own essence and practices. Philosophy's own indecidability (its deconstructive strategies and positions) is the bridge between its being and its objects, its passion and its reason, its place within the university and its view onto the world abroad. The textuality of philosophy is the elaboration of this indecidability: its texts are its views, and its views are its texts. Philosophy becomes itself when it is most something other. Its otherness is its textual identity.

The bar (*barre*) or barrier between what philosophy signifies and its signifying keeps it from becoming other than itself, keeps it from losing its identity, keeps it *for* itself. As philosophy establishes its own texts, it founds itself and its place within the university as that which is not itself, as that which is entirely other, as that which has no place in the leisurely, hallowed halls of the contemporary university. Philosophy has its reasons for being in the university and for justifying its degrees of otherness from itself—its Ph.D.s and its D.Phil.s—but it also has its reasons for looking in on the university, for its concerns about the well-being of the university with all its fields and domains. Philosophy has its reasons for wanting to know beyond, across, and between what it itself is and what it is not. Philosophy has its reasons for examining its own foundations as well as those of everything else. Philosophy has its reasons for being itself as well as being *other* than what it is. These are the reasons that make up the text of philosophy. They are the reasons that reason doesn't know about; *car la philosophie a ses raisons que la raison ne connaît point*—philosophy has its reasons which reason doesn't know at all.[6]

NOTES

CHAPTER 1: FROM HERMENEUTICS TO DECONSTRUCTION

1   See E. D. Hirsch, *Validity in Interpretation* (New Haven: Yale University Press, 1967). Henceforth cited in the text as *Validity*.

2   See Roman Ingarden, *The Literary Work of Art* (1931), trans. Georges G. Grabowicz (Evanston: Northwestern University Press, 1973). Henceforth cited in the text as *LWA*.

3   Hans-Georg Gadamer, *Truth and Method* (1960), trans. and ed. Garrett Barden and John Cumming (New York: Seabury, 1975). While page references are to this early English edition (henceforth cited in the text as *TM*), a new and improved 1990 version, translated by Joel Weinsheimer and Donald G. Marshall, is also published by Seabury.

4   See Paul Ricoeur, *Hermeneutics and the Human Sciences*, ed. and trans. John B. Thompson (Cambridge: Cambridge University Press, 1981). Henceforth cited in the text as *HHS*.

5   See F. de Saussure, *Course in General Linguistics* (1916), trans. Wade Baskin (New York: McGraw-Hill, 1959).

6   Roland Barthes, *Elements of Semiology* (1964), trans. Annette Lavers and Colin Smith (New York: Hill and Wang, 1968).

7   See Martin Heidegger, *Being and Time* (1927), sec. 34, trans. John Macquarrie and Edward Robinson (New York: Harper and Row, 1962).

8   The Heideggerian theme of a being's relation to Being will be reiterated at various junctures in subsequent chapters. For an earlier reading of this theme, see Hugh J. Silverman, *Inscriptions: Between Phenomenology and Structuralism* (London and New York: Routledge, 1987), chap. 16. Since the present study has an interwoven sequential and supplementary relationship to *Inscriptions*, subsequent references here will be cited with the relevant chapter(s) as *Inscriptions*.

9   See Martin Heidegger, "The Origin of the Work of Art" (1935–36; first published in 1950; amended, with an afterword by Hans-Georg Gadamer, in 1960), in *Poetry Language Thought*, trans. Albert Hofstadter (New York: Harper and Row, 1971), pp. 17–87. Henceforth cited in the text as *PLT-OWA*.

10 See Jacques Lacan, *Écrits* (1966), trans. Alan Sheridan (New York: Norton, 1977).

11 The theoretical practice of a hermeneutic semiology—clarified further as a juxtapositional deconstructive hermeneutic semiology—will be developed in detail

throughout the course of the present study. See *Inscriptions*, chaps. 19 and 20 for a preliminary formulation.

12 See Roland Barthes, "From Work to Text" (1971), in *Image/Music/Text*, trans. Stephen Heath (New York: Hill and Wang, 1977), pp. 155–64. Henceforth cited in the text as *IMT-FWT*.

13 Jacques Derrida. "Plato's Pharmacy" (1968), in *Dissemination* (1972), trans. Barbara Johnson (Chicago: University of Chicago Press, 1981), pp. 63–171. Henceforth cited in the text as *Dissemination*.

14 Jacques Derrida, "Differance" (1968), in *Speech and Phenomena and Other Essays on Husserl's Theory of Signs*, trans. David B. Allison (Evanston: Northwestern University Press, 1973), pp. 129–60. Henceforth cited as *Différance*. The 1967 *Speech and Phenomena* itself will be referred to as *SP*.

CHAPTER 2: SEMIOTICS AND HERMENEUTICS

1 As indicated in the previous chapter, but also as developed in *Inscriptions*, especially the final chapter (chap. 20) entitled "For a Hermeneutic Semiology of the Self."

2 See Carlo Sini, *Semiotica e filosofia: Segno e linguaggio in Peirce, Heidegger e Foucault* (Bologna: Il Mulino, 1978). Also see Sini's *Images of Truth*, trans. Massimo Verdicchio (Atlantic Highlands: Humanities Press, 1992).

3 See Martin Heidegger, "Logos (Heraclitus, Fragment B 50)," in *Early Greek Thinking*, trans. David Farrell Krell and Frank A. Capuzzi (New York: Harper & Row, 1975), pp. 59–78. Henceforth cited in the text as *EGT*.

4 Martin Heidegger, "Language" (1950), in *Poetry Language Thought*, pp. 189–210. Henceforth cited in the text as *PLT-L*.

5 A more detailed discussion of Heidegger's "Origin of the Work of Art" can be found in Part II: chapter 5.

6 Heidegger, *On the Way to Language* (1959), trans. Peter D. Hertz (New York: Harper & Row, 1971). Henceforth cited as *OWL*.

7 Dante Alighieri, *Vita Nuova*, trans. Barbara Reynolds (Middlesex: Penguin, 1969), p. 29. Henceforth cited in the text as *VN*.

8 Roland Barthes, *Writing Degree Zero* (1953), trans. Annette Lavers and Colin Smith (Boston: Beacon, 1967). Henceforth cited as *Degree Zero*.

9 Roland Barthes, "The Death of the Author" (1968), in *Image/Music/Text*, p. 142. Henceforth cited in the text as *IMT-DA*.

10 Roland Barthes, *S/Z* (1971), trans. Richard Miller (New York: Hill and Wang, 1974). Henceforth cited as *S/Z*.

11 See Charles Sanders Peirce, *Philosophical Writings of Peirce*, ed. Justus Buchler (New York: Dover, 1940, 1955).

CHAPTER 3: HERMENEUTICS AND INTERROGATION

1 Maurice Merleau-Ponty, *Le Visible et l'invisible* (Paris: Gallimard, 1964). English translation by Alphonso Lingis as *The Visible and the Invisible* (Evanston: Northwestern University Press, 1968), p. 105. Henceforth cited in the text as "*VI*" and *VI-tr.*, respectively.

2 Oliver Goldsmith, *She Stoops to Conquer* (eighteenth century drama)

3 Heidegger, "Aletheia (Heraclitus, Fragment B 16)" (1943), in *Early Greek Thinking* (1975), p. 122.

4   The notion of visibility as the chiasmatic relating of the visible and invisible is developed further in the next chapter and in the context of painting in chapter 15.

CHAPTER 4: INTERROGATION AND DECONSTRUCTION

1   Maurice Merleau-Ponty, "Le Doute de Cézanne," in *Sens et non-sens* (Paris: Nagel, 1947), pp. 15–44. Translated by Patricia A. Dreyfus and Hubert L. Dreyfus as "Cézanne's Doubt,"in *Sense and Non-Sense* (Evanston: Northwestern University Press, 1964). Henceforth cited as *SNS* and *SNS-tr.*, respectively.
2   Maurice Merleau-Ponty, "L'Oeil et l'esprit" (Paris: Gallimard, 1961). Henceforth cited in the text as *OE.* Translated by Carleton Dallery as "Eye and Mind" in *The Primacy of Perception*, ed. James M. Edie (Evanston: Northwestern University Press, 1964), pp. 159–90. Henceforth cited as *EM.*
3   Jacques Derrida, "Restitutions de la verité en pointure," *Macula*, nos. 3–4 (1978), pp. 11–37.
4   Jacques Derrida, *La Verité en peinture* (Paris: Flammarion, 1978). Translated by Geoffrey Bennington as *The Truth in Painting* (Chicago: University of Chicago Press, 1987). Henceforth cited as *Verité* and *TP*, respectively.
5   See Meyer Schapiro, "The Still-Life as a Personal Object—A Note on Heidegger and Van Gogh," in *The Reach of Mind: Essays in Memory of Kurt Goldstein, 1878–1965* (New York: Springer, 1967).
6   See *Conversations avec Cézanne*, ed. P. M. Doran (Paris: Macula, 1978), esp. pp. 23–80. Henceforth cited in the text as *Cézanne.*
7   Hubert Damisch, "Le Versant de la parole," in *Bulletin de Psychologie*, vol. 18, nos. 3–6 (November 1964). The volume is entitled *Maurice Merleau-Ponty à la Sorbonne*," pp. 105–108. A two-volume translation by James Barry, Jr., and Stephen H. Watson as *Merleau-Ponty's Sorbonne Lectures*, edited by Hugh J. Silverman, is in preparation for publication by Humanities Press. The first volume is projected for 1994.
8   For the passage from the ninth letter, see *Cézanne*, p. 57.
9   In fact, Merleau-Ponty cites B. Dorival, *Paul Cézanne* (Paris, 1948).
10 The paradigm case of rendering vision into painting is self-portraiture. See chapter 15 for a more detailed reading of self-portraiture.
11 See chapter 13 in which Derrida's reading of Meyer Schapiro's reading of Heidegger's reading of Van Gogh's shoes painting(s) is given further attention.

CHAPTER 5: ENFRAMING THE WORK OF ART

1   Dante Alighieri, "Inferno," *The Divine Comedy*, trans. John Ciardi (New York: New American Library, 1954), p. 106.
2   Roland Barthes, *The Pleasure of the Text* (1973), trans. Richard Miller (New York: Hill & Wang, 1975).

CHAPTER 6: WRITING AT THE EDGE OF METAPHYSICS

1   See Jacques Derrida, *Speech and Phenomena* (1967); *Of Grammatology* (1967), trans. Gayatri Chakravorty Spivak (Baltimore: Johns Hopkins University Press, 1976) [henceforth *Grammatology*]; and *Writing and Difference*, trans. Alan Bass (Chicago: University of Chicago Press, 1978).

2   See Jacques Derrida, *Edmund Husserl's Origin of Geometry: An Introduction* (1962), trans. John P. Leavey (New York: Nicholas Hays, 1977). A new edition has been published by the University of Nebraska Press (Lincoln, 1989). Henceforth cited as *IOG.*

3   See Jacques Derrida, *Positions* (1972), trans. Alan Bass (Chicago: University of Chicago Press, 1982), for these interviews with Houdebine and Scarpetta, and with Julia Kristeva. Henceforth cited as *Positions.*

4   See Derrida, *Dissemination* (1972), and *Margins of Philosophy* (1972), trans. Alan Bass (Chicago: University of Chicago Press, 1982). Henceforth cited as *Margins.*

5   See Jacques Derrida, "The Parergon," trans. Craig Owens, *October*, no. 9 (Summer 1979), pp. 3–40. See especially p. 33. Incorporated into *Truth in Painting* (1978), pp. 16–147; *Verité*, pp. 19–168.

6   Jacques Derrida, *La Carte Postale: de Socrate à Freud et au-délà* (Paris: Aubier-Flammarion, 1980), p. 536. Henceforth cited in the text as *Carte postale.*

7   See *Les Fins de l'homme: à partir du travail de Jacques Derrida* (Paris: Galilée, 1981), and especially, Jacques Derrida, "D'un ton apocalyptique adopté naguère en philosophie," pp. 445–86.

8   See Jacques Derrida, "The *Retrait* of Metaphor," in *Enclitic*, vol. 11, no. 2 (Fall 1978), pp. 5–33. Henceforth cited in the text as *Retrait.*

9   See Jacques Lacan, "Seminar on 'The Purloined Letter,' " trans. Jeffrey Mehlman, in "French Freud: Structural Studies in Psychoanalysis," *Yale French Studies*, no. 48 (1972), pp. 38–72; and Jacques Derrida, "The Purveyor of Truth," trans. Willis Domingo, James Hulbert, Mosche Ron, and Marie-Rose Logan, in "Graphesis: Literature and Philosophy," *Yale French Studies*, no. 5 (1975), pp. 31–113.

10 See Barbara Johnson, "The Frame of Reference: Poe, Lacan, Derrida," in *The Critical Difference: Essays in the Contemporary Rhetoric of Reading* (Baltimore: Johns Hopkins University Press, 1980), pp. 110–46.

11 Harold Bloom et al., *Deconstruction and Criticism* (New York: Seabury Press, 1979). See especially the essays by Paul de Man, "Shelley Disfigured," pp. 39–73, and Jacques Derrida, "Living On: Border Lines," pp. 75–176. Henceforth cited as *DC.*

12 Jacques Derrida, *The Archeology of the Frivolous* (1973), trans. John P. Leavey (Pittsburgh: Duquesne University Press, 1980). Henceforth cited as *AF.*

13 See Martin Heidegger, *The Question of Being*, trans. Jean T. Wilde and William Kluback (New York: College & University Press, 1958).

14 See *Inscriptions*, chap. 16.

15 See Martin Heidegger, *Introduction to Metaphysics*, trans. Ralph Manheim (New Haven: Yale University Press, 1959), and *The End of Philosophy*, trans. Joan Stambaugh (New York: Harper & Row, 1973).

16 See *Inscriptions*, chap. 17. See also Rodolphe Gasché, "Deconstruction as Criticism," in *Glyph 6* (1979), pp. 177–215.

CHAPTER 7: TEXTUALITY AND LITERARY THEORY

1   Jean-Paul Sartre, *What Is Literature?* (1947), trans. Bernard Frechtman (New York: Harper and Row, 1965). A new edition , edited by Stephen Ungar is published by Harvard University Press, 1988.

2   See Barthes, *Writing Degree Zero* (1953).

3   See Claude Lévi-Strauss, "The Structural Study of Myth," in *Structural Anthropology*, trans. Claire Jacobson and Brooke Grundfest Schoepf (New York: Basic Books, 1963), pp. 206–31.

4   See Michel Beaujour, "For a Science of Literature," *Punto de Contacto/Point of Contact*, vol. 1 , no. 4 (1977), pp. 4– 11.
5   See, for example, Samuel R. Levin, *Linguistic Structures in Poetry* (The Hague: Mouton, 1962) and the papers collected in *Linguistics and Literary Style*, ed. Donald C. Freeman (New York: Holt, Rinehart and Winston, 1971).
6   Michael Riffaterre's *Essais de stylistique structurale* (Paris: Flammarion, 1971) is the classic document for the theory of the intertext. See also his *Semiotics of Poetry* (Bloomington: Indiana University Press, 1978).
7   Roman Jakobson's essay "Two Aspects of Language and Two Types of Aphasic Disturbances," in *Fundamentals of Language* (The Hague: Mouton, 1971), pp. 69–96, is one of the key reference loci for contemporary studies of metaphor and metonymy. In the analytic philosophical tradition, the issue is treated by Max Black in *Models and Metaphors* (Ithaca: Cornell University Press, 1962) following I. A. Richards's notion of "tenor and vehicle" in *The Philosophy of Rhetoric* (New York: Oxford. 1936). The rhetorical tradition, including Aristotle, Quintillian, and Fontanier, offers grounding for the Group µ (J. Dubois, F. Edeline, J. M. Klinkenberg, P. Minguet, F. Pire, and H. Trinon) study: *Rhétorique générale* (Paris: Larousse, 1971). Perhaps the most significant contemporary study of metaphor is Paul Ricoeur, *The Rule of Metaphor*, trans. Robert Czerny with K. McLaughlin and J. Costello (Toronto: University of Toronto Press, 1977). John Searle's "speech act" modifies J. L. Austin's "illocutionary act." Searle attests to the compatibility of linguistic performatives with Ferdinand de Saussure's conception of *langue* as opposed to the expected *parole*. See John Searle, *Speech Acts: An Essay in the Philosophy of Language* (Cambridge: Cambridge University Press, 1969), and John Austin, *How to Do Things with Words* (New York: Oxford University Press, 1962). In addition to various articles by Richard Ohmann and Stanley Fish, see, for instance, Mary Louise Pratt, *Toward a Speech Act Theory of Literary Discourse* (Bloomington: Indiana University Press, 1977).
9   See, for example. the essays in *The Computer and Literary Style*, ed. Jacob Leed (Kent, Ohio: Kent State University Press. 1966).
10   Notably the work of Paul Ricoeur, *The Symbolism of Evil*, trans. Emerson Buchanan (Boston: Beacon, 1969); *Freud and Philosophy*, trans. Denis Savage (New Haven: Yale University Press, 1971); *The Conflict of Interpretations*, ed. Don Ihde (Evanston: Northwestern University Press, 1974); and Hans-Georg Gadamer, *Truth and Method*. See also Richard E. Palmer, *Hermeneutics: Interpretation Theory in Schleiermacher, Dilthey, Heidegger and Gadamer* (Evanston: Northwestern University Press, 1969), and Kurt Müller-Vollmer, *Toward a Phenomenology of Literature: A Study of Wilhelm Dilthey's Poetik* (The Hague: Mouton, 1963). Some valuable recent collections of essays on hermeneutics include *Interpretaton of Narrative*, eds. Mario J. Valdés and Owen J. Miller (Toronto: University of Toronto Press, 1978); *The Hermeneutics Reader: Texts of the German Tradition from the Enlightenment to the Present*, ed. Kurt Müller-Vollmer (New York: Continuum, 1985); *Hermeneutics and Modern Philosophy*, ed. Brice Wachterhauser (Albany: SUNY Press, 1986); *The Hermeneutic Tradition: From Ast to Ricoeur*, along with *Transforming the Hermeneutic Context: From Nietzsche to Nancy*, eds. Gayle L. Ormiston and Alan D. Schrift (Albany: SUNY Press, 1990); *Hermeneutics and Deconstruction*, eds. Hugh J. Silverman and Don Ihde (Albany: SUNY Press, 1985); and *Gadamer and Hermeneutics*, ed. Hugh J. Silverman (New York and London: Routledge, 1991).
11   Ernest Jones, *Hamlet and Oedipus* (New York: Anchor, 1949) is the classic study.

William Phillips has collected together many other important essays in this domain in *Art and Psychoanalysis* (New York: Meridian, 1957).

12 See Sartre, *Baudelaire* (1947), trans. Martin Turnell (New York: New Directions, 1950), Sartre, *Saint Genet* (1952), trans. anon. (New York: New American Library, 1963), and Sartre, *Mallarmé, or the Poet of Nothingness* (1986), trans. Ernest Sturm (University Park: Penn State University Press, 1988).

13 See Georg Lukacs, *Goethe and His Age*, trans. Robert Anchor (New York: Grosset and Dunlap, 1963); Max Horkheimer and Theodor W. Adorno, *Dialectic of Enlightenment*, trans. John Cumming (New York: Seabury, 1972); Lucien Goldmann, *The Hidden God: A Study of Tragic Vision in the* Pensées *of Pascal and the Tragedies of Racine*, trans. Philip Thody (New York: Humanities Press, 1964); and Jan Kott, *Shakespeare Our Contemporary* trans. Boleslaw Taborski (New York: Anchor, 1966).

14 See Northrop Frye, *Anatomy of Criticism* (New York: Atheneum, 1957).

15 See René Girard, *Violence and the Sacred*, trans. Patrick Gregory (Baltimore: Johns Hopkins University Press, 1977).

16 In referring here to Geoffrey H. Hartman's *The Unmediated Vision* (New York: Harcourt Brace and World, 1954), I am not overlooking his subsequent considerations of structuralist and post-structuralist criticism, as demonstrated in *Beyond Formalism* (New Haven: Yale University Press, 1970), *The Fate of Reading* (Chicago: The University of Chicago Press, 1975), and *Criticism in the Wilderness* (New Haven: Yale University Press, 1980)—and then, *Saving the Text: Philosophy/-Derrida/Literature* (Baltimore: Johns Hopkins University Press, 1981).

17 The discussion here builds upon and refers to issues raised in the first chapter of the present study—particularly the question of divergence and difference.

18 See Ingarden, *The Literary Work of Art* (1931), and Robert Magliola, *Phenomenology and Literature: An Introduction* (West Lafayette: Purdue University Press, 1977), esp. Part II, chap. 2. [Henceforth cited in the text as *Pheno&Lit.*]

19 See Silverman, "Review of Dufrenne's *The Phenomenology of Aesthetic Experience*, trans. E. S. Casey et al. (Evanston: Northwestern University Press, 1973)," *The Journal of Aesthetics and Art Criticism*, Vol. 33, no. 4 (Summer 1975), pp. 462–64 and Silverman, "Dufrenne's *Phenomenology of Poetry*," *Philosophy Today*, Vol. 20, no. 4 (Spring 1976), pp. 20–24.

20 René Wellek and Austin Warren, in their now classic *Theory of Literature* (New York: Harcourt, Brace and World, 1956), distinguish between extrinsic and intrinsic approaches to literature. Intertextuality, as introduced by Julia Kristeva and employed by Michael Riffaterre and others, is established according to what W. K. Wimsatt and Monroe Beardsley (in the article on "Intention" for Shipley's *Dictionary of World Literature*) call "internal evidence." For theorists such as Claude Lévi-Strauss, different versions of the same mythical structure indicate relations between texts which are established according to both internal and external evidence—even to the extent that the distinction itself has no continuing applicability.

21 Jonathan Culler, *Structuralist Poetics* (Ithaca, New York: Cornell University Press, 1975), p. 3. Henceforth cited as *StructPoetics.*

22 See Hirsch, *Validity in Interpretation* (1967), and *The Aims of Interpretation* (Chicago: University of Chicago Press, 1976). Magliola discusses Hirsch along with Husserl and the Fregean *Sinn/Bedeutung* distinction in Part II, chap. 1 of his book.

23 Hirsch's notion of "significance" (which is only what the text means to me as reader) does not come into play here since it is distinct from both "meaning" and "signification."

24 See Barthes, *S/Z* (1971), and Culler, *StructPoetics*, p. 203.
25 Culler, *StructPoetics*, p. 118. Here Culler draws upon Barthes's *Critique et verité* (Paris: Éditions du Seuil, 1966).
26 Culler, p. 118, citing Barthes's *Critique et verité*, p. 57.
27 Balzac, "Sarrasine" in *S/Z*, pp. 221–54.
28 Barthes, *S/Z*, p. 151; "To Write: lntransitive Verb?" *The Structuralist Controversy*, eds. Eugenio Donato and Richard Macksey (Baltimore: The Johns Hopkins University Press, 1972), pp. 134–56. For another discussion of the middle voice but within a different framework, see the last chapter of Derrida's *Speech and Phenomena*, especially pp. 94–98. In both cases, the aortist in Greek serves as a model.
29 A hermeneutic semiology announces itself at the turning point, the hinge, or the interface between signification and meaning, reading and interpretation, text and expression. The "indecidable" is situated at the point where the reader signifies and the text interprets. Making sense of that indecidable can go under the name of deconstruction, which typically also incorporates Jacques Derrida. See further: *Inscriptions*, chap. 17: "Self-Decentering: Derrida Incorporated." The question of the indecidable has already been outlined here in some detail at the end of chapter 4.

CHAPTER 8: THE LANGUAGE OF TEXTUALITY

1 Paul de Man, "Shelley Disfigured," in *DC*.
2 Edward Said, "The Problem of Textuality: Two Exemplary Positions," in *Aesthetics Today*, ed. Morris Philipson and Paul J. Gudel (New York: Meridian/New American Library, 1980), p. 89. Henceforth cited in the text as *PT*.
3 See chapter 6, section IIb for a detailed account of "indecidables."
4 Derrida, "Limited Inc. a b c ...," in *Glyph 2* (Baltimore: Johns Hopkins University Press, 1977), pp. 162–254. A more recent version of this essay has been published by Northwestern University Press (1988), trans. Samuel Weber and Jeffrey Mehlman, ed. Gerald Graff as *Limited Inc* (1988). It was finally issued in French as *Limited Inc* (Paris: Galilée, 1990).
5 See chapters 9–11 for the role of "autobiographical textuality" in these three texts.

CHAPTER 9: AUTOBIOGRAPHICAL TEXTUALITY AND THOREAU'S *WALDEN*

1 Henry David Thoreau's *Walden: or Life in the Woods* (1960 edition) is a text which would play an important role in my own autobiography—were I to write one. [See Hugh J. Silverman, "An Essay in Self-Presentation," in *American Phenomenology*, ed. Calvin O. Schrag and Eugene Kaelin (Dordrecht: Kluwer, 1989), pp. 374–83.]
   Thoreau was born in Concord, Massachusetts, in 1817—I was born not far from there about a century and a quarter later. Like Thoreau I grew up in the countryside within the environs of Boston. Since I had a penchant for both philosophy and literature, Thoreau's *Walden* suited my fancy most appropriately. During my adolescence, I read the book eagerly, and just as an Englishman might return on occasion to Shakespeare, a Frenchman to Montaigne, and a German to Goethe, I read *Walden* as, for me, the paradigm of American letters. Since then my reading has taken me far from the New England terrain where I grew up and was educated. I now return to this textual homeland in order to develop the space and limits of its autobiographical textuality.
   Thoreau's text is henceforth cited as *Walden*.

2   Georges May, *L'Autobiographie* (Paris: Presses Universitaires de France, 1979).

3   See, for instance, James Olney, ed., *Metaphors of Self* (Princeton: Princeton University Press, 1972), and Karl Joachim Weintraub, *The Value of the Individual: Self and Circumstance in Autobiography* (Chicago: University of Chicago Press, 1978).

4   Thoreau is cited once in Elizabeth W. Bruss, *Autobiographical Acts* (Baltimore: Johns Hopkins University Press, 1976); twice in an essay included in George P. Landow, ed., *Approaches to Victorian Autobiography* (Athens: Ohio University Press, 1979); and briefly in James Olney, ed., *Autobiography: Essays Theoretical and Critical* (Princeton: Princeton University Press, 1980).

5   For a further elaboration of autobiographical temporality, see chapter 11.

6   Sigmund Freud, *An Autobiographical Study*, trans. James Strachey (New York: Norton, 1950), p. 43.

7   Michel de Montaigne, "To the Reader," *The Complete Essays*, trans. Donald Frame (Stanford: Stanford University Press, 1958), p. 2.

8   Jean-Jacques Rousseau, *The Confessions*, trans. J. M. Cohen. (Harmondsworth, Middlesex: Penguin, 1954), p. 17.

9   Giambattista Vico, *The Autobiography*, trans. Thomas Goddard Bergin (Ithaca: Cornell University Press, 1944), p. 111.

10 Johann Wolfgang Goethe, *The Autobiography*, vol. 1, trans. J. Oxenford, ed. K. J. Weintraub (Chicago: University of Chicago Press, 1974), p. 3.

11 Henry Adams, *The Education of Henry Adams* (Boston: Houghton Mifflin, 1918), p. 3.

12 Paul de Man, "The Epistemology of Metaphor," in *On Metaphor*, ed. Sheldon Sacks (Chicago: University of Chicago Press, 1978), pp. 11–28.

13 See, for instance, Edward S. Casey, *Imagining: A Phenomenological Study* (Bloomington: Indiana University Press, 1976); "Imagining and Remembering," *Review of Metaphysics*, vol. 31, no. 2 (1977), pp. 187–209; and Hugh J. Silverman, "Imagining, Perceiving, and Remembering," *Humanitas*, vol. 14, no. 2 (1978), pp. 197–207.

14 Eugène Ionesco, *Present Past/Past Present*, trans. Helen R. Lane (New York: Grove, 1971).

15 Jean-Paul Sartre, *Between Existentialism and Marxism*, trans. John Matthews (New York: Pantheon Books, 1974).

CHAPTER 10: TRACES OF AUTOBIOGRAPHICAL TEXTUALITY IN NIETZSCHE'S *ECCE HOMO*

1   Friedrich Nietzsche, *Ecce Homo*, trans. Walter Kaufmann (New York: Vintage, 1967), p. 221. Henceforth cited as *EH-WKtr*.

2   R. J. Hollingdale, "Introduction," to Nietzsche, *Ecce Homo* (Harmondsworth: Penguin, 1979), p. 7. Henceforth cited in the text as *EH-RHtr*.

3   See Friedrich Nietzsche, *Ecce Homo* (Frankfurt: Insel, 1977), pp. 39–40.

CHAPTER 11: THE TIME OF AUTOBIOGRAPHY: LÉVI-STRAUSS'S *TRISTES TROPIQUES*

1   "D'une façon inattendue, entre la vie et moi, le temps a allongé son isthme." Claude Lévi-Strauss, *Tristes Tropiques* (Paris: Plon, 1955), p. 55. Translation by John and

Doreen Weightman (New York: Atheneum, 1974), p. 44. Subsequent references to *Tristes Tropiques* in the English translation are cited as *TT*.

2   See also Hugh J. Silverman, "Un Egale deux ou l'espace autobioqraphique et ses limites" in *Le Deux*, ed. M. le Bot (Paris: 10–18, 1980), pp. 279–302. An English version appeared in *Eros: A Journal of Philosophy and Literary Arts*, vol. 8, no. 1 (June 1981), pp. 95–115, as "The Autobiographical Space and Its Limits."

3   The most notable exception was his journey to New York during the Second World War when he taught in exile at what is now called the New School for Social Research.

4   Roland Barthes asserts that the same writing can occur in different epochs—as long as writing *(écriture)* is understood as occurring at the intersection of style and language *(langue)*. While the writing of one's own life may take place in different temporal contexts within the general historical time in which autobiography prevails, individual style and cultural language tend to specify the time of the narrative.

5   Adjacent to autobiographies are diaries, journals, notebooks, and memoirs. The memoir approximates (and is sometimes identical with) the autobiography because it is written from a position which reviews a large span of one's life. However, the memoir often focuses on a particular topic, such as war, years in office, days as an actor, etc. The diary, journal, and notebook tend to be written in installments with items entered daily or some approximation thereof. They chronicle the life on the basis of many short-term segments. Although these neighboring types exhibit a personal chronological time, the span is delimited and does not need to fulfill many of the characteristics ascribed to full-scale autobiographies.

6   Benvenuto Cellini, *La Vita* (Torino: Einaudi editore, 1973), p. 7. English translation, as *The Autobiography*, by George Bull (Harmondsworth, Middlesex: Penguin, 1956), p. 15.

7   To confirm Cellini's view, one need only consider that Descartes published his *Discourse on Method* at the age of forty-one; Rousseau began writing his *Confessions* at the age of fifty-two; John Stuart Mill embarked upon his *Autobiography* at forty-seven and completed it at the age of sixty-six; Sartre wrote *Words* when he was fifty-nine; Roland Barthes published his *Roland Barthes* at the age of sixty; and Bertrand Russell reserved the period between ninety-five and ninety-seven for his *Autobiography*. There are of course exceptions: Kierkegaard wrote *The Point of View for My Work as an Author* (published posthumously) at the age of thirty-five.

8   William Butler Yeats, "Preface" to "Reveries over Childhood and Youth," in *The Autobiography of William Butler Yeats* (New York: Macmillan, 1965), opening unnumbered page.

CHAPTER 12: THE SELF-INSCRIPTIONS OF SARTRE AND BARTHES

1   See Jean-Paul Sartre, *The Words* (1963), trans. Bernard Frechtman (Greenwich, Conn: Fawcett, 1964). Henceforth cited as *Words*.

2   See Roland Barthes, *Roland Barthes* (1975), trans. Richard Howard (New York: Hill and Wang, 1977). Henceforth cited in the text as *RB*.

3   See, for example, the 1976 Sartre interview with Leo Fretz in Hugh J. Silverman and Frederick A. Elliston, eds. *Jean-Paul Sartre: Contemporary Approaches to His Philosophy* (Pittsburgh: Duquesne University Press and Hassocks, Sussex: Harvester Press, 1980), pp. 221–39.

4   Jean Paul-Sartre, *Sartre, un film réalisé par Alexandre Astruc et Michel Contat* (Paris:

Gallimard, 1977); *Sartre by Himself*, trans. Richard Seaver (New York: Urizen Books, 1978). Henceforth cited as *Sartre by Himself*.

5   Francis Jeanson, *Sartre dans sa vie* (Paris: Seuil, 1974), pp. 89–93.

6   Liliane Sendyk-Siegel, *Sartre: Images d'une vie* (Paris: Gallimard, 1978). The latter is henceforth cited as *Sartre: Images*. See chapter 14 for further discussion of these photographs of Sartre.

7   "Photobiographical textuality" is also developed at length in chapter 14.

8   See Sartre, "From Poet to Artist," in *The Family Idiot*, vol. 2, trans. Carol Cosman (Chicago: University of Chicago Press, 1987), pp. 315–435.

9   See *Inscriptions*, chap. 11, entitled "Sartre and the Structuralists."

10 See specifically: Sartre, *Les Mots*, ed. David Nott (London: Methuen, 1981), pp. ix–xxi.

11 Roland Barthes, *Michelet* (Paris: Seuil, 1954).

12 Barthes, "*Barthes puissance trois*," *La Quinzaine Littéraire* (March 1-15, 1975).

13 See Louis Marin, *Utopics: The Semiological Play of Textual Spaces*, trans. Robert Vollrath (Atlantic Highlands: Humanities Press, 1990), and also *Inscriptions*, chapter 19, for the relation between atopia and utopia.

CHAPTER 13: THE AUTOBIOGRAPHICAL TEXTUALITY OF HEIDEGGER'S SHOES

1   As indicated earlier, references to this text are given as "The Origin of the Work of Art" [*PLT-OWA*] which was first published in *Holzwege*. *Holz* is the abbreviation for the Klostermann edition of *Holzwege* (Frankfurt: Klostermann, 1980). The Reclam edition of *Der Ursprung des Kunstwerkes* (Stuttgart: Reclam, 1960), contains an afterword by Hans-Georg Gadamer, who edited the small student edition.

2   Paolo le Caldano, *Van Gogh: Tout l'Oeuvre peint*, 2 vols. (Paris: Flammarion, 1971).

3   Four of these five paintings are reproduced along with Derrida's essay entitled "Restitutions de la verité en pointure," in *Verité* (1978), pp. 291–436.

4   *Verité*, p. 432.

5   In the early versions of "The Origin of the Work of Art"—the lectures given in Freiburg and Zürich in 1935—Heidegger does not discuss the Van Gogh "shoes" painting. Along with the absence of the painting example is also the absence of the concomitant discussion about equipment. Between 1935 and 1936, Heidegger seemed to find it important to return to the question of *Zeug* (equipment) and to link this discussion to that of the shoes. Why Heidegger should be especially concerned with equipment, shoes, and the peasant life that accompany them remains to be developed in the context of Heidegger's unquestionably disconcerting National Socialist politics at the time.

6   See Jacques Derrida, *Spurs: Nietzsche's Styles*, trans. Barbara Harlow (Chicago: University of Chicago Press, 1978). Henceforth cited in the text as *Spurs*.

7   Martin Heidegger, *Aus der Erfahrung des Denkens* (Pfullingen: Neske, 1954).

8   See Derrida, *Limited Inc.* (1977/1988) and also *Inscriptions*, chap. 17: "Self-Decentering: Derrida Incorporated."

CHAPTER 14: THE PHOTOBIOGRAPHICAL TEXTUALITY OF THE PHILOSOPHER'S BODY: SARTRE/HEIDEGGER

1   Diane Meller Marcovicz, *Martin Heidegger: Photos* (Stuttgart: Fey, 1978), and Liliane Sendyk-Siegel, *Sartre: Images d'une vie* (Paris: Gallimard, 1978).

2   For an account of Husserl's view of the body in relation to his theory of the self, see *Inscriptions*, chap. 1: "The Self in Husserl's *Crisis*."

3   See *Sartre by Himself* (1977).

4   André Breton, *Manifesto of Surrealism*, p. 21.

5   See Jean-Paul Sartre, Philippe Gavi, and Pierre Victor, *On a raison de se révolter* (Paris: Gallimard, 1974).

CHAPTER FIFTEEN: THE VISIBILLTY OF SELF-PORTRAITURE: MERLEAU-PONTY/CÉZANNE

1   English translations of Merleau-Ponty's essay are mine. However, see also *EM* in Carleton Dallery's translation.

2   Among these commentaries on Merleau-Ponty's account of painting, none of the following say anything about self-portraiture: Gary Brent Madison, "La Peinture," *La Phénoménologie de Merleau-Ponty* (Paris: Klincksieck, 1973), pp. 89–124; Michel Lefeuvre, "Les Arts," *Merleau-Ponty au délà de la phénoménologie* (Paris: Klincksieck, 1976), pp. 353–64; James Gordon Place, "The Painting and the Natural Thing in the Philosophy of Merleau-Ponty," *Cultural Hermeneutics*, vol. 4 (1976), pp. 75–91; Mikel Dufrenne, "Eye and Mind," *Research in Phenomenology*, vol. 10 (1980), pp. 167–73; and Véronique M. Fóti, "Painting and the Re-Orientation of Philosophical Thought in Merleau-Ponty," *Philosophy Today*, vol. 24, no. 2 (Summer 1980), pp. 114–20. The only mention and discussion of self-portraits is in Marjorie Grene, "The Sense of Things," *Journal of Aesthetics and Art Criticism*, vol. 38, no. 4 (Summer 1980), pp. 377–89. She cites the case of Courbet rather than Cézanne but only mentions mirroring briefly. When commenting upon Grene's essay, Harrison Hall in "Painting and Perceiving," *Journal of Aesthetics and Art Criticism*, vol. 39, no. 3 (Spring 1981), pp. 291–95, misses the issue of self-portraiture altogether.

3   "Cézanne's Doubt" was first published in *Sens et non-sens* (Paris, 1947), as "Le Doute de Cézanne."

4   Jacques Lacan, *Écrits:* (Paris: Éditions du Seuil, 1966), pp. 93-100. Translated as "The Mirror Stage as Formative of the 'I,'" in *Écrits: A Selection*, trans. Alan Sheridan (New York: Norton, 1977), pp. 1-7.

5   Maurice Merleau-Ponty, *Consciousness and the Acquisition of Language*, trans. Hugh J. Silverman (Evanston: Northwestern University Press, 1973).

6   Jacques Lacan, *Écrits*, p. 95.

7   Michel de Montaigne, "Au Lecteur," *Essais* (Paris, 1962), p. 1. The French passage reads: "Je veus qu'on m'y voie en ma façon simple, naturelle et ordinaire, sans contantion et artifice: car c'est moy que je peins." The standard English translation is by Donald M. Frame in *The Complete Essays of Montaigne* (Stanford: Stanford University Press, 1958), p. 2.

8   Jean-Jacques Rousseau, *Les Confessions* in *Oeuvres Complètes*, vol. 1 (Paris: Gallimard, 1959), p. 3.

9   See the previous section on "Autobiographical Textualities."

10 A celebrated M. C. Escher lithograph entitled "Drawing-Hands" shows two hands drawing (or writing) each other. Each hand has an artist's pencil in its grasp and they simultaneously give rise to each other. Escher demonstrates what it would mean to achieve the paradoxical condition of making the-hand-that-writes-itself visible. But these hands are not writing a life as autobiography. Their visibility lies more in the establishment of their existence than in the articulation of their identity.

11 For an account of photo-biographical textuality, see chap. 14. The parallel between self-portraiture as autobiographical visibility and photobiographical textuality in relation to the body of the other, as in Sartre and Heidegger, should now be clearer.

CHAPTER 16: THE TEXT OF THE SPEAKING SUBJECT: MERLEAU-PONTY/KRISTEVA

1 Response to a question concerning the role of Merleau-Ponty in Kristeva's account of the speaking subject raised during her graduate seminar and again in a private conversation while she was visiting distinguished professor at SUNY/Stony Brook during the Fall 1988.

2 See the account in Louis Althusser, "Freud and Lacan," in *Lenin and Philosophy and Other Essays*, trans. Ben Brewster (New York: Monthly Review Press, 1971), pp. 189–219.

3 Julia Kristeva, *Revolution in Poetic Language*, trans. Margaret Waller, with an Introduction by Leon S. Roudiez (New York: Columbia University Press, 1984), p. 29. Henceforth cited as *RPL*.

4 Maurice Merleau-Ponty, *Prose of the World*, ed. Claude Lefort, trans. John O'Neill (Evanston: Northwestern University Press, 1973). Henceforth cited as *Prose*.

5 Maurice Merleau-Ponty, *Signs*, trans., with an introduction, by Richard C. McCleary (Evanston: Northwestern University Press, 1964), p. 43. Henceforth cited as *Signs*.

6 For a further and more detailed discussion of Merleau-Ponty's theory of language, see *Inscriptions*, esp. chaps. 6 and 9.

7 Interestingly, although both Merleau-Ponty and Heidegger make the distinction between speaking and thinking, ultimately Heidegger links thinking with poetizing while at the same time resisting a consideration of either as a subject.

8 The issues of depression and melancholy are the focus of Kristeva's more recent writings, especially her study *Black Sun* (New York: Columbia University Press, 1989). Since it is outside the focus of this discussion, I only invoke this new direction in her work and its place in the present consideration of the semiotic so as to suggest an avenue for further investigation.

CHAPTER 17: WRITING ON WRITING: MERLEAU-PONTY/DERRIDA

1 See Michel Foucault, *The Order of Things*, trans. anon. (New York: Vintage, 1970).
2 See *Inscriptions*, chap. 5.

CHAPTER 18: NIETZSCHE/SCHOPENHAUER: ON THE UNIVERSITY

1 Friedrich Nietzsche, *Schopenhauer as Educator*, trans. James W. Hillesheim and Malcolm R. Simpson (South Bend, Ind.: Gateway Editions, 1965), p. 61. [Hereafter cited as *SE*.] Another translation of this text is available in Friedrich Nietzsche, *Untimely Meditations*, trans. R. J. Hollingdale (Cambridge: Cambridge University Press, 1983), pp. 127–94. A bilingual German-French edition is published as Friedrich Nietzsche, *Unzeitgemäße Betrachtungen*, III-IV, trans. Geneviève Bianquis (Paris: Aubier, 1976), pp. 15–169. This text will be cited in brackets for an indication of the corresponding German passages. In this case [*UB*, p. 96].

CHAPTER 19: MERLEAU-PONTY/BLANCHOT: ON PHILOSOPHICAL DISCOURSE

1 Maurice Blanchot, "Le 'Discours Philosophique,'" in *L'Arc: Merleau-Ponty*, no. 46 (1971), pp. 1–4. Henceforth cited as *DP*.

CHAPTER 20: DERRIDA/HEIDEGGER: ON THE TIME OF THE LINE

1 Martin Heidegger, *The Question of Being*, trans. Jean T. Wilde and William Kluback (New Haven, College and University Publishers, 1958). Henceforth cited as *QB*.
2 Derrida, "Living On: Border-lines," in *Deconstruction and Criticism* (1979).
3 Michel de Montaigne, "Of Experience," in *The Complete Essays*.
4 Francis Bacon, *Essays* (New York, Penguin, 1986).
5 Derrida, *Grammatology*.
6 See the general set of questions raised in *Philosophy and Non-Philosophy since Merleau-Ponty [Continental Philosophy-I]*, ed. Hugh J. Silverman, devoted to the topic. Also see *Inscriptions*, esp. chaps. 5–9.
7 Friedrich Nietzsche, *Thus Spoke Zarathustra*, trans. R. Hollingdale (New York, Penguin, 1969).
8 See Heidegger, "Time and Being," in *On Time and Being*, trans. Joan Stambaugh (New York, Harper & Row, 1972), and Derrida, "Ousia and Grammē," in *Margins*.
9 See, for instance, Albert Hofstadter, "Enownment," *Boundary 2*, no. 4 (1976), pp. 357–77, and his "Translator's Introduction" to Martin Heidegger, *Poetry Language Thought*.
10 Heidegger, "What Are Poets For?" in *PLT*, pp. 91–142. Although delivered on the twentieth anniversary of Rilke's death in 1946, the essay was first published in *Holzwege* (1950).
11 Derrida, "Survivre," in *Parages* (Paris, Galilée, 1986), pp. 117–218.
12 Maurice Blanchot, *L'Arrêt de mort*. English translation by Lydia Davis as *Death Sentence* (New York, Station Hill, 1978).
13 Derrida, *De l'esprit* (Paris, Galilée, 1987). English translation by Geoffrey Bennington and Rachel Bowlby, *Of Spirit: Heidegger and the Question* (Chicago: University of Chicago Press, 1987).
14 In this connection, I should like to remember Professor Philip Rhinelander (Professor Emeritus of Philosophy and Humanities at Stanford University), who died on March 20, 1987, at the age of 79. He was my Doktor Vater.

CHAPTER 21: FOUCAULT/DERRIDA: ON THE ORIGIN(S) OF HISTORY

1 Michel Foucault, *The Order of Things*, trans. anon. (New York: Vintage, 1970).
2 See *Inscriptions*, chap. 18: "Foucault and the Anthropological Sleep."
3 Edmund Husserl, "The Origin of Geometry," in *The Crisis of the European Sciences and Transcendental Phenomenology*, trans. David Carr (Evanston: Northwestern University Press, 1970), pp. 353–78.
4 Foucault, "Nietzsche, Genealogy, History" (1971), in *Language, Counter-Memory, Practice*, trans. Donald Bouchard and Sherry Simon (Ithaca: Cornell University Press, 1977), pp. 139–64. Henceforth cited as *NGH*.

5   Michel Foucault, "Discourse on Language," in *The Archaeology of Knowledge*, trans. Alan Sheridan Smith (New York: Pantheon, 1972), pp. 215–37.
6   Friedrich Nietzsche, *Genealogy of Morals*, trans. Walter Kaufmann (New York: Penguin, 1967).
7   See the detailed discussion of Heidegger's "The Origin of the Work of Art," and particularly the question of "origin" in chapter 5.

CHAPTER 22: PHILOSOPHY HAS ITS REASONS...

1   Blaise Pascal, *Pensées* (bilingual ed.), trans. H. F. Stewart (New York: Modern Library, 1947), pp. 342–43.
2   Pascal, p. 343.
3   For a further discussion of "indecidables," see again chapter 6: IIb.
4   Martin Heidegger, "What Are Poets For?" in *Poetry Language Thought*, trans. Albert Hofstadter (New York: Harper & Row, 1971), p. 92.
5   Jacques Derrida, "The Principle of Reason: The University in the Eyes of Its Pupils," *Diacritics*, vol. 13, no. 3 (Fall 1983), p. 6.
6   I am grateful to Jacques Derrida for reminding me, on the occasion of the first presentation of this essay, that Heidegger, in *What Is Called Thinking?*, made the link between thinking (*Denken*) and thanking (*Danken*): that thinking involves "taking to heart." But if philosophy, here, takes the place of the heart, then the question, Derrida's question, as to the difference between thinking and philosophy becomes crucial. Making the bridge between philosophy and thinking, taking the place of the heart and taking to heart, inscribes the difference that might, one would hope, bring philosophy and thinking together.

BIBLIOGRAPHY

Adams, Henry., *The Education of Henry Adams*. Boston: Houghton Mifflin Co., 1918.

Althusser, Louis., *Lenin and Philosophy and Other Essays*. Trans. Ben Brewster. New York: Monthly Review Press, 1971.

Austin, J. L., *How to Do Things with Words*. New York: Oxford University Press, 1962.

Bacon, Francis., *Essays*. New York: Penguin, 1986.

Barthes, Roland., *Writing Degree Zero* (1953). Trans. Annette Lavers and Colin Smith. New York: Hill and Wang, 1968.

——————., *Michelet*. Paris: Seuil, 1954.

——————., *Elements of Semiology* (1964). Trans. Annette Lavers and Colin Smith. New York: Hill and Wang, 1968.

——————., *Criticism and Truth* (1966). Trans. Katrina Pilcher Kenneman. Minneapolis: University of Minnesota Press, 1987.

——————., *S/Z* (1970). Trans. Richard Miller. New York: Hill and Wang, 1974.

——————., *The Pleasure of the Text* (1973). Trans. Richard Miller. New York: Hill and Wang, 1975.

——————., *Roland Barthes* (1975). Trans. Richard Howard. New York: Hill and Wang, 1977.

——————., *Image/Music/Text*. Trans. Stephen Heath. New York: Hill and Wang, 1977.

Beaujour, Michel., "For a Science of Literature," *Punto de Contacto/Point of Contact*, vol. 1, no. 4 (1977): 4–11.

Black, Max., *Models and Metaphors*. Ithaca: Cornell University Press, 1962.

Blanchot, Maurice., "Le 'Discours Philosophique'" in *L'Arc: Merleau-Ponty*, no. 46 (1971): 1–4.

——————., *L'Arret de Mort*. Trans. as *Death Sentence* by Lydia Davis. New York: Station Hill, 1978.

Bloom, Harold, et al. *Deconstruction and Criticism*. New York: Seabury Press, 1979.

Bruss, Elizabeth W., *Autobiographical Acts*. Baltimore: Johns Hopkins University Press, 1976.

Caputo, John D., *Radical Hermeneutics: Repetition, Deconstruction, and the Hermeneutic Project*. Bloomington: Indiana University Press, 1988.

Casey, Edward S., *Imagining: A Phenomenological Study*. Bloomington: Indiana University Press, 1976.

——————., "Imagining and Remembering," *Review of Metaphysics*. vol. 31, no. 2 (1977), pp. 187–209.

—————., *Remembering: A Phenomenological Study*. Bloomington: Indiana University Press, 1987.

Cellini, Benvenuto., *La Vita*. Torino: Einaudi editore, 1973. *The Autobiography*. Trans. George Bull. Harmondsworth, Middlesex: Penguin, 1956.

Cézanne, Paul., *Conversations avec Cézanne*. Ed. P. M. Doran. Paris: Macula, 1978.

Culler, Jonathan., *Structuralist Poetics*. Ithaca: Cornell University Press, 1975.

—————., *On Deconstruction: Theory and Criticism after Structuralism*. Ithaca: Cornell University Press, 1982.

Damisch, Hubert., "Le Versant de la parole." *Bulletin de Psychologie*, vol. 18, nos. 3–6 (November 1964): 105–8.

Dante Aligheri., *Vita Nuova*. Trans. Barbara Reynolds. Middlesex, England: Penguin, 1969.

—————., *The Divine Comedy*. 3 vols. [*The Inferno, The Purgatorio, The Paradiso*] Trans. John Ciardi. New York: Mentor, 1970.

Deleuze, Gilles, and Félix Guattari., *Anti-Oedipus: Capitalism and Schizophrenia* (1973). Trans. Robert Hurley, Mark Seem, and Helen Lane. New York: Viking Press, 1977.

—————., *Thousand Plateaux: Capitalism and Schizophrenia* (1980). Trans. Brian Massumi. Minneapolis: University of Minnesota Press, 1987.

De Man, Paul., "The Epistemology of Metaphor." *Critical Inquiry*, vol. 5, no. 1 (Autumn 1978): 13–30.

—————., "Shelley Disfigured," in *Deconstruction and Criticism*. New York: Seabury, 1979.

Derrida, Jacques., *Edmund Husserl's Origin of Geometry: An Introduction* (1962). Trans. John Leavey. Lincoln: University of Nebraska Press, 1989.

—————., *Of Grammatology* (1967). Trans. Gayatri Chakravorty Spivak. Baltimore: Johns Hopkins University Press, 1975.

—————., *Speech and Phenomena, and Other Essays on Husserl's Theory of Signs* (1967). Trans. David B. Allison. Evanston: Northwestern University Press, 1973.

—————., *Writing and Difference* (1967). Trans. Alan Bass. Chicago: University of Chicago Press, 1978; London: Routledge and Kegan Paul, 1978.

—————., *Dissemination* (1972). Trans. Barbara Johnson. Chicago: University of Chicago Press, 1981; London: Athlone Press, 1981.

—————., *Margins of Philosophy* (1972). Trans. Alan Bass. Chicago: University of Chicago Press, 1982; Hassocks: Harvester Press, 1982.

—————., *Positions* (1972). Trans. Alan Bass. Chicago: University of Chicago Press, 1982; London: Athlone, 1982.

—————., *The Archeology of the Frivolous: Reading Condillac* (1973). Trans. John P. Leavey. Pittsburgh: Duquesne University Press, 1980.

—————., *Glas* (1974). Trans. John Leavey and Richard Rand. Lincoln: University of Nebraska Press, 1986.

—————., "The Purveyor of Truth." Trans. Willis Domingo, James Hulbert, Mosche Ron, and Marie-Rose Logan. In *Graphesis: Literature and Philosophy: Yale French Studies*, no. 51 (1975), pp. 31–113.

—————., *Spurs: Nietzsche's Styles* (1976). Trans. Barbara Harlow. Chicago: University of Chicago Press, 1979.

—————., "Ou commence et comment finit un corps enseignant." In Dominique Grisoni, ed. *Politiques de la philosophie*. Paris: Grasset, 1976.

—————., "L'Âge de Hegel." In *Qui a Peur de la philosophie?*. Paris: Flammarion, 1977.

—————., "Fors. The English Words of Nicolas Abraham and Maria Torok." Trans. Barbara Johnson. *The Georgia Review.* vol. 11, no. 1 (Spring 1977), pp. 64–116.

—————., *Limited Inc., a b c...* (1977). Trans. Samuel Weber. Baltimore: Johns Hopkins University Press, 1977. Published as a supplement to *Glyph 2, Johns Hopkins Textual Studies.* Republished by Nortwestern University Press, 1988.

—————., "Coming Into One's Own." In *Psychoanalysis and the Question of the Text*, ed. Geoffrey Hartman. Baltimore: Johns Hopkins University Press, 1978.

—————., "Restitutions de la verité en pointure," *Macula.* nos. 3–4 (1978): 11–37.

—————., *The Truth in Painting* (1978). Trans. G. Bennington and I. McLeod. Chicago: University of Chicago Press, 1987.

—————., "The *Retrait* of Metaphor." Trans. F. Gasdner et al. *Enclitic*, vol. 2, no. 2 (Fall 1978): 5–34.

—————., "Scribble." Preface to Warburton, *Essai sur les hiéroglyphes.* Paris: Aubier-Flammarion, 1978.

—————., "Living On: Border-lines" (1979). Trans. J. Hulbert. In *Deconstruction and Criticism.* Ed. Harold Bloom et al. New York: Seabury Press, 1979.

—————., "La philosophie des Etats généraux" in *Les Etats généraux de la philosophie.* Paris: Flammarion, 1979.

—————., "Title (to be announced)." *Substance.* no. 9 (1979): 3–40.

—————., "The Law of Genre." Trans. Avital Ronnell. *Critical Inquiry.* vol. 7, no. 1 (1980), pp. 55–81. And in *Glyph 7.* Baltimore: Johns Hopkins University Press, 1980.

—————., *The Post Card: From Socrates to Freud and Beyond* (1980). Trans. Alan Bass. Chicago: Chicago University Press, 1987.

—————., "The Deaths of Roland Barthes" (1981). Trans. Pascale-Anne Brault and Michael B. Naas. In *Philosophy and Non-Philosophy since Merleau-Ponty. Continental Philosophy-I*, ed. Hugh J. Silverman, 259–96. London and New York: Routledge, 1988.

—————., *The Ear of the Other: Otobiography, Transference, Translation: Texts and Discussions with Jacques Derrida* (1982). Trans. Peggy Kamuf. New York: Schocken Books, 1985.

—————., "Interview with Derrida" (1982). In *Derrida and Différance*, ed. David Wood and Robert Bernasconi. Evanston: Northwestern University Press, 1988.

—————., "Of an Apocalyptic Tone Recently Adopted in Philosophy," Trans. John P. Leavey. *Semeia*, vol. 23 (1982). *Oxford Literary Review.* vol. 6, no. 2 (1984): 3–37.

—————., "The Time of a Thesis: Punctuations." In *Philosophy in France Today*, ed. Alan Montefiore. Cambridge: Cambridge University Press, 1982.

—————., "*Geschlecht*—Sexual Difference, Ontological Difference." *Research in Phenomenology*, vol. 13 (1983): 68–84.

—————., "The Principle of Reason in the Eyes of its Pupils." *Diacritics*, vol. 13 (Fall 1983): 3–20. *Graduate Faculty Philosophy Journal* (New School for Social Research), vol. 10 (Spring 1984): 5–45.

—————., "Deconstruction and the Other." Interview with Richard Kearney. In Richard Kearney, ed., *Dialogues with Contemporary Continental Thinkers.* Manchester: Manchester University Press, 1984.

—————., "Devant la loi." Ed. A. Phillips Griffiths. In *Philosophy and Literature.* Cambridge: Cambridge University Press, 1984.

—————., *Feu la cendre.* Firenze: Sansoni, 1984. Paris: Des femmes, 1987.

—————., "Mes Chances/ My Chances." In Joseph Smith and William Kerrigan, eds. *Taking Chances*. Baltimore: Johns Hopkins University Press, 1984.

—————., "Mochlos ou le conflit des facultés." *Philosophie*, no. 2 (April 1984), pp. 21–53.

—————., "No Apocalypse, Not Now." Trans. Catherine Porter and Philip Lewis. *Diacritics*. Vol. 20 (Summer 1984), pp. 20–31.

—————., *Otobiographies: l'enseignement de Nietzsche et la politique du nom propre*. Paris: Galilée, 1984.

—————., *Signéponge/Signsponge*. Trans. Richard Rand. New York: Columbia University Press, 1984. (Parallel French and English translation.)

—————., *Droits de regards*. Photographs by M. F. Plissart with an essay by Jacques Derrida. Paris: Minuit, 1985.

—————., "Des Tours de Babel." Trans. Joseph F. Graham. In *Difference in Translation*, ed. Joseph Graham. Ithaca and London: Cornell University Press, 1985. 165–207. [Also includes French text, pp. 209–48.]

—————., "Les Langages et les institutions de la philosophie." *Texte* (1985): 9–39.

—————., "Letter to a Japanese Friend" (1985). In *Derrida and Différance*, ed. David Wood and Robert Bernasconi, . Evanston: Northwestern University Press, 1988.

—————., "Préjugés—devant la loi." In *La faculté de juger*. Paris: Minuit, 1985.

—————., "Racism's Last Word." Trans. Peggy Kamuf. *Critical Theory*, vol. 12 (Autumn 1985).

—————., *Memoires: For Paul de Man*. Trans. Cecile Lindsay, Jonathan Culler, and Eduardo Cadava. New York: Columbia University Press, 1986.

—————., *Parages*. Paris: Galilée, 1986.

—————., "Survivre." In *Parages*. Paris: Galilée, 1986.

—————., *De l'esprit: Heidegger et la question*. Paris: Galilée, 1987. Trans. by Geoffrey Bennington and Rachel Bowlby as *Of Spirit: Heidegger and the Question*. Chicago: University of Chicago Press, 1989.

—————., *Psychē,. Inventions de l'autre*. Paris: Gallimard, 1987.

—————., *Ullyse gramophone: deux mots pour Joyce*. Paris: Galilée, 1987.

—————., *Du droit à la philosophie*. Paris: Galilée, 1990.

—————., *A Derrida Reader: Between the Blinds*. Ed. Peggy Kamuf. New York: Columbia University Press, 1990.

—————., *Jacques Derrida*. By Geoffrey Bennington and Jacques Derrida. Paris: Seuil, 1991.

De Saussure, Ferdinand. *Course in General Linguistics* (1916). Trans. Wade Baskin. New York: McGraw-Hill, 1959.

Descartes, René., *Discourse on Method*. Trans. F. E. Sutcliffe. Harmondsworth: Penguin, 1968.

Descombes, Vincent. *Modern French Philosophy*. Trans. L. Scott-Fox and J. M. Harding. Cambridge: Cambridge University Press, 1980.

Donato, Eugenio and Richard Macksey, eds. *The Structuralist Controversy*. Baltimore: Johns Hopkins University Press, 1972.

Dorival, B., *Paul Cézanne*. Paris, 1948.

Dubois, J. et al., *Rhétorique générale*. Paris: Larousse, 1970.

Dufrenne, Mikel., *Phenomenology of Aesthetic Experience* (1952). Trans. Edward S. Casey et al. Evanston: Northwestern University Press, 1973.

Dufrenne, Mikel., *In the Presence of the Sensuous*. Trans. Mark Roberts and Dennis Gallagher. Atlantic Highlands, N.J.: Humanities Press, 1987.

Eagleton, Terry., *Criticism and Ideology*. London: New Left Books, 1976.

Eagleton, Terry., *Literary Theory: An Introduction*. Oxford: Blackwell, 1984.

Eco, Umberto., *A Theory of Semiotics*. Bloomington: IN: Indiana University Press, 1976.

Elliston, Frederick A., ed. *Heidegger's Existential Analytic*. The Hague: Mouton, 1978.

Fóti, Véronique M., "Painting and the Re-Orientation of Philosophical Thought in Merleau-Ponty." *Philosophy Today*, vol. 24, no. 2 (Summer 1980): 114–20.

Foucault, Michel., *The Order of Things: An Archaeology of the Human Sciences* (1966). Trans. anon. New York: Vintage, 1970.

—————., *The Archaeology of Knowledge* (1968). Trans. Alan Sheridan Smith. New York: Pantheon, 1972.

—————., "Nietzsche, Genealogy, History." In *Language, Counter-Memory, Practice*, 139–64. Trans. Donald Bouchard and Sherry Simon. Ithaca: Cornell University Press, 1977.

Freeman, Donald C., ed. *Linguistics and Literary Style*. New York: Holt, Rinehart and Winston, 1970.

Freud, Sigmund., *An Autobiographical Study*. Trans. James Stachey. New York: Norton, 1950.

Frye, Northrop., *Anatomy of Criticism*. New York: Atheneum, 1957.

Gadamer, Hans-Georg. *Truth and Method* (1960). Trans. and ed. Garrett Barden and John Cumming. New York: Seabury Press, 1975. Revised translation by Joel Weinsheimer and Donald G. Marshall. New York: Seabury, 1990.

Gasché, Rodolphe., "Deconstruction as Criticism:" In *Glyph 6* (1979): 177–215.

—————., *The Tain of the Mirror: Deconstruction and the Philosophy of Reflection*. Cambridge: Harvard University Press, 1986.

Girard, René., *Violence and the Sacred*. Trans. Patrick Gregory. Baltimore: Johns Hopkins University Press, 1977.

Goethe, Johann Wolfgang. *The Autobiography*. 2 vols. Trans. J. Oxenford. Ed. K. J. Weintraub. Chicago: University of Chicago Press, 1974.

Goldmann, Lucien. *The Hidden God: A Study of Tragic Vision in the* Pensées *of Pascal and the Tragedies of Racine*. Trans. Philip Thody. New York: Humanities Press, 1964.

Grene, Marjorie., "The Sense of Things." *Journal of Aesthetics and Art Criticism*, vol. 38, no. 4 (Summer 1980): 377–89.

Hall, Harrison., "Painting and Perceiving," *Journal of Aesthetics and Art Criticism*, vol. 39, no. 3 (Spring 1981): 291–95.

Hartman, Geoffrey., *The Unmediated Vision*. New York: Harcourt, Brace and World, 1954.

—————., *Beyond Formalism*. New Haven: Yale University Press, 1970.

—————., *The Fate of Reading*. Chicago: University of Chicago Press, 1975.

—————., *Criticism in the Wilderness*. New Haven: Yale University Press, 1980.

—————., *Saving the Text: Philosophy/Derrida/Literature*. Baltimore: Johns Hopkins University Press, 1981.

Harvey, Irene E., *Derrida and the Economy of Difference*. Bloomington: Indiana University Press, 1986.

Heidegger, Martin., *Being and Time* (1927). Trans. John Macquarrie and Edward Robinson. New York: Harper and Row, 1962.

Heidegger, Martin., *Introduction to Metaphysics* (1935/1953). Trans. Ralph Manheim. New Haven: Yale University Press, 1959.

—————., *Holzwege* (1950). Frankfurt: Klostermann, 1980.

——————., *Early Greek Thinking* (1950, 1954). Trans. David Farrell Krell and Frank A. Capuzzi. New York: Harper and Row, 1975.

——————., *Aus der Erfahrung des Denkens.* Pfullingen: Neske, 1954.

——————., *What is Called Thinking?* (1954). Trans. Glenn Gray and Fred Wieck. New York: Harper and Row, 1972.

——————., *The Question of Being* (1956). Trans. Jean T. Wilde and William Kluback. New Haven: College and University Publishers, 1958.

——————., *Satz vom Grund.* Pfullingen: Neske, 1957.

——————., *On the Way to Language* (1959). Trans. Peter D. Hertz. New York: Harper and Row, 1971.

——————., *Der Ursprung des Kunstwerkes.* Stuttgart: Reclam, 1960.

——————., *Nietzsche* (1961). 4 vols. Trans. David Farrell Krell, et al. New York: Harper and Row, 1979–85.

——————., "Time and Being" (1962). "The End of Philosophy and the Task of Thinking" (1964). In *On Time and Being* (1969). Trans. Joan Stambaugh. New York: Harper and Row, 1972.

——————., *Poetry Language Thought.* Trans. Albert Hofstadter. New York: Harper and Row, 1971.

Hirsch, E. D., *Validity in Interpretation.* New Haven: Yale University Press, 1967.

——————., *The Aims of Interpretation.* Chicago: University of Chicago Press, 1976.

Hofstadter, Albert, "Enownment," *Boundary 2*, vol. 4 (1976): 357–77.

Horkheimer, Max and Theodor W. Adorno, *Dialectic of Enlightenment.* Trans. John Cumming. New York: Seabury, 1972.

Hoy, David Couzens. *The Critical Circle: Literature and History in Contemporary Hermeneutics.* Berkeley and Los Angeles: University of California Press, 1978.

Husserl, Edmund., "The Origin of Geometry." In *The Crisis of the European Sciences and Transcendental Phenomenology.* Trans. David Carr. Evanston: Northwestern University Press, 1970: 353–78.

Ingarden, Roman., *The Literary Work of Art* (1931). Trans. Georges G. Grabowicz. Evanston: Northwestern University Press, 1973.

Ionesco, Eugene., *Present Past/Past Present.* Trans. Helen R. Lane. New York: Grove, 1971.

Jakobson, Roman., "Two Aspects of Language and Two Types of Aphasia." In *Fundamentals of Language.* The Hague: Mouton, 1971.

Jeanson, Francis., *Sartre dans sa vie.* Paris: Seuil, 1974.

Johnson, Barbara., "The Frame of Reference: Poe, Lacan, Derrida." In *The Critical Difference: Essays in the Contemporary Rhetoric of Reading.* Baltimore: Johns Hopkins University Press, 1980.

Jones, Ernest., *Hamlet and Oedipus.* New York: Anchor, 1949.

Joyce, James., *Portrait of the Artist as a Young Man* (1916). New York: Viking, 1964.

Kierkegaard, Søren., *The Point of View for My Work as an Author.* Trans. Walter Lowrie. New York: Harper & Row, 1962.

Kristeva, Julia., *Revolution in Poetic Language.* Trans. Margaret Waller. Introduction by Leon S. Roudiez. New York: Columbia University Press, 1984.

——————., *The Kristeva Reader*, ed. Toril Moi. New York: Columbia, 1986.

——————., *Black Sun.* New York: Columbia University Press, 1989.

Kofman, Sarah., *Lectures de Derrida.* Paris: Galilée, 1984.

Kott, Jan., *Shakespeare Our Contemporary.* Trans. Boleslaw Taborski. New York:, Anchor, 1966.

—————., *The Eating of the Gods*. Trans. Boleslaw Taborski. New York: Vintage, 1974.

Lacan, Jacques., "Seminar on 'The Purloined Letter.'" Trans. Jeffrey Mehlman. In *French Freud: Structural Studies in Psychoanalysis, Yale French Studies*, no. 48 (1972): 38–72.

—————., *Écrits*. Paris: Seuil, 1966. Trans. Alan Sheridan. New York: Norton, 1977.

Landow, George P., ed. *Approaches to Victorian Autobiography*. Athens: Ohio University Press, 1979.

Le Bot, Marc, ed., *Le Deux*. Paris: 10–18, 1980.

Le Caldano, Paolo., *Van Gogh: Tout l'Oeuvre peint*. 2 vols. Paris: Flammarion, 1971.

Leed, Jacob, ed., *The Computer and Literary Style*. Kent, Ohio: Kent State University Press, 1966.

Lefeuvre, Michel., *Merleau-Ponty au délà de la phénoménologie*. Paris: Klinksieck, 1976.

Levin, Samuel R., *Linguistic Structures in Poetry*. The Hague: Mouton, 1962.

Lévi-Strauss, Claude., *Structural Anthropology*. Trans. Claire Jacobson and Brooke Grundfest Schoepf. New York: Basic Books, 1963.

—————., *Tristes Tropiques*. Paris: Plon, 1955. Trans. John and Doreen Weightman. New York: Atheneum, 1974.

Llewelyn, John., *Beyond Metaphysics?* Atlantic Highlands, N.J.: Humanities Press, 1985.

—————., *Derrida on the Threshold of Sense*. London: Macmillan, 1986.

Lukács, Georg., *Goethe and His Age*. Trans. Robert Anchor. New York: Grosset and Dunlap, 1968.

Lyotard, Jean-François., *The Postmodern Condition: A Report on Knowledge*. Trans. Geoff Bennington and Brian Massumi. Minnesota: University of Minnesota Press, 1984.

—————., *The Lyotard Reader*. Ed. Andrew Benjamin. Oxford: Blackwell, 1989.

Madison, Gary Brent., *La Phénoménologie de Merleau-Ponty*. Paris: Klinksieck, 1973.

Magliola, Robert., *Phenomenology and Literature: An Introduction*. West Lafayette, Ind.: Purdue University Press, 1977.

—————., *Derrida on the Mend*. West Lafayette, Ind.: Purdue University Press, 1984.

Marcovicz, Digne Meller., *Martin Heidegger: Photos*. Stuttgart: Fey, 1978.

Marin, Louis., *Utopics: The Semiological Play of Textual Spaces*. Trans. Robert Vollrath. Altantic Highlands, N.J.: Humanities Press, 1990.

May, Georges., *L'Autobiographie*. Paris: Presses Universitaires de France, 1979.

Melville, Stephen., *Philosophy beside Itself*. Minneapolis: University of Minnesota Press, 1986.

Merleau-Ponty, Maurice., *Phenomenology of Perception* (1945). Trans. Colin Smith. London: Routledge and Kegan Paul, 1960.

—————., *Sense and Non-Sense* (1947). Trans. Hubert L. Dreyfus and Patricia A. Dreyfus. Evanston: Northwestern University Press, 1964.

—————., *Consciousness and the Acquisition of Language* (1949–50). Trans. Hugh J. Silverman. Evanston: Northwestern University Press, 1973.

—————., "The Experience of Others," (1951–52). Trans. Fred Evans and Hugh J. Silverman. In *Merleau-Ponty and Psychology*, ed. Keith Hoeller, 33–63. Atlantic Highlands: Humanities Press, 1993.

—————., *The Primacy of Perception*, ed. James M. Edie. Evanston: Northwestern University Press, 1964.

—————., *L'Oeil et l'esprit* (1960). Paris: Gallimard, 1964.

—————., *Signs* (1960). Trans. Richard C. McCleary. Evanston: Northwestern University Press, 1964.

————., *The Visible and the Invisible* (1964). Trans. Alphonso Lingis. Evanston: Northwestern University Press, 1968.

————., *Prose of the World* (1969). Trans. John O'Neill. Evanston: Northwestern University Press, 1973.

————., *Texts and Dialogues*, ed. Hugh J. Silverman and James Barry, Jr. Atlantic Highlands, N.J.: Humanities Press, 1992.

Mill, John Stuart., *Autobiography*. In *Essential Works of John Stuart Mill*, ed. Max Lerner, 9–182. New York: Bantam, 1961.

Montaigne, Michel de., *The Complete Essays*. Trans. Donald M. Frame. Stanford: Stanford University Press, 1957.

Müller-Vollmer, Kurt., *Toward a Phenomenology of Literature*. The Hague: Mouton, 1963.

Müller-Vollmer, Kurt, ed., *The Hermeneutics Reader: Texts of the German Tradition from the Enlightenment to the Present*. New York: Continuum, 1985.

Nietzsche, Friedrich., *Schopenhauer as Educator* (1874). Trans. James W. Hillesheim and Malcolm R. Simpson. South Bend, Ind.: Gateway Editions, 1965. Also in: *Untimely Meditations* (III), 127–94. Trans. R. J. Hollingdale. Cambridge: Cambridge University Press, 1983. Bilingual German-French edition: *Unzeitgemäße Betrachtungen*, III-IV, 15–169. Trans. Geneviève Bianquis. Paris: Aubier, 1976.

————., *Thus Spoke Zarathustra* (1883–5). Trans. R. Hollingdale. New York: Penguin, 1969.

————., *On the Genealogy of Morals* (1887). Trans. Walter Kaufmann. New York: Vintage, 1967.

————., *Ecce Homo* (1889). Trans. Walter Kaufmann. New York: Vintage, 1967.

————., *Ecce Homo*. Trans. R. J. Hollingdale. Harmondsworth: Penguin, 1979.

Norris, Christopher., *Deconstruction: Theory and Practice*. London: Methuen, 1982.

————., *The Deconstructive Turn: Essays in the Rhetoric of Philosophy*. London: Metheun, 1983.

————., *The Contest of Faculties: Philosophy and Theory after Deconstruction*. London: Methuen, 1985.

————., *Derrida*. London: Fontana Modern Masters, 1987.

Olney, James, ed., *Metaphors of Self*. Princeton: Princeton University Press, 1972.

————., *Autobiography: Essays Theoretical and Critical*. Princeton: Princeton University Press, 1980.

Ormiston, Gayle, and Alan Schrift, eds. *The Hermeneutic Tradition: From Ast to Ricoeur*. Albany: SUNY Press, 1990.

————., *Transforming the Hermeneutic Context: From Nietzsche to Nancy*. Albany: SUNY Press, 1990.

Palmer, Richard E., *Hermeneutics: Interpretation Theory in Schleiermacher, Dilthey, Heidegger, and Gadamer*. Evanston: Northwestern University Press, 1969.

Pascal, Blaise., *Pensées*. Trans. H. F. Stewart. New York: Modern Library, 1947.

Peirce, Charles Sanders., *Philosophical Writings of Peirce*, ed. Justus Buchler. New York: Dover, 1940, 1955.

Phillips, William, ed., *Art and Psychoanalysis*. New York: Meridian, 1957.

Place, James Gordon., "The Painting and the Natural Thing in the Philosophy of Merleau-Ponty." *Cultural Hermeneutics*, vol. 4 (1976): 75–91.

Pratt, Mary Louise., *Toward a Speech Act Theory of Literary Discourse*. Bloomington: Indiana University Press, 1977.

Richards, I. A., *The Philosophy of Rhetoric*. New York: Oxford University Press, 1936.

Ricoeur, Paul., *The Symbolism of Evil*. Trans. Emerson Buchanan. Boston: Beacon, 1969.

—————., *Freud and Philosophy*. Trans. Dennis Savage. New Haven: Yale University Press, 1970.

—————., *The Conflict of Interpretations*. Ed. Don Ihde. Evanston: Northwestern University Press, 1974.

—————., *The Rule of Metaphor*. Trans. Robert Czerny with K. McLaughlin, and J. Costello. Toronto: University of Toronto Press, 1977.

—————., *Hermeneutics and the Human Sciences*. Ed. and trans. John B. Thompson. Cambridge: Cambridge University Press, 1981.

Riffaterre, Michael., *Essais de stylistique structurale*. Paris: Flammarion, 1971.

—————., *Semiotics of Poetry*. Bloomington: Indiana University Press, 1978.

Rousseau, Jean-Jacques., *Les Confessions*. In *Oeuvres complètes*, vol. 1. Paris: Gallimard, 1959. *The Confessions*. Trans. J. M. Cohen. Middlesex, England: Penguin, 1954.

Russell, Bertrand., *Autobiography*. London: Unwin, 1975.

Ryle, Gilbert., *The Concept of Mind*. London: Hutchinson, 1949.

Said, Edward., "The Problem of Textuality: Two Exemplary Positions." In *Aesthetics Today*, ed. Morris Philipson and Paul J. Gudel, 87–133. New York: Meridian/ New American Library, 1980.

—————., *The World, The Text and the Critic*. Cambridge: Harvard, 1983.

Sallis, John, ed., *Deconstruction and Philosophy: The Texts of Jacques Derrida*. Chicago: University of Chicago Press, 1987.

Salusinsky, Imre., *Criticism in Society: Interviews with Jacques Derrida, Northrop Frye, Harold Bloom, et al.* London: Methuen, 1987.

Sartre, Jean-Paul., *The Transcendence of the Ego: An Existentialist Theory of Consciousness* (1936). Trans. Forrest Williams and Robert Kirkpatrick. New York: Noonday, 1972.

—————., *Being and Nothingness: A Phenomenological Essay on Ontology* (1943). Trans. Hazel Barnes. New York: Washington Square Press, 1956.

—————., *What is Literature?* (1947). Trans. Bernard Frechtman. Secaucus, N.J.: Citadel Press, 1965.

—————., *Baudelaire* (1947). Trans. Martin Turnell. New York: New Directions, 1950.

—————., *Saint Genet* (1952). Trans. anon. New York: New American Library, 1963.

—————., *The Words* (1963). Trans. Bernard Frechtman. Greenwich, Conn.: Fawcett, 1964.

—————., *The Family Idiot* (1971–72). 5 vols. Trans. Carol Cosman. Chicago: University of Chicago Press, 1981, 1987, 1989, 1991, 1992.

—————., *Between Existentialism and Marxism*. Trans. John Matthews. New York: Pantheon Books, 1974.

—————., *Sartre, un film réalisé par Alexandre Astruc et Michel Contat*. Paris: Gallimard, 1977; *Sartre by Himself*. Trans. Richard Seaver. New York: Urizen Books, 1978.

—————., *Mallarmé, or the Poet of Nothingness* (1986). Trans. Ernest Sturm. University Park: Penn State University Press, 1988.

Sartre, Jean-Paul, Philippe Gavi, and Pierre Victor., *On a Raison de se révolter*. Paris: Gallimard, 1974.

Schapiro, Meyer., "The Still-Life as Personal Object—A Note on Heidegger and Van Gogh." In *The Reach of Mind: Essays in Memory of Kurt Goldstein, 1878–1965*. New York: Springer, 1968.

Schrag, Calvin O.,and Eugene Kaelin, eds., *American Phenomenology*. Dordrecht: Kluwer, 1989.

Searle, John., *Speech Acts: An Essay in the Philosophy of Language*. Cambridge:, Cambridge University Press, 1969.

Sendyk-Siegel, Liliane., *Sartre: Images d'une vie*. Paris: Gallimard, 1978.

Silverman, Hugh J., "Dufrenne's *Phenomenology of Aesthetic Experience*," *The Journal of Aesthetics and Art Criticism*, vol. 33, no 4 (Summer 1975): 462–64.

—————., "Dufrenne's Phenomenology of Poetry." *Philosophy Today*, vol. 20, no. 4 (Spring 1976): 20–24.

—————., "Imagining, Perceiving, Remembering," *Humanitas*, vol. 14, no. 2 (May 1978): 197–207.

—————., "Autobiographizing." *Partisan Review*, vol. 47 (1980): 142–46.

—————., "Un Égale deux ou l'espace autobiographique et ses limites." In *Le Deux*, ed. Marc le Bot, 279–302. Paris: 10–18, 1980.

—————., *Inscriptions: Between Phenomenology and Structuralism*. London and New York: Routledge, 1987.

—————., "An Essay in Self-Presentation." In *American Phenomenology*, ed. Calvin O. Schrag and Eugene Kaelin, 374–83. Dordrecht: Kluwer, 1989.

—————., "Merleau-Ponty's New Beginning: Preface to *The Experience of Others*." In *Merleau-Ponty and Psychology*, ed. Keith Hoeller, 25–31. Atlantic Highlands: Humanities Press, 1993.

Silverman, Hugh J. and Frederick A. Elliston, eds. *Jean-Paul Sartre: Contemporary Approaches to His Philosophy*. Pittsburgh: Duquesne University Press, 1980.

Silverman, Hugh J. and Don Ihde, eds. *Hermeneutics and Deconstruction*. Albany: SUNY Press, 1985.

Silverman, Hugh J. and Donn Welton, eds. *Postmodernism and Continental Philosophy*. Albany: SUNY Press, 1988.

Silverman, Hugh J., ed. *Philosophy and Non-Philosophy since Merleau-Ponty* [*Continental Philosophy-I*]. London and New York: Routledge, 1988.

Silverman, Hugh J., ed. *Derrida and Deconstruction* [*Continental Philosophy-II*]. London and New York: Routledge, 1989.

Silverman, Hugh J. and Gary E. Aylesworth, eds. *The Textual Sublime: Deconstruction and its Differences*. Albany: SUNY Press, 1989.

Silverman, Hugh J., ed. *Postmodernism—Philosophy and the Arts* [*Continental Philosophy-III*]. New York and London: Routledge, 1990.

Silverman, Hugh J., ed. *Gadamer and Hermeneutics* [*Continental Philosophy-IV*]. New York and London: Routledge, 1991.

Silverman, Hugh J., ed. *Writing the Politics of Difference*. Albany: SUNY Press, 1991.

Sini, Carlo, *Semiotica e filosofia: Segno e linguaggio in Peirce, Heidegger e Foucault*. Bologna: Il Mulino, 1978.

—————., *Images of Truth*. Trans. Massimo Verdicchio. Atlantic Highlands, N. J: Humanities Press, 1993.

Sturrock, John, ed., *Structuralism and Since: From Lévi-Strauss to Derrida*. London: Oxford University Press, 1979.

Thoreau, Henry David., *Walden: Or Life in the Woods* (1854). New York: New American Library, 1960.

Valdés, Mario J., and Owen J. Miller, eds. *Interpretations of Narrative.* Toronto: University of Toronto Press, 1978.

Vico, Giambattista., *The Autobiography.* Trans. Max Harold Fisch and Thomas Goddard Bergin. Ithaca: Cornell University Press, 1944.

Wachterhauser, Brice, ed. *Hermeneutics and Modern Philosophy.* Albany: SUNY Press, 1986.

Weintraub, Karl Joachim., *The Value of the Individual: Self and Circumstance in Autobiography.* Chicago: University of Chicago Press, 1978.

Wellek, René, and Austin Warren., *Theory of Literature.* New York: Harcourt, Brace and World, 1956.

Wood, David., *Deconstruction of Time.* Atlantic Highlands, N. J.: Humanities Press, 1988.

Yeats, William Butler., *The Autobiography of William Butler Yeats.* New York: Macmillan, 1965.

ABOUT THE AUTHOR

Hugh J. Silverman is professor of Philosophy and Comparative Literature at the State University of New York at Stony Brook. He has held visiting appointments at New York University, Duquesne University, the Université de Nice (France), the University of Warwick (England), the University of Leeds (England), the Università di Torino (Italy), and the UniversitätWien (Austria). He was executive co-director of the Society of Phenomenology and Existential Philosophy (1980-86) and is currently executive director of the International Association for Philosophy and Literature (since 1987).

Author of *Inscriptions: Between Phenomenology and Structuralism* (Routledge, 1987), and numerous articles and essays in continental philosophy, aesthetics, and literary theory, he is editor of *Piaget, Philosophy and the Human Sciences* (Humanities, 1980), and *Writing the Politics of Difference* (SUNY Press, 1991); and coeditor of *Jean-Paul Sartre: Contemporary Approaches to His Philosophy* (Duquesne, 1980), *Continental Philosophy in America* (Duquesne, 1983), *Descriptions* (SUNY Press, 1985), *Hermeneutics and Deconstruction* (SUNY Press, 1985), *Critical and Dialectical Phenomenology* (SUNY Press, 1987), *The Horizons of Continental Philosophy: Essays on Husserl, Heidegger, and Merleau-Ponty* (Nijhoff/Kluwer, 1988), *Postmodernism and Continental Philosophy* (SUNY Press, 1988), *The Textual Sublime: Deconstruction and Its Differences* (SUNY Press, 1989), and Merleau-Ponty's *Texts and Dialogues* (Humanities, 1992).

Professor Silverman is also editor of the Routledge *Continental Philosophy* series, in which five volumes have now appeared: *Philosophy and Non-Philosophy since Merleau-Ponty* (1988), *Derrida and Deconstruction* (1989), *Postmodernism—Philosophy and the Arts* (1990), *Gadamer and Hermeneutics* (1991), *Questioning Foundations: Truth/Subjectivity/Culture* (1993).

INDEX